New Jersey:
A Mirror on America

by
John T. Cunningham

*A grant from the NJ
Historical Society partially
underwrote the research and
writing of this book — a
book worthy of New Jersey's
long and remarkable past,
the people who helped shape
that past, and modern New
Jerseyans who continue to
make history.*

Updated by
Patricia Cunningham

Cover by
Jay Cunningham

Afton
Publishing Co., Inc.
PO Box 1399
Andover, NJ 07821-1399
Toll Free 1-888-238-6665
Fax 973-579-2842
www.aftonpublishing.com

This book depends as much on pictures as it does on words. The illustrations both amplify the text and demonstrate evolving styles of illustrative materials. Picture captions expand the meaning of the text, rather than merely identifying the illustration. Text, pictures, and captions thus are three meshing parts. It is difficult to obtain contemporary paintings or engravings of colonial and Revolutionary War New Jersey. A few are available including 1776 British drawings of New York harbor and the November scaling of the Palisades to attack Fort Lee (both owned by the New York Public Library). Most of the colonial and Revolutionary War illustrations, however, are from 19th century paintings, engravings, or books.

Illustrative material derived from each period of history was used as much as possible to provide the changing visual dimension of the 19th, 20th, and 21st centuries. Many 19th century engravings concerning New Jersey were found in out-of-state journals, particularly *Harper's Weekly, Leslie's Illustrated Weekly, Harper's New Monthly Magazine, The Century Magazine,* and *Scribners Monthly*, all published in New York. Most of the illustrations in the text will be familiar to those thoroughly conversant with New Jersey history. The bulk of the illustrations are from the author's own collection of books, pictures, engravings, photographs, and maps, compiled over a thirty-year period. Many are from the collection of Jay Cunningham. Others were copied, with permission, or purchased from libraries or museums around the state particularly the State Library, The New Jersey Historical Society, Rutgers University Library, Newark Public Library, Newark Museum, Morristown Library, Drew University, Monmouth County Historical Association, Camden Historical Society, Princeton University Library, Trenton Public Library, Madison Public Library, and the Morris Museum of Arts and Sciences. Some materials from the picture collection of the Library of Congress are included. Acknowledgement is made to all these institutions, and to many others throughout the state, for their continuing interest in preserving the pictorial record of New Jersey.

Table of Contents

Featured Maps

I'm From New Jersey

Each day hundreds of thousands of visitors speed across New Jersey's narrow waist. Their visits usually last exactly as long as it takes a train or automobile to run between New York and Philadelphia.

Few tarry, but they think they see New Jersey: a factory-lined flatland, characterized by smokestacks, steel rails, and express highways. Such a land is easy to forget.

Occasionally New Jerseyans encounter these visitors, say in New England, where great numbers of New Jersey people go each summer in search of change and quiet. The casual question, "Oh, you're from Jersey?" can put the New Jerseyan on guard. He or she is uneasily aware that the other probably means no compliment.

I know. As a native of New Jersey I once found myself constantly on the defensive explaining, for instance, whence the nickname "Garden State." I usually failed, because I, too, knew little of the real New Jersey.

Then the State became for me a full-time job. To my surprise and delight I found the land beyond the railroad tracks well worth the knowing.

It was this simple. My newspaper, the *Newark News*, assigned me to write on New Jersey's history and vitality. I am still at it (although the *News* has disappeared) and I am not on the defensive!

The years have taken me across every one of New Jersey's 7,836 square miles, through hundreds of factories, across thousands of acres of farmland, into the offices of more than thirty college presidents, and along one hundred and twenty-seven miles of the Jersey Shore in every season of the year.

I've seen giant machines spew forth beer bottles and bridge cables, and I've watched painstaking fingers make a gold brooch. I've seen corn picked under floodlights at 4 AM, and I've seen Miss America crowned at midnight. I've been with muskrat trappers in the lonely Salem County marshlands, with track walkers in the crowded Hudson County railroad yards, with an orchid grower inspecting his seemingly endless hothouses, with farm boys driving cows homeward on deserted Sussex County roads.

Giant trucks hem me in on the superhighways, but I know country lanes that lead to mountains and back roads that end at Atlantic beaches. Along these roads I've seen maple trees tapped for syrup in the spring, blueberries plucked in summer, cranberries harvested in fall.

If I despair at weekend traffic, I try to remember that New Jersey has been a pathway for more than three hundred years, and was one of the most strategic, most fought over, of the Thirteen States in the Revolution.

Certainly I neither scorn nor dismiss the familiar view of New Jersey from a train window. Those factories, rail yards, and crowded highways all add up to economic importance, even if they obscure the fact that off beyond eye's view there is both quaintness and charm for the finding.

JOHN T. CUNNINGHAM
Reprinted from an article
in National Geographic Magazine

A Mirror On America

New Jersey has been called "the Little Giant," but that cannot obscure the fact that it is tiny. Much said or written about the state must be viewed against that fact.

Only Hawaii, Connecticut, Delaware, and Rhode Island (in that order) are smaller. Alaska is seventy-five times as large; Texas is thirty-four times as big. If the United States were to be divided into states all the same size as New Jersey, there would be 416 rather than fifty stars on the American flag.

The square miles are not impressive. One county in California — San Bernardino — is two-and-a-half times as large as New Jersey — one county! Lake Superior is four times as big; Yellowstone National Park is almost half as large.

So, New Jersey scores no points in boasting about its size.

How, then, can this state expect to be appreciated among sister states? The answer lies in one word: variety.

New Jersey is varied in geography, climate, industry, and recreational opportunities. It is varied in history, politics, and modern problems. The story of New Jersey reflects, in miniature, much of the story of the United States.

Thus, to know New Jersey is to begin to know the story of the nation and the world. There is no better place to start, no better mirror on America.

Yet, United States history seldom gives New Jersey its due. Colonial history is traditionally told and retold in terms of settlements in Virginia and New England. The American Revolution is usually a retelling of patriot leaders in Massachusetts and Virginia.

United States history tells of a nation using changing sources of power, from water wheels to steam, to create an industrial nation. Railroads rolled westward, to weld together the states into a nation that stretched from the Atlantic to the Pacific. North fought South to preserve that nation.

After the Civil War, European immigrants flocked to these shores to give muscle and talents to both industry and agriculture. Inventors turned their imaginations loose.

War ravaged the twentieth century world, completely involving the United States. Two wars in Europe and conflicts in Korea and Vietnam killed the old dream of isolation.

Changes swept through twentieth century America. Trucks and automobiles nudged aside the railroads. People fled outward from the cities, leaving festering troubles behind. Soon enough, the "country life" also bogged down in traffic, pollution, crowding, and taxes.

By 1976, when the United States paused to commemorate the two-hundredth anniversary of the United States Constitution, this nation had become urban. Challenges beset nearly all the land: pollution of air and water, traffic snarls, declining cities, rising taxes, diminishing fuel supplies, soaring inflation, and the evident need to insure human rights for all people.

That, in brief, is the dramatic story of the United States. It is also the story of New Jersey. This is the point: History happened here. Often it happened here first.

Location is the key to the exciting fullness of New Jersey's history. The state was destined by nature to be a midway state — wedged between the two finest natural harbors on the East Coast, between New York City and Philadelphia, between New England and the South.

That placement also is the chief reason why New Jersey's leading role in nearly every major historical movement tends to be omitted from national accounts of this nation's rise and development.

New Jersey's historical importance, as well as its modern vigor, unquestionably stems from New York City and Philadelphia. Both have from earliest days influenced the state's economy, culture, and patterns of living. Those cities also have always placed New Jersey in shadow.

Eastern New Jersey has revolved around New York; western New Jersey has been a satellite of Philadelphia for nearly three hundred years. In colonial days there actually were two colonies, East Jersey and West Jersey — and evidences of that deep split are still obvious.

To understand New Jersey, recognize that there really are two "Jerseys": "North Jersey" and "South Jersey." Neither appears on a map, but the division is almost as real as if there were a political boundary drawn from Burlington to Sandy Hook. North Jersey relies on New York City for its focus. South Jersey finds its center in Philadelphia.

North Jersey residents, say in Bergen, Passaic, or Essex counties, know almost nothing about Gloucester, Salem, or Cumberland counties. Gloucester, Salem, or Cumberland freely admit that they, in turn, seldom pay attention to the northern part of the state.

That polarization gives out-of-state cities the opportunity to dominate state thought. Is it any wonder that New Jersey labors under a continuing "identity crisis"?

Out-of-state journalists and TV announcers concentrate unimaginatively on the state's crime and its politics (ordinary fare in all states, really). If they were to look beyond the obvious, they would find the state's fascinating diversity.

Here are steep mountains, gentle rolling hills, cascading waterfalls, and long stretches of sandy white beaches. The state's topography is ever-changing; from the blue water lakeland of northern New Jersey to the Pine Barrens of southern New Jersey; from the rock cliffs of the Palisades to the flat fertile acres along the lower Delaware River.

The varied land creates contrasting climates. Cumberland County farmers plant onions in March while ice is still thick on Sussex County's lakes. South Jersey farmers harvest spinach in early November, even as winter's first snow dusts the Kittatinny Mountains.

This diversity of climate should be expected, for High Point is as far north as Hartford, Connecticut, and Cape May is on the same latitude as Washington, DC, even though High Point and Cape May are only 166 airline miles apart.

Winter temperatures have dipped to thirty-four degrees below zero and summer's heat has soared to a record 110°. About forty-five inches of rain falls each year on the state. Blizzards have dumped more than two feet of snow here in a single storm.

New Jersey's prime story has been its ability to attract and hold many kinds of people. In colonial days, this was a place of Dutch, Swedes, English, Scots, Irish, and Germans. Later, immigrants swarmed here from eastern and southern Europe.

Two twentieth century world wars swelled the numbers of African American residents in the state, particularly in the cities. Here they joined other longtime African American residents, many of whom could trace their ancestors in this country back to pre-Revolution years.

Increasing numbers of Puerto Ricans, Cubans,

and other Hispanic people have made New Jersey a permanent home, particularly since World War II. New Jersey's Asian American population has increased in more recent years.

All come to New Jersey to work and to improve their prospects for a good life. They come in search of a better life for their children.

That story of human diversity can easily be found throughout New Jersey in architecture, in foods, in national celebrations, in place names.

Sturdy stone colonial Dutch houses are not difficult to find in Bergen County. Handsome eighteenth century brick houses are plentiful in Salem County, as are wooden pre-Revolution colonial mansions.

The contributions of varied people are found in the cathedrals, churches, and temples they have built — some small and simple, others large and ornate.

Differing national tastes in foods are evident — from kielbasa and wurst to lasagna, from egg roll to sweet potato pie and arroz con pollo. Varied national cultures are perpetuated in festivals, holidays, and folk dances.

Names underscore the immigrant influence. These tell of many national backgrounds in politics and box scores, on shop signs and in newspaper columns. No state knows a greater variety of people than New Jersey.

The twentieth century brought two world wars and "small wars" in far-off Korea, Vietnam, and Kuwait; a people gone lawlessly mad for alcohol in the 1920s; an economy sunk in the unprecedented Depression of the 1930s, a republic trying to find an adequate meaning of the word "liberty"; a nation that could set a man on the moon and yet find little money for its cities.

As the United States and New Jersey approached the twenty-first century, people were so dependent on computers they feared massive shutdowns of vital and emergency systems if the computers couldn't handle "00" in a date. The shutdowns were averted; communication became increasingly efficient as more and more New Jerseyans connected with the rest of the world on the Internet.

The twenty-first century arrived with newly incredible perplexity. It brought with it a new kind of war and new challenges for the United States — and New Jersey — to find their places in the world in a new millennium.

New Jersey's eight and a half million people now live in the most densely populated and most urban of all the fifty states. Modern New Jersey mirrors a look into America's future, for urbanization is the coming way of the nation. (Even Anchorage, Alaska, has a "flying traffic reporter.")

Kenneth A. Gibson, former mayor of Newark, expressed the urban dilemma most clearly: "Wherever American cities are going, Newark will get there first."

The former mayor might well have said, "Wherever America is going, New Jersey will get there first." Urban America arrived in New Jersey long ago — with its noise, crowding, pollution, and problems, and its challenges and opportunity.

Encouragingly, much open land persists in New Jersey despite the spread of highways and the sprawl of cities. This is yet a place of hardwood forests and dense pine woodlands. Perhaps the most startling little-known fact about "urban" New Jersey is that about forty-two percent of the state is still covered by forests.

Is New Jersey really the "Garden State"? New Jersey has lost much of its farmland and will continue to lose more, but the NJ Farmland Preservation Program assures the protection of many farmland acres.

New Jersey correctly can be called "the urban laboratory of America." This urban state yet has the chance to prove that — given enough imagination and dedication — humans can live in harmony with their environment.

Possibly the "laboratory" might prove that it can't be done. Either way, the choice will be made throughout the nation — and New Jersey will be forced to choose first. New Jersey again will make history.

So, look into the mirror of New Jersey. Find reflections of the past — not always glorious, not always noble, for history is far more than merely the triumphs of yesteryear. Find, as well, the emerging face of America's future.

The mirror might or might not say that New Jersey is the fairest of them all, yet its reflection of America will fascinate in all its complexity, in all its changing moods.

'That's their problem, not ours!'

The Imaginary "Identity Crisis"

The easiest way for a comic or a TV "news" announcer to get a laugh (in New York City or Philadelphia, at least) is to regard New Jersey as a barren wasteland inhabited by gangsters, simpletons, and polluters. Woody Allen once observed that "a certain intelligence governs our universe, except in certain parts of New Jersey." New York Magazine *called the Holland Tunnel New Jersey's "road to civilization." New York TV commentators show visible amusement at the very mention of New Jersey.*

New Jersey politicians, believing what the across-the-river critics repeat, long have dwelled on the need to cure what they label an "identity crisis."

Apparently the low out-of-state opinions do not depress New Jerseyans. Surveys show that state's residents are very high on New Jersey.

Bill Canfield, retired Newark Star Ledger *cartoonist, interpreted people-versus-the-politicians in the drawing to the left.* The Star Ledger *commented editorially: "Perhaps the politicians who dwell on this dreary, negative phrase (identity crisis) are too far removed from the people... and reality."*

The media has done much in recent years to "promote New Jersey." A radio station, NJ 101.5 (97.3 in South Jersey); a magazine, *New Jersey Monthly*; and TV Stations, NJN and News 12 New Jersey, all devote themselves to covering New Jersey news and issues. New Jersey still, however, often finds itself a ready target for a good laugh.

Chapter One - Six Faces Of New Jersey

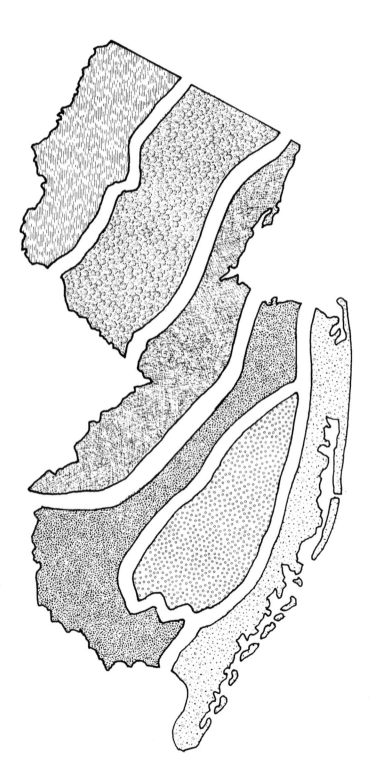

Little New Jersey offers lakeland ice boating and ocean surfing, thoroughbred horse farms and pounding factories, lonely swamplands and crowded cities. It is a place of wild orchids and cranberry bogs, flat vegetable fields and rolling dairylands, oak forests and pine woodlands.

This is a state of rugged mountains and blue water lakelands, thundering waterfalls and salt water bays, craggy rock ridges cast up by ancient volcanoes, and serene valleys gouged out by glaciers in times long past.

New Jersey is where the Palisades rise magnificently above the Hudson River, and where the Delaware Water Gap is a reminder that in time a river can cut relentlessly through the hardest stone. This is a place of Sandy Hook and Cape May, the Great Swamp and Brigantine National Wildlife Refuge, Island Beach and High Point Park.

Nature worked hard to fashion this land called New Jersey. Sometimes it used the violence of pre-historic times, more often it smoothed the surface in a gentle day-to-day wearing of water and wind against the earth. Nature's work is never done; each day the beaches of the Jersey Shore are arranged and rearranged by ocean tides. Often, too, the beds of rivers are changed, if ever so slightly, by raging rainstorms.

New Jersey, with a terrain that varies from mountains to seashore, is in miniature a cross-section of the varied landscape of the nation. Such a varied land is not easy to know, yet in knowing New Jersey there comes understanding of the way landforms affect people — and the way people adapt to the land.

There is one approach to knowing New Jersey's land. The state can be readily sectioned into six parts — to the north, mountainland, highlands; the intense corridor of cities across the middle; and to the south, prime farmland, the Pine Barrens, and the Jersey Shore.

Those are the "six faces" of New Jersey. Although they blur into one another on the edges, each is very different from the others.

The Mountain Country

New Jersey's highest spot — 1,803 feet above sea level — is defined by a 220-foot-tall granite monument. The impressive monument is 30 feet square at the base and can be seen from 20 miles away.

Huge slabs of rock, folded in layers across the slope of the Kittatinny Mountains near Pahaquarry, typify New Jersey's rugged, unconquered mountain country.

Winter pounds furiously at the northwest corner of New Jersey, jamming thermometers in the Kittatinny Mountains down into the 20s — below zero. Snow sweeps across the peaks and valleys. Ice slicks the roads. Some years, winter begins early in November; some years the cold seems never to end.

Then spring arrives. Cattle return to graze on the slopes. Streams swollen by melting snow coil down the rocky slopes. Wildcats sound their calls in the warming nights. By day, timber rattlesnakes sun themselves on the rocky eastern face of the mountains.

This is mountain country all right, rugged and wild, still unconquered.

Seen from a distance, the Kittatinnies are doubly remarkable. The long crest seems level and usually appears dark blue in color. The hue is so distinct that early settlers called these the "Blue Mountains," the name by which the formation still is known in Pennsylvania. (In New York, the ridge bears the Indian name, Shawungunk.)

The mountain averages about 1,600 feet above sea level along its entire length, although it rises to 1803 feet at High Point, the state's loftiest height.

Kittatinny Mountain has resisted change. Only two major roads cross the slopes in the thirty-six mile-long mountain. Route 206 follows an old Indian trail through Culvers Gap. Route 23 twists up the mountain in sweeping curves to reach High Point.

From the monument atop High Point, the eye takes in a dense green hardwood forest falling away in every direction — north, deep into New York State; west, to the distant Pennsylvania horizon; and east and south through Sussex and Warren counties.

That rich green woodland endures because the state owns two-thirds of the ridge between High Point and Delaware Water Gap. State-owned High Point Park and Stokes State Forest provide wide varieties of outdoor recreation. Worthington State Park, adjacent to the Gap, is also in state hands. It is not developed, but resolute hikers can climb the steep

9

The famed Delaware Water Gap (above), gouged down 1,100 feet by the river, has changed little since the engraving below was sketched in 1872.

mountainside to see Sunfish Pond sparkling atop the ridge.

Monument To Powerful Forces

More than 200 million years have gone into molding the Kittatinnies. Some geologists maintain that the original Appalachian Mountains (of which the Kittatinny ridge is part) rose 30,000 feet above sea level topping the modern Himalaya Mountains, highest in the world.

Other geologists argue that continuing erosion kept the ancient slopes to a height not much greater than the present. Either way, the Kittatinnies are a lasting monument to crunching forces that long ago shattered thick layers of rock and folded them upward into mountains.

The tremendous forces that make a mountain are revealed in Delaware Water Gap, the scenic wonder of the Kittatinnies and one of the best-known natural formations in the United States.

Shared by New Jersey and Pennsylvania, Delaware Water Gap is evidence of the subtle strength of water. Here, over millions of years of time, the river wore constantly at the hard rock. Now the Gap is 1,100 feet deep. The Gap's walls show how the Kittatinnies were formed. The rock layers appear crumbled and folded by nature as if they had been so much taffy.

Hikers on the famed Appalachian Trail know the Kittatinnies best. That trail begins in Maine and wends 2,028 miles to the end in Georgia. The section through New Jersey is too arduous for most people, but a feel for the splendid walkway can be experienced easily at Sunrise Mountain in Stokes State Forest.

Sunrise Mountain really should be called "Sunrise Lookout" for it is part of the Kittatinnies. Appalachian Trail hikers labor for miles over a boulder-strewn path to enjoy the view from Sunrise Mountain. Less athletic nature enthusiasts can drive up, park, and walk a few feet to get the same vista.

Valleys To Stir The Senses

Below to the east spreads the beautiful Kittatinny Valley, flat and broad as far as the Hamburg and Pochuck mountains to the east. Tiny houses and barns dot the valley. Holstein cows, appearing as little more than specks in the distance, graze in the pastures.

The valley is dairyland, a place of red barns, white silos, green grass, and placid cows. Southward, a viewer

Water works its magic in the Kittatinnies, here in Buttermilk Falls splashing down the west slope.

11

sees Culvers Lake, vividly blue against the emerald green of the fields.

West of the Kittatinnies, the Minisink Valley levels off to the Delaware River. Few settlers have called the valley home, yet tradition says that more than 300 years ago Dutch adventurers came to dig copper just north of Delaware Water Gap.

These Dutchmen struggled south from Kingston, New York in the 1650s. They built a trail through what they called a "howling wilderness" to carry their copper to market the long way around via Kingston. That trail is said to be the first long distance road in the New World. The copper mine site can still be seen, and the "Old Mine Road" is paved for modern travel.

Long unknown to most New Jerseyans, except occasional Sunday drivers on the Old Mine Road, the Minisink Valley became the battle ground for an epic struggle in the 1960s and the early 1970s between conservationists and the United States Government.

Fight For Minisink Valley

The battle for Minisink Valley began after the Army Corp of Engineers announced plans in 1960 to build a giant dam at Tock's Island in the Delaware River. This would have created a huge reservoir north nearly to Port Jervis. The Corps moved in, bought properties, and leveled houses.

The Tock's Island project would have served two worthwhile purposes. The reservoir would have supplied badly needed water for New Jersey, New York, and Pennsylvania. It would also have controlled floods that have periodically devastated the area. Hoping to lessen the opposition to the plan, the Corps of Engineers revealed plans in 1965 to build a giant recreational area beside the reservoir.

Conservationists reacted in horror to the ecological havoc they believed the project would wreak on the sparsely settled area. They said, with truth, that the recreational area would create monstrous traffic problems on narrow mountain and valley roads. Worse, sanitation problems likely would overwhelm a rural section of the state that had no modern sewerage facilities.

The conservationists won against overwhelming odds. New Jersey, New York, and Delaware voted in 1975 against building the dam, despite Pennsylvania's continuing support for the project. Federal officials were forced to set aside plans for the reservoir, although the United States Government now owns most of the valley. The recreational area will remain, greatly scaled down.

So, for a time, the Kittatinny Mountains and its valleys remain quite as they have been for thousands of years. The scenery is still exceptional, the air is clean, the roads uncrowded.

This idyllic situation may not last. Interstate Highway 80 is complete, coast-to-coast, and the New Jersey portion veers through Delaware Water Gap. The future of the Kittatinny Mountains and Valley already is being set in the traffic-clogged highway.

Tiny Sunfish Pond, atop the Kittatinny Mountains, stirred a classic nationwide conservation battle in the 1960s that would have made Henry David Thoreau proud. Few had heard of Sunfish Pond before that time. Only the hardiest of hikers along the Appalachian Trail had seen the crystal-clear, half-mile-long pond in state-owned Worthington Forest. Then, in 1961, the state sold Sunfish Pond to two utility companies that planned to use it as a storage reservoir for making electrical power. One of the last pure glacial lakes in the nation appeared doomed.

A handful of Sunfish Pond admirers began to fight back against well-financed, politically powerful opponents. Interior Secretary Stewart L. Udall, an avowed friend of nature lovers, warned in 1966 that the pond could not be saved. The undaunted conservationists, led by the Lenni Lenape League, fought on against heavy odds. Reams of mimeographed "Save Sunfish Pond" literature flooded across the desks of newspaper editors, politicians, and conservationists in all parts of the nation. Gradually a public outcry built up, prompting the New Jersey legislature to buy back Sunfish Pond, with promises to keep it in its wilderness state.

Sunfish Pond lives, still beyond the sight of all but the hardiest of hikers — but apparently also beyond the reach of those who would destroy it.

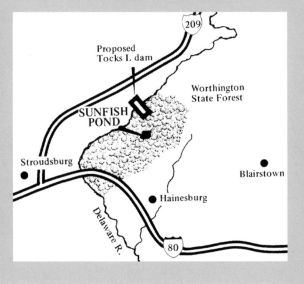

Battle For Sunfish Pond

Where Hills Rise High

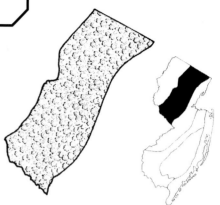

Far across the valley, below Sunrise Mountain in the Kittatinnies, the Highlands start to rise. New Jersey began in those Highlands, formed more than two billion years ago when great boulders were pushed above the surface of ancient seas.

Looking east and south from Sunrise Mountain atop the Kittatinny Ridge, the eyes see a series of irregularly shaped, thickly wooded mountains on the far side of the valley. Those immediately in view are Pochuck Mountain and the Pimple Hills. In "Pochuck" and "Pimple," New Jersey's Highlands begin.

It is fitting that these two first-seen parts of the Highlands are called "mountain" and "hills," for the Highlands measure somewhere between mountains and high hills. The top Highland ridge rises 1,496 feet above sea level near Vernon. Other ridges, near Spruce Run and the Delaware River, are only about 500 feet.

Here, nearly two billion years ago, New Jersey rose from the sea.

Tremendous boulders were pushed slowly upward from the floor of the prehistoric sea. The boulders rose ever higher, until at last they peeped above the surface to form land. The oldest part of New Jersey — the Highlands — had appeared.

Nothing has pushed these stout Highlands aside, not in two billion years. Time rounded and smoothed the many high mountains, and then covered them with forests. Passing centuries scoured out the valleys and carpeted them with green growth. Beneath the surface tidying up, the original hard rock remains.

The Highlands are part of a long range of similarly rounded mountaintops and deep valleys between northern New England and the South. Vermont visitors who see New Jersey's Highlands have exclaimed, on first sight, "Why, this is like New England!"

In fact, New Jersey gets much the best of that highest possible Vermont accolade, for some of Vermont's Green Mountains rise nearly 4,400 feet above sea level. It is not a totally undeserved compliment, however, for this is beautiful country.

Similarity to New England is most marked in winter, especially in Vernon, where one of the largest ski resorts in the East spreads over the slopes of Hamburg and Wawayanda mountains.

New England is blessed (from a skier's viewpoint) with far more snow than New Jersey. But Mountain Creek Ski Area proprietors lessen the deficiency with snow-making machines that powder the Sussex County hillsides from as early as late November until sometimes early April.

Skiing has become a major New Jersey sport, thanks mainly to the development of snow-making machines that powder the trails when nature fails to cooperate. Scores of snowmakers dot the hills in New Jersey's Highlands. The machines operate at night, pouring forth new snow before the ski lifts begin to carry crowds up the slopes.

New Jersey's Lakeland

Nearly every important New Jersey lake is cupped within the Highlands (excepting only Culvers, Owassa, and Swartswood, all nearby in the Kittatinny Valley). The largest Highland lake — and by far the largest in the state — is Lake Hopatcong, nearly seven miles long. The shoreline is cut by so many deep coves that the distance around Hopatcong is more than forty miles.

Lake Hopatcong was once two small ponds. A dam was built at the southern end in the 1830s to provide water for the Morris Canal, joining the ponds into one handsome jewel of a lake. The dam site is now Hopatcong State Park.

Nearly every lake in the Highlands is either artificial or was partially enlarged by a dam. The chief exception is Green Pond. Despite the "pond" name, this is a deep, natural lake, more than two and a half miles long and up to fifty feet deep.

Several other lakes were created or expanded to supply water for the Morris Canal. Both Cranberry and Musconetcong were built solely for the canal.

Greenwood Lake, shared by New Jersey and New York State, was enlarged.

Most other lakes in these mountains owe their existence to more personal desires or needs. They were made in the 1920s for summer recreation, but now most provide year-round housing. Such lakes include Lake Mohawk, Highland Lakes, Mountain Lakes, a variety of small lakes near Denville, and several lakes in the Butler-Pompton Lakes area.

Where Rivers Begin

Water is a dashing hallmark of the Highlands. Brooks that begin as springs atop the rolling hills gain speed as they head down the mountain. They gain more water from other brooks, and then race downward to join rivers headed for the sea.

There are Highland streams of note, especially the Musconetcong River, flowing briskly southwestward from Lake Hopatcong to the Delaware River; the Rockaway and Pequannock rivers, bubbling rapidly eastward to join the Passaic; and the Ramapo, surging southward from upper Bergen County, also headed

14

Lake Hopatcong was surrounded by unexplored forests when this engraving was made in the 1850s, about 20 years after two small ponds were combined. The lake has retained the same size and shape ever since. Thousands of homes now line the shores and boats crowd the water, but Hopatcong remains beautiful.

for the Passaic.

A most unusual evidence of river origin occurs at Hilltop Presbyterian Church on a Highland hill at Mendham. Rain that strikes the north roof of the church drains off into the Passaic River. Rain pattering on the southward shingles finds its way to the Raritan River.

Plentiful Highland streams attracted dam builders of another sort early in the late nineteenth and early twentieth centuries. Seeking ample water supplies for urban use, Newark and several other major northern New Jersey towns constructed reservoirs at Oak Ridge, Clinton, Canistear, and Wanaque to store Highlands water.

Jersey City also reached out for Highlands water, building its reservoir at Boonton early in the twentieth century. Much more recently, the State constructed reservoirs at Spruce Run and Round Valley in Hunterdon County.

The Glow of Iron

Pompton Lake, begun when the Pompton River was dammed to provide water power for a pre-Revolution forge, introduces another element of the Highlands: iron. This was the most vital resource of these mountains for more than two hundred years.

Early settlers in Newark and Elizabeth, in about 1700, heard Indian tales of "Succysunny" (meaning "black stone") found near what is now the town of Succasunna. Prospectors crossed the Highlands to seek the black stone in about 1710. Soon after, iron forges were built in "The Hollow" (modern Morristown) and at Hanover.

Within fifty years, forges and furnaces were started between Ringwood, near the New York State border, and Bloomsbury, in Warren County. These provided colonial ironware for arms during the Revolution. Ringwood, Oxford, and Dover became centers for ironmakers in the nineteenth and twentieth centuries. There was scarcely a place within the Highlands where fortunes did not at one time or another rise and fall with the flickering flames of the glowing iron furnaces.

The Highlands had everything that early ironmakers needed — plentiful supplies of good ore, ample forestland for fuel, limestone to hasten melting of the ore, and powerful streams to provide power for the forges. Forests were significant factors. It has been estimated that a single forge "fire" consumed one thousand acres of woodland annually.

Gradually the forge fires diminished, particularly after easily mined iron was discovered near Lake Superior in Minnesota in the 1870s. The western ore

Paradise For Rock Hounds

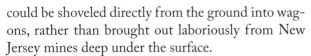

Mention Franklin, New Jersey to geologists anywhere and expect instant attention — for no area in the world has produced as many minerals as this Sussex County region.

Franklin won fame as one of the world's foremost producers of zinc between 1848 and 1954. In that period, at least 212 different minerals were found at the site, including several never found anywhere else. Forty-two were first found at Franklin.

Many of Franklin's minerals glow (or fluoresce) in a wide variety of colors under ultraviolet light, prompting the town to call itself "The Fluorescent Mineral Capital of the World."

Science classes from schools and colleges regularly visit Franklin and nearby Ogdensburg. They tour the Franklin Mineral Museum and the Sterling Hill Mining Museum. Some prospect at the outdoor mineral dump.

Zinc mining at the Sterling Mine started in 1852 and continued until 1986. Now an historic site, the museum allows visitors to walk through underground tunnels, view fluorescent minerals, and see authentic mining artifacts.

You can also see some of Sterling Hill Mine's 340 different kinds of minerals in the Hall of Geology at the Smithsonian Institution in Washington, DC.

could be shoveled directly from the ground into wagons, rather than brought out laboriously from New Jersey mines deep under the surface.

Spurts of production in World War I and World War II were nothing more than temporary stimulants for the ironmakers. All the mines were either closed or on standby status by 1970. The Mt. Hope Mine, where a vertical shaft is sunk half a mile into the earth, announced in 1976 plans to reopen, but this never materialized. Two hundred years before, Mt. Hope helped supply arms to Washington's army.

Ironmakers may be only biding their time. Ore still buried in the Highlands is estimated to total as high as 600 million tons.

Mining is just another story of the past. The lakelands no longer have huge summer boarding houses or the numerous public amusement parks of the early 20th century. Ice is no longer cut and loaded aboard long strings of freight cars for shipment to city restaurants and hotels.

Instead, the Highlands have become places where people want to live. Interstate Highways 78, 80, and 287 pour streams of people out to their homes in the evening and take them back to work in the flatlands to the east the next morning.

Governor James McGreevey signed the Highlands Preservation Act in August 2004. This law protects the resources of the Highlands, especially the drinking water that supplies more than half the state's population.

Change doesn't matter in the Highlands. An area with more than two billion birthdays can cope with anything that mere humans plan.

The Vidal Corridor

New Jersey's chief crossroads are in Middlesex County where the New Jersey Turnpike and the Garden State Parkway, both built in the 1950s, exchange traffic in a complex system of bridges, ramps, and toll booths. This exchange lies almost exactly between two of New Jersey's "new" cities — Edison and Woodbridge.

Geography's direct effect on people is seldom more clearly seen than in New Jersey's twenty-mile-wide corridor between the Hudson and Delaware rivers. Two wide, deep rivers predestined great ports on either side; a level plain between the ports ensured that this area would vibrate with transportation and industrial activity.

This is New Jersey's vital corridor. This is where people live, work, attend college, seek culture, shop, conduct state government, and clog the roads with their automobiles and trucks.

This corridor contains every major New Jersey city, two-thirds of all its industries, most of its colleges and universities, most of the transportation network, and most of the research laboratories. More than half of all New Jerseyans dwell here, and here are most centers of culture, the most important financial houses, and the state's political pulse.

The corridor is not new. In 1880, when census

The Passaic River plunges 70 feet at Paterson in a spectacular cascade (that can be frozen in place by a cold winter). In 1791 these falls provided the power for America's first planned industrial city.

takers first described New Jersey as urban, the area already contained about two-thirds of the people and about two-thirds of the industry.

There probably is no more busy, dynamic, confusing twenty-mile-wide strip of land in all the world than this avenue that runs from the George Washington Bridge southwestward to Camden.

Rigid boundaries cannot be fixed, for this hectic path grows wider each year as people and industry force it outward. It spills westward into the foothills, south and east toward the level Coastal Plains.

Industry At The Fall Line

The corridor's western portion is in the Piedmont ("foot of the mountains"). Including the Piedmont in the vital corridor is logical, since colonial industry began here. Streams tumbling out of the Piedmont hills quickly were harnessed to power grindstones, saws, looms, and other machines in the lowlands.

That place where streams and rivers of the Piedmont pick up speed then drop rapidly to sea level is called the "fall line." This might include intermittent rapids, such as those at Little Falls, or a thundering cascade, such as the Great Falls at Paterson.

Paterson's falls gather momentum atop a rocky ledge, then drop 70 feet into a confined gorge in a dazzling display of raw power. In 1791, when

Alexander Hamilton and several associates foresaw the infant United States needed industry to prosper, they recognized that the Great Falls could supply power for Paterson, America's first planned industrial city.

Water power was the major need of industry. Also necessary to commerce was the level land between the Delaware and Hudson rivers. New York City (known first as New Amsterdam) was founded on the Hudson in the 1620s; Philadelphia was started on the Delaware in 1682. Those would be the markets and the ports.

In northwestern New Jersey, steep hills and rugged mountains cut off quick movement east and west. Southeast, the dense pine woodland known as the Pine Barrens was a place that colonial travelers avoided, even dreaded.

How different history would have been if New Jersey's high hills had run from High Point to Cape May, effectively blocking movement between the Hudson and Delaware! But history is shaped by terrain. That meant, for middle New Jersey, an inevitable role as a corridor over which would pass people whose ideas would affect the United States and the world.

The Roots Go Deep

Roots go deep in that strip. New Jersey's first town, Bergen, was founded by the Dutch in 1660.

Here are views of three New Jersey cities: the Capitol complex in Trenton (left), downtown of the biggest city, Newark (below), and Camden's Wiggins Waterfront Park along the Delaware River (lower right).

Nearly 150 years later, Bergen became Jersey City. Elizabeth was founded late in 1664 as New Jersey's first English-speaking town; Newark dates to 1666. Government began here; New Jersey's first Assembly met in Elizabeth in 1668.

Control of the artery helped determine the winning of the American Revolution. The region saw constant conflict for five years.

Then the inventive dreamers came: John Stevens, who built America's first railroad locomotive at Hoboken in 1826; John Philip Holland, a Paterson school teacher who made the first practical submarine in 1878; Thomas Edison, who perfected the electric light at Menlo Park in 1879; and the Rev. Hannibal Goodwin, who perfected flexible photographic film in his Newark parsonage in 1887.

Railroads ruled the corridor before 1850. Industry followed the rails, in bewildering complexity: machine makers, metal refiners, food canners, furniture makers, textile weavers, clothing manufacturers; makers of chemicals, oil products, explosives, and almost everything else known to humanity.

Twentieth and twenty-first century wonders are part of the story of this strip. Many of the pharmaceutical advances since the 1920s were discovered here — vitamins, "wonder" antibiotics, sulfa drugs, and other disease killers. Flights into space were pioneered in the corridor's research laboratories.

This is a place of learning. Rutgers University, once confined to "the banks of the old Raritan" in New Brunswick now also has major campuses in Newark and Camden. Princeton thrives in Ivy League dignity in the middle of the corridor's frantic pace. Seton

Hall, Fairleigh Dickinson, New Jersey Institute of Technology, Stevens, Montclair, and other campuses are part of the highly-populated region.

Return From The Hills

This long, narrow strip of real estate between Bergen and Camden counties continues to flex New Jersey's muscle. Unfortunately, opportunity and congestion go hand in hand; people might flee to the upper hills or to the Jersey Shore to rest by night, but by day, they return to make a living.

Sometimes the living is won as much in the morning and evening "rush hours" as in the actual work hours. Automobiles, trucks, and buses vie for decreasing space on the New Jersey Turnpike, the Garden State Parkway, and other major highways. Each day the "rush" slows to a snail's pace.

Nothing illustrates the corridor's transportation maze better than a small area near Newark Liberty International Airport. Nearby are Port Newark and Port Elizabeth, so close that a high school outfielder could easily throw a ball from the airport to the piers.

New Jersey Turnpike and the Jersey Central Railroad lie between the airport and the docks. Perhaps at no other place in the world are a major airport, superhighway, busy railroad, and crowded docks so bunched together.

The corridor is not all business. There is beauty here too — in the blossoming dogwood trees of the Piedmont, in the cherry blossoms in Newark and Belleville's Branch Brook Park, in the marshlands of the Great Swamp, in parts of the Jersey Meadows between Newark and Hackensack, and everywhere in the Watchungs.

Beauty is in the mind of the viewer. There is a nighttime glow along the New Jersey Turnpike, where jets spring into sudden flame at the refineries, and then lapse into darkness; in the necklaces of lights on bridges and in the after-midnight luster of the docks at Newark and Elizabeth; in the changing light patterns at Newark Liberty International Airport.

Look eastward at night from Eagle Rock Mountain in Essex County for more beauty. Millions of lights shine in the valley below, where a high percentage of New Jersey's people live. The valley at 9 PM looks like a giant fireplace, slowly burning down into a soft bed of embers as the night wears on.

By morning, the embers will fade. The valley will hum again its song of work.

America's First County Parks

Few New Jersey assets are more precious than the Essex County Park system, started in 1895 as the first county park system in the United States.

Today the system's 5,726 acres of parkland serve millions of people, but in 1895 the proposal to spend $2.5 million to buy county parkland was met with astonishment.

The Essex County Park Commission bought land — two large swamps in the northern and southern sections of Newark; two huge areas of isolated mountain woodland atop the First Mountain, beyond even the trolley lines; and many other small patches of land throughout the county.

Branch Brook and Weequahic parks emerged from the swamps. Eagle Rock and South Mountain reservations were formed from the mountain woodlands.

Some editors criticized purchase of swamps and "distant mountainland," but most approved. The Newark **Daily Advertiser** *called the parks "a beautiful prospect — lovely in contemplation, lovelier still in the realization."*

The wisdom of the 1895 purchase is almost beyond calculation. The parks give densely populated Essex County a place to relax. The "beautiful prospect" of 1895 has come true, and the idea of county parks has spread to most other counties in New Jersey.

The Garden Strip

New Jersey's southwestern corner — "the Garden Spot" — begins a recurrent cycle of planting and harvesting every spring. Vegetable fields are so huge that the tender new plants must be set in the earth from special planting machines.

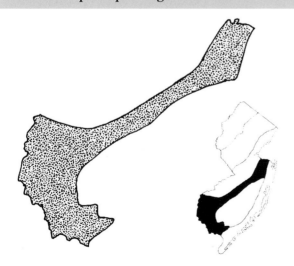

Really now, visitors ask, how does New Jersey dare put *Garden State* on its license plates? They admit that the state has a noble historical heritage and that twenty-first century industry is evident, but the "Garden State" nickname strikes them as quaint — at best.

The "Garden State" reputation depends mostly on a semicircle of fertile land around the northern and western edge of the Pine Barrens. It begins just west of Red Bank in Monmouth County, an area of horse farms, and runs down through parts of Mercer, Burlington, Camden, Gloucester, Salem, and Cumberland counties.

From the standpoint of history, current and past, the nickname is valid. Farmers continue to prosper in densely populated New Jersey on farms well away from the beaten path that most travelers take across the state.

New Jersey ranks among the top three states in the nation in producing cranberries and blueberries. Large southern New Jersey orchards annually produce hundreds of thousands of baskets of peaches and apples. Our farms produce fresh market sweet corn, spinach, head lettuce, escarole and endive, snap beans, tomatoes, bell peppers, asparagus, cabbage, eggplant, and cucumbers. Our processing vegetables include tomatoes, carrots, cucumbers, green peas, snap beans, lima beans, and sweet corn.

Return To Horsepower

Not all New Jersey horsepower is in automobiles. Our horses gallop along bridle paths, in pastures, and down the stretch of racetracks. Some owners show their horses off in horse shows.

Horse breeding revived in New Jersey when betting on horse races was legalized in 1939. Increasing interest in horses prompted many former poultry or dairy farmers to convert their farms to horse raising. New Jersey ranks as a national leading breeder of purebred horses. Our stallions rank among the top sires in the nation. Our yearlings sell at higher than national average prices.

An unusual aspect of New Jersey's horse picture is a handsome training center, near Gladstone (Somerset County), where the United States Equestrian Team has trained since 1962 for the Olympics, the PanAmerican Games, and other international competitions.

The Horse Park of New Jersey in Allentown hosts a variety of competitions and equestrian shows including national championships.

Horses bred on New Jersey farms continually stand out nationally. Horse breeding calls for extensive green pastureland. Monmouth, Burlington, and Camden counties all have room for the noble steeds.

Urbanization pushes constantly against the vegetable fields, the orchards, and the horse farms. Homes, shopping centers, and industry slowly have replaced bean fields and apple orchards for the past fifty years. Yet, despite intense real estate pressures and the high costs of farming, many farmers stand fast.

Farmers For Three Centuries

Farming traditions have survived here for more than three centuries. Swedish settlers along the Delaware River sowed seeds and planted fruit trees in the 1640s. When John Fenwick led the first English Quaker settlers into Salem County in 1675, he called this "a land of milk and honey."

The passing centuries made agriculture ever more dominant. South Jersey agricultural history was filled with tales of 1,000-pound hogs and 2,000-pound beef cattle fattened for nineteenth century Philadelphia markets.

By 1875, Burlington, Camden, Salem, and Cumberland counties proudly traded on their reputation as "the garden spot of the Garden State." Each summer the dirt roads that led to the Camden ferries were clogged with wagonloads of vegetables and fruit that would cross the Delaware River to Philadelphia's fresh markets.

By 1900, tomato canneries in Camden, Swedesboro, Bridgeton, and several other South Jersey towns competed hotly for the tons of juicy tomatoes grown in nearby fields. Gloucester County's peaches and apples found ready markets in Philadelphia, New York, and even Boston and Baltimore.

Specialization became the way of farming life, sometimes to the ruination of the farmer. Monmouth County soared to prominence as the nation's leading producer of early-season white potatoes, and then floundered through periods of boom and bust. High prices encouraged overproduction, which in turn ruined profits. Fewer acres were planted, prices rose, farmers overplanted; the ruinous cycles went on and on.

Monmouth turned its attention now to raising fine horses, a tradition dating to colonial days when Colt's Neck produced some of the nation's great race horses. Modern horse breeding and nearby Monmouth Race Track rely on each other. Across the state, in Camden

Seabrook Farms became the largest agricultural processor in New Jersey, at one time freezing the crops of nearly 60,000 acres of farmland in southern New Jersey. Its acres were so large that low-flying plans were needed to dust the crops. Seabrook Farms operated until 1982.

County, similar horse farms sprang into being after the Garden State Race Track was built in the 1940s.

Monmouth County farmers have also turned to another specialized product — nursery stock. Certified nurseries abound in Monmouth County and also in Cumberland County.

Where Food And Industry Mix

Agriculture and industry began to mix more than a century ago. The first large-scale canning of tomatoes began in Camden in 1869 when Abraham Anderson and Joseph Campbell began packing the noted beefsteak tomato "so large that only one was packed to a can."

Campbell began buying all the tomatoes that South Jersey farmers produced. Then, in 1897, the company expanded its purchase of local tomatoes even more. That year it introduced condensed soup at 10 ½ ounces for a dime." Tomatoes were the first to be condensed into soup. Soon the soup line included

all kinds of vegetables as well as beef and chicken.

Another South Jersey name became famous when Charles F. Seabrook introduced scientific farming to Cumberland County in the 1840s. He started freezing vegetables and fruit in 1933. Seabrook Farms became the largest agricultural processing business in New Jersey and one of the largest in the world.

It was fitting that agriculture and industry merged in the food processing plants. The two clashed head-on throughout the area in competition for land and labor.

Industry was no stranger here. America's first successful glass manufactory was established in Salem County in 1739. The Bridgeton-Millville-Vineland triangle became one of the nation's major glass centers, producing millions of bottles daily and hiring thousands of employees.

Industry spread slowly, particularly along the Delaware River. Deepwater, in Salem County, boasted the largest chemical plant in the western hemisphere. Two large petroleum refineries located in Paulsboro and Westville. Camden became an electronics and industrial center. All the way north to Burlington and beyond teemed with industrial activity.

Farewell To Farmers?

Immediately after the New Jersey Turnpike sliced through the region in the 1950s, farmers had to ponder whether it was better to continue plowing the soil or to sell their land to the highest bidders among real estate developers and factory builders. Many decided to reap the rich, quick money harvest. For a time, the state lost two or three farms a week to developers.

The orchards and asparagus fields of Gloucester County have been drastically reduced. The vegetable farms of Cumberland County are seriously threatened. Most of the huge chicken farms are but memories. Homes now sprout where only asparagus shoots or pepper plants grew sixty years ago.

All is not lost, however. Vegetables and fruits are still harvested here in considerable quantities. Competition from other farm sections of the nation, high labor costs, and rising land taxes have cut steadily into farm profits.

The Garden State as a region of many small farms may well disappear within your lifetime. Some large operations will continue to farm the land, but personal farming, as depicted in poetry and history, is a dying vocation. It takes a determined, overworked farm family to continue in the face of progress, mechanization, and low income.

Sadly, when farmlands disappear, everyone loses. Farm prices rise. Water supplies are threatened as homes and factories increase their demands. Roads are crowded; air and water are polluted. The lush green farmland no longer exists to please the eye and enrich the spirit.

Enjoy the Garden Spot while it lasts.

Saving New Jersey's Farms

Pioneers are still present in New Jersey's farmlands — but now they work to keep farmers on the land rather than clearing pasturelands for new farms.

As the nation's most densely populated state, New Jersey lost farms to developers at the rate of sixty-five acres every day for twenty-five years. When farms disappeared, everyone lost.

New Jersey recently has pioneered ways to keep satisfied farmers on the land. It is not easy. How can a farmer not be tempted when a developer offers him enough money for his land that he might never have to work again?

The state eased taxes for farmers in 1964, taxing acres for farm value rather than what the land might bring if an industry or home developer bought it. The State Department of Agriculture then proposed in 1973 that billions of dollars be spent to buy one million acres of farmland to keep it forever in agricultural use.

That was too rich for New Jersey taxpayers, but in 1977 a pilot program was set up in Burlington County to buy as many acres as possible for $5 million. Farmers who sold to the state could continue farming.

The Farmland Preservation Program continues — preserving some farms for eight years and others for life. The State Agriculture Development Committee (SADC) administers the program in voluntary cooperation with the counties, municipalities, and farm owners.

We know New Jersey voters want our farmers to stay. They continually allow their tax dollars to go toward keeping farms by voting yes for Farmland Preservation Bond Issues. The Preservation Program has sufficient funds to continue in the twenty-first century.

Nature's uncertain rainfall forced New Jersey farmers to install extensive, and expensive, irrigation equipment in their fields.

The Pine Barrens

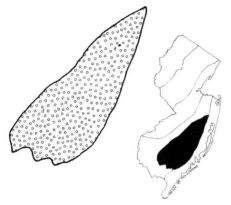

From the lookout tower in the big mansion at Batsto, the eyes wander in every direction — North, East, South, West, or to any of the countless points between.

Immediately below is the little village of Batsto. Beyond, reaching to the most distant horizon in all directions, only a vast area of treetops can be seen. A wisp of smoke might drift lazily upwards here or there. Nothing else indicates life in the unbroken greenness — not a house, not a road, not a person to be seen.

Out there, mysterious and challenging, is New Jersey's most unusual region. This is the Pine Barrens, a famed forest that covers about one-fourth of the state.

Seldom has an area been so misnamed. The undeserved reputation began more than three centuries ago. Settlers who could not grow their usual grains, hay, or vegetables in the sandy soil dismissed the area as "barren." The sand made travel difficult, even on horseback. It became traditional to shun the region, even fear it.

Pine *Barrens*, indeed! Here is a land that supports incredible varieties of plants — little-known flowers such as turkey beard, pyxie moss, at least thirty-five different kinds of wild orchids, golden crest, sundews, insect-eating pitcher plants, and at least 400 other varieties of wild flowers. It is a land of cranberry bogs and blueberry plantations.

Here, too, are more than 150 kinds of birds, deer, muskrats, raccoons, several kinds of rare frogs, flying squirrels, beavers, and several species of harmless snakes. The rarest creature is the Pine Barrens Tree Frog, found only here and in two other small, isolated colonies in North Carolina and Georgia.

Pitch Pine And Scrub Oak

The basic tree in the woodland is the pitch pine, some of which once grew as tall as eighty feet. Now, because of repeated forest fires — a persistent threat in every dry season — few pines are more than fifty feet tall. Most average thirty to forty feet. Intermingled are scrubby oak trees — scraggly and undernourished — not the vigorous, proud oaks of song and legend.

Slowly-moving coffee-colored streams meander through the midst of thick cedars in the Pine Barrens.

Botanists from many parts of the world converge on the Pine Barrens to study and to catalogue the area's abundant and often rare plants. One hope of botanists is to see the scarce diminutive *Curly Grass Fern*, found in the Pine Barrens and nowhere else in the United States!

The Pine Barrens is truly nature's meeting ground. At Sim Place Bog, east of Penn State Forest in Burlington County, botanists seek out the very rare southern yellow orchid in early August. This is the northernmost home of the flower. Close by, within sight of the yellow orchid, one can find bearberry — a plant normally associated with the frozen Arctic tundra!

Witmer Stone, a noted South Jersey naturalist, surveyed Pine Barrens flora in 1910. He found that sixty plants usually associated with Canadian provinces reach their southern limit in the Pine Barrens, and 164 "Southern" (Virginia to Florida) species reach their northernmost limits here.

The Unchanging Woodland

Seventy-five years ago the Pine Barrens was measured at about 1.3 million acres. Today it is nearly the same in size, despite the encroachment of roads, industry, and public buildings.

To visualize the magnitude, trace the perimeter on a map. Start at Freehold, go east to the Garden State Parkway, then south nearly eighty miles to Dennisville in Cape May County. Swing west to Parvin State Park beyond Vineland, north past Berlin and Wrightstown, and then back to Freehold.

That encompasses about 1,900 square miles. Only a few known town names appear within the perimeter: Lakewood, Mays Landing, Millville, Vineland, Hammonton, and Egg Harbor City.

Elsewhere, place names reflect a simple past: Herman, Green Bank, Bulltown, and Pleasant Mills; Penny Pot, Milmay, Dorothy, and Apple Pie Hill; Atsion, Indian Mills, Red Lion, and Blue Anchor; Blue Bell, Double Trouble, and Roosevelt City; Retreat, Bamber, Prospertown, and Georgia.

The pine woodland seems to hide villages and crossroad towns. Small wonder, for an area as large as this can also take on military installations or state parks and scarcely seem touched.

Consider the Fort Dix Military Reservation in Pemberton Township. Begun during World War I, the reservation now covers 31,000 acres in Burlington County. Millions of Americans remember training days at Fort Dix. Few ever saw the wild orchids. To them, "barrens" is a perfect name.

Fire: The Worst Enemy

The worst enemy of the Pine Barrens is fire that can destroy with a ferocious power. In the spring of 1963, an extended drought spread dread throughout the region. When fire came, powerful winds fanned the flames across nearly 190,000 dry acres. It was the largest wildfire in the region's recorded history.

Spurred by a hot dry wind at its tail, a pineland wild

Machines stir up a cranberry bog in the Pine Barrens, forcing berries to float on the flooded area where they can easily be harvested. Cranberries continue to be an important crop in the Pine Barrens. Such mechanization is the chief way for southern New Jersey farmers to survive.

fire devours everything before it. Such a fire can come up to a wide concrete highway, where it might reasonably be expected to stop. In an angry roar of seeming frustration, it shoots red-hot sparks thousands of feet ahead, finds tinder-dry food, and blazes onward. Many fires burn the surface of macadam roads.

A pine woodland blaze is no place for a tourist. Even experienced firefighters know fear: fire destroys humans, too, with brutal suddenness. One blaze in 1936 killed five trained firefighters.

Nature eventually soothes the fiery wounds and spreads greenery on the charred floor. Indeed, forest fires even encourage certain types of orchids to flourish. Fire is an old, old terror in the Pine Barrens and might even have led Indians and original colonists to suspect the earth itself.

One remarkable fire-caused sight is the so-called "Plains," nearly 15,000 stunted acres east of Brendan T. Byrne (formerly Lebanon) State Forest. Growth seldom exceeds twelve to fifteen feet in this lonely, forsaken place. Most trees are only four to six feet tall.

Long ago, it was believed that the "Plains" were jinxed by evil spirits or poor soils or both. Most scientists today blame fire. Repeated burnings in eight-to-twelve-year cycles apparently account for the shrunken, desolate area.

Water, Water, Everywhere

Water runs everywhere within the Pine Barrens. Streams are over-flowing, even in dry weather. Some, such as the Mullica, Tuckahoe, and Great Egg Harbor rivers, Cedar Creek, and Toms River, are fine for canoeing.

Lush Pine Barrens growth is near the waterways

(that means practically anywhere). Here grow the dark green cedar forests, their roots cooled by the sphagnum moss of the surrounding swamps. Here cranberry bogs dot the area. Here flow mahogany-colored waters as clean as any in New Jersey.

Underlying the sandy soil is a vast reservoir of almost unlimited pure water, enough to supply at least a billion gallons daily. New Jersey officials recognized the value of that water in 1954 when they bought the 97,000-acre Wharton Tract in Burlington, Atlantic, and Camden counties.

The Pine Barrens remains a place for all seasons. Spring brings the stately wild laurel. Summer coaxes wild orchids into bloom and makes the blueberry plantations rich with color. Autumn finds the trees filled with chattering birds harvesting fall berries and seeds amid the fall foliage. Winter snow emphasizes the deep green leaves of holly trees mingling with the long-needled pines.

Pressures to "develop" the Pine Barrens frequently are heard. An effort to save much of the region was strengthened, on November 10, 1975, when Congress created the Pinelands National Reserve, the first such reserve in the nation. A year later, Governor Byrne appointed a New Jersey Pinelands Commission to supervise 1.1 million acres in the reserve. The reserve includes fifty-six municipalities and seven counties.

Many thousands of people pass the eastern fringe of the Pine Barrens each day in summer. Thousands more stream eastward from Camden or Trenton. They rush through the pine forests and see them as a barrier, not an attraction.

The automobiles whiz on, bound for the Jersey Shore, which is as much sought after as the Pine Barrens is shunned.

Imagine buying 97,000 acres of pine woodland, two villages, parts of three rivers, several "ghost towns," and enough underground water to supply all southern New Jersey.

The State of New Jersey did that in 1954 when it purchased the so-called Wharton Tract for $3 million. The tract spreads through three counties — Atlantic, Burlington, and Camden. Its area — 156 square miles — is much larger than Essex County's total of 128 square miles.

Joseph Wharton, a Philadelphia industrialist and financier, began assembling acreage in 1876, hoping to raise such warm weather crops as sugar, cotton, and sugar beets. The experiments failed.

In 1891, Wharton expressed the hope that water on his land could be used for Philadelphia's needs. The New Jersey legislature passed a law prohibiting such a use.

The land lay idle after Wharton's death in 1909. Then, in 1954, Alfred E. Driscoll, former governor, spearheaded a successful drive to buy the vast tract, primarily for the water potential.

Acquisition of the Wharton Tract more than doubled the state's parkland total in 1954. Since then, millions of visitors have enjoyed the tract's hunting, fishing, hiking, camping, canoeing, and other recreational activities.

Naturalists from many parts of the world visit to see the hundreds of flowers and shrubs growing beneath the towering pine trees. They must hike or ride Jeep-type vehicles over sandy trails, since only one major highway cuts through the preserve.

The most frequented spot within the Wharton Tract is Batsto, a village that has resisted forest fires and depressions for more than one hundred and fifty years. Batsto once produced iron and glass, and then became a "ghost village" until the state acquired the tract.

Threats to the Pine Barrens are constant, but in the Wharton Tract, the pines, the water, and the history are safe.

Water and pine trees are the two main components of the Pine Barrens, the last remaining large area of unspoiled woodland in the State of New Jersey.

A Golden Strand

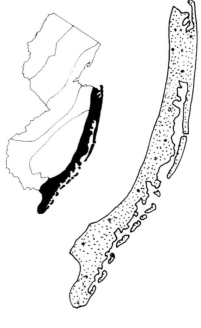

Who really knows the Jersey Shore, that fabled 127 miles of oceanfront stretched between Sandy Hook and Cape May Point? Who knows this coast, in all its moods, all its seasons, all its variety?

Sandy Hook, long a secret defensive outpost but now a state park, is startlingly different from Wildwood or Atlantic City. Cape May's stately Victorian air is in sharp contrast with Asbury Park's beachfront. No one place truly characterizes the Jersey Shore.

The Jersey Shore is actually several types of coastline, beginning with Sandy Hook in the north. Now about seven miles long, the Hook is still being enlarged by sea-carried sand. It has quadrupled in size since it was first explored in 1665, and the old lighthouse, near the tip of the Hook when built in 1762, is now one-and-a-half miles inland.

Southward, from Long Branch to Manasquan Inlet, mainland New Jersey meets the ocean directly. Despite Herculean efforts to restrain it, the Atlantic Ocean has pounded that coast back more than a thousand feet in recorded time — as much as thirty feet in a single savage thrust.

South of Point Pleasant, the oceanfront changes

again. Beginning at Bay Head, a long, thin peninsula juts southward, parallel to the mainland, for more than twenty miles. This peninsula includes state-owned Island Beach State Park as well as a string of resort towns.

From Barnegat Inlet, where old Barnegat Lighthouse stands as the best-known Jersey Shore symbol, every resort area south to Cape May is on an island. Long Beach Island advertises that it is "four miles at sea," but few people realize that Atlantic City is also an island town.

The mainland touches the ocean again at Cape May City, although that resort occasionally calls itself an "island" because the Cape May Canal technically cuts it off from the mainland.

Waves chew constantly at the Cape May mainland. In 1804, Commodore Stephen Decatur, a Cape May vacationer, calculated the distance from Atlantic Hall to the edge of the beach to be 334 feet. Twenty-five years later, ocean tides splashed against the foundations of Atlantic Hall. The ocean had claimed 334 feet in twenty-five years.

Gold Beside The Waves

Visitors have responded to the variety for more than two centuries. In 1766, when one Robert Parsons sought to sell his 54-acre Cape May plantation, he praised "the Sea Shore, where a number resort for health and bathing in the water." Long Branch attracted its first boarding house visitors in 1788.

Eighteenth century visitors walked, rode horseback, or made the trip in wagons hauled through the Pine Barrens. Nineteenth century visitors arrived mainly by railroad car, and it was a railroad that brought Atlantic City into being in 1854. Today's visitors jam the Garden State Parkway or Atlantic City Expressway on their way to their favorite patches of sand.

The Jersey Shore is big business. Summer cottages are always at a premium for summer rentals. The boardwalks are crowded night and day. The beaches at the most popular resorts are packed with umbrellas, beach chairs, towels, and broiling bodies. Vacationers jet ski, parasail, surf the waves with their boards or bodies, wind surf, fish from the shore, board boats to fish at sea, swim, and relax on the beach.

About sixty separate communities line the oceanfront, but not more than a half dozen are genuine boardwalk towns, where the bright lights of night compete with the bright sun of day. Most of the resorts offer little more than sand and sunshine.

Many who travel to the shore never see the sand and surf; some never see the sun. Atlantic City attracts many to its dazzling casinos year-round. They come from near and far to gamble, dine in the fancy restaurants, and enjoy the world-renown entertainment.

One person's seaside pleasure is another's boredom. People who love Avalon or Stone Harbor in Cape May County wouldn't go near Atlantic City. That doesn't disturb Atlantic City supporters, most of whom have never even heard of Avalon or Stone Harbor. Small matter: there is room enough and variety enough for all.

Nature Ignores Mortgages

The Atlantic Ocean gives the Jersey Shore its beaches, its charm, its stimulation, and its value. The ocean also disputes minute by minute, year by year, those who claim to own the seacoast.

Developers ignore the ocean's periodic, terrifying warnings. They slice away dunes and build castles on the uncertain sands. Buyers eagerly take out mortgages to ensure themselves of beachfront cottages. Nature ignores mortgages, just as it ignores every attempt to keep the swirling waves in check. Nature expects cooperation, not opposition.

A comprehensive study of Jersey Shore erosion, made in 1923, showed that in a 100-year period the ocean had eroded away 5,521 acres. Some of the sand was carried off to build up a new 3,025 acres in other places, such as Sandy Hook. The remaining 2,496 acres — enough for nearly eleven million king-sized beach towels — simply vanished into the ocean.

Most of the damage occurs after the summer visitors have gone home. Severe storms usually slash the shore between late September and early November. One exception was a March 1962 storm that probably was the most severe the oceanfront has ever experienced.

The New Jersey Shore has only one real story: Ocean against sand. People are a passing phase. Usually

Fishermen relish the off-season tranquility of the Jersey Shore as much as summer beach-goers revel in its brilliant white sands and inviting surf.

the ocean is relatively mild, but it can snarl and rip and destroy, especially when humans attempt to build counter to its will.

The ocean very seldom erupts during the summer. It calms down in June, July, August, and September, entertaining visitors with a majestic, controlled show under warm blue skies.

Then surf and sand become the Jersey Shore, a beacon for vacationers. The storms, the history, are of little concern to those who love this golden strand only in summertime.

Barnegat Light, finished in 1857, stands 168 feet tall and is painted red and white (above). Long Beach Island vacationers affectionately call the light "Old Barney."

Modern-day geological changes are evidenced in the beaches guarded by lighthouses at the northern and southern tip of the Jersey Shore. The ocean has given enough beach to Sandy Hook that its lighthouse (bottom, left) has appeared to move 1 ½ miles away from the ocean while Cape May Lighthouse (above) looks down at an eroding shoreline. Landings along the climb to the top of the lighthouse explain and depict the ongoing erosion stealing the beaches. The picture below, taken from the top of the lighthouse in November 2005, dramatically shows what erosion and storms can do. The bunker, made of reinforced concrete, with 6-foot roof and walls, was built on dry beach in 1942 — 900 feet from the ocean.

Interpretive nature trails through Island Beach State Park offer access to the bay (left) and the ocean (right).

Island Beach: Sea Coast Bargain

Henry Phipps, a partner of Andrew Carnegie's Pittsburgh steel ventures in the 1920s, could afford to indulge himself. If he wanted ten miles of beachfront along the Jersey Shore, he could buy it — as he did in 1926 when he acquired title to all of Island Beach.

Island Beach had lingered as a name, although the section had been just the lower end of a long peninsula since 1812. Until then, the area was really an island, since a channel through the peninsula allowed ships to sail into Toms River. A wild storm closed the channel in a single night.

Someday, Phipps thought, he might develop the property. The Depression killed that idea, Phipps died, and World War II came. By 1950, as the Jersey Shore was beginning a period of frenzied development, this strip of seacoast was much as it had been through all time.

New Jersey officials reacted quickly in 1952, after a real estate developer sought to buy Island Beach. The state paid $2.7 million for what the National Park Service termed "the last remaining significant stretch of natural beach and dune land in the Northeastern United States." It was a precious bargain!

The ten-mile-long state-owned park preserves the natural state. There is a public swimming area and one mile of life-guarded beach in the northern part, near Seaside Park. Public access is also allowed for fishing, bird-observing, biking, and strolling the interpretive nature trails.

The natural area is an intriguing reminder of what the Jersey Shore was like when the first settlers came more than 375 years ago. Dunes rise high over the beachfront. Near Barnegat Bay on the west side Spanish oaks and holly trees thrive, and beach plums are a reminder of colonial days.

With a permit, you can drive a four-wheel drive vehicle onto the beach at the southern end of the park (left) and fish within view of Barnegat Light (right). Signs remind you to keep off the dunes.

The Original People

Fearless, strong, handsome, proud: those were terms used by explorers to describe New Jersey's first settlers, the Lenape, often called "The Original People."

The first Europeans to see the Lenape close up were those aboard the ship that Giovanni da Verrazano sailed into New Jersey waters in 1524. The crew wrote of the Lenape:

"They came without fear aboard our ship. This is the goodliest people and of the fairest conditions that we have found in this our voyage."

These Lenape impressed da Verrazano's men with their size: "They exceed us in bigness." Native Americans were not yet all lumped together as "red men," for the account continued: "They are the color of brass, some of them inclined to whiteness, others are of yellow color."

Men and women alike were "very handsome and well favored," according to the da Verrazano account. They wore their hair "carefully trimmed." The women were portrayed "as well mannered as any women, and of good education."

In short the Lenape were not savages.

Lenape tribes had been here for 10,000 years or more by the time the first Europeans set foot on the New World. The Lenape had traveled far. They left their native land — in what is now Siberia — and walked, through many centuries and countless

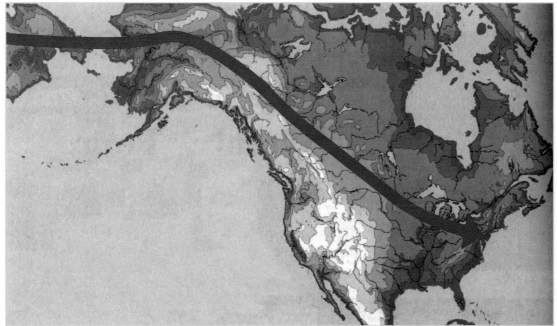

Many generations of Lenape walked for thousands of years before settling in New Jersey or, as they called it, *Scheyechbi*, "Land Along Water."

Before the European explorers arrived, the only boats the Lenape had seen were their dugout canoes. (The photo above was taken at The Lenape Village, Historic Site of Waterloo, Stanhope.)

generations, halfway around the world to settle what is now New Jersey.

They won the land fairly. They first survived as wandering hunters, battling without fear even the giant mastodons and other prehistoric beasts that were here when the Lenape arrived.

Long before the Europeans arrived, the Lenape ceased their nomadic wanderings. They settled in scattered villages facing swiftly-running streams, built homes and community centers, fashioned tools for farming, and made utensils for cooking.

Village life centered on the long house, where tribal ceremonies were held. Private homes were simple. The framework consisted of green saplings bent over, fastened at the top, and then covered with bark, skins, or grass mats. A hole in the roof let smoke from interior fires escape. Platforms around the edges served as beds or seats.

The Lenape, as children of nature, approached life simply. They wore animal skins in winter and as little as possible in summer. They were, according to the da Verrazano account, "all naked save a cover of deerskin." Men and women adorned themselves as necessary, with male vanity even more evident than female. Both wore beads, earrings, and arm bands. Men painted their faces for various ceremonies, from thanksgiving to preparation for war.

Food consisted of whatever was close at hand — animals felled by spears or arrows or caught in traps, fish speared in streams, vegetables from well-tended gardens, berries from the woods, and shellfish from the ocean.

Most students of Lenape life agree Lenape marriages usually lasted. Family tasks were divided. Men hunted, fished, built the houses, and fought possible enemies; women tended the gardens, cooked the food, made the clothes, and tended the young children.

Children never interrupted their parents — but, in turn, adults also waited courteously for others to finish speaking. Hospitality was constant; a pot of food always simmered on the fire, signifying the family would share what it had with strangers.

Tribes carefully respected hunting and fishing rights, and the Lenape believed in peace. Warring tribes called them "The Old Women," not necessarily in scorn, for the Lenape interceded often in wars between other major tribes.

These peace-loving, hospitable Native Americans welcomed European settlers and permitted them to share the bounties of the land. The Lenape probably had no awareness they were "selling" land when the newcomers offered cash or trinkets in exchange for huge pieces of property, assuming they were merely sharing hunting and fishing grounds.

The number of Native Americans in New Jersey when the first Dutch and Swedish settlers arrived, between 1620 and 1640, is estimated at about 2,000. Within less than a century, fewer than 500 survived. Some moved north or west; most died from evils brought by the Europeans.

Smallpox and measles, both imported from Europe, hit the Lenape fiercely. One epidemic in the 1680s swept away the Lenape so fast there was not time even to bury the dead. Alcohol and guns killed or ruined many others.

The Lenape grew ever weaker, ever more despised by their conquerors, ever more insecure, and ever more dependent on those who displaced them. When the Lenape were offered a reservation in the Pine Barrens at Brotherton in 1758, only about 200 were left to take advantage of the offer.

Later, beset with starvation, cold, and misery, the Lenape were invited to join others of the tribe who had migrated to Lake Oneida in New York. Come, said the New Yorkers, and spread your mats before "our fireplace, where you will eat with your grandchildren out of one dish and use one spoon."

The surviving Lenape accepted the offer in 1802. Brotherton fell into ruin. There is now scarcely a trace of the Lenape at the site, now renamed Indian Mills.

In time, the Lenape traveled westward to live on reservations in or near Oklahoma. A few won fame as scouts for exploring parties headed for the Pacific Coast.

Little tangible remains of New Jersey's Native Americans. None of their clothing exists. No houses stand, since the flimsy saplings and hides or bark vanished with time. Archeologists have uncovered evidence of their villages and burial places, as well as arrowheads, weapons, ornaments, and bits of pottery.

The Lenape left their mark in melodic place names: Raritan, Passaic, Hackensack, and Rockaway; Manahawkin, Manasquan, Absecon, and Navesink; Kittatinny, Hopatcong, Watchung, and Ramapo; Pompton, Whippany, Alloway, and Tuckahoe.

Lenape names are spelled and pronounced the way early settlers believed the Lenape spoke, but the poetic place names are worthy of keeping even in the corrupted versions. Through them, the Original People are still part of the land.

Interpretations of the original people are as varied as the artists who depicted them. Through the years, the Lenape have been shown as everything from boldly savage to timidly primitive. The paintings and sketches on this page underscore the artistic differences. The artist who painted the *Purchase of Newark* (upper left) imagined a "warrior" with head shaved except for a center tuft. Similar Lenape appear (left) in a Trenton State College mural that represents a 1758 treaty between the Lenape and the State of New Jersey. Directly above is Oratam, chief of the Hackensacks.

Probably closer to fact are 17th century sketches. A lone Lenape (upper right) appeared on a Dutch map drawn in 1656 by Adrian Van der Donck. The Lenape family (center) was sketched by Swedish observer Johan Campanius Holm in the 1640s. A modern State Museum portrayal of a Lenape women hoeing uses the primitive look.

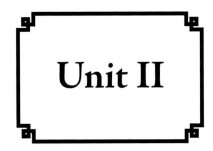

Unit II

President Roosevelt was not quite correct. All Americans, even pure-blooded Native Americans, are descended from immigrants. The Lenape came here from what is now Siberia, many thousands of years before Europeans dared sail westward on the Atlantic Ocean.

Immigration is the basic story of the United States. In time, wave after wave of European immigrants followed the Lenape. A relative few came to a wilderness as 17th century colonists; most came two centuries later to work in an industrial America.

Except for millions of Africans cruelly kidnapped and brought to America as slaves, most immigrants expected to exchange a miserable homeland for a land where dreams came true.

The dreams were many. Early explorers sought a westward water passage to India, the storied land of easy riches. Some of the earliest settlers were adventurers, lured by thoughts of gold. Many yearned for a place where they might find freedom from religious persecution.

Some of the early European settlers were forced to board ships bound for the New World. They were debtors, the political prisoners, and white servants who were promised freedom after several years of service. These people did not come voluntarily, yet most of them recognized a new world offered more chance than the filthy slums of London or the foul jails of Europe.

The first colonists were a mixed group — Dutch and Swedes in New Jersey, English debtors in Georgia, English Puritans in Massachusetts, English Catholics in Maryland.

Others followed, chiefly for religious reasons: English Baptists, Quakers, and Methodists; French Huguenots, German Lutherans, Scotch Presbyterians. By the time of the American Revolution, New Jersey had as mixed a group of colonists as any of the colonies.

Crossing the Atlantic Ocean in the 17th and 18th centuries was an ominous undertaking. The wild storms of the North Atlantic and the miserable accommodations aboard tiny ships were bad enough. There were other terrors. Tales persisted of giant sea monsters. Moreover, many people were not convinced the world was round. Stories of fierce, hostile Indians were common.

A Nation Of Immigrants

Yet men, women, and children set out on the journey, believing they were giving up persecution for freedom. It is important to know these were the bold dissenters — the rebels who felt so strongly about their beliefs they would face almost any danger to practice them.

Most colonists sought personal freedom on their own terms. That quest for "freedom" often meant finding a haven from which all dissenters from the "true faith" would be forever excluded. Yet, their beliefs in liberty saw nothing wrong with slavery.

Many of the Puritan founders of Massachusetts grew disenchanted with what they felt was a growing spoilage of their religion. They pressed west and south, always seeking some place where they might install their rigid system in which church and state were one. They roamed — to Connecticut, Long Island, and finally to New Jersey in the 1660s.

The people who brought America into being were daring, independent, rebellious, even cantankerous. A common bond among the families was the memory of suffering at home, whether by mistreatment in a debtor's prison or as a result of religious persecution.

Naturally these colonists, who braved danger for their beliefs, were angered by English attempts to govern them from 3,000 miles away. The settlers considered themselves English, but they ignored governmental orders, opposed governors appointed by the king, and argued incessantly in their own colonial governments.

The years passed. New generations of Americans were born on this side of the Atlantic. They listened to their parents and grandparents and warmed to stories of the daring gamble for freedom rather than dimly remembered glories of the "homeland."

These generations of native-born Americans became less and less attached to an England they had never seen and never expected to see. They encountered "England" only in the persons of red-coated soldiers who appeared occasionally to back up orders from a distant government. A new breed of "Americans" was emerging. The seeds of revolution were planted a century or more before July 4, 1776. By then, most of those who would decide on revolution were members of families that had been in the New World 125 years or more. They had enjoyed the fruits of freedom. Eventually they would have to decide whether they would fight to keep it.

United States		New Jersey	
Columbus discovers America	1492		
Ponce de Leon discovers Florida	1513		
		1524	Verrazano sees New Jersey
Jamestown settled	1607		
		1609	Hudson explores New Jersey coast
1st African slaves sold in Virginia	1619	1626	New Amsterdam founded
Massachusetts Bay Colony founded	1630		
Maryland settled	1633		
Connecticut settled	1635		
		1638	New Sweden established on Delaware River
English capture Dutch fort at New Amsterdam	1664	1664	English take over NJ and give it a name
		1675	Quakers found their first New World colony at Salem
William Penn founds Philadelphia	1682	1702	East and West New Jersey united
		1745	Land riots rock New Jersey
Georgia founded	1733		
French and Indian (Seven Year) War begins	1754		
Stamp Act Congress	1765	1765	NJ opposes Stamp Act
Declaration of Independence	1776	1776	American forces score major victories at Trenton & Princeton
Battle of Saratoga	1777	1777	Battle of Red Bank (Fort Mercer)
Siege of Savannah	1778	1778	Battle of Monmouth
Siege of Charlestown	1780	1780	Washington spends worst winter at Morristown
		1780	Battle of Springfield
Victory at Yorktown	1781		
Treaty of Paris established American independence	1783	1783	Congress receives Treaty of Paris at Nassau Hall, Princeton

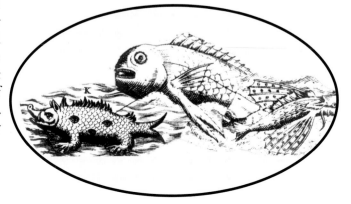

Chapter Two - New Holland And New Sweden

United States		New Jersey	
Magellan begins voyage around world	1519		
Verrazano explores North Atlantic Coast	1524	1524	Verrazano sails into New Jersey waters
Virginia settlement started	1607	1609	Hudson anchors at Sandy Hook
Pilgrims found Plymouth	1620		
Minuit buys Manhattan	1626	1626	New Amsterdam (including NJ area) begins
		1633	First permanent Dutch settlers at Pavonia
First Connecticut settlement	1636	1638	New Sweden founded
New England Confederation established	1643	1643	Dutch massacre Indians at Pavonia: Indian wars begin
First group of Jews in New Amsterdam	1654	1655	Dutch seize Swedish settlements on Delaware
		1660	Bergen becomes New Jersey's first organized village
English subdue New Amsterdam	1664	1664	New Jersey founded and named

Henry Hudson's little Dutch Ship, the *Half Moon*, left the docks of Amsterdam in April 1609 and headed northwest across the Atlantic Ocean. Out there, somewhere, Hudson was certain there was a water route to China.

A previous expedition failed to prove Hudson's theory, but the Dutch East India Company had faith in this English captain hired to lead the way to fortune. Hudson, in turn, trusted the English aides he enlisted to guide this ship across the perilous Atlantic.

One of those English aides, Robert Juet, ensured Hudson's place in history by keeping a careful journal of the voyage. There is evidence that Juet kept the record to prove he had not joined mutineers aboard the ship, but thanks to Juet's writings, the memory of Henry Hudson is preserved.

Within a month of sailing, trouble threatened the *Half Moon*. Frightened by the dense fog, the raging storms, and the icebergs of the North Atlantic, the crew turned mutinous between May 5 and May 19. Hudson agreed to their demand the ship turn south to warmer, safer waters.

The *Half Moon* was off Cape Cod by early August. It sailed south to the Virginia coast, and then

◇◇◇◇◇◇◇◇◇◇◇◇◇◇◇◇◇◇◇◇◇◇◇

Passage To The Indies

Christopher Columbus proved in 1492 that a ship could sail west, at least for 2,500 miles, without falling off the edge of what many feared was a flat earth.

Columbus gambled the earth was round, for the stakes were high. If a water route to India and China ("The Indies") could be found by sailing westward, the nation sponsoring the voyage would be rich beyond the wildest fables. Hopefully, the land Columbus reached would be the "West Indies."

The race to "The Indies" was on. England hired Giovanni and Sebastian Caboto (or Cabot), Italian navigators, to sail westward along the coast of a new world in 1498. Giovanni da Verrazano, another Italian, sailed a French ship westward in 1524.

Verrazano maneuvered his vessel into what is now New York harbor in the fall of 1524 to get what probably was the first close-up view of present-day New Jersey. He decided this was no short cut to the Indies and probably no place that

offered hope for quick riches. He sailed away.

The centuries-old search for the legendary wealth of the Indies obscured the natural riches of a new continent — the unlimited open spaces, the fertile soil, the thick forests, the abundance of game, and the clean, swift-flowing streams.

European kings encouraged private companies to send expeditions to the New World. Spain, England, and Holland all set tiny bands of adventurers ashore in the greedy hunt for treasure.

Gold prospectors, fur traders, and soldiers never found the chests of coins and jewels or the spices and tapestries of the Indies, but those adventurers prepared the way.

Soon others would follow, to farm rather than dig for gold. The Dutch would venture westward across the Hudson River into what would become New Jersey. Not long after, Swedes would settle along the Delaware.

These people had come to stay and to work. They would make the difference. The colony of New Jersey would be born.

reversed course on August 16 and moved north before the prevailing winds. The crew had been at sea for four months: faith in their captain was dangerously low again.

Excitement and joy raced through the ship on August 28, the day Juet scribbled word that a "great bay" had been sighted. Perhaps the opening to the Indies was found at last! Hopes were dashed within minutes when the *Half Moon* went aground on a sand bar in what is now Delaware Bay off Cape May.

Hudson backed the ship off the shoal and resumed sailing north. This time, the happy crew gazed at the "islands in our sight." When Juet wrote that, he was looking at the string of islands between modern Cape May and Barnegat Inlet.

"A Pleasant Land To See"

Juet noted "we saw a great fire" inland on September 2. Somewhere in that darkness, he knew there were other human beings. Juet logged details of the land — the mouth of Barnegat Inlet and "high hills to the north" (either the Navesink Highlands or Staten Island). He wrote enthusiastically:

"This is a very good land to fall with, and a pleasant land to see."

Hudson anchored the *Half Moon* inside Sandy Hook Bay, on September 4, to seek fresh water and to give the crew some rest. Soon, Juet wrote, "the people of the country" (the Lenape) came aboard "and brought green tobacco, and gave us of it for knives and beads." The Lenape were "well dressed" and "very civil," Juet recorded.

Two days later, a search party left the boat to explore the bay. The sailors returned in the afternoon carrying the lifeless body of John Colman, shot through the neck by a Native American arrow. Colman was buried on Sandy Hook, the first European known to have been buried in the area.

Hudson left Sandy Hook and moved northward up a broad, unexplored river beneath the towering cliffs. The *Half Moon* struck shallow water near the site of modern Albany. Once again Hudson learned the sad fact: this was not the passage to India either.

The *Half Moon* headed downstream on September 23, as Juet scribbled descriptions of the land, its thick forests, and the Indians (significantly, he now called them "savages"). The Dutch ship left the

With flags flying, pennants waving, and friendly Native Americans paddling nearby, the *Half Moon* sailed past the towering Palisades in September 1609. This voyage by Captain Henry Hudson gave Holland its claim to the land on both sides of the river that was named for the captain.

North American mainland on October 4 and reached Holland late in November.

Disappointed Dutch East India Company officers found no wealth in the *Half Moon's* hold, but Hudson had given Holland a valid claim in the New World. Juet's journal preserved Hudson's role in colonial exploration. Others would remember Hudson by naming a river and a New Jersey county in his honor.

Piracy And "Trifling Trade"

Investors in the East India Company were casually curious about Juet's notes on "good furs" and the copper ornaments worn by the Indians. More to their liking was mention of a "white green cliff" (probably the Palisades) that held, Juet thought, either a "cop-

per or silver mine." That was more like it.

A few Dutch treasure hunters or fur traders might have landed in New Amsterdam (now New York) before 1615. One or two of them might have ventured briefly into the forests west of the Hudson River in present-day Hudson or Bergen counties before 1620, but none seriously considered settling here.

Control of New Amsterdam passed into the hands of the Dutch West India Company, founded in 1621 to wage piracy on Spanish ships and to conduct a fur trade with the Indians. Colonization had very low priority.

One company report showed furs brought in only sixty *thousand* Dutch guilders a year, compared with sixty *million* guilders from piracy. Rumors of a possible peace treaty with Spain as a means of promoting colonization brought vigorous company protests. Peacetime colonization, the directors argued, would mean only "trifling trade with the Indians."

New Amsterdam was not forgotten completely. Captain Cornelius Jacobsen Mey (for whom Cape May is named) brought thirty families to the area in 1624. The captain spread his followers thinly, from Fort Orange (now Albany) to the Fresh (Connecticut) River and all the way to a tiny settlement on the Delaware River. It proved how "trifling" colonization could be.

Settling a Wilderness

Mey took two families and eight single men up the Delaware River and set them ashore on an island (now Burlington Island). They were the first European settlers on New Jersey soil. Mey found the climate charming "like Holland" and gave several land areas his own name.

Two years later, in 1626, the Dutch established a trading post at what they called Fort Nassau, near modern Gloucester. A Dutch ship visited the Delaware in 1630 and found both Burlington Island and Fort Nassau abandoned. The settlers had vanished, probably having walked through the New Jersey wilderness all the way back to New Amsterdam.

Peter Minuit concluded his famous bargain purchase of the Island of Man-a-hat-ta ("Heavenly Island") from the Indians in 1626. He gave the natives trinkets worth $24 (in currency of the time). At least it was evidence of his earnest desire to seek peace before colonization.

Getting colonists was harder than buying land. The Dutch West India Company complained Dutchmen were so satisfied at home they would not emigrate to New Amsterdam "on an uncertainty." The company told the government it simply could not supply enough colonists for such "wild and uncultivated countries."

Finally, in 1629, the company hit on a scheme. A sponsor (called a patroon) who would pay to send 50 emigrants to the New World within four years would be given a large grant of land. A patroon would have complete control over the lives, behavior, and earnings of his charges. It was not a happy prospect for anyone except the patroon.

Inspired by the chance to become richer and more powerful than ever, a few wealthy Dutchmen agreed to the proposal. Few of their countrymen responded to the patroon's call to exchange comfortable lives for what seemed to be little more than slavery in America.

"Land Of The Peacock"

New Jersey's first permanent residents settled on the property of patroon Michael Pauw, an Amsterdam town official. He was granted a fine site that included most of present day Hoboken and Jersey City. Several Indian trails converged on the Pauw property at the point where canoes could cross to Manhattan.

Pauw's family history provided a name for his vast new estate. The Latin name for Pauw is *pavo* so the Amsterdam owner named his holdings "Pavonia" — meaning "Land of the Peacock." Pauw never left

Holland himself and never found anywhere near fifty persons to occupy his land.

Thanks entirely to one Cornelius Van Vorst, Pauw's director, the "Land of the Peacock" had two houses and a rather substantial number of settlers by 1633. Van Vorst brought his wife, a grown son, Jan; several other children, and several grandchildren.

Van Vorst was no ordinary hired estate manager. He spoke two languages, was hardy and resourceful, and was pleased to be in the Land of the Peacock. When Pauw failed to find fifty emigrants for his estate, he had to give Pavonia back to the West India Company, in 1634. The Van Vorsts did not care who owned the land. They chose to stay in America.

The Van Vorsts built their houses close to the salt marsh along the Hudson. Son Jan traded with the Native Americans for furs, and on one trip home to Holland he took along thousands of beaver skins to sell. Those furs did more to sell the advantages of America than all the patroon promises.

Something of a diplomat, Van Vorst knew he must keep in the good graces of the company officials. He invited the colony's governor and the church minister over from Manhattan Island, in 1636, to share a shipment of rare wines just received from Holland. The wine unfortunately made tempers flare and harsh words were shouted.

When his guests were about to depart for Manhattan, Van Vorst shot a gunfire salute into the air to show there were no hard feelings in Pavonia. A spark

No sketch exists of Dutch settlements in what is now Hudson County, but this old woodcut of a New Amsterdam setting shows a typical Dutch area. There would have been a few scattered homes, barns, fruit trees, and perhaps a boat or two being built. Atop the nearest high hill, a windmill would have been turning to provide energy to pump water or to turn mill wheels.

from the gunpowder landed on his thatched roof, set fire to the house, and it burned to the ground. As evidence of Van Vorst's standing in New Amsterdam, the house was rebuilt at government expense.

Tensions Mount

Governor William Kiefft arrived in 1638 with instructions to expand the fur trade. Settlements were begun in modern Hoboken, Ridgefield Park, and Old Tappan. On New Year's Day, 1641, Aert VanPutten leased "a certain bowerie named *Hoboquin*" for ten years.

VanPutten cleared his land and built a house. He brought to Hoboken twenty-eight large cattle, "besides various more stock, swine, goats, etc. and sheep, together with many of his fruit trees." He settled down in style with his wife, children, and servants and, in 1642, built America's first brewery at Hoboken.

The scattered population west of the Hudson River lived in uneasy fear of the natives. Traders were warned not to exchange alcohol for furs. The warning was ignored and drunken natives, once a rarity, became more numerous. Additionally, the natives became more aggressive, causing one official to warn against "admitting them to the table, laying napkins before them, presenting wine to them, and more of that kind of thing."

Tension mounted. Dutch settlers girded for possible attack. Fear gripped the entire populated region west of the Hudson River. A showdown was near, and when it came in the winter of 1643 the blame lay entirely with the Dutch.

Massacre In Pavonia

Governor Kiefft decided he must prove to the natives who ruled the territory. He chose the night of February 25, 1643 to unleash a surprise attack on a large group of natives encamped at Pavonia. Captain David DeVries wrote an eyewitness account of the slaughter that resulted from Kiefft's decision to make the natives "wipe their chops."

"Let this work alone," DeVries warned Kiefft. "You will go to break the Indians, but it is our nation you are going to murder."

Kiefft was in no mood for warnings. He ordered eighty Dutch soldiers to cross the river to "drive away and destroy the savages." The governor added piously: "Spare as much as it is possible their wives and children." Kiefft concluded by asking God to "bless the expedition."

DeVries, who remained in New Amsterdam, recalled the brutal massacre: "About midnight I heard a great shrieking and went to the ramparts of the fort and looked over to Pavonia, saw nothing but firing and heard the shrieks of the savages murdered in

The exaggerated 17th century woodcut on the right, probably meant to show the bravery of Dutch colonizers, portrayed an attack on the natives. One such assault, as that at Pavonia on February 25, 1643, caused the natives to rip down Dutch emblems before rampaging through the area in fiery retaliation.

their sleep."

Before the night was over, eighty Native Americans were dead. Sounds of the prolonged savage butchery sent chills of fear and disgust through Dutch homes. The berserk soldiers ignored Kiefft's order to spare women and children. One account told of children "slain while fastened to their little boards." Another told of youngsters being thrown in the river to drown. When parents waded in to save them, Dutch guns felled young and old.

Many of Kiefft's subjects vigorously protested the slaughter. One wrote: "This is indeed a disgrace to our nation."

The Natives Retaliate

The Dutch massacre set the entire frontier aflame. In retaliation, the Hackensacks, joined by thousands of warriors from other tribes, rampaged through nearly all the Dutch territory, killing and burning as they went. Not a settlement was safe between the Raritan and Connecticut rivers.

Aert VanPutten's family at Hoboken was wiped out except for Mrs. VanPutten, who managed to escape. VanPutten, away from home, was killed on his sloop while trading with Native Americans in Shrewsbury Inlet. His children and servants were murdered. The farm was destroyed — cattle, horses, sheep, and swine slain; and the barns and house burned. The natives spared only the brewery.

Spring brought a temporary cessation of the warfare. The Native Americans accepted Dutch peace terms and went home to sow their gardens. The truce did not last. The natives harvested their corn in the late summer, and then returned to the warpath.

The raids on the frontier settlements continued for nearly eighteen months before a permanent truce was secured in 1645. Nearly everything west of the

Dutch settlements in the New World centered on New Amsterdam on the southern tip of Manhattan Island. On the left, a 19th century woodcut recaptures the appearance of the fort on the eastern edge of town commanded by Captain David DeVries. The drawing on the right shows the towering city hall and the great dock as they appeared in 1679.

Penelope And Her Stout Family

Dutch newlyweds named van Princis had a wild introduction to America in 1640. A raging storm wrecked their ship off Sandy Hook. Most of the survivors walked overland to New Amsterdam.

Penelope van Princis stayed on the beach to nurse her ill husband. Natives attacked, killed the husband, and left Penelope unconscious with a fractured skull, mangled left arm, and slashed stomach. Friendly natives found the girl, nursed her back to health, and helped her reach friends.

Four years later, Penelope married Richard Stout, an English sailor who left his British ship in New Amsterdam when his enlistment expired. The couple moved to Middletown in Monmouth County — not far from where Penelope nearly died.

Remarkably, considering the wounds she suffered, Penelope van Princis Stout gave birth to seven sons and three daughters. When she died in 1712, Mrs. Stout left 492 living descendants. Today thousands of descendants trace themselves back to Penelope, a Stout-hearted woman indeed.

43

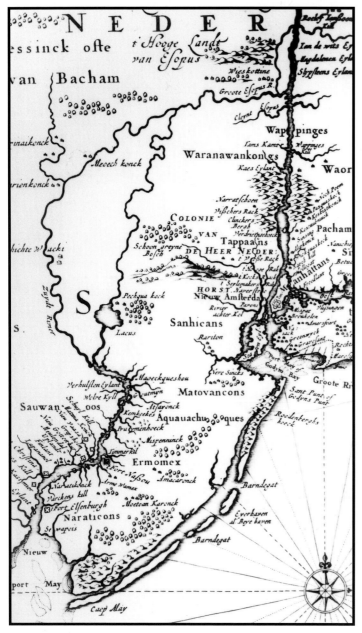

This portion of a map drawn in 1656 by Adrien Van der Donck shows the area that is now New Jersey. The shape of New Jersey is quite clear, although the Delaware (or Zuydt) River wanders vaguely to the northwest. Several Dutch and Swedish forts are marked along the Delaware River. Staten Island (or Eylandt) is shown, as is Manhattan. Peculiarly, Nieuw Amsterdam is shown on the west side of the Hudson River. Settlements appear near what are now New Brunswick and the northern part of Monmouth County.

Mountains are correctly placed to the northwest, and a large woodland (the Pine Barrens) covers much of the southern part. Yet Van der Donck also showed high hills in Cape May and along most of the northern shore. This is strange, since his rendering of the offshore islands is otherwise reasonably correct.

Considering the information and the equipment available in 1656, the map is remarkable in its detail.

Hudson River lay in ruins. Blackened remains of farms were a stark proof of DeVries' prediction "our nation" would be murdered. Uneasiness about possible native raids pinned the Dutch close to the Hudson River. Few Hollanders chose to emigrate to New Amsterdam. Holland's venture in the New World was in danger of oblivion.

The Delaware River was open to any nation ready to challenge the scant Dutch attempts at colonization. When Sweden decided to join the European pursuit of riches and glory in America, it chose the Delaware River for the venture.

New Sweden On The Delaware

Sweden's King Gustavus Adolphus emerged as Europe's leading military figure by welding Sweden, Finland, Estonia, and Latvia into one Scandinavian union. Sweden could dream of further conquests, and except for more warfare in Europe, it might well have challenged Holland as early as 1624.

Sweden's ambitions were aided by Hollanders dissatisfied with Dutch attempts to colonize America. William Usselinx, one of the founders of the Dutch West India Company, approached King Gustavus in 1624 and urged him to start a Swedish colony on the Delaware River.

Gustavus also had a surprise visit in 1626 from Peter Minuit, who had just returned from his celebrated low-cost purchase of Manhattan Island. Minuit suggested the king found a Delaware River colony, "which might be named Nova Swedia" (New Sweden). Minuit volunteered to lead the expedition personally. His requirements were small — one vessel and a dozen soldiers.

For his part, Minuit promised to return with "4500 or 6000 beaver skins." King Gustavus agreed with Minuit's declaration this would be "a large capital from so small a commencement." However, Sweden's involvement in the Thirty Years' War in Germany postponed Minuit's plan for nearly a dozen years. The delay robbed New Sweden of most of its chance to survive.

Dutchmen Plant Sweden's Flag

Except for granting a charter and supplying two ships and a few soldiers, Sweden invested very little in founding New Sweden when it finally got around to colonization in 1637.

Minuit raised most of the necessary money,

getting about half in Holland. He and his Dutch associates bought supplies in Holland, hired Dutch crews, and signed on Dutch captains to pilot two Swedish ships.

Holland did not seem disturbed by this open Swedish proposal to occupy land the Dutch claimed. Indeed, Minuit's two ships put into Holland for repairs, and when they sailed on New Year's Eve 1637 six Dutch colonists bound for New Amsterdam were aboard as passengers.

Minuit guided his two ships into Delaware Bay in mid-March 1638. He established Fort Christina near what is now Wilmington, Delaware, and then bought a strip of riverbank land from the natives. Minuit informed the Dutch he was merely stopping by to pick up wood and water before resuming his voyage "to the West Indies."

Before summer's end, Minuit set out for Sweden to get more supplies and settlers. He left behind 25 soldiers in the log enclosure at Fort Christina. Minuit vanished at sea in a hurricane, and with his disappearance New Sweden lost its premier promoter.

"The Swedes Still There"

Fort Nassau's Dutch soldiers, curious about the Swedish promises to leave, reported they went down river "some time afterwards." They "found the Swedes still there." A garden behind the fort was filled with "salads, pot herbs, and the like."

The Dutch soldiers asked the Swedes "whether they intended to stay there." The Swedes excused themselves for various reasons. The Dutch said, "it became apparent, from their building a fort, what their intentions were."

The men of Fort Nassau said they made several protests about the "intolerable insolence," but the protests had "as much effect as the flying of a crow overhead."

Peter Ridder, another Dutchman in Swedish uniform, replaced the lost Minuit. He tried to interest Swedish blacksmiths, shoemakers, brickmakers, carpenters, and similar artisans to join him in the New World. They were not eager to leave home, so army deserters and political prisoners were rounded up. A few soldiers and a clergyman also were with Ridder when he reached the Delaware colony in April 1640.

Ridder's plea for more settlers brought him more army deserters and others permitted to emigrate to America rather than serve jail terms. The latter included many Finns, whose crimes usually were no

Where Log Cabins Began
Swedish and Finnish settlers built America's first log cabins in the frontier beside the Delaware River in New Jersey and Delaware. Later, as new generations of Americans pushed westward, log cabins became identified with the western lands.

Log cabins were found in much of southwestern New Jersey. Two traveling Dutchmen, Jaspar Dankers and Peter Sluyter, wrote in 1679 of one such cabin near Burlington built "according to the Swedish mode." Swedish cabins, according to the Dutch wanderers, were "nothing less than entire trees, split through the middle or squared out of the rough." The timbers were notched at the ends and placed together with the notches at the corners of a building. Rough roofs were added. The simple one-room cabins had dirt floors. Windows were slits in the logs, usually closed with a sliding panel (a few wealthier Swedes enjoyed the luxury of glass windows). The doors were wide but low, forcing a visitor to stoop on entering.

C.A. Weslager, author of The Log Cabin in America, *notes that the oldest log cabin remaining in New Jersey is probably a portion of the Nothnagle House (above) near Repaupo in Gloucester County. It is thought to be the oldest in the Western Hemisphere. A corner fireplace and chimney, characteristic of the Swedish-Finnish cabins, are intact. The tall part on the right was added later.*

The state's best known log cabin (below) is on the grounds of the Hancock House at Hancock's Bridge in Salem County. It was moved to the present location from upper Salem County.

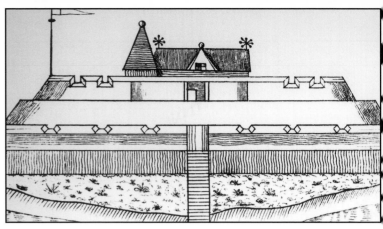

Johan Campanius Holm drew Swedish Fort Trinity as it appeared in the 1640s on a Delaware River bluff south of modern Wilmington. (right) Trinity was one of three Swedish forts on the river, including Fort Elfsborg in New Jersey.

Below: a group of Swedes in 17th century dress

more serious than burning timber on their own land in defiance of government orders. The newcomers also included several women and children.

The Finns made robust colonists, for they had little to lose. Finland had been conquered by Sweden. New Sweden's worst would be far better than what Finns might expect at home from old Sweden. The Finns were among the first to see America could be a land of personal opportunity.

A Giant For New Sweden

Struggling little New Sweden desperately needed a giant to lead it. One arrived, quite literally, on February 15, 1643 when Governor Johan Printz lumbered down the gangplank to succeed Ridder. Printz weighed 400 pounds, and some accounts describe him as being seven feet tall. He was the biggest colonist the New World ever would see.

The son of a Swedish clergyman and himself an ex-army colonel, Printz was considered by his enemies to be an arrogant, free-spending dictator. His friends believed his severe tactics were in New Sweden's best interests.

The Governor had none of the legendary fat man's good humor. When Indians called him "Big Tub" or "Big Belly," Printz swore if he had more soldiers, "with the help of God not a single savage would be allowed to live on this river." Those "savages" sold the Swedes and Finns enough grain to see them through several harsh winters.

Printz was an effective governor. He gave New

Sweden the only chance it had to survive. He moved rapidly to impress everyone in the Delaware River valley he was determined to save the colony.

Printz sent soldiers into what is now New Jersey to build Fort Elfsborg where a point of land juts out into the Delaware River (in what is now Salem County). The fort's guns forced intimidated Dutch sea captains to haul down their flags to ask permission to pass the Swedish guns. Fort Elfsborg momentarily made New Sweden a power on the east bank of the Delaware.

New Sweden Is Doomed

Printz's iron will was not enough to save the settlement. Ships seldom came from the homeland. One that arrived in the summer of 1644 brought such necessities as saws, pumps, grindstones, and tools as well as large bolts of cloth for flags and ten gilded flagpole knobs for a hard-pressed colony that had only about three or four places where a flag might be flown.

New Sweden was doomed by the lack of concern in the homeland. In a stretch of five years, not one Swedish ship sailed into Delaware Bay with provisions or more colonists. Printz complained constantly in letters to Sweden. He might as well have saved the ink.

As if Sweden's indifference were not enough to undo Printz, a new leader came to New Amsterdam to strike a death knell for the colony on the Delaware. The Dutch newcomer was the able Governor Peter Stuyvesant, whose awesome temper and unflagging energy made him a match for Printz.

New Amsterdam finally had the man capable of running a colony. When the one-legged Stuyvesant limped ashore on May 11, 1647, he vowed he would be "as a father over his children." Immediately, however, he commanded his "children" to stand bareheaded in his presence. He shouted in a "foul manner befitting the fish market" at those who opposed him. He stormed: "We derive our authority from God and the company, not from a few ignorant subjects."

Despite his love of power, Stuyvesant was an intelligent, colorful governor. He hobbled through the streets of New Amsterdam, his wooden leg tapping out a sound of authority across the wooden docks. The villagers called him "Old Peg Leg" or "Old Silver Nails," in mock homage to the silver nails in his wooden leg.

These nicknames were only whispered, for the New Amsterdam people feared Stuyvesant's tyranny. He told one group that threatened to appeal to authorities at home if he heard of another dissenter, "I will make him a foot shorter and send the pieces to Holland to let him appeal in that way."

Peg Leg Challenges Big Tub

"Old Peg Leg" decided in 1651 to challenge "Big Tub" for mastery of the Delaware River. The odds were heavily in Stuyvesant's favor — his people outnumbered the Swedes at least ten to one. Dutch supplies were ample, and New Sweden was weak and neglected.

Stuyvesant accompanied 120 men on a forced march overland to Fort Nassau on the Delaware on June 24, 1651. Eleven Dutch ships ignored the Swedish guns at Fort Elfsborg to sail up the river to join him.

To terrorize the Swedes and Finns, the Dutch fleet sailed up and down the river "drumming and connonading." In a futile gesture, Printz followed the enemy Dutch fleet up and down the river in his own small yacht. It was almost comic, and perhaps Printz meant it to be.

Later that year, the Dutch built Fort Casimir (now New Castle, Delaware) downstream from the Swedish strongholds. That made Fort Elfsborg's position untenable, and Printz withdrew his soldiers from the fort. Legend has it that marshland mosquitoes, rather than the Dutch invaders, ended Fort Elfsborg's days — but the sting *had* been bearable until the Dutch arrived.

Printz decided in 1653 that ten years of New Sweden's frustration were enough. He took his wife, four daughters, and about twenty-five other New Sweden settlers to New Amsterdam, where they boarded a Dutch ship for home. Printz promised to return or to send supplies and colonists within ten months.

Ironically, unknown to the departing Governor, Sweden was about to give its American colony the only substantial support it ever received. Some 250 colonists — about four times the number already in New Sweden — embarked in 1654, led by a new Governor, Johan Rising.

Rising made a fatal mistake on his way up the Delaware: he stopped to "conquer" Fort Casimir. He fired two cannon shots over the fort and a detachment of his soldiers entered the fort to accept surrender.

The Knights of Albion

England's Lord Plowden asked King Charles I, in 1634, for a huge piece of America that included all of modern New Jersey, Maryland, Delaware, and Pennsylvania. The king agreed, overlooking two important details: he gave almost exactly the same land to Lord Baltimore more than two years before, and it was land claimed by Holland.

Plowden then began one of the strangest episodes in colonial history. He advertised his empire widely, urging true believers to join his mythical "Knights of Albion," whose castle town would be near what is now Salem County.

The English lord planned to convert the "Twenty-three Kings" (supposed Indian chiefs of the area) to Christianity. He promised to use the Bible and the sword, both shown on his emblems. The sword was first in mind, since twenty-two of the twenty-three Indian "kings" on Plowden's medallion were shown as beheaded. The remaining one presumably would accept conversion and be spared.

Plowden's associates would be "Knights," in the legendary pattern of King Arthur's noble followers. Plowden himself would be "Edmund, by Divine Providence, Lord Proprietor, Earl Palatine, Governor, and Captain General of the Province of New Albion."

After his Lordship visited the Delaware River in 1642 (and saw both Swedes and Dutch in place), he issued pamphlets describing the virtues of his fanciful empire.

A modern reader of Plowden writings can almost imagine gales of laughter pouring from the Lord's English castle as he and his "Knights" gathered on winter evenings to sip ale and to plan their "Albion," but it was no joke to Plowden.

"Edmund by Divine Providence" (self-anointed) never got to use either the sword or the Bible in the New World. As he daydreamed, others settled the land without the need for fancy titles.

Governor Johan Printz, who reached New Sweden in 1843, weighed more than 400 pounds, as can be imagined from his portrait below. The natives called him "Big Tub," and both they and his colonists feared him. He went into towering rages in scolding his subjects, but his toughness was needed to keep the weak colony alive.

Stuyvesant Rules Supreme

Infuriated by the loss of Fort Casimir, Stuyvesant waited a year to put together a fleet that carried 317 soldiers to the Delaware. Fort Casimir's Swedish defenders surrendered meekly in September 1655. A few days later, Fort Christina also capitulated without a shot being fired. New Sweden was dead.

Stuyvesant offered the conquered settlers a generous choice: go home peacefully or stay and continue to farm the land. Most of New Sweden's officers sailed for home. Most of the others stayed on, unconcerned about who governed the region as long as they were free to work the soil.

Stuyvesant had no time to enjoy his bloodless conquest. Natives surrounding New Amsterdam once again had been roused to fury while Stuyvesant was away. Their anger was triggered by the senseless murder of a young native girl who tried to pick a ripe peach from a New Amsterdam orchard.

Five hundred enraged natives besieged New Amsterdam, demanding revenge. Turned back, the rampaging natives recrossed the Hudson River and "in the twinkle of an eye" Hoboken and Pavonia were aflame. In three days, more than 100 settlers were killed, 150 were carried into captivity, and another 300 made homeless.

Stuyvesant reacted quickly, more in anger at his own people's folly than at the natives' behavior. He ordered everyone west of the Hudson River to live in villages, "like our neighbors of New England." Failure to obey meant a heavy fine. Stuyvesant banned houses with straw roofs or wooden chimneys, as a precaution against fires that might be started by flaming native arrows.

Nearly all of the families living in what is now Hudson County followed Stuyvesant's orders. In 1660, they established Bergen as New Jersey's first organized village. (Old Bergen is now Bergen Square in the heart of Jersey City.)

New Amsterdam Prospers

New Amsterdam, from the Hudson to the Delaware, prospered under Stuyvesant's rigid rule. Demand for dock space on Manhattan Island grew steadily. By 1660, hundreds of immigrants from a number of European nations arrived every year. The island of Manhattan had become America's first haven for immigrants.

The newcomers included people from Germany,

France, and other parts of northern Europe, fleeing religious persecution or other restrictions on their personal liberties. They were in America not to seek fortunes, but to work farms and enjoy independence. Some moved west of the Hudson river in search of open spaces.

New settlers also occupied open lands on both sides of the lower Delaware River, finding room among Swedes and Finns scattered throughout the area. Stuyvesant urged settlement on the east (New Jersey) side of the river where, he wrote, the land was "good and fertile."

Holland authorities forced many to sail to New Amsterdam, including little children from the alms-houses. The children were "bound out" to families already in America — that is, they were obliged to become servants or farmhands until they had worked out their freedom. Stuyvesant asked for more such workers, "but if possible, none ought to come less than 15 years of age and somewhat strong."

Stuyvesant also contacted Puritans in Connecticut and Long Island, inviting them to settle in New Amsterdam. A few, including Robert Treat, who later founded Newark, came to discuss terms, but the Dutch gesture failed.

New England Puritans insisted that their government must operate within their own village churches, with the villages being independent of one another. They would not submit to Dutch rule — or any rule in any way.

Farewell To New Amsterdam

A man as intelligent as Stuyvesant surely realized New Amsterdam was living on borrowed time. Just as New Sweden was taken over by the Dutch, so both were destined to be conquered whenever England decided to take action.

The English based their claims to all of North America on the voyages they had sponsored for the Cabotos (Cabots). New Amsterdam, the only non-English territory between Virginia and Massachusetts, irritated Great Britain.

The prolonged Civil War that swept the Stuarts out of the royal palace stalled England's serious attempts at colonization for many years. The return of the Stuarts to the throne in 1660 finally gave England the peace necessary to plan and execute the colonizing of America.

King Charles II (a Stuart) summoned his brother, the Duke of York, on March 12, 1664, to present him

More than a match for New Sweden's big governor was New Amsterdam's Peter Stuyvesant. He came in 1647, limping ashore on his wooden leg. Stuyvesant berated his colonists, dared them to disobey him, and showed his anger when anything went wrong. He was exactly what the Dutch required to gain a foothold in America.

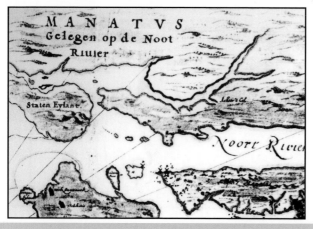

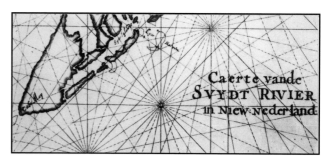

Dutch Rivers, English Names

Although Dutchmen first explored and settled the two rivers on either side of New Jersey, both are named for Englishmen.

Henry Hudson, an English captain aboard the Dutch ship **Half Moon,** *explored both sides of the peninsula in 1609. Long after, his name was given to one river. In 1610, after Captain Samuel Argall sailed from Virginia to explore the coast, he named the lower river for Lord De la Warre, governor of Virginia. De la Warre remained in this country less than a year and never ventured north of Virginia, but a bay, a river, a state, and an Indian tribe all honor a lord whose historical contributions to the area were nil.*

Portions of early maps (above) show Dutch names for the streams were the North (or Noort) River and the South (or Suydt) River.

Dutch Hero: Born In Newark, NJ

No Dutch character ever became better known worldwide than Hans Brinker, winner of the Silver Skates. He was born in the imagination of Mrs. Mary Mapes Dodge of Newark, who had never been closer to Holland than New York.

Mrs. Dodge, left a widow with two sons at age thirty-seven, began writing in 1864 to support her family. Constantly occupying her mind was a charming young Dutch boy who she had been inventing since she read the classic history, **Rise of the Dutch Republic.** *"Hans Brinker" became the hero of a carefully researched story of Holland, its history, and its people. The book became a smash success. It has gone through scores of printings, has been translated into many languages, and became a Walt Disney movie.*

When Mrs. Dodge visited Holland in 1881 for the first time, she asked a book clerk there to suggest a reliable book on the country. He handed her, without knowing who she was, a Dutch translation of **Hans Brinker.**

all the land between the Connecticut and Delaware rivers. Ignoring any possible Dutch claims, Charles gave the Duke absolute power to govern "as he shall think to be fittest for the good of the adventurers and inhabitants there."

Two months later, the Duke sent Colonel Richard Nicolls westward to the New World with four ships and an army of 450 soldiers. His orders were clear: subdue the Dutch. Once he accomplished this, Nicolls could rule as deputy governor.

Nicolls sailed his fleet into New Amsterdam harbor in mid-August and went ashore to demand surrender. Peter Stuyvesant wanted to fight, but ninety-three leading citizens petitioned him not to take the risk. "Let it be so," said Stuyvesant, but he delayed a week before hauling down the Dutch flag on August 27.

Stuyvesant left the fort, followed by his soldiers, with banners flying and a military band bringing up the rear. The stubborn old governor reportedly declared sadly, "I had rather be carried to my grave."

English soldiers moved into the fort. Nicolls renamed the New Amsterdam area New York to honor the Duke of York. The new governor offered the Dutch generous terms to stay on their land, and most of them swore allegiance to the new government. Stuyvesant went home to Holland, and then returned to live in New York.

Nicolls dispatched Sir Robert Carr to the Delaware River to force surrender of the colonists there. The river forts offered no resistance, but in an unnecessary display of force, Carr's men killed or wounded several settlers.

New Sweden and New Amsterdam vanished by name in 1664, but Swedish and Dutch traditions lived on. The two opposite borders of New Jersey were greatly influenced, for many decades to come, by the serious settlers.

New Sweden and New Amsterdam were not failures, except in the eyes of European investors. The Swedes, Finns, and Dutch who first colonized the area decided to stay. They recognized that America offered them a vital chance for freedom, no matter what flag — Dutch, Swedish, or English — flew over the nearby forts. This was home.

A circular slab bearing the date 1784 above the front door of "Old Swedes Church" in Swedesboro marks the last major Swedish effort in New Jersey. Swedesboro was known as Raccoon when Swedes built a log church on the same site. That lasted for eighty-six years before the Rev. Nicholas Collin goaded church members into donating funds for a substantial brick structure. He designed the new church himself.

Dr. Collin was transferred to Philadelphia in 1786, ending Swedish influence in town. Episcopalians acquired the building and renamed it Trinity Church.

Etching by Charles X. Harris, drawn in 1908, sought to recapture the tense atmosphere in August 1664, when Peter Stuyvesant reluctantly surrendered New Amsterdam to a vastly superior British invasion force. His English conquerors impressed Stuyvesant; after a visit back to Holland, he returned to live out his life in New York.

Chapter Three - Trouble In The Jerseys

United States			New Jersey
England solidifies control of American coast	1664	1664	Land grants to Elizabeth, Monmouth settlers
		1665	Philip Carteret becomes NJ governor
		1666	Newark, Piscataway, Woodbridge founded
		1668	1st NJ Legislature meets
French explore Mississippi River	1673	1675	Quakers settle Salem
		1676	New Jersey becomes two colonies
Philadelphia founded	1682	1702	East, West Jersey united
England's Molasses Act limits colonial trade	1733	1738	NJ separated from NY and gets own governor
		1745	Severe land riots start
Albany Congress discusses unified colonial defense	1754		
French and Indian (Seven Years) War begins	1756		

Firmly established in the old Dutch fort in New York by late August 1664, Governor Richard Nicolls faithfully set out to improve what he considered was still the valuable property of the Duke of York. More than anything, the area needed settlers.

Nicolls concluded that his best chance of attracting new people lay in promoting the green marshes and heavily wooded hills west of the Hudson River. He reasoned the soils of Connecticut and Long Island were too poor to attract farmers. He dismissed the Hudson River region as too cold.

The Governor thus looked west to the region he named Albania, again honoring the Duke of York, who happened also to be the Duke of Albany (in England). Nicolls obviously had no idea his patron, the Duke, already had named the land New Jersey — and given it away.

Nicolls circulated invitations throughout the other colonies, urging people "to set out a town and inhabit together" in Albania. Nicolls guaranteed limited religious liberty, provided such freedom did not disturb Protestants. He also permitted self-government and self-taxation — rights that soon would lead to bitterness and bloodshed.

Prospective Albanians were required to purchase

◇◇◇◇◇◇◇◇◇◇◇◇◇◇◇◇◇◇◇◇◇◇◇

The Day Of Birth

New Jersey was both born and christened on June 23, 1664.

That day, the Duke of York summoned to his London palace two longtime friends, Lord Berkeley and Sir George Carteret. He had written a deed for a handsome gift for the pair — all of the land between the Hudson and Delaware rivers. That set the boundaries for a definite colony.

The Duke also ordered the tract must be called "New Cesarea or New Jersey." The name paid homage to Carteret's stubborn defense of the Isle of Jersey in the English Channel during the British civil war that just ended.

Lavish gifts of vast tracts of American land, bestowed with little awareness of their true value, were common for the Duke. Berkeley and Carteret were among a group given the Carolinas in 1663. Now they had their own real estate to colonize and to govern.

The Carolinas and New Jersey were considered little more

than real estate speculations. America was no place for royalty to visit, much less a place in which to live.

New Jersey's birthday had lasting impact. Not only was it a casual transfer of property, but it also threw New Jersey property and politics into a tangle that even today is unresolved.

The trouble stemmed from the Duke of York's apparent forgetfulness. A month before he gave the land to Berkeley and Carteret, he sent Sir Richard Nicolls to overcome the Dutch, settle the area, and govern the large territory between the Connecticut and Delaware rivers.

So, conflict was inevitable. Berkeley and Carteret, for their part, treated their gift so casually that within a dozen years the colony was hopelessly severed in two. If one seeks reasons for New Jersey's split personality, the place to start is June 23, 1664.

James, the Duke of York and Albania, enjoyed the high living and casual government that marked England after his Stuart family (or House of Stuarts) was restored to power in 1660. The Duke's lavish clothing and adornment in this portrait proved the strict ways of the Puritans had vanished from royal favor.

The House of Stuart began to rule England in 1603, after more than 250 years of governing Scotland. The Stuarts believed they had absolute (or "Divine") power, bestowed on them by God. King Charles I sought to rule England with an iron hand.

Led by Oliver Cromwell, the Puritans rebelled in 1642. They took over the government, beheaded King Charles I in 1649, and crowned Cromwell as king. The rest of the Stuarts and their followers fled to France and to offshore islands — including the Isle of Jersey in the English Channel.

The Stuarts returned in 1660. Charles, the eldest son, became King Charles II. James was named Duke of York and Albania. The "Restoration" of the Stuarts was at first a time of relief for the people of England after nearly 20 years of Puritan rigidity. Immorality and high living became the fashion among England's royalty.

Followers of the Stuarts were rewarded for wit and cleverness rather than intelligence or wisdom. Great gifts of valuables or land (such as New Jersey) were common.

James lacked the imagination and caution of his brother Charles. He was reckless and self-centered. He became king in 1685, but was forced to flee within four years.

the property from the natives after getting land grants from Nicolls. The governor urged that at least eight families locate in each town, a reasonable number of people for colonial America.

Land At Bargain Prices

Two groups of Long Islanders recognized the bargain that Nicolls offered. One group, from Jamaica, applied for a tract along the Arthur Kill in what is now Union County. The other, from Gravesend, sought property along Raritan Bay.

Nicolls amiably agreed to both proposals. He promised to give the new settlers "all due encouragement in so good a work."

The Jamaica hopefuls wasted no time. Nicholls gave them permission, on September 25, 1664, to ne-

gotiate with the Native Americans. That transaction was finished within a month and the Long Islanders possessed property vaguely described as "between the Raritan and Passaic rivers." It reached inland for thirty-four miles, beyond modern Bernardsville and Somerville.

From the standpoint of the Long Islanders, the purchase was a matter of shrewd bargaining. Consider the price paid to the Native Americans in a deal typical of colonial purchases:

Twenty fathoms [about 120 feet] of trading cloth, two coats, two glens, two kettles, ten bars of lead, and twenty handsful of gunpowder — plus 400 fathoms [2,400 feet] of wampum shells to be paid within one year.

The Raritan Bay transfer proceeded more slowly, but on April 8, 1665 Governor Nicolls approved the "Monmouth Patent," or land grant.

Governor Philip Carteret's chilly reception from colonists along the Arthur Kill highlights this mural by Howard Pyle in the Essex County Courthouse. Carteret, with his followers and servants on the right, waits as an aide reads a proclamation making Philip New Jersey's governor. Their fine clothing, weapons, and equipment contrast sharply with the rustic appearance of the town's founders.

It ran from Sandy Hook westward to the Raritan River, cut southwest twelve miles, and from there went straight east to the Atlantic Ocean. The Indians received the usual trinkets and weapons.

Trek To Albania

The Long Islanders eagerly occupied their marvelous new properties. Some Jamaica people might have been on their property as early as November 1664, exploring the sweet grassy marshes or marveling at the autumn foliage on the hills rising to the westward. A few began felling trees for logs to build the first crude huts.

Families arrived in the spring of 1665, long before the dogwood flowered on the Watchung Mountains or the beach plums bloomed on Sandy Hook. They probably made the trip in small boats, carefully calculating what goods might be safely transported across the open waters. Livestock likely was ferried from Long Island to New York, then ferried again across the Hudson River, and finally herded overland to the new settlements.

Early records of the first two English settlements in Albania are vague. The Arthur Kill outpost had no name at first. Two towns — Shrewsbury and Middletown — were planned in the Monmouth area. Rhode Island Quakers and Baptists joined the Long Island Puritans in Monmouth, providing the colony's first religious mix. However, the colonists beside the Arthur Kill were determined to keep their town entirely Puritan.

Two families — the Ogdens at Arthur Kill and the Stouts in Monmouth — typified those first English settlers. Both families were strong leaders in their towns and both were large in number. The two families became important in New Jersey history.

John Ogden, born in England in 1609, settled on Long Island before 1640. He gained attention as a bricklayer and stonemason in 1642 by building a large stone church in New Amsterdam. He and his wife, Jane, brought five sons, aged 12 to 26, to the village beside the Arthur Kill.

The Stouts were from Gravesend. Their Long Island family head was John, but the Monmouth leader probably was son Richard, whose family was one of the first five to occupy the area. Richard Stout and his wife, Penelope, had seven sons and three daughters, a sizable contribution to the fledgling community.

Trouble In Paradise

Albania seemed a paradise. The rivers were sparkling clean, with just enough rapids inland to provide waterpower for sawmills and grain mills. Thick forests were alive with game of every kind. Salt marsh meadows provided pastureland for cattle, pigs could root along the muddy riverbanks, and the soil was deep and fertile.

This might well have been the Eden that these wandering colonists had long been seeking. The founders at both Raritan Bay and the Arthur Kill happily began laying out towns, drawing for favored lots, and planning for more settlers. They governed themselves, completely at ease about their futures.

Suddenly, in July 1665, an unexpected jolt hit Albania.

Berkeley and Carteret, either ignoring or unaware of Nicolls, chose Philip Carteret to be their New Jersey governor in the spring of 1665. Philip, a twenty-six-year-old bachelor and a distant relative to Sir George Carteret, was dispatched to govern the colony. He was ordered as well to collect rents for parcels occupied by settlers.

Young Carteret's arrival in New York stunned Nicolls. Thirteen months had elapsed since the transfer of New Jersey to the Duke's friends, yet not a word of the transaction had reached the colony. Albania had never really existed. Governor Nicoll's hopes were shattered.

Nicolls wrote angrily to the Duke of York "all of the improvable land" lay west of the Hudson. That land had "the fair hope of rich mines," Nicolls argued, and could accommodate twenty times more people than Long Island. He asked in wonderment: "Why had the Duke given it away?"

Nicolls' letter did no good. Carteret was here to stay — and if his surprise stopover in New York astounded Nicolls, imagine the consternation on the Arthur Kill a few days later when Carteret's ship dropped anchor and the new governor came ashore.

One account has it that Carteret was greeted by "the cheering of all the townsfolk gathered at the landing." That is extremely unlikely. He represented a serious threat to their titles gained from Nicolls and the Indians, their liberties, their beliefs. What was there to cheer?

Carteret's contingent of about fifty men and women from the Isle of Jersey probably doubled the size of the colony. Eighteen were servants, considered social inferiors. Many of the newcomers were French-speaking Roman Catholics, a status certain to make the Puritans unhappy.

The new governor also brought a name for the village: Elizabethtown, to honor Sir George Carteret's wife. That might have been cause for celebration, although it more likely stirred further feeling that Berkeley and Carteret were interfering.

Tradition says the unwelcomed governor made the best of things. He shouldered a hoe to prove that he, too, was a farmer, and then strode into the village, servants and townspeople trudging behind. If anyone suspected that with eighteen servants available Philip was not about to be a gardener, the notion was carefully hidden.

The long arm of English authority had reached across the ocean. Paradise on the Arthur Kill was endangered.

New Guarantees, New Towns

Philip Carteret read to the settlers promises from Berkeley and Carteret, now called the "Proprietors" (or owners). They guaranteed a popularly elected assembly and freedom to follow personal beliefs "in matters of religion." Only the Assembly would levy taxes. On the surface, these were acceptable to the colonists.

There was one catch: Philip also brought the disturbing news that every settler must pay the proprietors one half penny annually for every acre owned. There were indignant grumblings; these Englishmen transplanted in America were not used to paying anything to the English lords. The complaints were muffled, for the rents would not start until March 25, 1670.

Carteret wooed other New Englanders. Puritans from Branford and Milford, Connecticut founded Newark in the spring of 1666. They hoped they finally found the quiet backwater where they could place a town where their Congregational Church ruled both government and spiritual life. They had been seeking such a place in America for forty years.

Late that December, Carteret also approved sale of the lower portion of the Elizabethtown tract. Puritans from New Hampshire bought part of it and founded Piscataway. Other Puritans, from Massachusetts, bought the rest and established Woodbridge.

Thus, within less than thirty months after the Dutch surrender, New Jersey had seven towns, including the Dutch town of Bergen. Each, again including Bergen, was patterned after the New England type of village: compact, centered on a meeting house or church, with public lands set aside for markets, pastures, and militia training.

Crime, Taxes, And Rebellion

Governor Carteret waited three years before instructing each town to send "two able men" to New Jersey's first Assembly in Elizabethtown on May 26, 1668. The few settlers along the Delaware were asked to send two representatives (or burgesses as Carteret called them) to join fourteen from the seven towns in the eastern area.

The burgesses (meaning "free man") finished their work in five days. First they occupied themselves with crime and punishment, providing death penalties for witches and "undutiful" children. All men between sixteen and sixty were ordered to be ready for militia duty. Every town was made responsible for a "fence viewer," who saw that fences were strong enough to keep cattle from wandering into gardens or village streets.

Recognizing central government needed funds, the burgesses agreed to tax each town £5 annually, payable in produce (wheat, corn, etc.). Storms of protest greeted the tax in every town. These people were not about to be taxed, with or without representation.

Antitax feeling centered on the governor. The second Assembly informed Carteret, in November 1668, the people would not pay taxes. Spokesmen also told him they resented "your expectations that things must go according to your opinions." The meeting broke up in disorder. Seven years would pass before another Assembly met.

Swift and sure, punishment took many forms in strict colonial New Jersey — humiliation in the stocks, ducking, public penance, and whippings.

The Revolution Of 1672

Carteret was in deep trouble. Monmouth residents refused to swear loyalty to Berkeley and Carteret, fearing they might lose rights gained in the Monmouth Patent. Faced with such flaring dissension, Carteret foolishly demanded payment of rents to the proprietors on March 25, 1670.

The rents should not have been a surprise. Carteret had mentioned them five years before. The time to pay had come. The governor's Elizabethtown neighbors led the opposition, maintaining their deeds from the Indians protected them against rents.

Newark alone agreed to pay and assessed each landholder "a just share and proportion of wheat." However, instead of recognizing Newark's wheat symbolized friendly compliance, Carteret peevishly insisted on payment in gold or silver.

Enemies surrounded Carteret. Finally, in what was called "The Revolution of 1672," the townspeople overthrew the established government. They summoned their own Assembly, on May 14, 1672, and declared Carteret was no longer governor.

Fired by their own boldness, the revolutionists replaced Philip with James Carteret, the weak second son of Sir George. James happily accepted the grandiose title of "President of the Country."

Frightened, Philip sailed for England. There, he vowed "to cure this wound by speedy medicine which delay may cause to gangrene." Back home, he received support all the way up to King Charles. Before Philip Carteret could return in triumph to Elizabethtown, a brief incident had to be played out with the Dutch.

War broke out between England and Holland early in 1673. The Dutch took the opportunity to dispatch a fleet to New York, where English Commander Manning surrendered without firing a shot. The Dutch renamed New York as New Orange, but by the spring of 1674 England had retaken the thinly-defended fort.

Quakers Find A Haven

Philip Carteret returned to America in 1675, filled with forgiveness. The Dutch interlude may have alarmed his once-rebellious subjects, for they turned polite. The proprietors agreed rents could be satisfied with "country pay" (corn, wheat, etc.) rather than gold — although they insisted the fees must be paid.

Governor Carteret found Lord Berkeley in deep personal and financial difficulty in England. Berke-

Our Town On The Passaic

Thirty families fell silent, on May 18, 1666, as their little boats slowly moved up the river the Indian called Passaic. They were Puritans, on the move again, hoping for a promised land where they might found a town in which church and government were one.

The crude little craft that brought the Milford settlers to New Jersey rode dangerously low in the water. The families aboard averaged five or six children, plus several animals, a limited amount of household goods, and a few fruit trees.

The spiritual shepherd of the newcomers, Reverend Abraham Pierson, was a wanderer if ever there was one. Born and educated in England, Mr. Pierson came to Lynn, Massachusetts in 1639 and had been seeking religious isolation ever since. He and his wife had eight children: one born in Lynn; three in Southampton, Long Island; and four in Branford, Connecticut.

The townspeople loved and respected Pierson, even as they feared his unrelenting preaching on sin, fire, and salvation. They named "Our Town on the Passaic" Newark (or New Ark) in honor of Mr. Pierson's former home in England, Newark-on-Trent.

Newark's first families lived for a year or more in crude shelters, little more than sod huts. The boats plied regularly between the Passaic River and Connecticut, bringing more people, household goods, supplies, plants, and animals. By June 1667, there were sixty-four families in town, totaling between 350 and 375 persons.

These original Newarkers ranged from babes in arms to aged men and women who had been searching for religious peace in both England and America for more than seventy years. Their skills were as various as their ages, and every skill was needed — none more so than the skills of women and older girls in making cloth, tending gardens, and preserving food.

Establishing streets that still exist, the town fathers plotted the rising town after New Haven, Connecticut. They followed an Indian trail north and south for Broad Street, 132 feet wide — the widest street in all of colonial America. Two militia training grounds were laid out, and a public market place was set aside.

Settlers drew lots for property, after setting aside six acres in the center of town for the meeting house and cemetery. Every able-bodied man had to work on the meeting house — with the most labor expected from the wealthiest males.

Finished in the spring of 1670, the first meeting house was crude, Puritans hated ornamentation, so there were no stained glass windows, steeple, bell, or altar. The building would serve as a place of worship, a site for town meetings, a town school, and if necessary, a fort.

Success of the colony called for every person to follow a standard routine. A boy named Thomas Johnson was hired as town drummer in September 1668. His drum beat announced daybreak, when all hard-working people must be stirring. At night, his drum announced bedtime.

Johnson drummed men to work on village projects, routed late risers out of bed on Sunday mornings, and beat out a cadence for marching to church services or racing to the meeting house in case of danger.

Apparently some either did not hear Thomas Johnson drum or chose to ignore it. The town minute books recorded the names of those who "refused to go when warned" of work and those who missed town meetings.

The town needed a grist mill. To get one, it offered twenty-four acres of land, timber to build the mill, £20 annual pay, and exclusive rights to build other mills. It took almost two years to find someone with the necessary skills.

Quickly it became evident the inner circle of Puritans lacked many of the skills needed to build Newark. Persons of various religious beliefs came — to build boats, start a saw mill, and barter their handcrafts for the good of the community.

The ideal of an isolated religious town reserved only for a few fell by the wayside. People marching to the beat of different drums — not only Thomas Johnson's — would change Newark.

ley offered to sell his half of New Jersey to meet his debts. Eager to buy was the Society of Friends — or Quakers — who had prayed for just such a chance.

Quakers needed a haven somewhere. They angered Englishmen because they ignored church ritual and refused to bear arms. New Jersey's liberal treatment of Quakers in Shrewsbury had been impressive. When Berkeley's share became available, Quaker representatives grabbed it.

Berkeley sold his share for £1,000, a tiny sum for what would turn out to be more than 4,500 square miles of land. The buyer was Major John Fenwick, a newly converted Quaker and a former officer in the British army. Fenwick apparently was the front man for a group of Quakers.

So much land could set even Quakers to quarreling. Several bickered so embarrassingly long with Fenwick over ownership of the New Jersey property that William Penn was asked, in February 1674, to help decide the dispute. That was Penn's first appearance on the American scene.

Penn and the other arbiters granted Fenwick only one-tenth of the land bought from Berkeley "only" all of modern Salem and Cumberland counties, or about 850 square miles.

Time Of Two Jerseys

Fenwick continued complaining so loudly about his "small" share that Penn told him in exasperation:

"Away with vain fancies, I entreat thee. Fall closely to thy business ... make the best of what thou hast. Thy grandchildren may be in the other world before what land thou hast alloted will be employed."

Following that sage counsel, Fenwick decided to profit from his acres. He printed glowing reports of his new colony, hoping to entice settlers to buy land and sail with him. In America, Fenwick assured prospective buyers, a person could travel for hundreds of miles "and never hear the least complaint." He did not mention he had never been there.

About fifty passengers were aboard when Fenwick's expedition sailed in the summer of 1675. Mrs. Fenwick stayed home, but the passengers included two married Fenwick daughters, their husbands and children, a son, and an unmarried daughter. Fenwick also brought ten servants; he too would colonize in the grand manner.

The storm-battered ship reached Delaware Bay in the autumn, slipped up stream (now Salem Creek), and dropped anchor two miles inland. Fenwick gazed out on his colony and named it Salem (from the Hebrew word *Sholom*, meaning peace).

Fenwick paid the Indians the usual guns, rum, clothing, blankets, and cheap jewelry. He laid out a wide street from the wharf on Salem Creek, and by winter his followers were comfortably housed. He planned to start villages at Cohanzick (now Greenwich) and Finn's Point, near where the Swedes had built their ill-fated Fort Elfsborg.

John Fenwick built this house on a knoll at Ivey Point on Fenwick's Creek in 1677 as the center of a pleasant riverfront estate. The house was taken down in 1830, and nothing remains of Fenwick's once-beautiful 6,000 acre estate in Salem County.

Anxious to attract more people (to whom he could sell his real estate), Fenwick wrote home of his "happy country" where people "never know what sickness is." He declared enthusiastically:

"If there be any terrestrial Canaan, 'tis surely here, where the land floweth with milk and honey!"

The Splitting Of A Colony

Fenwick's propaganda was stronger than his title to the land, for the Duke of York refused to recognize Berkeley's sale. William Penn realized a clear-cut division of the province of New Jersey was necessary. He pressed Carteret for an agreement.

Penn, three other Quakers, and Carteret agreed to a split on July 1, 1676 (almost exactly one century before the signing of the Declaration of Independence). New Jersey was divided along an indefinite line from Little Egg Harbor to the northwest corner.

The Quakers received about 4,600 square miles of land and the entire east bank of the Delaware River. Carteret retained only about 3,000 square miles in his "half." However, because the land had not been surveyed, both sides could only guess at the exact amounts of land involved.

The deal was not nearly as one-sided as the square miles might indicate. George Fox, founder of the Quaker movement, had traveled across the western part of New Jersey in 1672 and described it as total wilderness. At most, there were only twenty or thirty Swedish and Finnish families in the entire area.

By 1676, even with Fenwick's colony, there probably were not 400 people in all of West New Jersey. Newark alone had about twice that number in East New Jersey.

New Jersey now had become two colonies: East New Jersey and West New Jersey. Thus, for twenty-six years, until the two were reunited in 1702, there were two governments and two capitals on the little peninsula.

"Power To The People"

The Quakers earnestly set out to make their portion of America attractive to much-needed settlers. Prospective colonists were offered liberal terms, based on the principle government must guarantee "power to the people."

That power was spelled out — in those words — in a remarkable document issued in March 1677:

The Concessions and Agreements of the Proprietors, Freeholders and Inhabitants of the Province of West New

Two mighty veterans from pre-colonial days have long outlived settlers buried beneath their boughs. The Basking Ridge Oak in a Presbyterian Church yard, above, is estimated to be more than 400 years old. The Salem Oak in a Quaker cemetery, below, already was more than a century old when John Fenwick and his settlers sailed up Salem Creek in 1675.

Jersey in America. Many of the liberties written into the Declaration of Independence nearly a century later were in the *Concessions.*

The Quaker document guaranteed secret balloting for the annual election of 100 Assemblymen and ten "commissioners of state." The only limiting provision on the legislators was that West New Jersey actions must not conflict with English laws.

Freedom of speech was guaranteed in legislative debate. Meetings would be open, so citizens could be "witness of the votes and inclinations of their representatives."

Also guaranteed were trial by jury, equal tax assessments, swift punishment of false witnesses, and freedom from illegal arrest or imprisonment for debt. Admirably, in an age when most Europeans regarded

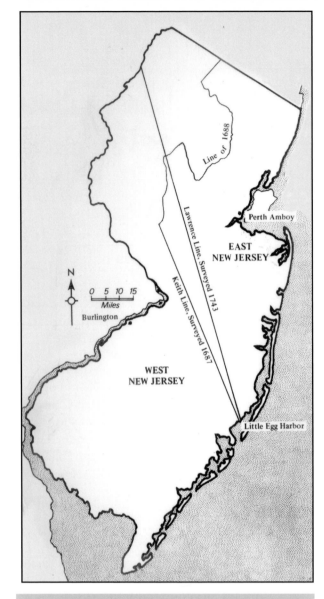

Purchase of West New Jersey by Quakers in 1676 created two provinces split along an uncertain boundary. George Keith surveyed a dividing line in 1687, but he was stopped after reaching what is now Three Bridges; Quakers argued the division was uneven. A vague compromise boundary was run from Three Bridges to the Hudson River. This situation lasted until 1743 when John Lawrence ran a line accepted by both sides.

Indians as "savages," trials of Indians would be before a jury of six Indians and six settlers.

Above all, the Quakers ensured religious freedom: "No man, nor number of men on earth, have power or authority to rule over men's consciences in religious matters." That was the strongest guarantee in any of the colonies.

A Town Called Burlington

Two companies of English Quakers — one from London, the other from Yorkshire — accepted the terms and sailed from London aboard the ship *Kent* early in the summer of 1677. King Charles II gave the ship his blessing, a gesture not appreciated by the Quakers. Charles, as much as anyone, was responsible for their sufferings.

About 230 men, women, and children were crowded into cramped, moist quarters below deck on the *Kent*. There they ate and slept for most of the two-month voyage. Goats, swine, and poultry were penned on the deck above. Furniture, weapons, tools, seeds, and trinkets for trading with the Indians were in the hold below.

The low-riding ship moved up the Delaware River in late August and dropped anchor at Raccoon Creek. Swedish settlers already in place welcomed them and introduced them to the Indians as a beginning toward negotiations for land.

Some of the weaker and older passengers moved in with Swedish families in their simple huts, but most of the newly-arrived Quakers spent the fall and winter in hastily built bark houses similar to Indian wigwams. The company bought from the Indians a huge tract of land along the Delaware River from about modern Trenton south forty-five miles along the river. They laid out a town called Burlington along High Street. The Yorkshiremen lived east of High Street, the Londoners west.

More settlers came; by 1681 more than 1,400 Quakers lived in West New Jersey. That year Burlington became the capital of the province. A jail went up in the capital town in 1682, followed in 1683 by the courthouse. Punishment came before government, even in liberal Burlington.

The Quakers pushed outward. Mahlon Stacy went up river in 1679 to found the town at "ye falls of the Delaware" that later would be called Trenton. Thomas Farnsworth founded Farnsworth's Landing (now Bordentown) in 1682. Others paddled up the Rancocas Creek soon after 1700 to found Mount Holly beneath a holly-covered hill.

Two Colonies, Two Capitals

When George Carteret died in 1680, his East New Jersey holdings soon were divided. For a short time, in 1682, Quakers controlled both East and West New Jersey, but they made no effort to govern the eastern part. By then, William Penn had decided to found Philadelphia on the west bank of the Delaware River. His interest shifted west from New Jersey.

Engraving on the left depicts English Quakers going ashore on the ice from the ship *Shield* in 1678. They arrived at Burlington as part of the constantly arriving new settlers who started a string of Delaware River towns between Trenton and Salem.

Facsimile of title page from the *Concessions and Agreements*, a remarkably liberal document issued in 1677 to guarantee Quaker settlers of West New Jersey a far-reaching set of liberties. Many of the rights incorporated in the *Concessions* became part of the freedoms written into the Declaration of Independence a century later.

More landowners (or proprietors) bought shares in the East New Jersey venture. Much of the area became little more than a highly profitable real estate enterprise as far as the absentee English owners were concerned.

The East New Jersey proprietors located their capital at "sweet, wholesome and delightful Ambo (or Amboy) Point" on Raritan Bay in 1684. Two hundred oppressed Scots, mostly Presbyterians, emigrated to the Point in 1688. They called their town New Perth, to honor the Earl of Perth, who had given them permission to leave Scotland. Soon "New Perth" and "Ambo Point" were blended into Perth Amboy.

New Jersey now had two colonies, two governments, and two capitals, connected by a narrow, rutted road across the level ground between Perth Amboy and Burlington. The pattern was set. Outward from that road, both Jerseys grew in leisurely fashion.

Elizabethtown's young families slowly moved outward to found new towns on the west of town — out to where springs gushed across the field (Springfield), out to the "West Fields," or to the plains where Scots had settled (Scotch Plains). New generations of Newarkers moved westward up the slopes of the Orange Mountains.

The Pine Barrens impeded Quaker movement eastward from the Delaware, for settlers shunned the sandy pinelands soil as barren. Along the coast, only a few hardy fishermen and whale hunters frequented the sandy ocean beaches. They were mainly squatters and beachcombers, far removed from society's centers of culture, religion, and government.

The Concessions and Agreements of the Proprietors Freeholders and Inhabitants of the Province of West New Jersey in America: Chapter 1

New Jersey's two oldest businesses, whose corporate seals are shown above and below, are the East New Jersey Proprietors of Perth Amboy (founded in 1682) and the West New Jersey Proprietors of Burlington, established five years later.

By law, the two firms have full title to all unclaimed lands in New Jersey. The ownership stems from 1664, when the Duke of York gave all of New Jersey to Lords Berkeley and Carteret.

Through the centuries, the two boards sold off most of their holdings and occasionally granted themselves dividends. At first the dividends were huge land areas, but more recently the dividends have been very small cash dividends, if anything.

The land ownership is not just a matter of ancient history, however. Anyone putting together a large piece of ground— for a military installation, a highway route, an airport, or any other major use —finds the truth of that. Surveys will disclose a small unclaimed triangle here, a long strip there, a corner somewhere else, left because of errors in old surveys. All such pieces belong to the proprietors.

These days the interests of the proprietors are mainly historical and ceremonial. Fees for securing title are nominal and are used to maintain the "home offices" in the old provincial capitals of New Jersey.

Skills To Build A Colony

Industry had begun. Ironmakers started a forge at Tinton Falls in Monmouth County in 1674. Leather makers were busy in Elizabethtown and Newark before 1680; Elizabethtown soon became known as the "mother of tanners" because of the large numbers of leatherworkers who journeyed to other colonies to found their own businesses.

Sawmills and gristmills hummed in many towns before 1680. Docks at Newark, Elizabethtown, Perth Amboy, Burlington, and Salem all bustled with ships. Whaling had become a major industry in Cape May by 1698, when three whaling companies were reported as bringing in "prodigious, nay — vast — quantities" of "oyle and whalebone."

The emerging colony needed people with mechanical abilities to balance those who arrived only with farming skills or those gentlemen who admitted they possessed no skills at all.

The East New Jersey proprietors hired George Scot as a publicist in 1685. Scot described the richness of the land. He also underscored the need for skilled people:

"All sorts of tradesmen may make a brave livelihood there, such as carpenters, shipwrights, ropemakers, smiths, brickmakers, tailors, coopers, millwrights, joiners, shoemakers, and such like."

African slaves or white servants often supplied skills and muscles. Some colonists, such as Carteret and Fenwick, arrived with bonded (or indentured) servants who were obliged to work several years for their freedom. Slaves were imported without any promises of rights or liberties.

Perth Amboy became one of the major towns for selling slaves imported directly from Africa. Boatloads of bonded white servants were sent to Philadelphia or New York, where the young servants were dispatched to work in the surrounding countryside, including New Jersey.

Bonded servants often were worked harder than slaves, for landholders knew they would lose the bonded laborers in time. Slaves were considered personal property, to be conserved if possible for longer periods of time.

Many servants and slaves learned trades and became skilled craftsmen or artisans. They helped to run the mills and operate the forges. They helped to build fine mansions. They worked on the roads and labored on the farms. These unknown, unsung people were the real "builders" of early America for they contributed most of the actual muscle and much of the talent.

One Jersey Out Of Two

Squabbles erupted constantly, chiefly over the question of whether the New Jersey colonists owed rents to the English proprietors. That issue forced Governor Philip Carteret from office in 1672. Every year, at rent time, there was only surly compliance with the proprietors' demands.

Some 250 New Jerseyans signed a petition to King William III, in 1700, asking him to appoint a governor able to mediate the constant disputes "between the proprietors and the inhabitants of Your Majesty's Province." Anger rose throughout the colony.

The controversy soon became violent. Mobs surged through the streets, threatening officers of the King and invading courthouses to disrupt trials. A sheriff was attacked in Monmouth County. Judges were "grossly abused" in Newark, and a mob of seventy angry Burlington citizens drove officials from office in March 1701.

Frightened and dismayed, the proprietors in both East and West New Jersey approached Queen Anne shortly after she became monarch in 1702. The proprietors agreed to relinquish their right to govern if the Queen would protect their rights to the land.

Her Majesty agreed, and on April 17, 1702 the provinces of East New Jersey and West New Jersey were united under royal rule. William Penn protested that unification was surrender "knavishly contrived to betray the people." His opinion was not heeded; New Jersey had become a united colony again.

Queen Anne combined New Jersey and New York under one governor. A Council, composed mainly of New Jersey proprietors, and an Assembly, limited to those who owned at least one thousand acres of land, would aid him. It was far from government "of the people" or "for the people."

The Queen recognized New Jersey's split nature by ordering the Assembly to alternate its meetings between Burlington and Perth Amboy. There was neither expectation nor hope the governor ever would live in either of the New Jersey towns.

Shadows Across The Province

Only the proprietors benefited from Queen Anne's action. New Jersey, although united politically, was possibly more divided than ever socially. The Queen

Except for Quakers, very few colonial New Jerseyans would have answered yes to the question posed in the above symbol of an English antislavery society.

Slavery certainly did not trouble church leaders, the opinion makers of the day. African slaves were segregated in church balconies and buried in far corners of cemeteries, "lest when the trumpet of resurrection sounded there be a disagreeable confusion of persons."

Slavery began early in New Jersey. Dutch settlers enslaved Native Americans, and the original English colonists of 1661 acquired African slaves. Richard Morris of Shrewsbury had more than sixty slaves by 1680 for his mill and plantation.

Queen Anne encouraged slavery in 1702 by asking the Royal African Company of England to "have a sufficient supply of merchantable negroes, at moderate rates." Perth Amboy became a center of the slave trade.

Slaves were considered as mere property, to be exchanged, sold, or included in wills along with furniture, buildings, and livestock. When the Rev. Samuel Finley president of the College of New Jersey, died in 1766, his will included "two negro women, a negro man, and three negro children" all to be sold.

The first actual count of slaves, in 1737, showed 3,981 in a population of 47,402 — one slave for every twelve people. Bergen County's Dutch farmers particularly used African labor, although slaves were common elsewhere. In 1758, a report stated nearly every house in Perth Amboy "swarmed with black slaves."

If slavery did not concern most church-goers, it did deeply anger Quakers. By 1740, they sought full abolition of slavery in answer to the question of the slave: "Am I not a man and a brother?"

Lewis Morris, appointed governor of New Jersey in 1738, was the first "native son" to lead the colony.

showed further contempt for the colony by forbidding anyone "to keep a press for printing."

Queen Anne believed "great inconvenience may arise by the liberty of printing in our said province," meaning that New Jerseyans were troublesome enough without a newspaper to spread rebellion. The colony had to read New York and Philadelphia papers for information, news, and leadership.

With no newspaper, magazine, or even a press for printing announcements, New Jersey began to fall into the shadows of its neighboring colonies. The series of royal governors who ruled both New York and New Jersey seldom put the latter in first place.

Governor Robert Hunter, who ruled from 1710 to 1719, was an exception. He liked New Jersey well enough to build a house here and even talked of retiring in the colony (although he did not). The people of New Jersey returned his affection; when a large section of Burlington County became a new county in 1714, it took the name Hunterdon.

Affection for Hunter did not stop the New Jersey Assembly from quarreling with him, as it did with all authority. As early as 1707, one of Queen Anne's agents, Robert Quarry, surveyor general of customs, wrote the Assemblymen would not be satisfied until they could "send representatives to sit in the Parliament of Great Britain!" Hunter warned "these colonies would wean themselves [from England] when they came of age."

Governor William Burnet, who succeeded Hunter, recognized a spirit of independence was abroad in New Jersey. He told belligerent legislators, in 1721, they were not quarreling with him, but "directly with His Majesty, whose instructions you have entirely disregarded."

A Native Son For Governor

Lewis Morris, a brilliant, argumentative Assemblyman, went personally to London in 1734 to plead for a New Jersey governor independent of New York. Few listened; Morris returned two years later, thoroughly discouraged.

Then, in January 1738, an English ship brought unexpected news: New Jersey had been granted a governor of its own — Lewis Morris. The choice pleased nearly everyone in the colony. Morris was one of their own — native-born, forthright, and friendly with rich and poor alike. In his bouts with Crown-appointed governors he had won a reputation as an outspoken liberal and independent thinker.

Morris soon found his native-born status gave him no advantage. The Assembly fought him as stubbornly as it had battled the England-born governors. It refused Morris's pleas for an adequate militia, for more paper money, and for nearly everything else that the governor proposed.

By 1744, Morris in retaliation refused to consider any laws sent him by the legislators. They, in turn, became so divided that they could agree on only one measure "an act to encourage the destroying of crows, blackbirds, squirrels and woodpeckers." Governor Morris vetoed it.

Lewis Morris had been an influential, dedicated legislator for more than forty years, but New Jersey had changed greatly by the time he became governor. The population, that was about 12,000 when the Jerseys were united in 1702, had risen to 61,383 by 1745.

It was not merely a matter of population increase. The kinds of colonists had also changed. New Jersey had become home to the most varied population mix in all the New World.

By the middle of the eighteenth century, New Jersey was a place of Dutch, Swedes, and Finns; of people from New England and "old" England, Scotland, Ireland, and Wales; of families from Belgium, France, and Germany; of growing numbers of slaves from Africa.

Within the British segments there were sharp differences in religion in an age when religion was the chief element in life. The Britons were Presbyterians, Baptists, Anglicans, and Quakers, plus a small sprinkling of Roman Catholics. Among the Protestants, there was further argument about whether ministers should be trained abroad.

Bigotry and class distinction abounded. All Catholics, non-English, and non-whites were scornfully lumped together as "foreigners." Some of those foreigners were the backbone of two rising industries — iron and glass.

Iron ore was found at Succasunna in about 1700. A forge was started at Hanover in 1710, and by 1750 the Highlands from High Bridge to Ringwood were aglow with iron furnaces and forges. The Ringwood operation was especially "German," having been founded by the German Baron Peter Hasenclever, who imported other Germans to make the mines pay.

Deep in the forests of Salem County, Casper Wistar of Philadelphia saw that glass could be made from the fine local sand and plentiful wood supplies. He started America's first successful glass works at Wistarburg in 1739 — by importing four skilled glassblowers from Rotterdam. Wistarburg-trained blowers set up so many glassworks in other areas that the Salem town became known as "the cradle of American glass blowing."

Models Of Patience

Patience Lovell of Bordentown, who began modeling figures from bread dough as a child, became the best known female sculptor in all of colonial America.

Born in a modest Quaker home in 1725, Patience Lovell became a young woman of tremendous energy, described as being "tall, athletic, straight as an Indian."

She married a local farmer, Joseph Wright, in 1748 and bore him four children. When Wright died in 1769, Mrs. Wright moved to New York and opened a wax works. Then she sailed for England in 1772. Her exceptional talent, plus her saucy manners, made her a favorite of King George III and Queen Charlotte, both of whom she boldly called by their first names. In 1775, the **London Magazine** *said her statues were so incredibly lifelike that visitors were tempted to speak to them.*

Many Londoners visited Patience Wright's studio to be sculptured in wax. Her life-size wax statue of William Pitt, great British statesman and a friend of revolutionists in colonial America, still stands in famed Westminster Abbey in London.

During the Revolution, Mrs. Wright often passed on to Benjamin Franklin information that she received from the British court. After the war, she won acclaim in London and Paris. She died in London in 1786 just as she was planning a return to America.

More intercolonial traffic travelled through New Jersey than any other part of America. Despite miserable roads, slow ferries, and few bridges, people constantly surged between New York and Philadelphia. The crude horse-drawn cart of about 1720, right, was a great advance. By the time of the Revolutionary War, stagecoaches drawn by teams of horses dashed across the state between the Delaware and Hudson River ferries. The tavern (or inn) was the center of every village, and often the "village" was little more than the tavern where the coach stopped. A stage trip across New Jersey in 1760 required at least two overnight stops in wayside inns.

A Colony On The Move

Rivers and streams once were the major means of travel: front doors in most houses in early Salem County faced the water. Towns gradually spread away from the rivers into the hills and even into the edges of the Pine Barrens. In 1765, there were about sixty definable towns. Another thirty to forty crossroads villages existed without name.

New roads were needed to weave this colony together. The narrow Indian trails of 1700 were gradually widened into rough roads. Those thoroughfares were so poor that a Swedish traveler, Peter Kalm, noted in 1748 the people of New Jersey were "careless in mending" their roads.

Mud made travel a nightmare in spring and fall. Hard-baked ruts jolted travelers' spines in **summer**. Veteran travelers preferred to cross New Jersey in winter, when sleighs could glide over the snow and cross rivers on frozen ice — a great convenience in an age of few bridges.

In New Jersey's first century, a Philadelphia-New York trip meant time-consuming ferry crossings at South Amboy and Burlington, with a long miserable land trip between. An all-land route from Burlington to Paulus Hook (Jersey City) was not finished until 1764 — 100 years after New Jersey became an English colony. That land route was only a modest improvement, for there were no bridges across wide streams.

When coaches and wagons stopped overnight at crossroads inns, travelers brought excitement, news, and New York or Philadelphia newspapers. The inn was the political, social, cultural, and legal center of any town. It was town hall, courthouse, theater, news center, lodge hall, overnight stop, and restaurant — all under one roof.

Who Owned The Land?

Roads brought in new people to take up residence. Many of them merely settled, or squatted, on property without the formality of buying or leasing the acreage from the proprietors, who by law owned all property not previously sold.

That set the squatters on a collision course with the proprietors. The question that had been simmering for nearly eighty years came to a boil once again:

Who really owned the land — the King, the proprietors, the Indians, or the people who transformed the wild acres into fertile fields? Legally, the proprietors were right, and they had reason enough to be agitated. Those who had taken the land inhabited huge areas without permission. A 1735 survey in Hunterdon County revealed ninety-eight families occupying 13,000 acres without the slightest evidence of ever buying the land or of intending to do so.

The issue boiled over, in September 1745, when proprietors discovered one Samuel Baldwin cutting wood in the Horseneck, a swampy woodland in a bend of the Passaic River in western Essex County. Baldwin refused to pay a fine. The sheriff led him down the mountain to a Newark jail cell.

After church services on Sunday, September 19, a mob of 150 protestors swarmed into Newark, armed with clubs, axes, and crowbars. They shoved aside the sheriff, freed Baldwin from jail, and warned that pursuit or further arrests would bring "double the number" of rioters into town.

The following January, three Horseneck men were arrested and charged with being ringleaders in the September riot. True to their promise, the jail breakers returned, this time with more than 300 in their ranks. Twenty-six militiamen summoned to the jail never fired their guns; after all, these were friends and neighbors advancing. The mob had its way. The prisoners were released.

"Soft Words Turn Away Wrath"

The turbulence increased. Led by an outlaw named Amos Roberts, the belligerents expanded their operations in Essex County. By 1747, Roberts had set up his own rebel government. His "country" was divided into areas, with its own courts, militia, and tax collector. Roberts' prestige was such a New York newspaper account said Roberts was "reverenced as much as . . . a king."

The battle for squatter's rights spread far in the spring of 1747. Mobs stormed the Somerset County jail and threatened Morris County people who remained loyal to the proprietors. John Deare, Middlesex sheriff, wrote of a riotous throng that surged into Perth Amboy in July to free a prisoner. Deare said they came into town with "two fiddles playing," gave the sheriff a "grievous wound," struck the mayor, and "beat several of the others" before throwing open the jail doors.

Soft-spoken, Harvard-educated Jonathan Belcher

arrived in August 1747 to become governor of the strife-torn colony. The mobs threatened, and Roberts still boasted of his intent to drive "authority into the sea," but his power ebbed.

Belcher at first threatened to lead troops against the rioters, but he met with several dissenters and declared that "soft words turn away wrath but the wringing of the nose brings forth blood." The militants wrung few more noses. The riots were over, and the ringleaders fled from New Jersey.

Thoughts Of A Greater War

Tranquility, however uneasy, returned slowly. Thoughts turned to a greater war under way between France and England. It spread to North America (as the French and Indian War), and would in time reach the New Jersey shores of the Delaware River.

The New Jersey Assembly, pleading poverty, at first absolutely refused to send troops to help defend the Ohio Valley against the French. The war edged closer. Ominous news from New York's frontiers in 1755 ended the indifference. The Assembly voted to send 500 militia under Colonel Peter Schuyler to fight the French and Indians.

Spurred on by French promises, warring Indians slashed across the northern New Jersey frontier in 1755 and 1756. They killed several persons in Sussex County — including three members of the Swartwout family near Swartswood Lake. Thoroughly frightened, the Assembly voted to build and fortify a series of blockhouses along the upper Delaware River.

England announced plans, in 1757, to house 600 soldiers in private homes in Newark, Elizabethtown, and Perth Amboy. The Assembly, heeding reports that English soldiers carried diseases, loosened the purse strings. Funds were released to build barracks in Elizabethtown, Perth Amboy, New Brunswick, Burlington, and Trenton. (One still stands in Trenton.)

The French and Indian War temporarily muted the dissension and anger against the proprietors, the governors, and the King himself. Threats of Indian warfare made British soldiers welcome in New Jersey and elsewhere, although not in private homes. Militiamen went off to fight for the King.

Nearly a century had passed since England proclaimed New Jersey a colony. Many of the colonists grew restless in that secondary status, remembering the heady feeling of arguing with governors and royal officials. A new breed of independent American had been born.

As Governor Hunter had said forty years before, these stubborn Americans would "wean themselves when they came of age." They were maturing fast.

British soldiers parade through the gate of the high fence that surrounded the Trenton barracks in pre-Revolutionary days. This version, painted by William Pedrick in the 1890s, hangs in the Trenton Old Barracks to recall days when five such buildings were built in New Jersey.

Life Doth Pass

As runs the Glaſs
Mans life doth paſs.

The crude woodcut above, from a child's reading book dated 1727, sums up colonial life: rigorous, unyielding, with death the master of all.

Children were taught harsh realities along with their A, B, C's. For "R," they learned that "Rachel doth mourn, for her first born." For "T," the message was "Time cuts down all, both great and small."

Education was limited and illiteracy was common. Most girls and boys, if they went to school at all, learned only basic reading and writing. Few girls continued school beyond about age six (except among Quakers), but some boys received enough schooling to conduct business or church affairs.

It was believed that girls needed only enough arithmetic to count eggs, skeins of wool, yards of cloth, or the stitches in the cloth they wove. Such things, along with making candles and soap, churning butter, rearing the children, and tending the gardens, were women's work.

Men cleared the land, although young brides often labored beside their husbands. Men built the houses and furniture, plowed and planted the fields, harvested the crops, supplied the firewood, and tended the livestock.

Families were closely-knit, for each person, down to toddling children, had jobs vital to the family's welfare. Villages centered on the meeting house — a place of worship, the center of government, and the court where rigid punishment was given for a wide variety of crimes.

Play for play's sake was discouraged. Little girls soon gave up dolls to care for younger children. Boys learned to tend animals and to handle knives, fishing rods, and guns. All these mixed work and pleasure, with emphasis on work.

Children listened in gloomy quiet as adults lectured them — at home, in school, in church. Everyone kept them busy: sewing, spinning, hoeing, carrying wood, cleaning the barns, helping in the fields. They constantly heard of the virtues of manners, hard work, discipline, frugality, and religion.

Day-to-day existence was extremely difficult, at best. Tools were scarce. Everything had to be saved, for stores were rare and cash almost unknown. Every nail, board, candle, piece of soap, article of clothing, or nearly anything else, was handmade.

Death always lurked near. Women died often in childbirth: Rachel's mourning for her first born was not fictional. Many children died within a few hours or days of birth. Smallpox, measles, pneumonia, influenza, or blood poisoning carried off large numbers of people. Medical knowledge was closer to witch doctor days than to science.

Eroding brownstone grave markers in old cemeteries tell the story best. A stone or two might tell of someone who died in old age, but most markers were for infants or children dead before age ten; young mothers who died in childbirth, or young fathers felled by overwork, disease, or the ignorance of doctors.

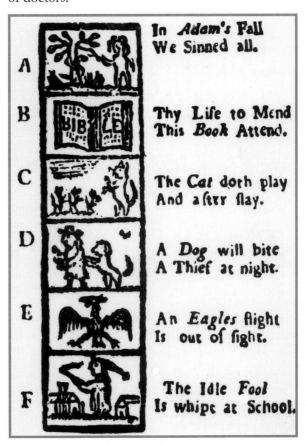

A page from *The New England Printer*, **that taught both the alphabet and religion, anticipated 20th century idiom with "eagle's flight" that is "out of sight."**

69

Man May Work From Sun to Sun

Morning's first rays of sun — or the roosters' first crow on rainy days — set men to work. They sliced the earth with crude plows drawn by oxen, the best of farm animals, and sowed seeds. Men and older boys felled towering trees, either to clear the land or provide fuel for heating, cooking, and cabin illumination. Some trees were sawed into beams or boards, with the master "sawyer" showering sawdust over his helper in the pit. Harvesting was backbreaking; getting in the crops on time was crucial. The loss of corn or wheat to blight or bad weather was disastrous. In the fall, apples were pressed into cider or apple whiskey (to fend off disease or help ward off the winter chill).

Each night in every season, as the sun set, the livestock had to be fed and watered, the stables cleared, and the fires banked. At least, then, man's work was done until next day's dawn.

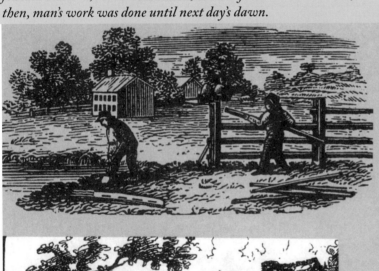

70

But Woman's Work Is Never Done

The woman often pitched in at harvest time, especially if rain threatened to ruin the ripened grain. She tended the "kitchen garden" (vegetables and fruits), with younger boys and girls to help. The newest baby was cradled in a nearby tree.

During her endless round of work, she churned the butter, made the candles and soap, spun, wove, and sewed the cloth. She dried fruits and vegetables for winter use. She cared for the children — and many years she faced the pain and danger of another birth.

At day's end, she served and cleared away supper as the man sat by the fire, smoking a pipe or perhaps laboriously reading the Bible. When she sat down, she spun yarn, knitted socks, or patched worn garments.

Her work ended only when everyone was asleep, and even then it was she who answered a sick child's call in the night.

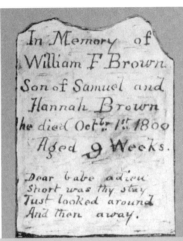

In Memory of
William F Brown
Son of Samuel and
Hannah Brown
he died Oct.r 1.st 1809
Aged 9 Weeks.

Dear babe adieu
Short was thy stay
Just looked around
And then away.

In Memory of David
Son of Mofes and
Elizabeth Ward who
Died Sep.r 12. 1776
Aged 4 years.

In Memory of
Margret Johnfton
Dau.tr of Robert
& Elizabeth Johnfton
Who Departed this
Life August 25.th 1775
Age 2 Years & 11 Days

Unas Dau.tr of
Samuel & Jane
Clizbe Dec.d May
15.th 1764 in ye 4.th
Year of her Age.

To Be Seen And Not Heard

Merely staying alive posed the greatest challenge to colonial children. The headstones above, all from Newark's original cemetery, give the story of early death: William Brown, dead at nine weeks; David Ward, gone at four years; Margaret Johnston, dead at two years and eleven days; Unas Clizbe, dead at four.

Children who survived were readied to be adults from the time they could understand words. They worked hard, for a three-year-old could pick stones from the garden. A five-year-old knew the difference between beans and weeds.

They played games, for a while — rolling hoops, flying kites, hide-and-seek, wrestling, or running. Boys fished, for food, not for sport. Girls stitched samplers, the better to learn sewing.

Schooling was slight: a "dame school," perhaps, or a church academy for a privileged few. The lessons were always clear: mind your manners, work hard, and prepare to die. Even the "words of four syllables" in their reading book stressed virtue.

He that ne'er learns his A, B, C,
For ever will a Blockhead be;

Ais   Bull   Cat

Words of four Syllables.

Ac·com·pa·ny	Accompany
Be·ne·vo·lence	Benevolence
Ce·re·mo·ny	Ceremony
Dif·con·tent·ed	Difcontented
E·ver·laft·ing	Everlafting

A Roof Over Their Heads

Except for the Swedes and Finns, who built log cabins — as they had in their native lands — New Jersey's first colonists waited impatiently until they could build in solid brick or wood. That was what they did in England.

Many colonial accounts tell of living for a winter or two in caves or crude huts, likely similar to the rough cave-like house shown above. It did not take long to build substantially; Robert Treat house in Newark (upper right) was completed sometime before 1672, when Treat left town.

The handsome red brick Trent House, topped by a copper roofed cupola, has stood in Trenton since 1719. The date of the Hancock House (below) in Salem County is clear in the multi-colored bricks, along with the initials of the builders (William and Sarah Hancock).

Regardless of the size of the house, great or small, fireplaces such as that (lower right) in the Van Veghten House in Somerset County supplied all heat, light, and energy for cooking and baking.

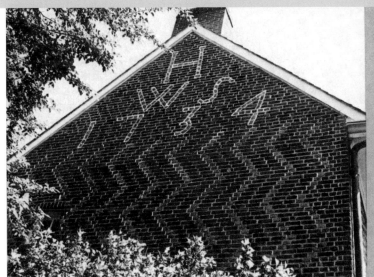

Chapter Four - Slow Road To Independence

United States			New Jersey		
George III starts reign as King of England	1763	1763	Gov William Franklin comes to NJ		
England passes Stamp Act	1765	1765	NJ people oppose stamps		
Stamp Act Congress meets	1765	1765	NJ divides at Stamp Act Congress		
The Boston Massacre	1770				
The Boston Tea Party	1773				
First Continental Congress meets	1774	1774	Greenwich Tea Party		
		1774	1st Provincial Congress meets in New Brunswick		
Battles of Lexington and Concord	1775	1775	Franklin seeks to keep NJ loyal to England		
(March) British leave Boston	1776	1776	(June) Franklin arrested by Provincial Congress		
Continental Congress adopts Declaration of Independence	1776	1776	(June) NJ picks 5 new delegates to congress		
		1776	NJ delegates back Declaration in unanimous show of enthusiasm		
		1776	NJ is third to adopt a Constitution		

Ice jammed the Raritan River and snow lay deep in the country roads, in late February 1763, as all of New Jersey — and Perth Amboy in particular — prepared to give warm greetings to new Governor William Franklin and his young bride.

Word had spread that the new governor had a wealth of qualifications, including the fact that his father was the illustrious Benjamin Franklin — that witty, wise, rebellious Philadelphia philosopher whose fame had spread to the far corners of Europe.

William had his own fine credentials, though. He had been well educated in Philadelphia and in England where he spent six years with his father. Young Franklin studied law at Oxford and was admitted to the English bar in 1758. His distinguished father undoubtedly opened some English doors for his son, but William had his own share of charm, intelligence, and wit.

New Jersey liked everything it heard about this thirty-two-year-old newcomer. One pleasing prospect was that Governor Franklin would be Philadelphia-minded, meaning that the west of New Jersey

◇◇◇◇◇◇◇◇◇◇◇◇◇◇◇◇◇◇◇◇◇

Loyal Englishmen All

Few New Jerseyans clamored for independence as the countdown began toward war with Great Britain. This colony had no John Adams, the passionate Massachusetts advocate of liberty, nor a Patrick Henry, whose eloquent outbursts set Virginia aflame.

Actually, there were few outspoken rebels in any of the thirteen colonies in 1770. Most, including Adams, Henry, Thomas Jefferson, and Benjamin Franklin, still considered themselves to be totally loyal Englishmen, subject to English laws, and under certain circumstances, even liable for English taxes.

New Jerseyans had shown a love of freedom for nearly a century. When Assemblymen fought with governors and proprietors, it was not rebellion against the Crown itself, but it was dangerously close. The mobs that broke into the streets to protest rents imposed by the proprietors were revolutionists.

There were good reasons why New Jersey voices were quiet as time ticked down toward a break with England.

Duties imposed by the British on imports hit port areas most severely. Since New Jersey depended on Philadelphia or New York ports, the impact was not direct.

New Jersey had no newspapers or printing presses to spread propaganda. A Boston newspaper could report overnight British indignities, real or fancied. New Jerseyans had to wait weeks to see if New York or Philadelphia newspapers cared to set forth their emotions.

This colony was slightly out of the mainstream of revolt as 1776 approached, but the reason was not a lack of leadership. Rather, in Governor William Franklin, New Jersey had probably the most skillful leader in all the colonies.

American-born William Franklin, the son of Benjamin, understood the yearnings for freedom, even though the colonists considered themselves to be English. Yet he also understood Great Britain's problems.

William Franklin kept his colony within reach of King George and Parliament. It was they who let it slip away.

would be most familiar to him. Every previous governor in the colony's century-long history had been oriented toward New York. Franklin had a qualification certain to appeal to the romantic-minded. He was accompanied by a young bride, Elizabeth. They met in England and were wed just before the Governor's ship sailed for America. Elizabeth had never seen the New World.

Time For A Honeymoon

The newlyweds reached Philadelphia on February 19. Four days later, they crossed the Delaware River and, in a horse-drawn sleigh, made the one-day dash to New Brunswick. They stayed there the night of February 24.

Perth Amboy hummed with excitement the next day. Early in the morning the Middlesex Troop galloped off to New Brunswick to escort the governor and his bride into the eastern capital of New Jersey. A "numerous concourse of people" waited in the frozen streets to greet them.

Perth Amboy's town fathers and the colonial legislators welcomed the governor in the best of spirits as befitted the start of both a new marriage and a hoped-for new relationship between governor and legislature. As the people stomped their feet to ward off the cold, they were warmed by Franklin's "inaugural address:"

"I thank you for your kind congratulations. The esteem which you so gratefully and justly express for my predecessors is no less agreeable to me. And wherever I may reside, which is as yet uncertain, I shall be glad of every opportunity of showing my regard for the City of Perth Amboy."

Anyone who speaks for less than a minute on a frigid day is a certain crowd pleaser. The crowd roared its approval and felt only slightly hurt after the ceremony when the Franklins left for Burlington, where they could rent quarters suitable for newlyweds. Burlington, the western capital, was much closer to Franklin's cultural and intellectual interests.

Tax The Americans

Franklin knew the governmental honeymoon would not last long. His Philadelphia years made him aware of the yearning for independence in America. His six years in England helped him know of the hardening in England's attitude toward the American colonies.

Bas-relief of William Franklin, the last Royal governor of New Jersey. The son of Benjamin Franklin, William came to the colony in 1763 eager to be fair to the people, but also determined to enforce English laws strictly.

The "numerous concourse of people" that rode out to greet the new governor in Perth Amboy took particular pride in the new barracks just completed in their town overlooking Raritan Bay.

Colonial New Jersey Counties

New Jersey had thirteen counties when Governor William Franklin reached the colony in 1763. Twin capitals in Perth Amboy and Burlington emphasized that East New Jersey and West New Jersey, while no longer official provinces, were very much in mind. To underscore the point, six of the eighteenth century counties were in East New Jersey and six in West New Jersey, with Sussex County divided between East and West.

Four of East New Jersey's colonial counties dated to 1683 when Bergen, Essex, Middlesex, and Monmouth were formed. Somerset was cut away from Middlesex in 1688 and Morris from Hunterdon in 1739.

West New Jersey also had four old counties — Salem, set up in 1681; Cape May, 1685; and Burlington and Gloucester, both 1686. Hunterdon broke away from Burlington in 1714, with vague boundaries that included modern Morris, Sussex, and Warren counties. Cumberland split from Salem in 1748. Then, in 1753, Sussex was formed from Morris County.

Eight pre-Revolution counties were named for areas in England: Essex, Somerset, Middlesex, Monmouth, Cumberland, Gloucester, Burlington, and Sussex. Cape May was named for Dutch Captain Cornelius Mey. Bergen was named for a town in Holland. Salem derives from the Hebrew word, *Shalom*, meaning peace. Two counties were named for colonial governors: Hunterdon for Governor Robert Hunter and Morris for Governor Lewis Morris.

Only four of the original county seats have changed. Somerset County's seat in 1763 was Millstone; it is now Somerville. Gloucester County's seat was Gloucestertown (Gloucester City); it is now Woodbury. Hunterdon's county seat at Trenton was shifted after the Revolution to Flemington. The Middlesex County seat was shifted from Perth Amboy to New Brunswick.

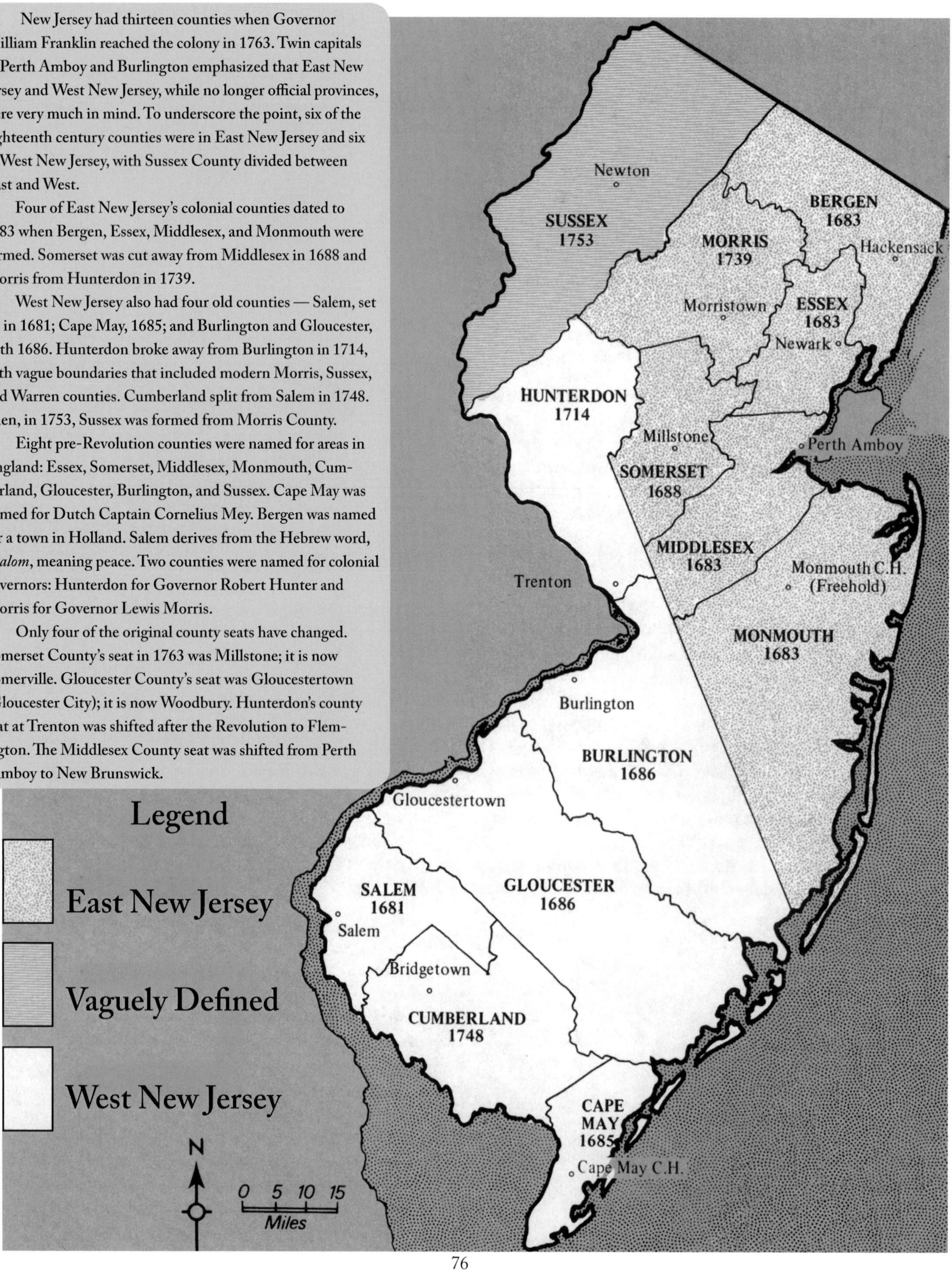

Legend

East New Jersey

Vaguely Defined

West New Jersey

N

0   5   10   15
Miles

Newton

SUSSEX
1753

BERGEN
1683

Hackensack

MORRIS
1739

ESSEX
1683

Morristown

Newark

HUNTERDON
1714

Millstone

Perth Amboy

SOMERSET
1688

Trenton

MIDDLESEX
1683

Monmouth C.H.
(Freehold)

MONMOUTH
1683

Burlington

BURLINGTON
1686

Gloucestertown

SALEM
1681

GLOUCESTER
1686

Salem

Bridgetown

CUMBERLAND
1748

CAPE
MAY
1685

Cape May C.H.

The possibility of new taxes on the colonies was being discussed as Franklin left England. The levies would be unpopular, but the governor had taken an oath to support the King and Parliament. He was determined to enforce the English law to the letter and to collect the taxes.

Unfortunately for Franklin, he assumed office just as the tax storm broke. British debts had doubled during the French and Indian War, and the advisers of King George III urged Parliament to tax the Americans to help pay the bills. They pointed out that most of the thirteen colonies had grown rich during the war.

Parliament responded in 1764 with the Sugar Act. It seemed innocent enough on the surface, actually cutting in half the taxes on molasses and other sugar products. However, for the first time, sugar and molasses smugglers would be prosecuted by British-run courts instead of friendly American neighbors inclined to acquittals.

The Sugar Act also prohibited trade directly with the French West Indies, a principal American market. New England was aghast. Molasses revenues from the West Indian trade were vital to New England's balance of trade. New Jersey was not much affected by the act.

A more stunning blow for New Jersey also came in 1764. Parliament forbade the issuance of colonial paper money, a move designed to discourage the colonial custom of adjusting money shortages by printing new paper currency. New Jersey, one of the leading paper money advocates, suddenly was saddled with debts and no way to print its way out of the crisis.

"November Is Dreaded"

Hard times came upon America. New Jersey, whose debts were the largest in all the colonies, was on the brink of financial ruin. Parliament struck again: effective November 1, 1765, colonists must pay for stamps on all legal documents, printed matter, playing cards, and licenses. Even college degrees must bear British stamps. The Stamp Tax was too much. Such a levy in the midst of a deepening depression proved England's lack of concern for conditions and attitudes in America. At a time when New York and Philadelphia newspapers were filled with notices of New Jersey farms for sale at ruinous prices, the tax was simply outrageous.

Even the most fervent supporters of England were appalled. Cortland Skinner of Perth Amboy,

Hatred mounted in New Jersey and the other colonies as the Stamp Act took hold. Cartoons in the Pennsylvania *Journal* in 1765 warned that the "fatal stamp" would be a crushing blow to the American economy. Colonists gleefully hailed the cartoon below, showing a tax collector tarred and feathered by Sons of Liberty under a "Liberty Tree."

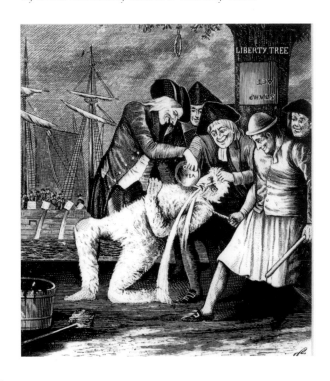

77

A North-West Prospect of Nassau-Hall, with a Front View of the Presidents House, in New-Jersey

By Any Name

Princeton University (by some other name) might easily be on the banks of the Raritan River at New Brunswick, and Rutgers University (by another name) might as easily be on the banks of the old Hackensack River.

Presbyterians, who wanted to train ministers in America rather than England, founded the College of New Jersey in Elizabeth in 1746. The college transferred to Newark within a year, and then in 1754 decided to move again. College trustees offered to locate in New Brunswick if townspeople would donate £1,000 plus ten acres in town and 200 acres of woodland within three miles of town.

As New Brunswick dallied, Princeton leaders quickly accepted the offer. The College of New Jersey moved to Princeton in 1756 and after several decades became Princeton University.

Meanwhile, the Dutch Reformed Church decided in 1766 to found Queens College to train its own ministers in America. In granting the charter, the state legislature split on a location, sixteen voting for Hackensack, sixteen for New Brunswick. The governor's vote finally gave New Brunswick its college.

Queens College changed its name to Rutgers College in 1825, honoring a small gift from Colonel Henry Rutgers of New York. When Rutgers became The State University in 1945, in a very roundabout way, a "College of New Jersey" finally reached the banks of the Raritan.

At any rate, by any name and by any location, New Jersey was the only one of the thirteen colonies to have two colleges founded before the American Revolution.

When Henry Dawkins made this copperplate engraving of Nassau Hall in 1764, the building was called "the largest stone building in all the colonies." The structure was the home of the College of New Jersey, founded in 1747 in Elizabeth, transferred to Newark a year later, and then moved to its permanent home beside muddy Nassau Street in 1756. The president's house, to the right, was finished the same year. Both buildings form the heart of the Princeton University campus.

who would choose to remain loyal to England when war broke out, wrote in October 1765: "Everything here is in the greatest confusion, and the first of November is dreaded."

Governor Franklin appointed William Coxe of Burlington as Stamp Officer. Coxe became a handy target for the wrath of his neighbors. He could not even rent a place for an office, lest it be "pulled down or burned." The Sons of Liberty warned Coxe if he handled the stamps, he would be treated "in such a way and manner, as perhaps will be disagreeable both to yourself and us."

New Jersey lawyers voted not to do any legal work requiring stamps. This was not as spectacular a move as the hot words and flaming torches of Massachusetts and Virginia, but it cut directly to the heart of the matter: no stamps, no taxes.

New York merchants promised to end all British imports until the Stamp Act was repealed. Philadelphia and Boston also endorsed the importation move, hoping that British merchants might be so crippled they would protest directly to Parliament. Caught between the ports of Philadelphia and New York, New Jerseyans automatically became non-importers without any say in the matter.

"Like A Speckled Bird"

Massachusetts took matters into its own hands. It invited all colonies to a Stamp Act Congress in New York on October 7, 1765. When New Jerseyans hesitated, lawyer Richard Stockton of Princeton argued if New Jersey was not represented, "We shall not only look like a speckled bird among our sister colonies, but shall say implicitly that we think it no oppression."

The reluctant Assembly agreed and dispatched Robert Ogden of Essex County, Henrick Fisher of Somerset, and Joseph Borden of Burlington to the Congress. Only two delegates voted against expressing the "rights and grievances of the colonies" in a written petition to King George. One was a Massachusetts delegate, the other was Ogden. When he returned to Essex County, infuriated neighbors forced him to resign from his Assembly seat.

Faced with such opposition — and, more to the point, with greatly reduced shipments to America — Parliament repealed the Stamp Act. The word reached New Jersey on April 3, 1766. Six weeks later, Governor Franklin joined Burlington residents in "demonstrations of joy." The Woodbridge Sons of Liberty also celebrated, after carefully expressing their "firm loyalty" to the King.

Now the tax-hungry British tried a new tack, the so-called Townshend Acts (named for Charles Townshend, Chancellor of the Exchequer). These taxes — on glass, paper, red and white lead, and tea — failed as miserably as the Stamp levies.

Colonial embargoes cut English sales to a trickle. Once more Great Britain backed down and, on March 5, 1770, repealed all but the tea tax. Tea immediately became socially undrinkable; many began drinking "New Jersey Tea," made from the dried leaves of the native wild shrub called red root.

Word of the tax repeal was slow in reaching America in a period when all messages were carried on slow-moving ships. Ironically, on the very day of the repeal of the Townshend Acts in England, British soldiers fired on a protesting mob on the Boston Common. Five persons were killed in what was called "The Boston Massacre."

Franklin Grows Uneasy

Neither the Boston Massacre nor the repeal of the Townshend Acts excited New Jerseyans particularly. They were far more incensed by New York merchants

New York State's boundary experts agreed with New Jersey's representatives on only one point in 1764: the two states joined at a point on the Hudson River at forty-one degrees latitude (near modern Northvale, New Jersey).

New Jersey claimed the northwest boundary should be at forty-one degrees, forty minutes (near present-day Calicoon, New York). Hah, retorted New York, the line really should be drawn to Reedy's Island in Salem County! The Yorkers said they would agree, however, to take only the land north of a line drawn from forty-one degrees latitude to modern Phillipsburg.

King George III appointed seven commissioners to settle the dispute. They agreed, in 1769, to draw the line from a point near what is now Port Jervis to the Hudson River. The survey, finished in 1774, split Greenwood Lake in half and gave New York State more than 200,000 acres that New Jerseyans long claimed as their own.

To make the injury worse, the line was resurveyed a century later and the 1874 surveyors found that the border line of 1774 veered a half mile out of a straight line — to the south. New Jersey lost more land, but it was far too late to go to war or to court over that.

The border stands, with New York much the richer.

who secretly imported British goods and sold them on the black market.

A Woodbridge group promised a coat of tar and feathers for anyone caught buying the New York merchandise. Graduates at the College of New Jersey attended the 1770 commencement in homespun suits to show they would not buy clothes from shady New York dealers.

Governor Franklin grew increasingly uncomfortable. His efforts to tread the thin line between his English superiors and his rebellious colonists earned him little but bitter complaints from both. His meetings with the legislature were a series of continuing quarrels. Yet the governor kept his head, trying to reason with both the King and his New Jersey subjects.

Benjamin Franklin compounded his son's troubles. In December 1773, King George removed Benjamin as head of the Post Office in America because of anti-British remarks. The father wrote his son to expect no more promotions. Forget the British, Benjamin advised; retire and "be well settled on your farm."

Young Franklin ignored his father's advice and clung to his Governor's post. When Bostonians dumped tea into the harbor in December 1773, William defended the British. Benjamin agreed with him the Tea Party was a violation of private property, but after that, father and son found less and less in common. Within a year they barely spoke to one another.

"The Cause Of All"

Political leaders were aroused. Acting on a Virginia proposal, the New Jersey Committees of Correspondence began, in February 1774, to communicate their rebellious thoughts from town to town. When the British closed the Port of Boston in June of 1774, the committees endorsed a Monmouth County resolution that Boston's cause was "the cause of all."

Seventy-two of the colony's leaders met in New Brunswick on July 21, 1774 to organize New Jersey's First Provincial Congress. After cautiously swearing allegiance to King George, the New Jerseyans boldly declared Parliament's tax laws were oppressive and illegal.

The Provincial Congress was illegal, of course. It had in effect seized the power of government and moved New Jersey into the mainstream of revolution. The Provincial Congress chose five delegates to attend the first Continental Congress that would assemble in Philadelphia on September 5, 1774. The

five were Stephen Crane, William Livingston, and John DeHart, all of Essex County; and James Kinsey and Richard Smith of Burlington.

The fiercely independent John Adams and other New Englanders dominated the First Continental Congress, but their goal was not yet an open break with Great Britain. Day after day, speakers stressed their rights as *Englishmen*, especially the basic right to be represented in Parliament.

"An Imaginary Tyranny"

New Jersey's Chief Justice Frederick Smyth, appointed by the King — and thus the very symbol of English law — inflamed an Essex County Grand Jury in November 1774 by denouncing the rebellious attitude sweeping the land.

"People are guarding against imaginary tyranny, three thousand miles distant," said Judge Smyth. He warned the jurors they might better study "real tyranny at our own doors." His tone was patronizing, as if he were chastising wayward children.

Grand jurors, who usually nodded their heads meekly at the utterance of any King's judge, reacted differently this time. Uzal Ward, foreman of the Essex jury, rose to reply. Judge Smyth listened in astonishment to the remarks of the foreman, that were as rebellious as any yet spoken in America:

We cannot think, Sir, that taxes imposed upon us by our fellow subjects in a legislature in which we are not represented is imaginary, but that it is real and actual tyranny…

We cannot think, Sir, that depriving us of the inestimable right of trial by jury — seizing our persons, and carrying us for trial to Great Britain, is a tyranny merely imaginary…

Nor can we think with your Honor that destroying charters, and changing our forms of government is a tyranny altogether ideal…

…In a word, Sir, we cannot persuade ourselves that the fleet now blocking up the Port of Boston, consisting of ships built of real English oak and solid iron, and armed with cannon and ponderous metal, with actual powder and ball; nor the army lodging in the town of Boston, and fortifications thrown about it… are all creatures of the imagination.

Chief Justice Frederick Smyth and his fellow judges listen in astonishment as Uzal Ward, foreman of an Essex County grand jury, boldly responds to Smyth's allegation in November 1774 that colonists were rebelling against an "imaginary tyranny." The scene is from a mural painted by Francis D. Millett in the Essex County Court House. Ward's stinging words to Smyth and the King's judges were as rebellious as any spoken in America to that time, yet they have been nearly forgotten.

The New York *Journal* carried the foreman's stinging words in full. It reported that the startled chief justice made "a very complaisant and conciliating reply." Judge Smyth's soothing words have not been preserved, but the grand jury's angry words demonstrated that New Jerseyans no longer feared the King's agents.

Tempest in The Tea Cups

Essex County was a focal point of rebellion for more than a century and the center of fiery street fighting as recently as 1745. Puritans founded the county, and their memory of forced exodus from England 150 years before lived on in family traditions. There was little affection here for English officials.

Rebellion also was in the air at the Presbyterian College of New Jersey in Princeton. Students stole tea from the school kitchen in January 1774 and burned it on campus in sympathy with Boston's tea vandals.

That cost student rebel Samuel Leake his chance to speak at commencement the following June.

Radical sentiment simmered as well in the little port of Greenwich on Cohansey Creek in Cumberland County. Tea brought Greenwich to the boiling point.

Captain J. Allen of the British ship *Greyhound* obviously expected no difficulty when he tied up at Greenwich on December 12, 1774 with his cargo of tea. The cargo was unloaded and stored in Dan Bowen's cellar. Angry residents of the river village set December 23 to discuss the tea publicly, but the meeting never took place.

Local activists, lightly disguised as "Indians," rode into town on the night of December 12. They broke open Bowen's cellar, removed the tea, and burned it in the street. The crackling, perfumed flames proved that rebellion was afoot even in the most unlikely places.

Seven of the tea burners were tried the following April before Chief Justice Smyth and a reluctant jury. Charged with putting together the jury panel

Cumberland County lay far off the beaten path as the showdown with England neared, but distance from the center of rebel thought did not keep independent spirits from flaming in the southern New Jersey area. The most impressive show of defiance occurred, on December 12, 1774, when Greenwich radicals burned British tea in their village square to show Great Britain the hated leaves could not be stored in their town.

That tea party was only one evidence of the antiBritish spirit. One of the tea burners, twenty-three-year-old Ebenezer Elmer, continued the fight in the *Plain Dealer* he began publishing at Cohansey Bridge (now Bridgeton) on Christmas Day 1775. The title from the paper's first issue is shown on the right.

Elmer's publication appeared every Tuesday and thus probably was New Jersey's first regular newspaper. It was handwritten, Elmer wrote, because "there is no press within reach." The *Plain Dealer* was tacked on the wall of Potter's Tavern (below).

Thomas Harris, a writer for the *Plain Dealer*, knew he could be hanged for his work. He signed his articles anyway, saying they were "wrote with my blood."

With pride in their tea burners and "Plain Dealers," Cumberland County's patriots rang their own liberty bell in joy after the Declaration of Independence was adopted. The old bell, lower right, is now in the county courthouse in Bridgeton.

was Sheriff Jonathan Elmer, brother of one of the accused. The foreman was Jonathan's nephew Daniel Elmer. The verdict for all was "not guilty." Greenwich justice in April 1775 did not include punishment for burning British tea.

A Thorough Government Man

Governor Franklin moved to Perth Amboy in 1773 to seek closer ties with the royal minded proprietors of East Jersey. He and Mrs. Franklin took over the handsome four-level Proprietary House late in 1774; it was the only fine home either had enjoyed in New Jersey.

Benjamin Franklin paid his last visit to William in September 1775. He long had labeled his son as a "thorough government man," although he admired his honesty. It was far too late for either to change. Benjamin was committed to radical action, William was loyal to the crown.

Embattled Governor Franklin pleaded with the Assembly in January 1775 to help ward off the impending "anarchy, misery, and all the horrors of civil war." He urged them to compile a list of grievances, promising to get them to the personal attention of King George.

Fearful that Franklin's pleading might persuade New Jersey to disapprove of the resolutions of the Continental Congress in Philadelphia, three New Jersey delegates to that Congress rode quickly to Perth Amboy to urge firmness. The Assembly stiffened and backed the Philadelphia actions.

Franklin was outraged. When the Assembly drew up its list of grievances, Franklin refused to forward the document. The infuriated Assembly itself forwarded the list to King George.

Eagerness for war grew. Patrick Henry demanded "liberty or death" as he shouted impatiently to Vir-

The Proprietary House

Governor Franklin found a Perth Amboy house that seemed ideal for a governor's home in 1763: the four-level "Proprietary House" on a high knoll overlooking Raritan Bay. The British government refused him funds to lease the place, so he bought a 575-acre farm near Burlington and traveled between the colony's two capitals.

The East New Jersey Board of Proprietors would have welcomed Franklin; they built this mansion with the candid hope that it would lure the colony's governors into full-time residence in Perth Amboy.

More than ten years elapsed between Franklin's first desire to live in the fine home and when he was able to lease it in September 1773. Mrs. Franklin liked the place; she wrote that "Amboy has been a very agreeable place" with "many joyous social evenings."

The governor's home featured a huge ball room, eighteen feet wide and paved with three-inch thick marble slabs. Other rooms were in the grand manner, with sixteen fireplaces providing heat. The Franklins lived in the house from October 1774 until June 1776 when the governor was arrested by the Provincial Congress and taken to Burlington.

The Proprietary House was in a state of ruin by 1784. Later it was enlarged and used as a hotel and a retirement home. The State of New Jersey bought the mansion in 1967 and restored the inside of the historic landmark to the opulence of Governor Franklin's time.

A Time For Hope

While much of the rest of New Jersey seethed in anger and despair, Pennsylvania Moravians came to the northwest mountain land in 1769 to found a town they called Hope (in what is now Warren County).

First things came first — a gristmill, and then a store and a tannery. Despite their deep religious feelings, the Moravians did not start their Hope church until 1781.

All ages and occupations were represented in Hope's first residents, but most were young and recently married. All town females wore plain dresses; colored ribbons denoted their status: pink for unmarried, blue for married, white for widows, red for children.

Hope's residents closely followed Moravian customs. The congregation was divided into "Economies" or "Choirs," according to age, sex, and occupation. Music was vital in community life; a trombone played for all affairs, joyful as well as somber.

The little village grew slowly, to a peak of 147 people in 1791. By 1799, the population had dwindled to eighty-four. Soon after, the Moravians sold their land and moved away, but buildings still remain in Hope Historic District from the time of the Moravian Hopefuls.

G: Tisdale ? el.   el fculp?—

The TORY'S Day of JUDGMENT

Anyone suspected of being loyal to King George faced such drastic punishment as this. "Tory's" were often denied fair trials, making them subject to the whims of vindictive neighbors.

ginians in March 1775, that "our brethren already are in the field!" A fast-riding dispatch rider from Massachusetts caused great excitement when he rode through New Jersey, on April 23, 1775, shouting news of the battles at Lexington and Concord four days earlier.

Newark leaders responded promptly. They resolved, on April 24, they were "willing at this alarming crisis to risk our lives and fortunes in support of American Liberty." Militia companies everywhere intensified their drilling on village greens. Perth Amboy's defiant militia marched past the Governor's home with "Colours, Fife and Drum" to make sure Franklin knew where their loyalties lay.

Franklin's Last Stand

The import of the news from Lexington and Concord seemed to escape Governor Franklin. Even as the militia marched outside his window, he urged the Assembly to accept England's offers of conciliation. The Assembly rebuffed him:

"We cannot suppose you to entertain a suspicion that the present house had the least design to desert the common cause, in which all America seems to be both deeply interested and firmly united."

Franklin's power had nearly evaporated, but so had the power of the Assembly. The New Jersey Provincial Congress, still an outlaw body, met in Trenton in

Benjamin Franklin's much copied snake severed into thirteen sections carried to colonists the very clear message: stay together or perish. New Jersey, in the middle, was a constant threat to rebel unity.

This 19th century drawing shows a very calm Governor Franklin sitting in his Perth Amboy living room while troops of the Provincial Congress place him under arrest.

May 1775 and took over the reins of government. It announced a regular system of elections for the first time in nearly seventy-five years and ordered all men between sixteen and sixty to enlist in the army.

Caught between two state governments, one legal and the other not, Franklin called the Assembly together at Burlington in November 1775. He asked for cooperation with England, and then plaintively asked whether he should remain in New Jersey. "It is high time that every man should know what he has to expect," he declared.

The alarmed Assembly assured Franklin that he should stay, and it petitioned King George to work to prevent "the effusion of blood." They asked the New Jersey delegation at the Continental Congress in Philadelphia to seek some way to return peacefully to England's good favor. New Jersey, the Assembly felt, wanted "a restoration of peace and harmony with the parent state."

"A Rope Of Sand"

Such peace talk worried the Continental Congress. Three members sped to Burlington to express the folly of dealing with King George. John Dickinson of Pennsylvania charged that New Jersey's action would tempt England to view the colonies as "a rope of sand." Dickinson carried the day; the Assembly tabled a proposed petition to the King.

Franklin knew that soon the trap would close on

him. A band of soldiers confirmed this on January 8, 1776. They beat on his door, awakened him from sleep, and told him the Provincial Congress wanted his pledge not to flee. Franklin agreed and won temporary amnesty.

Voters went to the polls on May 28, 1776 to choose a third New Jersey Provincial Congress. The mood was clear; every person elected was committed to independence. Franklin's base had vanished. Still unconvinced, he called on the now repudiated Assembly to meet with him on June 20, overlooking the fact that several members of the Assembly had already gone over to the rebel government.

The Provincial Congress was aroused when it gathered in Burlington on June 10. It sent Colonel Nathaniel Heard to Perth Amboy on June 17 to tell Franklin he had been removed from office. Heard was instructed to use "all the delicacy and tenderness" possible, but to make his message clear: Franklin was finished.

Franklin refused to accept parole in any place suggested by the Provincial Congress, so Heard arrested him on June 19 and took him to Burlington. The ousted Governor called his captors "desperate gamesters ... bent on an independent republican tyranny." Nobody listened. (Later, Franklin was sent to Connecticut under guard, and in 1778 he was permitted to go to New York where he worked for the Loyalist cause until the end of the war.)

Portraits of four of New Jersey's five signers of the Declaration of Independence exist. No certain likeness of John Hart has been found; a "portrait" painted in 1869 often has been erroneously cited as the "official" picture of Hart, a Hopewell farmer. Farmers rarely had their portraits painted in those days. More likely subjects were Clark and Stockton, lawyers; Witherspoon, president of the College of New Jersey; and Hopkinson, himself an artist.

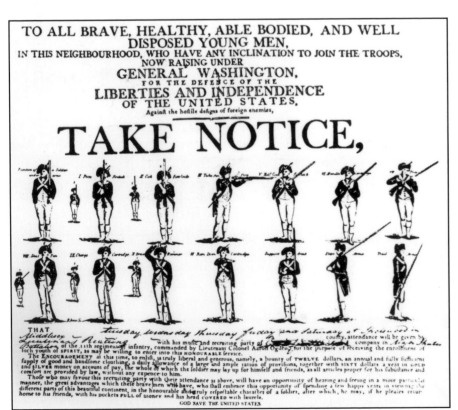

Young men who were "brave, healthy, able bodied and well disposed" were urged to sign up for the army. Soldiers on the recruiting poster were shown in a variety of military poses of the Revolutionary period. This poster leaned heavily on General Washington's fame and the much-admired military appearance of soldiers.

That Damned Old Rascal

Great Britain hated Governor William Livingston so intensely that, in February 1779, it offered "two thousand guineas and a life pension, for that damned old rascal, Governor Livingston, delivered dead or alive on Staten Island."

Livingston replied in a taunting fashion: "The British are as great blockheads as they are rascals for taking so much pain and running such risk to assassinate an old fellow whose place might instantly be supplied by a successor of greater ability and greater energy."

The 56-year-old governor might have been right about his energy in 1779, but he was totally wrong about his ability. There was no one in New Jersey — or in most of the nation — to match him for his intelligence, his keen wit, and his brilliant writing style.

Livingston was one of the wealthy, politically powerful New York Livingstons. He graduated from Yale in 1741 and married Susanna French of New Brunswick the following year. The couple had thirteen children before moving to Elizabeth in 1773 to enjoy "the pleasures of rural life."

Separation from England was not Livingston's major passion. There was so much fear in 1775 that he might oppose a declaration of independence that he was replaced in the Continental Congress. When independence was declared and Livingston was elected the first Governor of the State of New Jersey in June 1776, he avidly embraced the revolution. He and his family moved often to escape British troops intent on capturing him, but Livingston survived all British threats. He was re-elected annually until his death in 1790.

(From a painting.)

Five For Independence

New Jersey's Provincial Congress chose five new independence-minded delegates to the Continental Congress on June 22, 1776. They were Abraham Clark of Rahway, John Hart of Hopewell, Francis Hopkinson of Bordentown; and Richard Stockton and the Rev. John Witherspoon, both of Princeton. All were instructed to join at Philadelphia "in declaring the United Colonies independent of Great Britain."

New Jersey's delegation was an assorted lot. Self-educated Abraham Clark was called "the Poor Man's Counselor" because he willingly represented, without fee, those too poor to afford a lawyer. In contrast, Richard Stockton was one of the best educated and wealthiest attorneys in all the colonies.

John Hart was a farmer with little formal education, but he had earned the total respect of his neighbors. John Witherspoon, president of the College of New Jersey, was the only clergyman and the only college president in the Continental Congress. Francis Hopkinson, educated as a lawyer, was also an artist, a brilliant writer, and an accomplished songwriter.

The New Jersey delegation quickly made its presence felt in Philadelphia. Soon after Congress convened on July 1, Witherspoon heard a speaker declare the colonies were not "ripe for independence." The Princeton clergyman looked pointedly at the reluctant New York delegation and roared: "Some colonies are rotten for the want of it!"

The next day, July 2, all five New Jerseyans approved a resolution calling for the split from England. On July 4, they unanimously approved the Declaration of Independence. All five signed the Declaration when it was finally ready for signatures on August 2.

New Jersey Becomes A State

Meanwhile, back home, the Provincial Congress worked on a new constitution for the State of New Jersey that was about to be born. Jacob Green of Morris County and his committee began fashioning the constitution on June 24. Eight days later, on July 2, it was adopted by the New Jersey Congress.

It was a cautious document, saying guardedly that if a reconciliation took place between the United Colonies and Great Britain, "this charter shall be null and void." It was far from popular. Nearly half — thirty members — did not even vote on it. Thirty-five did vote, and of those, twenty-six approved. Thus, New Jersey's first constitution was adopted with only twenty-six out of sixty-five possible votes in favor.

Reluctance to make this additional show of defiance to England was understandable. New Jersey was only the third colony to adopt a constitution (New Hampshire and South Carolina were first and second). American independence was still a very delicate matter on July 2, 1776.

The constitution called for upper and lower houses — a Council and an Assembly — with annual elections on the second Tuesday of October. Each of the thirteen counties could elect three Assembly members and one Council member. All people who met property restrictions could vote, including women and African Americans, a rare privilege in eighteenth century America.

The Governor was to be elected by the legislature each year, a deliberate curtailment of his power. William Livingston of Elizabethtown was chosen as the first governor of the State of New Jersey despite strong opposition. Livingston had at first seemed lukewarm about independence.

However, when war became inevitable, Livingston wrote: "We have passed the Rubicon. We cannot recede, nor should I wish we could."

War had come. The Revolution would splinter the state. Individuals had to choose between revolt and loyalty to England. Soon the state would experience the actuality of battle, occupation by major armies, the suffering and starvation of war close to home.

New Jersey was astride the pathway between New England and the South. It could not escape being the crossroads of the Revolution.

Apostle Of Freedom

John Woolman of Mount Holly spent his life as a Quaker, avoiding all show and bluster, yet as the showdown with Great Britain approached, he became the foremost apostle of freedom — for all people — in the thirteen colonies.

Born to Burlington County Quaker parents in 1720, John Woolman worked with his 12 brothers and sisters on the family farm near Rancocas. He received little formal education but was an intensive reader.

He became a tailor at age 21. When he prospered and felt a growing desire for more wealth, he sold his shop and devoted his life totally to his religion.

Woolman became a bitter foe of slavery in 1742 when he was asked to write a bill of sale for an African American woman slave. He began a round of anti-slavery preaching that continued all the rest of his life.

Virginia planters heard the same firm denunciations of slavery that Woolman used in northern colonies. Many Quakers, North and South, freed their slaves after hearing Woolman speak.

Woolman believed that all persons were entitled to live in dignity. He wrote "we are the subject of like afflictions and infirmities of body, the like disorders and frailties in mind, the like temptations, the same death, and the same judgement."

He died in 1772 in England, where he went to preach. His words survive him, and his JOURNAL, reprinted more than 40 times, proves clearly he believed totally ALL human beings are created equal.

Artist F.A. Chapman sought in 1875 to capture the mood and spirit of a century before in his "Raising The Liberty Pole, 1776." As stalwart revolutionists tugged a new flagpole (the liberty pole) into position, young men signed up to fight. Cheering young women urged them on. To the left, disgruntled viewers, identified as lovers of King George by their dress and manner, showed dismay.

Mistress Yankee Doodle

Just as in the song Yankee Doodle *(when "father and I went down to camp to see the men and boys as thick as hasty pudding"), Jemima Condict of Orange rode into Newark with her father early in April 1775 to watch the Essex County militia drilling for war.*

Jemima, twenty years old, had started a diary three years before. On that training day in 1775, she wrote: "How soon they will be called forth to the field of war we cannot tell, for by what we hear the quarrels are not like to be made up without bloodshed."

Jemima realized something few others yet recognized or acknowledged: America was hastening down the road to war with England.

A few days later, Jemima wrote of the fighting at Lexington and Concord: "The regulars [the British] we hear shot first; they killed thirty of our men." She com-

mented: "Each day brings new troubles."

Jemima never mentioned major battles such as those at Trenton or Princeton. She noted the war's effects on her own town, wrote of several neighbor soldiers killed by Indians in September 1776 while on duty in Sussex County, and of a British raid in Essex County a year later that killed several local civilians.

Jemima Condict's diary, now owned by the New Jersey Historical Society, is unusual in many ways. It is one of the very few Revolutionary War diaries kept by a woman. It is literate and witty, and it shows an unusual grasp of what the war was about.

She did not see the end of the Revolution. Jemima stopped writing just before she married a soldier in the spring of 1779. She was stricken with disease and died seven months after her wedding day.

Chapter Five - World Turned Upside Down

United States		New Jersey	
British occupy New York	1776	1776	(Nov) Retreat across NJ
		1776	(Dec 26) Americans overwhelm Hessians in Trenton
British winter at New Brunswick	1777	1777	(Jan 3) Battle of Princeton
		1777	Americans winter camp at Morristown
British occupy Philadelphia; Americans at Valley Forge	1777	1777	Battle of Red Bank on the Delaware River
France becomes United States ally	1778	1778	(June 28) Battle of Monmouth
(Dec) British capture Savannah	1778	1778-79	American army camps at Middlebrook
		1779-80	American army returns to Morristown
Inflation soars, hurting American war effort	1780	1780	(June) Battle of Springfield
Surrender at Yorktown	1781	1781	American, French armies cross NJ on way to Yorktown
Treaty of Paris establishes American independence	1783	1783	Congress gets news of Treaty of Paris at Princeton

British troops stationed in colonial New Jersey barracks often marched across the village greens to an old fifing song, *The World Turned Upside Down*. The tune was prophetic, for the revolution now unleashed in America would in time turn the entire world topsy turvy.

War was a distant thing for New Jersey until July of 1776. The drilling of militia on the village squares had been fun; target practice had been a game. Now the game was over: the mighty British army was all too evident as it swarmed across Staten Island.

British General Howe waited until the summer was almost gone to make his move. Then, on August 22, he unleashed his British and Hessian soldiers to smash the American army at Long Island. Northward the Americans reeled, to Harlem Heights and all the way north to White Plains, New York by October. The fort at Paulus Hook (Jersey City) fell on September 23, the first New Jersey soil to be occupied by the enemy.

The victorious British paraded jauntily southward out of White Plains in November, headed for winter

◇◇◇◇◇◇◇◇◇◇◇◇◇◇◇◇◇◇◇

War In The Heartland

An eye-witness named Daniel McCurtin peeped out of his New York bedroom window at sunrise on June 29, 1776. His astonished eyes saw "something resembling a wood of pine trees trimmed… the whole bay was full of shipping as ever it could be. I thought all London was afloat."

All the speculation and wonder had come to an end. British General William Howe, who left Boston on March 17 on an unknown mission, brought his fleet of more than "one hundred sails" to New York. Soon his troops poured ashore onto Staten Island. The war had come to the heartland of America.

Here the conflict would be won or lost, for here were New York and Philadelphia, the two most prosperous cities in the land, built on the two finest harbors on the coast. Whoever controlled both harbors would win the war.

In between lay New Jersey. Obviously, whoever held this state could exert strong pressure — military, political, and economic — on both New York and Philadelphia. If

Howe had moved quickly across New Jersey, the thirteen states would have been cut in two.

When war came, many leading citizens, including Governor Franklin, became Loyalists (or "Tories"). Most Loyalists were judges, lawyers, doctors, merchants, or Episcopal clergymen. Loyalty to the Crown, however, was not limited to the wealthy and privileged. Many poor citizens preferred the established government.

There probably were as many Loyalists as there were Patriots in the state. The Quakers of southwestern New Jersey remained neutral for religious reasons. The Dutch in northeastern New Jersey had little feeling for either side. With the proper encouragement from Howe, New Jersey could have been swung to the British.

General Howe's army in New York harbor brought the war home. Soon, redcoated troops parading on Staten Island within sight of New Jersey must attack somewhere.

The time had come to choose sides, and fast.

Captain Archibald Robertson, British deputy quartermaster general, sketched this portion of the British fleet anchored between Staten Island and Long Island on July 12, 1776. This was the area from which the English forces would strike at Long Island on August 22, when British flatboats carried 15,000 men, along with their horses and cannon, across the water in two and one-half hours. (Spencer Collection, NY Public Library)

quarters in New York. General George Washington misread the maneuver as the start of an assault on New Jersey and hastened here with his troops. The Americans neared Fort Lee on November 14, "broken and dispirited," in Washington's words.

He had cause for worry. Few militiamen had turned out anywhere. So many soldiers were deserting that an officer declared Bergen County roads were filled with men "returning to their homes in the most scandalous and infamous manner." Washington himself had shown little talent except an ability to retreat without losing his army.

Terror On The Palisades

On November 16, British and Hessian soldiers overwhelmed Fort Washington in New York, just across the river from Fort Lee. They took more than 2,800 prisoners and captured large quantities of desperately needed supplies.

Four days later, English General Charles Cornwallis dealt the Americans an even more crippling blow. In one of the war's most daring exploits, he led several thousand soldiers across the Hudson River to Closter Dock in Bergen County. The Redcoats quietly scaled the face of the clifflike Palisades over a little-used path and raced toward Fort Lee.

The surprised, poorly disciplined Americans fled in terror. They left behind blankets and ammunition critically needed by Washington's army. Breakfast was still warm on the campfires when the British barged into the fort. The scampering soldiers had not even bothered to carry away warm clothing.

The fall of Forts Washington and Lee added up to a disaster. Within four days, the Americans suffered nearly 3,000 dead or captured. One hundred fifty cannon and 4,000 muskets were lost, as well as 400,000 cartridges and large stores of equipment.

Cold rain swept across the area, adding to the misery. America's existence was close to expiring in the deep mud of Bergen County. Washington's bedraggled army moved south. A Hackensack resident wrote of the wretched troops:

"They marched two abreast, looked ragged, some without a shoe to their feet, and most of them wrapped in their blankets."

The pitiful, beaten band straggled across the Passaic River at Acquackanonk (Passaic) on November 21, burned the bridge behind them, and headed for Newark. The hope of the nation rested on this ragged, disorganized military remnant. It was a flickering hope.

Times To Try Men's Souls

Strangely, Cornwallis failed to follow-up the bril-

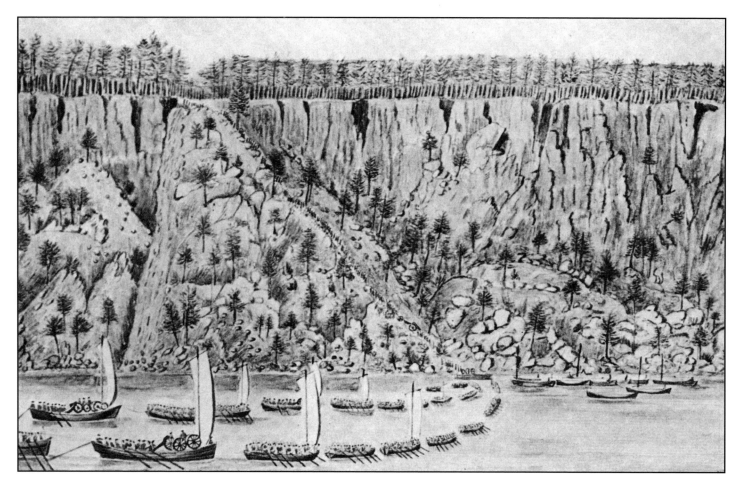

British strategy was at its most brilliant and British soldiers at their best on November 20, 1776 when they crossed the Hudson River, climbed the rugged face of the Palisades, and overwhelmed Fort Lee. This drawing of the operation, reportedly drawn on the scene by Lord Rawdon, shows troops crossing the Hudson in flatboats. Many of the soldiers are clambering up the rocky cliff, dragging their heavy equipment. (From the Emmet Collection, New York Public Library).

liant attack on Fort Lee. As the Briton dallied in Bergen County, Washington led his dispirited band into Newark on November 22. The exhausted army rested there for six days while Cornwallis paused indecisively to the north.

One American soldier in Newark understood what was happening. He was Thomas Paine, a former dweller in London's slums who fled to this country in 1774. Despite a total lack of previous experience, he had become a brilliant propagandist for the American cause.

Paine sat in front of a campfire in Newark on those cold, wet nights of November 1776 and began to scrawl the first unforgettable words of *The Crisis Papers*:

> *These are the times that try men's souls. The summer soldier and the sunshine patriot, will in this crisis, shrink from the service of his country; but he that stands it now, deserves the love and thanks of man and woman.*

Paine's words were prophetic. A determination to "stand it now" had set in for the bedraggled Americans who slipped out of the south end of Newark, just as Cornwallis paraded his sleek soldiers into the northern end of the town. Cornwallis rested again, permitting his troops to plunder the village.

Time To Escape

The American army stumbled southward, crossed the Raritan River into New Brunswick on November 29, and then reached a nearly deserted Princeton on December 2. Cornwallis still held back.

Cornwallis later admitted that "had I seen that I could have struck a material stroke by moving forward, I certainly should have taken it upon me to have done it." In fairness to the British general, his troops were bone weary, too.

Washington planned his strategy. As his retreating command neared the Delaware River, the general or-

92

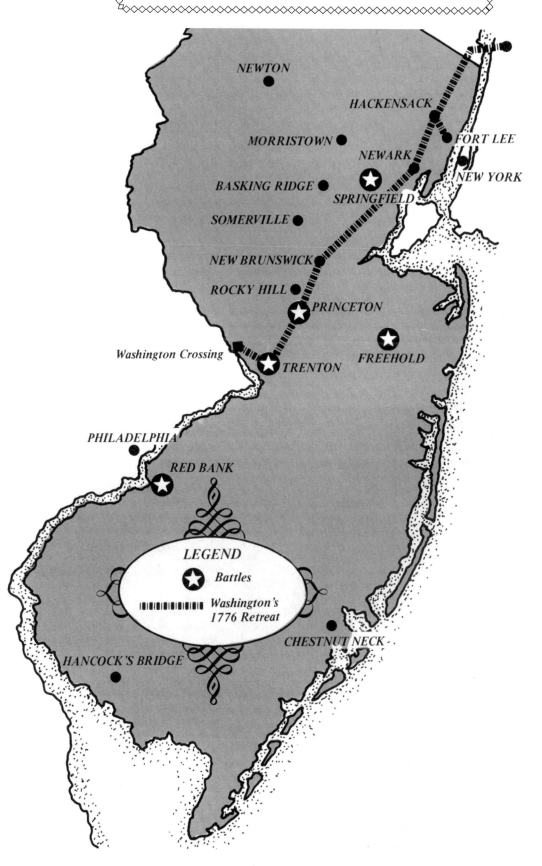

Revolution's Crossroads

NEWTON

HACKENSACK

MORRISTOWN

NEWARK

FORT LEE

BASKING RIDGE

SPRINGFIELD

NEW YORK

SOMERVILLE

NEW BRUNSWICK

ROCKY HILL

PRINCETON

Washington Crossing

TRENTON

FREEHOLD

PHILADELPHIA

RED BANK

LEGEND

★ Battles

||||||||||| Washington's 1776 Retreat

CHESTNUT NECK

HANCOCK'S BRIDGE

Thomas Paine began his immortal "Crisis" papers in front of a Newark campfire, but he is best remembered in New Jersey by this larger-than-life bronze statue in Burnham Park, Morristown (left). Paine's powerful words helped rally the dispirited, nearly beaten American army.

Bill Canfield's sketch (below) shows the sadness and the fear of Newark citizens as Washington and his dwindling army left Newark on November 28, 1776 on the long retreat toward the Delaware River.

dered Lieutenant Daniel Bray of Hunterdon County to round up every boat for thirty-five miles up and down the river. If the American army could cross the stream, quick pursuit would be impossible.

Meanwhile, General Howe hastened to New Jersey to take charge. Once on the scene, however, he showed no more ability or urgency to hunt down the enemy than Cornwallis. A cynical British supporter declared that Howe "had calculated . . . with great accuracy, the exact time necessary for his enemy to make his escape."

Finally, on December 7, the little Continental army was encamped on the west bank of the Delaware. There it sat "crouching in the bushes," as one lieutenant wrote, some "entirely naked." Washington declared, "most [are] so thinly clad as to be unfit for service." But they had won time.

"The Game Is Pretty Near Up"

Howe retired to the comforts of New York for the winter, convinced that the 1776 campaign was closed. He had only one nagging concern: his troops were spread too thinly across New Jersey between New Brunswick and Mount Holly. "The chain, I own, is too extensive," Howe confessed.

Across the Delaware, Washington feared December 31, when most enlistments would expire. His army would go home. On the bright side, General Charles Lee was leading a relief army of several thousand men across New Jersey toward the Delaware.

Lee despised Washington and said so openly in letters to friends in Congress. He answered the call for help by marching his army leisurely through the New Jersey Highlands. On December 13, Lee was taken prisoner at a house in Basking Ridge. (He was later exchanged, returned to the American army, and would appear again to haunt Washington).

The British were jubilant, believing that in Lee they had captured America's best general. Lee's capture proved to be a small loss, though. General John Sullivan took command and quickly marched the troops to join Washington faster than Lee had any intention of doing.

Washington calculated with Lee's men and other possible reinforcements, the American army would total 5,000 soldiers. If all those eligible for discharge on December 31 refused to re-enlist, the number would fall to 1,200. The Commander-in-Chief wrote his brother John: "I think the game is pretty near up."

Describing General Charles Lee as an enigma understates the character of the peculiar officer shown below in a caricature drawn by a contemporary. Lee delayed crossing New Jersey in December 1776, with troops greatly needed by the fading American army. He was captured (above) while breakfasting in Basking Ridge, was soon released, and returned to action to plague Washington at Monmouth on June 28, 1778.

One Who Was Loyal

James Moody of Sussex County wrote that he lived in the best climate in the happiest country in the world — until the Declaration of Independence was signed. He believed rebellion to be the "foulest of crimes."

According to his own account, written in 1783, Moody took "every possible precaution not to give offense" during the early days of the war. Late in March 1777, an armed mob of former friends attacked him, but Moody escaped.

The Sussex Tory led seventy-three "loyal" neighbors from Sussex County to New York to join the British in April 1777. He returned home in June, seeking more "loyal men." He claimed that 500 followed him (undoubtedly a highly exaggerated estimate).

Moody became somewhat of a legend in his own time. He led a daring raid on Tinton Falls in Monmouth County, in June 1778, to destroy a powder magazine. He spied constantly on the American army at Morristown in 1779-80, pilfering mail or examining army records.

In May 1780, Moody led a bold dash into Morris County to trap "someone of note" (probably Governor Livingston). That venture failed because one of Moody's men was captured, told all, and "blasted the whole project."

Soon after, Moody raided the New Town (Newton) jail to free a Loyalist prisoner. The illustration here, from Moody's book, portrays that action.

Moody never returned home to Sussex County. After the war, he joined other Loyalists in Nova Scotia.

While the British pursued the American army across New Jersey in late 1776, General Howe sought enlistments for Loyalist regiments. After two years service, Tory volunteers were promised fifty acres of land, where they might retire and enjoy life forever.

ALL INTREPID ABLE-BODIED

HEROES,

WHO are willing to ſerve His MAJESTY KING GEORGE the Third, in Defence of their Country, Laws and Conſtitution, againſt the arbitrary Uſurpations of a tyrannical Congreſs, have now not only an Opportunity of manifeſting their Spirit, by aſſiſting in reducing to Obedience their too-long deluded Countrymen, but alſo of acquiring the polite Accompliſhments of a Soldier, by ſerving only two Years, or during the preſent Rebellion in America.

Such ſpirited Fellows, who are willing to engage, will be rewarded at the End of the War, beſides their Laurels, with 50 Acres of Land, where every gallant Hero may retire, and enjoy his Bottle and Laſs.

Guerrillas Roam At Night

The Hessian troops, accustomed to the European military tradition of looting an occupied land, turned to stealing and vandalizing. The British soldiers also mistreated the inhabitants, although they usually were less brutal than their Hessian comrades-in-arms. Even the Tories who greeted the arriving British with open arms found themselves victimized. In Newark, a Loyalist named Nuttman hailed the Redcoats "with huzzahs of joy." The invaders promptly ransacked his house, stole his clothing, and even took the shoes off his feet. In Princeton, the British mistreated the populace and quartered their horses in the basement of Nassau Hall.

The acts of British and Hessian brutality actually helped turn the war around. Bands of armed civilians began retaliating, shooting any enemy soldier who dared venture out of New Brunswick or Trenton after dark. One Hessian stationed in Trenton wrote on Christmas Eve:

"We have not slept one night in peace since we came to this place."

Tory spies drifted into Trenton with vague rumors the Americans were planning some kind of major assault. British General James Grant, stationed at Princeton, advised Trenton's German commander on December 21 the town was "liable to be attacked at any moment." The commander, Colonel Johann Rall, scoffed at the warnings. "Let them come," he boasted.

The spies were right. Grant was right. The Americans were planning to cross the Delaware on Christmas Day to seize Trenton.

The First American Victory

Washington ordered Colonel Lambert Cadwalader to cross and attack near Mount Holly. General James Ewing's Pennsylvania troops and New Jersey militiamen would hit just south of Trenton, and Washington's main command of 2,400 men would strike north of the town.

Heavy clouds hung over the desperate Americans preparing on Christmas afternoon for the attack. The weather turned so ugly neither Cadwalader nor Ewing ventured across the river, a fact not learned by Washington until much later. Washington's little army would be crossing the dangerous ice-filled river alone.

The first Americans left the Pennsylvania side

A Country "Rich in Plunder"

The Hessian soldiers shown in this 19th century sketch mingled with camp followers and children during a forced march. They were luckier than most of the German soldiers, who generally were without friends or acquaintances in a strange land called America.

German soldiers were not in this country because of any passion for British principles. Rather, they had been sold to King George III in a series of treaties signed with German princes in 1776. The Germans (called Hessians after the province of Hesse-Cassel) came from several of Germany nearly 300 different territorial divisions.

The German princes were paid as if the Hessians were so many cattle. The soldiers themselves were given the same wages and benefits of British soldiers — low by any standard. If a Hessian soldier was killed, the German prince received a nice sum in payment, but the soldier's wife and family received nothing. For payment to a prince, three wounded counted as one killed.

About 30,000 Hessians eventually served in America and Canada. Although many, if not most, wore the British uniform against their will, they often fought bravely and well — at Trenton, Red Bank, Monmouth, and Springfield, among many places.

On the march across New Jersey in late 1776, Hessians were blamed for most of the looting, plundering, raping, and killing, although British troops were also seen running wild. If the Hessians behaved badly, it should have been small wonder. A British officer later testified the German soldiers reputedly were told they were headed for a country that was "rich in plunder," there for the taking.

at about 2 PM. It was long after midnight before all 2,400 men, their cannon, and a few horses were ferried to New Jersey. Sleet began pelting the area at about 4 AM on December 26, as two columns of soldiers advanced on Trenton. The cruel weather was a blessing in disguise. When the American army dashed into the Hessian-held town, the sleet slashed into the faces of the stunned, sleepy defenders and obscured their vision.

Slightly outnumbered and thoroughly outgeneraled, the Hessians fell back before the withering crossfire of this army that had materialized out of the storm. American cannon and musket fire swept through the Hessian ranks. Their much-vaunted discipline crumbled. They fled in disarray.

The battle ended in less than an hour. An American army won its first major victory at an amazingly low cost — only four soldiers wounded. The Hessians lost about twenty-five or thirty killed, another eighty wounded, and 918 taken prisoner. Colonel Rall, the once scoffing commander of Trenton, died a day later of wounds.

No Rest For The Weary

The American command briefly considered the heady possibility of marching against Princeton and New Brunswick, but decided against the risk. Herding their prisoners before them, the Continentals re-crossed to Pennsylvania. Three American soldiers froze to death in the boats on the return.

There was no time to rest, even for a few days. Soldiers drifted away as their enlistments ended. Washington decided to attack again. He led his dwindling army back across the Delaware on December 30 and ordered them to dig in along Assunpink Creek on Trenton's southern edge.

New Year's Day turned unusually warm, melting the hard, icy banks of the creek. As the red sun went down on January 1, the Americans awaited the British, fully aware the early January thaw was turning the area into a muddy trap for them.

Cornwallis hastened to Trenton with 8,000 soldiers. When he reached Assunpink Creek late on January 2, Cornwallis crowed he would "bag the old fox [Washington] in the morning." An aide, General William Erskine, protested: "If Washington is the general I take him to be, he will not be found there in the morning."

Weather again came to the American aid. Whistling winds drove the temperatures down and froze

Crossing The Delaware

No painting of an American event is better known than Leutze's Washington Crossing The Delaware *on the top of the opposite page. It has appeared in most high school history texts published in the past century. Many millions of people recognize the scene.*

The original painting, twenty-one feet long and twelve feet high, was painted in Dusseldorf, Germany, by Emanuel Leutze, a German artist who studied in Philadelphia as a young man and was familiar with the site of the crossing.

Leutze's massive painting covered 265 square feet of canvas. The finished work weighed more than 800 pounds. It was first exhibited in the Capitol of the United States in 1851.

Critics point out that Leutze's painting contains several inaccuracies — the boat is the wrong size and shape, his river is much more picturesque than the Delaware, and, most important, the 13-star flag was not adopted until seven months after the crossing.

All of these criticisms are true. Some art critics of the 1920s viewed the painting with such scorn its owner, the Metropolitan Museum of Art, withdrew it from display. Storms of protest forced the Museum to reverse its stand.

Despite such criticisms, the painting captures the emotional impact of the crossing. The ice floes, the misery on the faces of the soldiers, and the obvious command of Washington, all combine to make the canvas a memorable portrayal of the crucial importance of the Christmas Day crossing.

Other artists depicted the scene, as illustrated here. One etching, patterned after Leutze (except the boat is pointed the other way), shows the flag probably used in 1776. The small woodcut has everyone standing in the boats, an unlikely circumstance, in view of the treacherous current.

One painting (bottom right) shows Washington rallying his troops to smash at the Hessians in Trenton. The last sketch (bottom left) shows Washington visiting Colonel Johann Gottlieb Rall, the Hessian commander fatally wounded in the Trenton battle.

Rall died the day after the battle. The German commander, nicknamed "The Hessian Lion," was buried under a simple headstone that said: "Here lies Colonel Rall. With him, all is over."

This painting, owned by Princeton University, shows Washington at the close of the Battle of Princeton. On the ground behind Washington is General Hugh Mercer, fatally wounded in the action. Below is an interpretation of the battle, painted soon after the war by William Mercer, son of the stricken general.

the muddy roads solid. The "old fox" slipped silently away in the night, moving his army along a back road toward Princeton. Rags wrapped around the wheels of the cannon muffled the noise of movement. Beside Assunpink Creek, a few men were left to keep the fires brightly blazing and to dig noisily.

The deception worked. The outwitted British slept peacefully. Even the fire tenders and trench diggers were gone before the sun rose. Erskine wrote Washington's generalship that night "wrecked the British plans for the winter of 1776-77."

"A Fox Hunt, Boys!"

Delayed by ruts, stumps, and freezing mire, the Americans were still two miles short of Princeton at dawn on January 3. Washington dispatched General Hugh Mercer and 350 soldiers to destroy the bridge over Stony Brook as a means of delaying pursuit by the British. The main army pressed on toward Princeton.

British Lieutenant Colonel Charles Mawhood simultaneously rode out of Princeton with about 300 cavalrymen to reinforce Cornwallis. One of Mawhood's advance scouts brought the astonishing news an enemy force — Mercer's detachment — had appeared nearby. Mawhood ordered an attack.

The skilled, rested British troops sent the small American force flying. Mercer fell and was clubbed on the head (he died nine days later). Two small American cannon on a nearby hill momentarily stopped the enemy. Alerted by the noise of battle, Washington turned part of the main army back to face the British.

Washington spurred his horse across the field in advance of his troops, dashing recklessly between both lines. Bullets whizzed past Washington from both sides, prompting John Fitzgerald, a young staff officer, to cover his eyes so he would not see his leader fall. Miraculously when the smoke cleared, the general was untouched. Mawhood's force was withdrawing.

Joyously yelling, "It's a fox hunt, boys!" Washington galloped across the field in pursuit of the Redcoats. There was no time for gloating, however; Princeton itself needed prompt attention.

The Old Fox Scores Again

Two British regiments waited on the western edge of Princeton. When Major General John Sullivan hurled several American regiments against the British line, the Redcoats abandoned their cannon and bolted in disorder along a back road to New Brunswick.

Some of the British chose to fight on in Nassau Hall on the College of New Jersey campus. Lieutenant Alexander Hamilton's cannon blasted away at the windows of the sturdy stone building and Captain James Moore and a few soldiers broke down file doors. The British surrendered meekly, and Captain Moore had his revenge; his Princeton home had been ransacked by the British a few weeks before.

The Battle of Princeton ended in forty-five minutes. Washington estimated British losses at between 500 and 600, including about 300 prisoners. (Howe put the losses at 276 in a self-serving report to England.) The Americans suffered about thirty-five killed and seventy-five wounded. The "old fox" had triumphed again.

Some officers in the American command urged an attack on New Brunswick, where the British supposedly had £70,000 in gold. Cornwallis's huge army was nearing Princeton, "in an infernal sweat" (as General Henry Knox wrote). The American army needed rest far more than it needed gold. Washington turned toward Morristown.

The weary Americans plodded through Pluckemin and on toward the Morris County hills. They straggled into Morristown on January 6, 1777, and the winter campaign was over. Soldiers who only six weeks earlier were a beaten, disorganized band were now transformed into a victorious army.

Game Of Feint And Run

Morristown was a perfect winter headquarters. Most of its 250 residents actively supported the war. Iron for cannon and muskets was available in the mines to the northwest. Eastward, the rolling ridges of the Watchung Mountains offered protection in all

Early Warning System

Militiamen in the Watchung Mountains kept a constant watch on the broad plains in the valley below. By day, they shot cannon to signal the approach of British troops. By night, flaring beacons were lit to warn of enemy attack.

This early warning system eventually reached from West Point to Princeton, with three additional sites in Monmouth County. Central to the entire system was a string of beacons in the Watchungs, where the high slopes afforded a splendid view of the plains below.

General Lord Stirling of Basking Ridge, one of Washington's most trusted officers, apparently drew the basic plan (shown here, with Stirling's order: "the figure of Beacons will appear thus").

Stirling ordered the structures be about fourteen feet square at the base, rising in the form of a pyramid to about twenty feet high. The space inside and the spaces between the logs were filled with dry wood to insure instant flaming.

The lighting of any beacon was the signal to fire all the

others. Within minutes, a warning could be spread over hundreds of square miles, alerting militia forces as far away as the Delaware River.

Twenty-three of the beacons were described by Brigadier General Nathan Heard; that complete list of sites appears in A. E. Vanderpool's History of Chatham. *Some of these beacon locations now have modern communication or relay towers. Other sites are look-out spots in county or state parks.*

One of the major engagements of the war took place at Red Bank on the Delaware River, where Rhode Island troops inflicted heavy casualties in repulsing Hessian invaders. The battle delayed British control of the vital river for nearly a month. Some of the Rhode Islanders probably were African American soldiers, members of what later became a Rhode Island regiment of all African Americans.

directions.

Of the 3,000 soldiers who reached Morristown, only 800 answered roll call on January 19. General Greene called this "a shadow of a force." Cornwallis believed "the march alone will destroy his [Washington's] army." He was wrong again.

Enlistments picked up in the spring. The American regiments moved out of Morristown on May 26 to the outer rim of the Watchung Mountains, the better to watch His Majesty's forces on the plains below toward New Brunswick and Perth Amboy.

Howe dared not assault the Watchung stronghold. He tried instead a continuing game of feint and run. He sent detachments out to Scotch Plains, Elizabethtown, Spanktown (Rahway), Westfield, and as far as Somerset Court House. Small forces scampered out of the hills to hit, and then darted back up the slopes.

The British wearied of this cat and mouse game. Howe put his soldiers aboard ships and sailed for Philadelphia. They went via Chesapeake Bay, bypass-

ing a string of American fortresses on the Delaware River below Philadelphia.

"We Want No Quarter!"

Washington swiftly moved his army into Pennsylvania, seeking to delay Howe's entry into Philadelphia. He counted heavily on the Delaware River forts, and sent Colonel Christopher Greene and 400 Rhode Island soldiers into Fort Mercer at Red Bank on October 7, 1777. Greene's troops probably included some of the African American soldiers who later would comprise the famed Rhode Island "All-Negro" regiment.

Howe countered by sending Colonel Curt von Donop to level Fort Mercer. Shortly after noon on October 22, the Hessian commander reached the area, put his cannon in line, and readied his 1,200 Hessian soldiers for an attack. When von Donop shouted demands for surrender, Greene retorted: "We'll see King George damned first! We want no quarter!"

Von Donop drove his Hessians forward. The fort's unmanned outer posts fell quickly, but a maze of inner defenses exposed the attackers to merciless crossfire. Within forty-five minutes, at least 150 Hessians lay dead or wounded (some sources say the attackers sustained as many as 500 casualties). The wounded included von Donop, who died a few days later.

Fort Mercer could not be held indefinitely. Greene and his Rhode Islanders marched out on November 20, blowing the fort to bits as they left. Howe could settle down to the winter pleasures of Philadelphia. Washington had to settle for another harsh winter in the open, this time at Valley Forge, a day's march from the enemy.

Clinton Enters New Jersey

Great Britain grew weary of General Howe's lackluster performance in America. He was replaced in May 1778 by General Henry Clinton who brought orders to pursue the war vigorously. Clinton decided he must move from Philadelphia to New York.

He began to ferry 14,000 soldiers across the Delaware River on June 18, 1778. Along with them went a swarm of wives and camp followers. At times the British line stretched out for twelve miles. Alerted to the move, Washington immediately left Valley Forge, determined to make the British passage through New Jersey as costly as possible.

General William Maxwell's New Jersey troops were ordered to join General Philomen Dickinson, whose New Jersey Militia already was stinging the flanks of the long British columns. Maxwell and Dickinson's command of about 1,700 men soon was bolstered by some 600 sharp-shooting soldiers led by General Daniel Morgan of Virginia.

This advance American force avoided open battle. Instead, they fired on the cumbersome British column, and then darted away to hit elsewhere. Some of the militia moved well ahead of the British, destroying drinking wells and burning bridges to impede progress. Twenty-five woodsmen worked day and night felling trees across the enemy route.

The main American force of about 12,000 soldiers crossed the Delaware at Coryell's Ferry (now Lambertville) on June 21. No plan had yet been shaped to attack the British; many feared an American army would not be able to cope with a major English force on an open battlefield, where British tactics were respected and feared.

When the British army left Philadelphia to head across New Jersey for New York in June 1778, they met vigorous opposition. Woodchoppers felled trees across the British route, and mounted couriers raced through the countryside calling militiamen to arms.

Dame Whitall Stays Calm

Since Mrs. Ann Cooper Whitall lived in the same brick house at Red Bank for twenty-eight years, she was not about to move merely because a major force of Hessian soldiers approached the area in mid-October 1777. Rather, her concern was for the American soldiers who awaited the Hessian assault in nearby Fort Mercer.

Dame Whitall remained calm. As the first guns of battle roared, she picked up her spinning wheel, went to an upstairs bedroom, and began to spin.

Nearby on the Delaware River, two British ships opened fire on Fort Mercer. One cannonball went wide of its mark, smashed through a wall of the bedroom where Dame Whitall sat, and imbedded itself in the opposite wall. Considerably annoyed, Mrs. Whitall took her spinning wheel into the cellar and worked there until the battle ended.

When the guns became silent, the unruffled Mrs. Whitall went to the battlefield and bandaged the wounds of Americans and Hessians alike. She allowed herself the slight privilege of scolding the Hessians for coming to America to fight.

The battle did not harm Mrs. Whitall's health. She died in 1797 at the age of eighty-two.

General Washington arrives just in time to intercept a confused, disorganized General Charles Lee on the Monmouth battlefield. The painting by Emanuel Leutze (who also painted *Washington Crossing the Delaware*) catches the fiery sweep of the battle on June 28, 1778. The original is owned by the Monmouth County Historical Association.

"Society Of Midwives"

The American generals held a quarrelsome, indecisive council of war at Hopewell on June 24. Disgusted, Lieutenant Colonel Alexander Hamilton said the meeting "would have done honor to the most honorable society of midwives."

A day later, scouts reported Clinton turned slightly south toward an escape route at Sandy Hook. Washington stepped up the chase. His decision was made: he would meet Clinton on an open field if necessary.

The Marquis de Lafayette, twenty years old, was chosen to lead the American advance troops after General Charles Lee refused the assignment. Then the mysterious General Lee, who defied Washington in December 1776, changed his mind and asked for the command. His request was granted, and Lee was in command when the Battle of Monmouth began on June 28.

The day dawned blisteringly hot. Washington instructed Lee to attack at dawn, "acquainting him at the same time that I was marching to support him." Lee seemed "irresolute and confused" to his subordinates that morning. The battle swayed back and forth before noon, with Lee's forces doing little more

than jabbing at the British. In fairness to Lee, one of Washington's confusing orders also advised him against drawing the enemy "into a scrape."

At about noon, the British seized control of the field. Within an hour the American situation was nearly chaotic. By 1:30 PM, Lee was retreating in disorder. When Washington heard of the withdrawal, he dismissed it as rumor, although he galloped to the scene.

The rumor was true. Washington met the retreating Lee and the two argued heatedly in the midst of the confusion and noise. Lee promised to be "the last to leave the field," and wheeled his horse back into action. At about 3 PM, Washington ordered Lee off the battlefield, placing the soldiers under General Baron Freidrich Von Steuben.

Everything Under The Sun

Both armies fought savagely all afternoon, despite the incredible heat that felled soldiers with nearly the same deadliness of cannon shot and musket balls. The blazing sun created one of the lasting anecdotes of the American Revolution — the story of Molly Pitcher.

Molly Pitcher was really Mary Ludwig Hays, wife

Molly's Pictures

Molly Pitcher was a genuine American heroine, but how she actually looked is any artist's guess, as evidenced by the seven pictures on this page. Was she tall, slim, and young, as she appears to the right? Was she resolute, sturdy, plain, and resourceful, as the four pictures in the center of the page seem to agree? The painting on the lower left would indicate she was able to keep a certain glamour, even in the heat of battle (this vivid portrayal is in the Fraunces Tavern in New York). Or was she really the aging, roughly dressed, camp follower (called "Moll") as shown in the drawing on the lower right?

It really does not matter. Molly was real, and she was at the Battle of Monmouth. She was Mary Ludwig Hays, the wife of William Hays, a private in a Pennsylvania artillery company. Molly carried water to the thirsty soldiers. When her husband was injured, the indomitable wife dropped her pitcher and took his place at the cannon. No matter how she looked, Molly Pitcher was a woman of spirit, courage, and action.

of William Hays, a private in a Pennsylvania artillery company. As her husband manned the cannon, Molly carried water to parched soldiers. She filled her pitcher time and again. Tradition says soldiers called, "Molly, bring the pitcher!" and finally, just "Molly! Pitcher!" Mary Ludwig Hays earned an undying name and lasting fame.

Late in the day, William Hays was felled by a British bullet. Molly took his place at the cannon and proved herself capable of far more than carrying water. The Molly Pitcher story — part truth, part legend — will be told as long as the Battle of Monmouth is remembered.

The revived American troops were still advancing when darkness fell. They proved, on an open field, they were the match of the best the British could muster in America. The British departed first, marching over the Navesink hills under a new moon, and continued to New York by ship.

Both armies suffered severely. British losses were more than 500 killed or wounded, against more than 400 American casualties. One source also lists thirty-seven American and fifty-nine British deaths from sunstroke.

General Charles Lee was court-martialed on July 4 for his confusing tactics on the battlefield. He was found guilty and suspended from command for twelve months. He never fought again. Samuel Stelle Smith, a major modern authority on Monmouth, wrote that Lee's "rather harsh" conviction was due to "almost fanatical patriots."

When men and older boys raced off to fight, they left behind wives, daughters, children, and aged parents to carry on the vital, if unglamorous, work of the home front.

On The Edge Of War

The major fighting swung away from New Jersey for a time after the Battle of Monmouth. That did not end the conflict here — or lessen the need for constant vigilance.

War or no war, work had to continue on the home front. This was made doubly difficult because so many men were in the army at distant places. Cows had to be milked and springtime planting done. Mothers and young children had to tend the vegetable patches and harvest the ripened wheat or corn when the Minutemen answered a summons.

Families dreaded the sounds of gunfire. They feared every knock on the door when British and Hessian troops were reported near. They locked up horses and chickens when bands of ragged Americans appeared. Thievery was rampant.

Invading forces invariably steal and loot. "Friendly" Americans also often appropriated livestock, flour, blankets, meat, and rum in the name of "military needs." During the summer and winter of 1777-78, both sides rustled cattle off Salem and Cumberland county farms and herded them to Philadelphia or Valley Forge.

The war tore villages and townships apart socially and politically. Bands of Loyalist (Tory) troops organized by the British often struck within the state, especially when Washington's army was engaged elsewhere.

On March 22, 1778, several local Tories were among 300 pre-dawn British and Hessian raiders who surrounded Judge William Hancock's home at Hancock's Bridge in Salem County. British Major John Simcoe sent his attackers into the building. Before their night's work was done, thirty men were slain in the house. Simcoe later dismissed the massacre as a mere attempt to "chastise the rascals."

The Hancock house massacre, though horrendous, at least could have been considered a legitimate military operation. More notorious was the work of the "Pine Barren Robbers" who terrorized much of southern New Jersey during the war. They called themselves "refugees," to suggest they had heroically escaped from those who fought England. Most were, in fact, nothing more than opportunistic bandits.

Pleasures Of Middlebrook

The Raritan River Valley beckoned Washington to New Jersey for the winter of 1778-79. The first troops began arriving there on November 30, 1778. Eventually, between 8,000 and 10,000 soldiers were quartered in what was called the Middlebrook encampment.

Another force of about 1,600 gunners and sixty cannon was stationed at Pluckemin under General Henry Knox. Nearly all of the army's most distinguished officers occupied homes in Somerville, Bound Brook, Finderne, Pluckemin, and Bedminster.

Middlebrook offered a pleasant interlude for the army. The winter was mild. Wood was plentiful for building huts. Food was available, although during the winter soldiers were often forced to forage for enough to eat.

Washington reached the winter encampment on December 11, 1778, declaring he was ready "to indulge in more agreeable amusements." Mrs. Martha Washington joined her husband in the newly built Wallace House in Somerville. Many other wives joined their officer husbands for the winter.

Dr. James Thacher, an army surgeon, wrote on April 13, 1779: "We have passed a winter remarkably mild and moderate; since the 10th of January, we have scarcely had a fall of snow, or a frost, and no severe weather."

Such weather put the officers and their wives in a partying mood. Of all the many affairs, the most lavish was staged by General and Mrs. Henry Knox near Pluckemin, on February 18, 1779, to celebrate the first anniversary of the French alliance. Soldiers built a 100-foot-long pavilion for the ball, and the guests dined under thirteen arches, one for each state.

After a dinner of fine foods and expensive wines, General Washington and Mrs. Knox opened the dancing. General Knox wrote to his brother "we danced all night."

The winter faded into spring. Washington's thoughts were not diverted by the parties. He wrote on May 8: "Our army as it now stands is but little more than the skeleton of an army, and I hear of no steps that are being taken to give it strength and substance."

The troops left Middlebrook on June 3, headed for the Hudson River Valley. The summer of 1779 would be free of major battles anywhere in the North. British efforts were aimed at southern targets, particularly near Savannah, Georgia.

Another Morristown Winter

The main American army returned to Morristown for the winter of 1779-80. By December 9, nearly

General Washington bows to Mrs. Kitty Greene during one of the many parties staged by officers and their wives near Somerville during the mild winter of 1778-79.

A "Nest Of Freebooters"

Privateers who swarmed out of inlets to capture English merchant vessels along the Jersey Shore created panic among British commanders. The swiftly-sailing Jerseymen could cut a prized ship out of a fleet and within minutes be taking the prize to safety behind the inlets.

The privateers operated from Sandy Hook to Cape May throughout the war. Especially detested by the British were the privateer ships based at Chestnut Neck on the Mullica River, northwest of what is now Atlantic City. The seacoast village had several large warehouses for storing merchandise taken from captured enemy ships.

Commander Henry Colins of His Majesty's Navy decided "this Nest of Freebooters" must be smashed. He took 13 ships out of New York on September 30, 1778 and struck Chestnut Neck on October 6. The British burned every building in town and set fire to ten captured British prize ships anchored off Chestnut Neck.

The loss to the Americans was less than it might have been. Thanks to advance warning, several ships and most of the captured supplies had been moved up the Mullica. The British also had hoped to move inland to burn the Batsto ironworks, but that venture was abandoned when the local militia rallied.

107

10,000 men had arrived at Jockey Hollow, southwest of the town. That day, General Nathanael Greene wrote: "Our hutting goes on rapidly, and our troops will be undercover in a few days." Greene's optimism was totally unwarranted.

Washington reached Morristown on December 1, riding his horse through a frosted curtain of wind-driven snow. He headed for the Ford mansion, owned by the young widow of Colonel Jacob Ford, Jr. Washington and his staff took over all but the two rooms occupied by Mrs. Ford and her four children.

Twenty-eight snowstorms struck Morristown that winter, two of blizzard proportions, with howling winds, bitter cold, and lashing snow. For the only time in recorded history, the Hudson River froze from shore to shore so solidly sleighs could be driven between New York City and New Jersey. The *New Jersey Gazette* also reported horse-drawn sleighs rode from Trenton to Philadelphia on the Delaware River

Enterprise At Paulus Hook

Major Henry "Light Horse Harry" Lee of Virginia believed, in August 1779, the time had come to attack the British garrison holding the fort at Paulus Hook (now Jersey City). The fort had been in British hands since it was captured on September 23, 1776.

Lee begged General Washington for permission to launch the venture. Washington at first dismissed the "enterprise against Paulus Hook" as too dangerous, but finally gave permission. The Virginia major took about 400 infantrymen and a company of mounted soldiers out of New Bridge in Bergen County on August 18 at 9 AM.

The fourteen-mile trip took fifteen agonizing hours. Lee finally sent his troops surging against the fort at 3:30 AM on August 19. The British were overwhelmed, suffering nearly 200 casualties. Two Americans died.

Lee dared not tarry in the fort. He rallied his troops and took 159 prisoners back to New Bridge. Congress later awarded him a medal for his exploit.

ice. The Passaic and Raritan rivers were frozen to depths of six feet.

Dr. Thacher reached Morristown on December 14 and found snow already two feet deep. He saw soldiers "actually barefoot and almost naked." He declared: "Our only defense against the inclemency of the weather consists of brushwood thrown together."

Huts were not yet ready on January 2, when a blizzard struck. When the snow ended three days later, snow was four feet deep on the level and as much as eight feet in drifts.

Dr. Thacher wrote of the storm "no man could endure its violence for more than a few minutes without danger to his life." Some soldiers, he wrote, "were actually covered while in their tents, and buried, like sheep, under the snow."

"Almost Perishing For Want"

Most of the enlisted men had moved into crude huts by Valentine's Day in 1780. The tiny log structures were built around a large stone fireplace that provided both heat and light. Bunk beds of rough planking were along the walls. Some soldiers preferred to sleep in dirty straw on the earthen floor. The quarters were barely habitable, but for men who had been sleeping in the snow, they were palatial.

Days slid numbingly by. Little food reached the area. Thacher wrote the men often went "six or eight days entirely destitute of meat, and then as long without bread." The consequence was the soldiers "are too enfeebled to perform military duty or labor in constructing their huts."

Washington told the New Jersey legislature on January 8: "The present state of the army, with respect to provisions, is the most distressing of any we have experienced since the beginning of the war. For a fortnight past the troops, both officers and men, have been almost perishing for want."

Washington wearied of pleading with politicians. On January 8, he ordered several detachments of soldiers to visit leading officials in each county, begging them to send in bread and wheat.

If the officials showed any reluctance, Washington ordered the men to take the provisions "with as much tenderness as possible" along with wagons to carry the food. The message was clear: the food would be had at gunpoint if necessary. Officials cooperated, sometimes cheerfully.

Those unwilling to give might have been expected to sell, but Dr. Thacher pointed out even buying was

Shelter was the main need at Morristown as the winter of 1779-80 settled in. Soldiers felled trees and most were in log huts by February. The woodcut below, sketched in the 1840s, is a good representation of the Morristown encampment.

difficult because of runaway inflation. In 1780, one silver dollar was worth about thirty paper dollars.

New Jersey was not peculiar in its unwillingness to feed the army. Records indicate many Pennsylvania farmers near Valley Forge grew fat and sleek in the winter of 1777-78 by selling their products to the British in Philadelphia while soldiers in their own nation's army starved to death nearby.

The Cruelest Of Winters

The terrible severity of that winter of 1779-80 was difficult to describe, even for those who were there. General Johann de Kalb noted in February 1780: "Those who have only been in Valley Forge or Middlebrook during the last two winters, but have not tasted the cruelties of this one, know not what it is to suffer."

Many years later, in 1955, the distinguished Virginia Washington biographer, Douglas Southall Freeman, wrote without qualification that "the winter of 1779-80 at Morristown was a period of far worse suffering than the corresponding months of 1777-78 at Valley Forge."

Even if the weather had been warm, the food plentiful, and the clothing ample, the winter would have been a shocker. That winter the word came that one of America's greatest generals, Benedict Arnold, faced an army court-martial in Morristown.

Arnold was a man of courage. In the esteem of the army and Congress alike, he stood second only to Washington. Many felt he was the nation's finest field commander. Arnold was twice severely wounded in the same leg — at Quebec in 1775 and at Saratoga in 1777.

Arnold was charged with enriching himself and dealing leniently with Tories while military commander of Philadelphia in 1778-79. His trial began in the Dickerson Tavern in Morristown on December 23, 1779.

Arnold indignantly denied every charge, daring his fellow officers to challenge his military record. Despite his protestations, Arnold was found guilty on two minor counts. Washington was asked to reprimand the convicted general. He did so as gently as possible, trying to placate the enraged Arnold.

Arnold's passionate defense of himself and seeming hurt was only a pose. He had already secretly plotted for months with British officers to help overthrow the American cause. Eventually, in September 1780, his plot to turn West Point over to the British was uncovered. The once-proud American general fled to New York to gain British protection and thereafter to fight for the enemy.

"Hastening To Our Ruin"

There was some good news. The Marquis de Lafayette arrived in Morristown in May, bringing the cheering word a major force of six French warships and 6,000 trained French soldiers soon would land in Rhode Island to support the American cause.

Despite winter's surrender to spring, Washington despaired. He wrote on June 6, 1780: "One year rolls over another, and without some change, we are hastening to our ruin."

There was cause for pessimism. General Clinton

Every evidence proves the winter of 1779-80 at Morristown was by far the worst of the war. High winds swirled heavy snow across the hills, food and clothing were short, and morale was low. Artist Bill Canfield has emphasized the misery in this imaginative drawing of the scene.

won a smashing triumph over American defenders at Charleston, South Carolina in mid-May. Now he was back in New York, prepared to unleash a mighty army. Would he strike at Morristown? Or swing northward up the Hudson River?

A partial answer came on June 6, when Hessian General William von Knyphausen crossed from Staten Island to Elizabeth with 6,000 Hessian Jaegers, plus British and Tory troops. They marched westward toward Morristown the next day, hoping to break through at the "Short Hills gap" in the hills west of Springfield.

The enemy had returned in force, for the first time since the winter of 1776-77. Colonel Elias Dayton and his Third New Jersey Militia fought them, as Minutemen five years before had fought on the roads near Lexington and Concord. They used stone walls, barns, and bushes as temporary fortresses and poured withering fire into the invaders.

Knyphausen's forces fought their way into Connecticut Farms (now Union), and then stopped for three hours. Furious at the unexpected opposition they met, the Hessians put the torch to Connecticut Farms' houses and barns.

During the confusion, a British or Hessian soldier apparently believed he saw an American sniper in the home of the Rev. James Caldwell, an ardent local patriot. The soldier fired. His target was not a sniper but Mrs. Caldwell, who died a victim of mistaken identity. Mrs. Caldwell's killing aroused the militia to further effort. They forced Knyphausen's army back to Elizabeth.

The Battle Of Springfield

Knyphausen returned on June 23 with about 6,000 soldiers. General Nathanael Greene, heading about 1,500 American regulars, hoped for another outpouring of New Jersey militia from the villages west of Springfield. He was not disappointed, but the combined regulars and militia could only delay the Hessian commander. By noon his army was at Springfield.

Springfield's defenders relied at first on the seasoned Second Rhode Island Regiment. As the day wore on, other defenders emerged — Colonel Israel Shreve's Second New Jersey Regiment, Light Horse Harry Lee's Virginians, and Colonel Mathias Ogden's

110

First New Jersey Regiment. Hundreds of militiamen flocked into the valley to reinforce the line.

The person history recalls at Springfield is the Rev. James Caldwell, whose wife was killed in Connecticut Farms only sixteen days before. When American artillerymen ran out of wadding for their cannon, Parson Caldwell raced from his church carrying a load of hymn books by Isaac Watts. Flinging the Watts' *Hymnals* in front of the cannon for use as wadding, the parson yelled, "Give 'em Watts, boys!"

Knyphausen's soldiers set fire to Springfield. Nearly every building in town was burned, including Parson Caldwell's church. Then the Hessians and British retreated, dogged every step of the way by accurate militia fire. Before the withdrawal was over, the invaders had suffered more than 300 casualties.

Knyphausen wrote home: "I regret from the depths of my heart the great loss of the Jaegers took place to no greater purpose." A New Englander, Major Samuel Shaw of Massachusetts, declared Springfield was "Lexington repeated."

Mutiny in January

The war dragged on through the summer. Washington camped twice at Preakness from July 1 to July 29 and again from October 9 to November 27. Winter came and Washington moved his headquarters to Windsor, New York. He sent ten Pennsylvania regiments back to the huts built the winter before at Jockey Hollow.

These Pennsylvanians were discouraged and cynical — with good reason. Nearly six years had elapsed since the beginning of the war. They felt forgotten and abused. Major General ("Mad") Anthony Wayne, a favorite among the soldiers, urged Congress to provide food, pay, and decent clothing. Congress ignored him.

On January 1, 1781, the Pennsylvania troops mutinied at Jockey Hollow. They seized their weapons and vowed to march on Congress in Philadelphia. When some officers and a few non-mutineers tried to turn back the grim Pennsylvanians, the mutineers

Parson James Caldwell emerged from his Springfield Presbyterian Church on June 23, 1780, waving hymnals and urging soldiers to use them as wadding in their cannon. The original of this painting of the critical Battle of Springfield is owned by the Fraunces Tavern in New York.

This 19th century sketch shows Benedict Arnold fleeing to join British after his attempt to turn traitor was discovered. Arnold's defection stunned Americans.

Tempe Bedroom Guest

Troops in Morristown and Jockey Hollow were no novelty to Tempe Wick. Since late 1776, when the first soldiers arrived, they waved cheerfully as Tempe galloped by on her handsome horse.

The troops that returned for the winter of 1780-81 were sullen and rebellious, though. By January 1, 1781, they were ready for mutiny — and Tempe's steed was in their plans. Horses would be needed for a long trek across New Jersey.

Three American soldiers stopped Tempe as she rode through Jockey Hollow on New Year's Day. She lashed at the soldiers, escaped, and sped to her nearby home. There, according to a popular story, she led the horse into her bedroom, where she kept him for three weeks, feeding him with kitchen scraps.

The story is part truth, part legend. The Wick farmhouse still stands in the Morristown National Historical Park and Tempe's red cloak is in the park museum.

fired, killing Captain Adam Bettin and wounding two other officers.

Wayne ordered the men be supplied with food, and promised to accompany them to meet with Congress. The column headed south for Princeton and Trenton, where meetings with members of Congress satisfied the mutineers matters would improve if they returned peacefully to Morristown.

Some of the New Jersey Line at Pompton decided to imitate the Pennsylvanians. About 300 of them left Pompton on January 20 and walked overland to brigade headquarters at Chatham to demand better treatment. They went peaceably, and returned to Pompton quietly after being told their grievances would be heard.

Washington moved swiftly to quell the swelling mutinous spirit. Three of the Pompton protestors were chosen by lot to be executed. Twelve other mutineers were named to perform the grim job. One of the three chosen to die was pardoned, but the other two died under the gunfire of their fellow rebels. Mutiny in the colonies died with those two men of the New Jersey Line.

To Yorktown And Victory

Washington's full command marched across New Jersey for the last time in the dry days of late August 1781, headed for Yorktown, Virginia where the bulk of the British army under General Cornwallis was

Ignoring the entreaties of their officers, men of the mutinous Pennsylvania Line left Morristown on January 1, 1781 to march on Congress in Philadelphia.

trapped along the shores of the James River.

A hovering French fleet cut off British escape to the Atlantic Ocean. The Virginia militia hemmed in the British along the riverbanks. If Washington's regulars could reach Virginia in time, the British position would be untenable.

Marching with the weary American veterans were 5,500 fresh French soldiers, led by the Comte de Rochambeau. The well-equipped, well-trained French army won admiration as it filed along the dusty New Jersey roads from New York State to Parsippany.

On August 25, Washington veered southeastward to Chatham where, as a ruse, skilled French bakers were sent to build four huge brick baking ovens. The word was deliberately leaked to British General Clinton that the Americans and French would strike at the British in New York from Chatham.

Meanwhile, the French forces hastened south-ward through Whippany and Morristown, headed for Princeton. Suddenly, leaving the New Jersey Brigades behind to keep up the deception, Washington left Chatham on August 28 and hastened to join Rochambeau. The two armies forded the Delaware River on September 2 at a shallow point near Trenton. The outwitted British had no chance to follow.

The quick-moving force reached Williamsburg, Virginia on September 14, and then closed the circle on Cornwallis at Yorktown. By October 10, the British cause was hopeless. Cornwallis delayed a week, and then surrendered 7,500 soldiers on October 19, 1781.

The British army at Yorktown paraded slowly in defeat at Yorktown to the now-mournful tune of *The World Turned Upside Down*. Except for minor skirmishes, the war was over. The fight for independence had prevailed.

The "News" Of War

New Jersey's first two newspapers were started during the Revolution to propagandize the war effort. One, started in Burlington in 1777, died soon after the war ended. The other, begun in 1779, became the forerunner of the modern Elizabeth Daily Journal.

William Livingston, the state's first governor, decided in 1777 that New Jersey needed its own newspaper to spread revolutionary propaganda. He chose Isaac Collins of Burlington as editor and printer. Collins was a middle-of-the-roader. He published many materials for the British-backed government, but he also printed New Jersey's first State Constitution.

The New Jersey Gazette *began rolling off Collins' press on December 5, 1777. Governor Livingston was the Gazette's chief columnist and the state subsidized Collins until he could get 700 subscribers. Collins refused to be bullied into printing only propaganda. He wrote Livingston: "My ear is open to every man's instructions, but to no man's influence."*

On February 16, 1779, however, when Shepard Kollock began printing the New Jersey Journal *at Chatham, he fully accepted the frank fact he was being subsidized to print slanted news.*

Kollock resigned his commission as an army lieutenant to start the Journal. *The army gave him more than verbal support. He also received paper from scarce military supplies and was given large quantities of army rags to use in making his own paper.*

Army "news" in the Journal *was deliberately distorted to deceive the British in New York. For example, in the midst of the dreadful suffering at Morristown during the winter of 1779-80, Kollock wrote falsely the American troops were in fine condition.*

Although both papers existed mainly to aid the army, their columns gave a good account of life during the war — particularly in advertisements, essays, or letters to the editor. It was not good journalism, but it was better than nothing.

Princeton became the temporary capital of the United States from June 26 to November 4, 1783, after mutinous American troops forced Congress to flee from Philadelphia. Congress convened in Nassau Hall (below), scene of a savage battle in January 1777. Distinguished visitors often stopped by *Morven* (above), to visit the Stockton family.

Princeton: The Nation's Capital

Victory at Yorktown did not free the troops to return home, nor did it even mean improvement in their conditions. While soldiers still went without food or pay, Congress delayed in Philadelphia. Finally, in mid-June 1783, eighty mutinous Pennsylvania soldiers marched to Philadelphia to demand back pay as well as a date when they would be released from service.

The defiant soldiers surrounded Congress Hall on June 24, with drawn bayonets. They were in no mood for debate. Congress hastened away, to convene in Nassau Hall at Princeton on June 26, 1783.

Elias Boudinot, President of Congress, was born in Princeton and was a noted Elizabeth lawyer. His sister, Mrs. Annis Boudinot Stockton, lived in the handsome Princeton mansion called *Morven* (the official New Jersey governor's mansion from 1957 until 1981). Her husband, Richard Stockton, a signer of the Declaration of Independence, died in February 1781.

Princeton had only sixty to eighty houses, and its chief claim to fame was the little college, still battered from misuse by British troops in 1776. The village was hard-pressed to house and entertain Congress, but the lawmakers met in Nassau Hall for more than four months.

Congress summoned Washington to receive its official thanks. He and Mrs. Washington reached Rocky Hill outside of Princeton in mid-August. They stayed at *Rockingham*, a twenty-room house built by the late Judge John Berrian on a farm about four miles from Princeton.

A Time To Give Thanks

Washington rode into Princeton on the morning of August 26. He slowly guided his small horse through the throng of cheering admirers, pausing often to talk with veteran soldiers. The general entered Nassau Hall, where Congress continued to sit and to wear hats as evidence civilian government was superior to the military.

President Boudinot read a formal message of thanks. Washington replied briefly and walked quietly out of the hall. There was no applause. Congress immediately adjourned as the doors closed on the General. The doors were then thrown open, and Washington returned. Congress, freed of its official restraints, cheered him as lustily as had the crowds in

Huddy For White, Asgill For Huddy

Any soldier nineteen years old, wealthy, and unscathed in Revolutionary War action should have been able to greet each day in the summer of 1782 with pleasure, even as a prisoner of war. Captain Charles Asgill (shown to the right) was the exception. He feared any morning might be his last, despite the fact he was totally innocent of any wrongdoing, in battle or otherwise.

Tangled high level maneuvering brought the young captain to the edge of the hangman's platform. Captured at Yorktown in October 1781, he was routinely placed in a prison at Lancaster, Pennsylvania to await shipment home.

Then, on March 24, 1782, a cruel episode began. That day American Captain Joshua Huddy of Colts Neck was captured at Toms River. A week later, he was charged with murdering a Tory named Phil White, despite the fact Huddy was in prison at the time of the murder. Tory avengers hanged Huddy on a hill overlooking Sandy Hook Bay, shouting: "Up goes Huddy for Phil White!"

Washington demanded the British turnover the captain who had executed Huddy. When the demand was ignored, the American command ordered a British captain be chosen by lot to be hanged in retaliation. Asgil's number was drawn. He was taken to Chatham and told the noose was ready for his neck.

The case created an international sensation. Both Benjamin Franklin and King George III refused to help, but Asgill's plight became so poignant Washington asked Congress to decide whether the young captain must die. At this stage, the King of France personally asked Washington to free Asgil.

The French plea went to Congress by fast messenger. Many Congressmen first thought it was a false effort to save Asgill, but when the message was proved bona fide, Congress bowed to Washington, the King of France, and that part of the civilized world appalled by this cruel twist of postwar brutality.

the streets.

Word was received in Princeton, on November 1, the official treaty of peace had been signed at Versailles. Later that afternoon, the Netherlands minister to the United States addressed Congress and welcomed the United States into "the ranks of sovereign and independent powers."

Congress adjourned within three days. Washington appeared before his personal bodyguard of soldiers at Rocky Hill and read an emotional, affectionate message of farewell. A week later, he left for his Mount Vernon estate in Virginia. He had not been home since the summer of 1775.

The war was over, officially. Yet, as the new nation welcomed peace, there was widespread concern. Could this nation, where all persons were "created equal," really endure? No one was sure.

The Liberty To Fight

African American soldiers served with white neighbors in the Revolution, sometimes as free men, but often as slaves. An estimated 700 African American soldiers fought at Monmouth, and many saw action in other major battles. Two New Jerseyans are well remembered.

Jack Cudjo, a Newark slave owned by Benjamin Coe, served in Maxwell's New Jersey Brigade. He was listed (as John "Cujo") in the Register of Officers and Men in the Revolutionary War.

The Maxwell Brigade fought at Brandywine, Monmouth, Springfield, and Yorktown. After the war, Coe freed Cujo and gave him an acre of ground and a house on High Street in Newark.

Oliver Cromwell of Columbia, in Burlington County, served six years in the Second New Jersey Regiment, seeing action at Trenton, Princeton, Brandywine, Monmouth, and Yorktown.

Cromwell returned to Columbia after the war. He received a pension of $96, unusually large and particularly so for an African American soldier. He became a farmer and died in 1853 at the age of 106!

115

Unit III

Born in fiery revolution and toughened by adversity, the adolescent United States finally stood on its own in the family of nations in 1783. Others in that family admitted, often grudgingly, a new nation existed, even as they questioned openly whether it could survive.

Josiah Tucker, the brilliant English political economist, predicted in 1783 Americans would be "a disunited people till the end of time . . . they will be divided into little commonwealths or principalities, according to natural boundaries."

Tucker obviously wished the United States no good, but even the Count de Vergennes, the foreign minister of friendly France, observed in 1784 "the American Confederation has a great tendency toward dissolution."

There was no "United" States of America. The thirteen parts had bound themselves loosely together under the Articles of Confederation, carefully keeping power from the national government. Congress had no power to tax the states. It had no means of enforcing whatever laws it might adopt.

Questions plagued the thirteen states. Could New England's seafaring merchants compromise with the South's land-loving plantation owners? Could large, powerful Massachusetts and Virginia be concerned with the rights of such little states as New Jersey or Delaware?

Unless the answers were yes, the United States could not endure. Somehow, these widely varied states had to hammer out — and quickly — a framework of government within which all could dwell in some harmony.

One New Jerseyan, William Peartree Smith, echoed the general doubt in April 1783 when he wrote Elias Boudinot of Elizabethtown, then serving as President of the Continental Congress:

"I don't know whether it would not have been best for us all had he [George Washington] lain hold of the helm; for I am confoundedly afraid that the Stupid Crew [the states] will sink the ship, when escaped the storms and got safely to port."

Union of the states might begin with thirteen signers of an agreement, but the United States needed far more than a Constitution to knit the parts together.

Road conditions were so wretched it was difficult enough to journey from Hackensack to Haddonfield, much less from Boston, Massachusetts, to Charleston, South Carolina. Roads were often impassable. Few bridges spanned even the smallest

Can This Nation Long Endure?

streams; the great rivers could be crossed only on undependable ferries.

Large settlements were few. Boston, New York, and Philadelphia were not more than overgrown towns. Benjamin Franklin no longer could boast he knew everyone in Philadelphia, but that was more because his advancing years kept him close to his parlor than because of any rapid growth of his town. Sparsely settled New Jersey was little more than a series of widened crossroad villages linked together by slow-moving wagons.

Quick, easy travel was only one challenge. The young nation also needed the capability to produce its own products. The war had hardly ended before cheap British goods again flooded the American market, threatening to make the United States more dependent than ever on England.

America in 1783 was a nation of farmers, a "do-it-yourself land" where nearly every necessity of life was grown or made on the family farm. "Homespun" was a fact of life as well as a matter of pride.

Industry was insignificant. Iron "factories" were merely overgrown blacksmith shops. Glassworks rose unheralded and fell without any mourning for their collapse. Waterwheels turned millstones in little grain mills that served limited numbers of neighboring farmers.

Alexander Hamilton, the first Secretary of the Treasury, insisted if the United States ever were to be truly free, it must have a planned industrial system. Some region, he said, possibly the Great Falls of the Passaic (at what is now Paterson), had to be established where power could be found for an American industrial empire. Industry would provide work and encourage growth.

Westward, beyond the Appalachian Mountains, a vast, silent continent waited. Hunters and trappers brought back tales of purple mountains that rose above sprawling plains; of mighty rivers coursing through dense forests. A few Americans dreamed: someday, perhaps, they might go West.

But in 1783, the weak little United States was pinned down beside the Atlantic Ocean, barely able to call itself a nation. Here were thirteen states each different, each a mixture of local prides and jealous fears, each a blend of varied kinds of people. Unsure, unsafe, uncertain, the United States struggled toward maturity.

United States		New Jersey	
		1786	1st US steamboat sails in New Jersey waters
US Constitution adopted	1787	1787	New Jersey is third state to ratify Constitution
Washington elected President	1789		
1st Bank of US chartered	1791	1791	Paterson is 1st planned industrial town
War of 1812 begins	1812	1812	NJ militia alerted
Savanna 1st steamboat to cross Atlantic	1819	1819	Savannah engine made in Morristown
Missouri Compromise	1820		
Erie Canal completed	1825	1825	1st US locomotive runs in Hoboken
		1829	1st barges on Morris Canal
1st US railroad	1830		
		1831	1st railroad in NJ
Oregon trail opened to Pacific Ocean	1832	1832	1st daily Newspaper in New Jersey
		1838	Telegraph perfected in Morristown
Polk elected President	1844	1844	New State Constitution
Mexican War	1846	1846	1st organized baseball game played at Hoboken
Gold discovered in California by NJ man	1848	1850	Compromise of 1850
		1854	Railroad to Atlantic City
Lincoln elected, Civil War starts	1861	1861	NJ Brigade reaches Washington
Emancipation Proclamation	1863	1863	Rioters in NJ and NY protest draft
Lincoln re-elected	1864	1864	Candidate McClellan of W Orange wins NJ vote
Lincoln assassinated	1865	1865	NJ refuses to ratify 13th Amendment

Chapter Six - The Fight To Survive

United States		New Jersey	
		1784	Congress votes to make Trenton capital of US (later rescinded)
Washington bids nation farewell	1796	1796	1st major depression hits Paterson
Jefferson becomes President	1801	1801	Toll road era begins in NJ
Pike explores Colorado	1806	1806	Trenton bridge provides land route — Jersey City to Philadelphia
War of 1812	1812	1812	NJ militia alerted
		1814	James Lawrence of Burlington is Navy hero
Erie Canal opens	1825	1825	Work begins on Morris Canal; completed 1836
		1830	Camden & Amboy 1st state railroad
Idaho settled	1834	1834	D & R Canal opens
Panic of 1837	1837	1837	Depression hits mill towns
California statehood	1850		
Republican Party organized	1854	1854	1st train to Atlantic City
Panic of 1857	1857	1857	Factory workers suffer

Great Britain's mighty navy did not subdue the United States in the Revolution, but the war had scarcely ended before English ships began a subtle, innocent-looking counterattack. They unloaded a flood of British products on American docks, at prices far below comparable American-made goods. The competition was just too much; the American economy went into a tailspin.

In July 1782, a correspondent calling himself "a Plain Farmer" wrote in rage to the *New Jersey Gazette*: "Powder and ball, muskets and bayonets cannot conquer us, but we are to be subdued with British geegaws. We can deal with an open enemy; but now, like worms, they are eating through the bottom of the vessel, and we go down without seeing our destruction!"

The ruinous trade threatened New Jersey doubly, since the state lay wedged between the bustling ports of New York and Philadelphia. Goods flooded into the state from both sides. Already weakened by lessened post-war demands, New Jersey industry staggered toward collapse.

Iron forges and furnaces banked their fires, and grass began to grow in the streets of Ringwood and

◇◇◇◇◇◇◇◇◇◇◇◇◇◇◇◇◇◇◇◇◇◇◇

Binding The Wounds

George Washington wrote Governor William Livingston of New Jersey, in June 1783, urging him to help decide whether "the revolution must ultimately be considered a blessing or a curse — not to the present age alone, for with our fate will the destiny of unborn millions be involved."

The letter went to all thirteen governors, but it was especially meaningful in New Jersey. Here the war had raged for more than five years. Here troops had occupied the land.

Reminders of military presence could be seen everywhere between Bergen and Burlington: demolished houses and barns, wrecked churches, and the stone foundations of burned-out buildings. Orchards and pasturelands, trampled by warring armies, lay neglected.

A survey in 1782, by the New Jersey legislature, showed more than 2,000 known cases of British or Hessian actions against citizens in Bergen, Essex, Middlesex, Somerset, and Burlington counties. The survey also showed hundreds of properties ruined by American soldiers, especially in Bergen

and Morris.

The chasm widened between those who became revolutionists and those who remained loyal to Great Britain. Thousands of New Jerseyans chose the latter course. Most of the Loyalists fled to New York. Now, at war's end, they asked forgiveness and the right to return to their homes and farms. They found little sympathetic response, for hatred of Tories would not easily fade.

When their properties were seized and sold at public auction, most Tories fled to Nova Scotia or Canada to live out unhappy lives. The few who returned to New Jersey faced hostile neighbors or even infuriated mobs. The Loyalists paid the cruel price for siding with a loser.

In time, as the feelings lessened or as the Tories drifted away, the wounds healed. New Jersey renewed its struggle to maintain an identity in the midst of its ever more powerful neighbors.

118

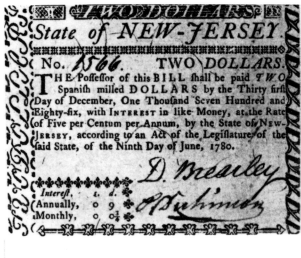

New Jersey's State Seal boasted from the start this was a place of "Liberty and Prosperity," with the horse's head and the three plows indicating farmers ran the economy. Boasts of prosperity did not make it so. New Jersey paper money, such as these bills issued in 1780 and 1781, had little acceptance in New York and Philadelphia. Interestingly, the 1780 bill is for two dollars, but the note issued a year later continues to use the British term shilling. Words made little difference; neither was worth much.

Batsto. Glassworks in the Pine Barrens closed down: the seven Stanger brothers who opened a glassworks at Glassboro in 1775 were in debtor's prison in 1780. Newark and Elizabeth leather makers found their markets gone.

Worsening the situation was rampaging inflation. Trying to keep pace, the state legislature printed large sums of paper money between 1783 and 1786. New York and Philadelphia merchants refused to accept New Jersey's currency, preferring their own state's money. The value of the New Jersey notes fell rapidly.

New Jersey Defies The Nation

To complicate matters, every state had the right to impose duties on the imported goods of another state, as if each were an independent nation. New York and Philadelphia treated New Jersey cabbages and pork exactly the same as china or spices imported from foreign countries. New Jersey countered by making Perth Amboy and Burlington duty-free ports, but few shippers took advantage of that generosity.

As the interstate wrangling deepened, heavy burdens fell on the nation as a whole. Indian wars had begun again on the western frontiers, and pirates attacked American ships in the Mediterranean Sea.

In September 1785, Congress asked the states to contribute $3 million to fight the threats to national security.

Each state was assessed according to ability to pay. New Jersey was taxed only $166,716, fair enough in view of the state's size. That Congressional levy provided the weapon New Jersey needed to stun the larger states.

The New Jersey legislature told Congress, on February 20, 1786, it would not pay one cent of its assessment until its complaints were heeded. Declaring New York had "ill used" their state for years, the New Jersey legislators called on a "weak and unjust" Congress to aid small states before asking for money.

Congress was shaken. If one of the smallest of the states could defy the federal government how could the United States justify its reputation as a federated nation in the eyes of the world?

A three-man Congressional committee hastened to Trenton to beg — not for the money, but for moral support. Charles Pinckney of South Carolina conceded New Jersey had a just grievance against New York. He argued that this, however, was not sufficient reason to threaten the very existence of the nation.

The legislature listened, and then agreed on March 17 to pay. It was only a moral victory for Congress, however, for New Jersey failed to forward the money (as did most other states, for that matter). Without the power to raise money, the nation barely clung to life.

Road To The Constitution

Virginia leaders recognized the peril. They asked each state to send representatives to Annapolis, Maryland in September 1786 "to take into consideration the trade and commerce of the United States." New Jersey joined Virginia, New York, Pennsylvania, and Delaware at the conference. New England ignored the gathering, as did the entire South except Virginia.

Trenton: Capital Of America?

James Madison of Virginia warned friends, in a letter written October 13, 1783, Trenton "is to become the future seat of the Federal Government" — the capital of the United States of America.

Every Northern state from New Hampshire to Delaware lined up behind Trenton. That was logical; in 1783 New Jersey was nearly the geographic midpoint of the 13 far-from-united States. Congress temporarily delayed the decision by voting to alternate annual sessions between Trenton and Annapolis.

Congress met in Trenton in November 1784, much to the delight of local tavern owners and shopkeepers. The French Arms Tavern was altered and redecorated to provide a meeting place.

On December 23, Congress voted in the French Arms Tavern to provide $100,000 for federal buildings. These would be erected in "a district not less than two, nor exceeding three, square miles on the banks of either side of the Delaware." That meant Trenton, beyond a doubt.

The lawmakers named a three-man commission to build "in an elegant manner, a federal house for the accommodation of Congress and the executive officers thereof." They could also erect a President's house and other buildings — if the total cost was under $100,000.

Trenton had only about one hundred buildings along its seven or eight dirt streets and town leaders glowed in anticipation. It was believed having Congress present might mean an extra $10,000 a month in trade. Property values soared.

George Washington, whose greatest feat probably was accomplished at Trenton on December 26, 1776, swung the pendulum southward by declaring by the time the federal buildings were finished, "it will be found that they are improperly placed for the seat of empire."

That, plus some dealing by Alexander Hamilton made Trenton's "Federal City" only a dream. Congress soon settled on a site beside the Potomac River, close to Washington's own Virginia home. The South had won.

The Annapolis convention proposed all states meet in Philadelphia the following May to "render the Constitution of the federal government adequate to the exigencies of the Union." Virginia appointed its delegates on November 9. Fifteen days later, New Jersey became the second state to endorse the Constitutional Convention.

Virginia dominated the early days after the convention began in May 1787. Its "Virginia Plan" proposed a strong federal government, with two legislative houses, one elected by popular votes and one selected by state legislatures. Representation would be based on shares of money paid to the national government or on the number of free inhabitants of each state.

New Jersey's William Paterson reacted angrily on June 10 to the Virginia Plan. He argued small states would be "more enslaved" than ever. Paterson declared, "Neither my state nor myself will ever submit to despotism or tyranny." The little state in the center of the nation had defied the rest of the land.

One Nation, Two Houses

Paterson offered a counter program — the New Jersey Plan — on June 15. It called for only one house of Congress with each state having equal representation regardless of size, a group of chief executives rather than one President, and limited control by Congress over a state's activities.

Alexander Hamilton, of New York, greeted this idea with scorn. He called it "the old Articles of Confederation with new patches." The New Jersey Plan, Hamilton said, was "pork, still, with new sauce." He was not far wrong.

However, the proposal provided the base for compromise. Small states used it as a lever to pry loose a compromise for two houses of Congress. One, patterned after the New Jersey Plan, would be the Senate where two Senators would equally represent each state. The House of Representatives, that would be based on population, stemmed from the Virginia Plan.

Four New Jerseyans signed the new United States Constitution on September 17, 1787 — Governor William Livingston, David Brearley, Jonathan Dayton, and Paterson.

Delaware ratified the Constitution first, followed by Pennsylvania, and then New Jersey. The center of the mid-Atlantic states was nearly in place. Eventually other states fell in line; a United States had at last

been achieved.

State legislators met at the Blazing Star Tavern in Trenton, on December 19, 1787, to give unanimous approval to the Constitution. A large crowd gathered outside the Trenton courthouse to cheer the action. The next day, a light infantry company fired thirteen rounds in salute to the thirteen states.

An Era Ends; Another Begins

Ratification of the Constitution signified the end of an old era and the beginning of a new one. The death of Governor William Livingston on July 25, 1790 also symbolized this.

Livingston was chosen governor after the State of New Jersey was officially created, on July 2, 1776, and was re-elected annually for fifteen years. The Rev. Alexander McWhorter of Newark, the state's foremost Presbyterian minister, summed up the loss of Livingston in the funeral oration:

"It is not a single family that this day mourns. It is not a single society, town or county … The head, the guide, the director, and he who held the helm of our government is no more."

William Livingston's brilliance truly steered New Jersey through its difficult formative years. Livingston was gone, but most felt comforted when William Paterson, warmly remembered for his championing of small states' rights at the Constitutional Convention, succeeded him.

The new leader faced stern challenges. New Jersey, mired beside its muddy cross-state roads, still without a pattern of industry or a port of its own, and still

"An admiring concourse" greeted George Washington as he passed through Trenton, on April 21, 1789, headed for New York to be inaugurated as President of the United States. All of Trenton (above) was clustered close to the Delaware River and Assunpink Creek. Washington crossed the creek, and then passed beneath a flower-bedecked archway bearing the message: The Defender of the Mothers Will Be the Protector of the Daughters.

Mariner.

Soap Boiler.

A Carpenter.

Hat-maker.

A Basket-maker.

A Bricklayer.

Baker.

A Cooper.

Currier.

A Smith.

A Wool Comber.

Shipwright.

122

deep in the shadows of New York and Philadelphia, had to find some kind of future for itself.

Industry For A New Nation

Alexander Hamilton, more than any other American, dreamed the United States might establish its own system of manufacturing. If the emerging nation had to depend on imported wares, he reasoned, it would become more dependent than ever on England and Europe.

Hamilton's hopes clashed with the tradition America could best succeed as a nation of independent farmers. Benjamin Franklin believed manufacturing was desirable only to use the "idle time of children." John Adams predicted in 1780: "America will not make manufactures enough for her own consumption these thousand years."

Manufacturing began in several areas on a small scale. Essex County was especially awake to the need for American-made goods, as proved in the annual Independence Day parade on July 4, 1788.

Marching up Newark's Broad Street that day, behind the fifes and drums and the aging war veterans, were twenty tanners, fifty cordwainers, eight stonecutters, and twelve blacksmiths: four scythe makers, eighteen wheelwrights, six silversmiths, fourteen tailors, and eight hatters; plus large numbers of furnace hands, nail makers, millers, and others.

They gathered from many miles around from the hills of Orange, the quarries of Belleville, the plateau of Bloomfield, and the streets of Newark. The diversity and extent surprised even those aware small industry thrived.

Most of the workers were from their own little one-man or two-man shops, usually little more than shacks set up behind the artisan's home through demand rather than plan. A farmer's handmade scythe might be so admired that a neighbor asked him to fashion another. Soon the scythe-maker might make three or four a month. If demand continued, he left his plow and made scythes full-time.

Power At The Great Falls

Such easy-come, easy-go industry was exactly what worried Alexander Hamilton. He envisioned, rather, a system of manufacturing in which a variety of full-time factories were clustered in one location to work together toward a planned industrial future.

Hamilton outlined his plan to Congress in his "Report on Manufactures" in 1791. He suggested the proposed industrial center be located in New York, Pennsylvania, or New Jersey. He clearly had one place in mind: The Great Falls of the Passaic River.

Thirteen years before, on July 10, 1778, Hamilton and General Washington stopped for lunch at the foot of the Great Falls. Hamilton never forgot the awesome power of the water plunging seventy feet through the rocky chasm.

New Jersey hastened Hamilton's dream on November 22, 1791, when the legislature approved a charter for the Society for Establishing Useful Manufactures. The Society (abbreviated as the SUM) invited proposals from New York, New Jersey, and

Alexander Hamilton first saw the Great Falls of the Passaic in 1778. The plunging waterfall stayed in his memory, and when he proposed a system of American manufacturers in 1791 that power was the key.

Work in New Jersey at the dawn of the 19th century called for skillful hands, since machines were almost unknown. Power came largely from windmills or waterfalls, despite the fact the first steam engine in America was installed at Arlington in 1753. The illustrations on the opposite page are all from a volume published in London in 1825: *The Book of English Trades and Library of the Useful Arts.* The variety of trades and occupations show one thing in common — an emphasis on craftsmanship. Little boys were apprenticed to such master mechanics at an early age and, after a long period of training, might hope to launch out on their own. Many grew tired of waiting, ran away, and signed aboard ships, hoping to earn the romantic title of "mariner." Most soon tired of the sea, where life was more a matter of swabbing decks than sighting the stars.

Pennsylvania.

An engineer hired by the SUM confirmed what Hamilton anticipated. Calling the Passaic River Falls "the best situation in the world," the engineer recommended the Society not look elsewhere.

First Planned Industrial City

The SUM accepted the engineer's appraisal, bought 700 acres at the Falls on May 17, 1792, and set out to build America's first planned industrial city. Hamilton showed both modesty and political wisdom by refusing to let the place be named for him. The Society settled for Paterson, to honor Governor William Paterson.

A noted French architect, Major Pierre Charles L'Enfant, was hired to design a city "to surpass anything yet seen in the country." He complied; his elaborate plans envisioned streets 200 feet wide, branching out from a center hub like spokes on a wheel.

Unfortunately, L'Enfant's imaginative design fitted neither the rough hills surrounding the falls nor the Society's meager budget. The major departed with his sketches, that served him well in 1801 when he laid out a federal city, called Washington, DC, on the flat lands beside the Potomac River.

Peter Colt, state treasurer of Connecticut, succeeded L'Enfant in February 1793. He had scant reason to believe Hamilton's vision would soon become reality. The SUM had raised only half its proposed capital of $500,000. Fewer than fifty people lived within sound of the thundering falls, and none of them had the slightest industrial experience.

Colt went to work. He hired laborers to dig a raceway to lead water from the falls to wheels in a cotton factory carpenters hammered together. The carpenters finished long before the raceway diggers, so Colt turned to a primitive power — oxen plodding on a treadmill. The cotton factory became known scornfully as the "Bull Mill."

Colt imported skilled craftsmen from England, Scotland, and Ireland. All went well until 1796, when a SUM employee absconded with $50,000 when sent to England to buy machine parts. The bulls stopped plodding. Raceway diggers laid aside their shovels. The mill stopped. Paterson, "the industrial city," knew its first cycle of boom and bust.

Bogged Down By The Roadside

Boom times would return to Paterson, as would days of bust. Before any industrial cycle could begin again anywhere, however, traffic threatened to bog down completely in the insufferable New Jersey highways.

The state had roads aplenty by 1790. They radiated outward from a variety of centers — Paulus Hook (Jersey City), Newark, Morristown, New Brunswick, Trenton, Burlington, Salem, and Cooper's Ferry (Camden). On paper, a traveler could get almost anywhere.

The trouble was with road maintenance. The responsibility still lay with those whose properties fronted on the roadside, a holdover from colonial laws. Occasionally a roadside neighbor cared enough to throw a few logs or loose stones in very deep holes, but far more than such rare gestures were needed to lift a state out of the mud.

An anonymous road user, calling himself "A Traveler," wrote dramatically to the *New Jersey Journal* in 1793:

"Thy inhabitants, oh State, are respectable — thy senators are wise — thy militia is formidable — thy daughters are fair; but some of thy ways are bad. Whoever travels the road from Stony Brook to Rocky Hill does it at the hazard of his life."

Who was to blame? Perhaps, the "Traveler" went on sarcastically, it was Princeton doctors who hoped to treat bones broken by riding the rough roads. If that were so, "Traveler" declared, "They Ought to get their bones broken!"

The "Traveler" was not alone in his complaints. A trip anywhere was long, dirty, and hazardous. One stagecoach rider wrote, in 1795, that a journey from New Brunswick to Trenton was so jolting "many of us could scarcely stand."

Crossing Their Bridges

Negotiating the roads was bad enough. Crossing the streams was worse. Stagecoach drivers sent their teams splashing across rock-strewn stream beds, often thoroughly soaking and rattling the passengers. There was a pause at wider streams, such as the Raritan, Passaic, or Hackensack rivers, to await the convenience of the lordly ferryman.

A 1779 law forbade ferrymen to "deny or unnecessarily delay the speedy carrying over of any passenger." However, since most ferryboat operators also operated the tavern bar at the ferry landing, it was common for boat schedules to be altered so waiting passengers might be well supplied with stimulants for the ferry trip.

Cross-state travelers won a large measure of independence in 1795. Long wooden toll bridges were finished that year across the Raritan, Passaic, and Hackensack rivers. The tolls brought few protests. The costs were more than regained in the time saved at the bar while waiting for the errant ferryman.

The bridges across the Passaic and Hackensack rivers were built simultaneously — 492 feet across the Passaic and 980 feet across the Hackensack. A causeway made of logs, covered by thin layers of sand and gravel, linked the spans.

The bridge across the Raritan River was on a grand scale. Thirteen stone pillars supported the 990-foot wooden roadway. Completion of the Raritan River bridge made it possible to travel from Paulus Hook, on the Hudson River, to Burlington, on the Delaware, without waiting at three ferry landings.

These impressive achievements led to the greatest bridge of the time, started in May 1804, to span the Delaware River at Trenton. Horse drawn vehicles began rumbling over the mighty Trenton bridge after "elaborate exercises" on January 30, 1806. The structure was a wonder of the age — 1,008 feet from entrance to entrance, nearly one-fifth of a mile long. This bridge resisted the onslaught of river floods, fire, and traffic for seventy years.

Thus, by 1806, a traveler could speed across country without a ferry stop between Philadelphia and the riverbank opposite New York. The legislature gave travelers a choice of ferries by extending the road from the bridges to Hoboken as well as Paulus Hook (Jersey City).

Tolls, Tolls, Everywhere Tolls

Since bridge fees did not disconcert travelers, road promoters suggested toll highways. Pay-as-you-go road fever raged through the states, starting in New England and sweeping southward until New Jersey's first toll road charter was granted in 1801.

That charter was for the Morris Turnpike, to run from Elizabeth to Milford, Pennsylvania, via Springfield, Morristown, Succasunna, Stanhope, and Newton. Businessmen were promised a stagecoach passenger on the toll road could be in New York "sometime before nightfall" if he boarded the coach that left Morristown at 6 AM.

The state chartered fifty-one turnpikes between 1801 and 1829, nearly all of them north of a line from Perth Amboy to Burlington. Only about half ever were finished, but 550 miles of toll roads were started before the turnpike fever subsided.

Two major roads were started in 1806 — one from Morristown to Phillipsburg by way of the exclusive summer resorts atop Schooley's Mountain, the other from New Brunswick to Phillipsburg by way of Somerville and Clinton. The latter was called The New Jersey Turnpike, a name revived nearly 150 years later when the modern New Jersey Turnpike was built north and south across the state.

Turnpike owners gained broad powers. They could take over existing roadbeds or could condemn property as they pleased. They could erect a "pike," or barrier, at intervals on the road and "turn the pike" aside only on payment of a toll. Tolls averaged about one cent per mile per horse (a half cent per mile for a rider on horseback).

Wonder of wonders, a stagecoach could speed from Jersey City to Philadelphia in less than two days after this bridge was completed over the Delaware River at Trenton in 1806. Nearly one-fifth of a mile long, this was the most impressive of four major New Jersey bridges built between 1795 and 1806.

Toll highways were the rage in northern and central New Jersey between 1801 and 1829. A total of fifty-one toll roads were built in that period. Travelers paid a toll (top) and the "pike" (gate) was turned; hence the name "turnpike." Rates were carefully listed (center), along with rules of the road. Great flocks of sheep and cattle swirled dust across the turnpikes.

Turnpike users had one break: they could use any toll road free on the way to church or to work. Most local people used parallel free roads, thus "shunning the pike." (A back road between Madison and Chatham, called "The Shunpike," recalls those days of toll avoiders.)

Drovers, Coaches, And Conestogas

Toll roads pumped life into New Jersey's economy. Great caravans of grain-filled wagons rolled, in season, down the New Jersey Turnpike to the docks at New Brunswick, where fast sailing sloops waited to carry the golden wheat to New York. Other wagons headed for markets in Newark, Elizabeth, or New York.

Drovers from the back country herded their sheep, beef cattle, and fat hogs eastward. Moving only a few miles a day, the herds were driven through Morristown and Chatham, through the Short Hills gap, and on to the markets at Newark.

Each night the livestock was herded into pens outside a village inn. Drovers, who yearned for a night's lodging in a real bed, usually smelled so much like their herds they were ordered to sleep with their animals.

Stagecoaches linked villages and towns, for America was starting to roll. Drivers were heroes. They reined their strings of steaming horses to a stop in front of a tavern with a great show of strength and noise. A loud horn sounded the approach of the daily stage; people raced to see the snorting horses, the shining coach, and the strangers who might alight.

Huge, brightly painted Conestoga wagons rumbled over the roads. Often the covered wagon and its team of six horses stretched sixty feet from end to end. John Parke, owner of a small cotton factory in Paterson, sent his products over the roads in multicolored Conestoga wagons. His gaudy signs painted on the canvas tops were rolling advertisements.

The War of 1812 brought prosperity to farmers and mill owners alike and increased traffic on the roads and bridges. The federal government spent $2 million on freightage in New Jersey, hiring 4,000 wagons and 20,000 horses. It spelled prosperity, but it turned the roads between New Brunswick and Trenton into "hopeless ruts and quagmires."

New Jersey's economy could not grow on its toll roads alone. John Stevens of Hoboken had an alternative — but who wanted to hear, in 1812, of his strange notion that steam engines could run on tracks, dragging passengers and freight behind them?

Paul Svinin, a Russian traveler who visited the United States between 1811 and 1813, painted this water color of the "Diligence Stage" at Trenton near the Delaware River. The stage raced between Philadelphia and Jersey City, carrying mail and passengers. (The Metropolitan Museum of Art).

A Fool For Steam Wagons

Stevens applied for a railroad charter from the New Jersey legislature in 1811. The legislators turned him down. Soon after, Stevens tried to interest New York promoters in a "steam wagon" line from Albany and Lake Erie. They laughed: "Stevens is making a damned fool of himself over steam wagons!"

Then, in 1812 (before there was a railroad anywhere in the world), Stevens published an amazing pamphlet "to prove the superior advantages of railway and steam carriages over canal navigation." He envisioned a steam engine "moving with a velocity of 100 miles per hour," although admitting "in practice it may not be advisable to exceed twenty to thirty miles per hour."

Railroads would "intimately connect" all states, Stevens said. Farmers and industrialists would enjoy lower costs. Armies could be transported rapidly across land in case of war. Newspaper editors snickered, one writing "if the contraption doesn't blow up, it will terrify livestock to death." John Stevens, then sixty-two years old, knew more about steam than any man in America.

Stevens had looked on with interest in 1786 when John Fitch of Trenton launched America's first steamboat on the Delaware River, twenty years before Robert Fulton's famed *Clermont* steamed up the Hudson River. One of Fitch's boats ran between Philadelphia and Trenton until 1790, but Fitch lost money despite 3,000 hours of accident-free service. America was not ready for steam.

Poor John Fitch

America's age of steam transportation began on the Delaware River in 1786 when John Fitch operated the steamboat shown above under a charter granted by New Jersey — America's first exclusive grant for steam navigation.

Connecticut-born John Fitch sailed under an evil star. He tried many trades unsuccessfully before coming to Trenton in 1767. Nine years later he had a thriving business, making guns for the army. The British burned his factory in 1776, and once again he was penniless.

Fitch's 1786 steamboat was successful, but the world was not ready for such fast movement. He built a twenty-ton steamboat in 1786 and gave several Congressmen a ride up the Delaware. Congress did not respond with funds.

Fitch had a steamboat in regular service between Philadelphia and Burlington in 1788, but few passengers bought tickets. By 1792, Fitch was described as "an abject, despised, insulted, heartbroken man."

Drifting to Kentucky, Fitch suffered more failure. The kindest reference to him was "Poor John Fitch." He committed suicide in 1798. His achievements are eclipsed by the myth Robert Fulton invented the steamboat.

"Don't Give Up The Ship!"

James Lawrence, born in Burlington in 1781, was expected to follow his father, Judge John Lawrence, into the law. Instead, James went to sea and became one of the foremost heroes of the War of 1812.

Young Lawrence tried law studies in his brother's office, but enrolled in the US Navy before he was seventeen. He worked his way up, and when war broke out with England in 1812, he was a captain.

Lawrence commanded the *Hornet*. His first exceptional feat was a rousing victory over the British ship *Peacock* early in 1813.

Soon after, Lawrence was assigned to command the *Chesapeake*, berthed at Boston. On May 30, 1813, Lawrence sailed to challenge the British ship *Shannon*. The two clashed in fiery combat on June 1.

The superior *Shannon* blasted the American vessel. Captain Lawrence suffered a grievous wound.

Tradition says Lawrence cried to his crew: "Don't give up the ship!" Soon, however, the *Chesapeake* surrendered. Lawrence died four days later.

Ignoring the fact that the toddling United States was totally unprepared for war, powerful "War Hawks" in Congress cried for another clash with England. They got their wish in 1812, at a time when the US Navy had only ten ships and the army consisted of 10,000 ill-equipped soldiers.

Such a force could not possibly protect the long United States coastline, and New Jersey especially feared imminent attack because of its strategic location between New York City and Philadelphia. No town of significance existed along the Jersey Shore; British forces might be landed anywhere.

New Jersey faced twin handicaps. The militia was little more than a social organization, trained at occasional alcoholic frolics. Worse, a strong "peace party," led by manufacturers and merchants, opposed the war. In November 1812, the State Assembly denounced the war as "inexpedient, ill timed and most dangerously impolitic." It suggested France as a more likely enemy.

The war was well underway in January 1813, when Governor Aaron Ogden urged efforts be made to strengthen the militia. A fort was built near the Sandy Hook Lighthouse, and cannon were placed elsewhere along the long Hook. A fort was built on the nearby Atlantic Highlands, where a semaphore "telegraph" was established to send messages to New York.

Great Britain set up a tight blockade between

Sandy Hook and Cape Charles in Virginia and effectively sealed off Delaware Bay. Small ships occasionally slipped through the blockade, but the British tactics were highly successful.

Two British forays into southern New Jersey led to minor incidents. When the enemy tried to get fresh water from Lily Lake in Cape May, residents worked day and night to cut a ditch from the bay to let salty sea water into the lake. Local militia foiled British troops seeking cattle in the marshes near Port Elizabeth. Neither Lily Lake nor Port Elizabeth really changed the war's course, but they showed the area was ready.

Governor Joseph Bloomfield took seriously his role as commander-in-chief, usually considered a mere ceremonial post. At one point he led 8,000 troops, including many New Jerseyans, to Plattsburgh, New York to help ward off a British attack.

Before the war ended, militiamen from every county were on the alert. Regiments were trained at Paulus Hook (Jersey City) and sent to Staten Island or the Atlantic Highlands. A large militia detachment was stationed at Cape May.

British troops never invaded New Jersey. The major enemy, thrust against Washington, DC in August 1814, showed an all-out effort probably could have conquered the feeble United States. No such effort was made. The war ended in 1815.

Stevens Turns On The Steam

Stevens built his own steamboat in 1798. He finished a 100-foot-long steamboat, the *Phoenix,* in 1808, a year after Fulton drove his *Clermont* up the Hudson. That trip earned Fulton undue credit for "inventing" the steamboat, and more important, gained Fulton's backers a monopoly on Hudson River water transportation.

The *Phoenix* was built as a Hudson River ferry. Blocked by the monopoly, Stevens ordered his ship out on the Atlantic Ocean, headed for Philadelphia by way of Delaware Bay. The *Phoenix* survived; John Stevens had another first — the first steam-powered vessel to cruise on an open sea.

Steam railroads dominated Steven's thoughts. In 1814, he made the nation's first railroad survey. He walked the route — from New Brunswick to Cranbury, and then (according to Steven's diary) to Trenton — "by way of the Devil's Brook, the Hide's Town [Hightstown] Road, and so to Princeton, up to Rowland's Tavern and the Ten Mile Stone; past the Quaker Wood by Jacob Haw's stable." When the walk ended in Trenton, Stevens treated himself to a cigar and a shot of whiskey.

Anyone that stubborn, durable, and inventive deserved a hearing. The New Jersey legislature gave Stevens America's first railroad charter in 1815. No backers invested money in the project.

Hoping to attract capital, Stevens built America's first railroad locomotive (or "Steam Wagon") and ran it over a 630-foot circular track at Hoboken. The "Wagon" reached a top speed of twelve miles an hour and easily climbed a thirty-inch slope to prove it could run uphill.

The Steam Wagon attracted interest, but by 1825 New Jersey and the rest of the nation had another transportation passion: canals. New Jersey was about to get two of the heralded waterways.

Canal To Climb Mountains

George P. Macculloch, a Morristown schoolteacher, conceived one of the most unusual of all canals in 1822 as he sat fishing at Lake Hopatcong. He envisioned a canal running west from Lake Hopatcong to tap Pennsylvania's coal fields and running east to carry Morris County iron products to Newark and New York City.

Macculloch sold bankers on his idea, and digging began on October 15, 1825. Within a year, 1,100

America's First Air Voyage
Jean Pierre Blanchard's gaudy, star-spangled balloon bounced to Earth in Deptford Township, New Jersey on the morning of January 9, 1793 and successfully completed America's first air voyage.

A veteran of many balloon ascensions in Europe, the French daredevil took off from Philadelphia exactly forty-six minutes previously. George Washington witnessed the takeoff and gave Blanchard a signed letter.

Blanchard recorded his thoughts and actions as he and his traveling companion, a little black dog, soared toward New Jersey. At a height of 5,812 feet, Blanchard's heart beat faster. The dog became uneasy, but quieted down when fed a biscuit. Blanchard sipped a bit of wine. Washington's letter helped Blanchard convince Deptford farmers he was not to be feared. They loaded him, his dog, and his balloon on a wagon and returned all to Philadelphia.

workmen with scores of mule teams worked their way over the mountains with picks and shovels.

Lake Hopatcong was raised five feet by a dam built to connect two smaller ponds. Water was brought from Greenwood Lake to supply a portion of the canal. Two new lakes, named Musconetcong and Cranberry, were formed, and water began to flow through the Morris Canal by the summer of 1829.

The waterway was an engineering marvel. By 1836, a combination of locks and inclined planes carried barges from sea level at Newark and Jersey City, up to Lake Hopatcong, a rise of 914 feet, and then down the Musconetcong River valley to Phillipsburg, a decline of 760 feet. That meant a total rise and fall of 1,674 feet in ninety miles. Few engineering feats surpassed this mountain-climbing canal.

When the first boats tied up for winter in 1829, a major, and eventually fatal, weakness was in clear focus. Ice froze the waterway from end to end, rendering it

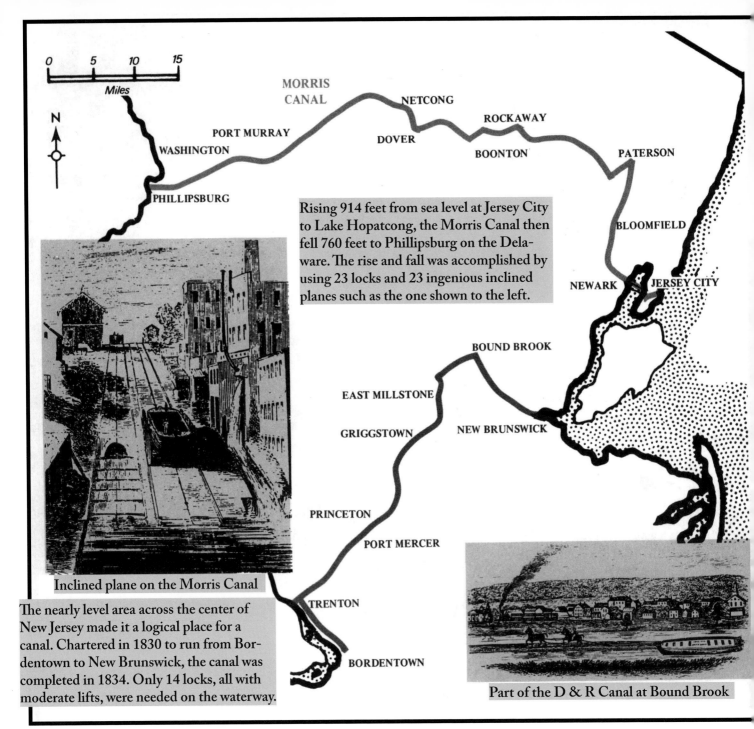

Rising 914 feet from sea level at Jersey City to Lake Hopatcong, the Morris Canal then fell 760 feet to Phillipsburg on the Delaware. The rise and fall was accomplished by using 23 locks and 23 ingenious inclined planes such as the one shown to the left.

Inclined plane on the Morris Canal

The nearly level area across the center of New Jersey made it a logical place for a canal. Chartered in 1830 to run from Bordentown to New Brunswick, the canal was completed in 1834. Only 14 locks, all with moderate lifts, were needed on the waterway.

Part of the D & R Canal at Bound Brook

temporarily useless.

The canal transformed its region. Pennsylvania coal burned new life into Dover, Boonton, and other Morris County "iron towns." Paterson knew prosperity again. Filled with industry, power, and population expansion, Newark was chartered as New Jersey's first city in 1836, the year the canal was completed.

Waterway Across The Waist

The Morris Canal defied logic. It ran over impossible terrain to link towns that in 1831 were not important. Far more sensible would be a canal to join the Delaware River and Sandy Hook Bay — connect-

ing Philadelphia and New York City.

Such a canal would traverse level ground, thus requiring only a few locks. It would link central New Jersey's key towns, and it could bring Pennsylvania coal to New York City more cheaply than the Morris Canal.

Backers for a mid-state canal began pushing for the right to build as early as 1804, but had to wait until 1830 to get their Delaware & Raritan Canal charter. Digging the forty-three-mile long passage from Bordentown to New Brunswick, by way of Trenton and Bound Brook, was so easy the canal was finished in 1834. It required only fourteen locks.

The first barges passed through the D & R Canal

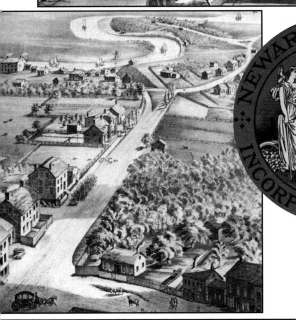

New Jersey was nearing remarkable change, thanks to railroads and steamboats, but when these views were painted the state still had a bucolic look. Hoboken's dock (top) featured simplicity when a artist visited in about 1830. Newark (left) in 1825 was an emerging town where dogs and cattle ran in the streets and a windmill still spun in the meadows. Camden (lower left) in 1810 was known only as "Cooper's Ferry" and retained the beauty of simple days. The capitol at Trenton stood in an open field, in 1810, and horses could be hitched to posts near the front door. Soon all would change; in 1836 Newark became the state's first incorporated city.

the Camden & Amboy Railroad, over almost exactly the same route as the canal. Significantly, the railroad stock sold out within ten minutes. The canal stock was not fully sold until more than a year after it was issued.

Stevens Dream Comes True

John Stevens' dream of a New Jersey railroad came to fruition in the Camden & Amboy. His sons, Robert and Edwin, backed the Camden & Amboy, and the father gave a party to celebrate the charter. John was then eighty years old, but his spirits at the party were described as being "as sparkling and abundant as the champagne."

Robert Stevens knew the flimsy rails on the original railroads were dangerous. Only flat strips of iron, the rails often broke loose to curl up through the bottoms of moving cars. Stevens invented the T-rail (the heavy type of track still used) as well as the familiar

in May 1834. The first commercial cargo consisted of lumber and stone headed south for the new state penitentiary at Trenton. At the same time, Pennsylvania coal headed north for New York City furnaces.

Successful from the start, the Delaware & Raritan lasted a full century. The seventy-foot-wide waterway needed few changes in its long life, since it was far more suited to industrial haulage than the much more narrow, shallow Morris Canal. Coal could be carried from Pennsylvania to New York City in less than two days, compared to five days on the Morris Canal.

The only threat to the Delaware & Raritan Canal's bright future became clear on the day the waterway was chartered. That day the legislature also chartered spikes that hold the rails to wooden cross ties.

Robert Stevens went to England in 1831 to persuade George Stephenson to build him a ten-ton locomotive. Stephenson, then the world's best-known locomotive builder, delivered the engine to Bordentown several months later.

The engine arrived in a bewildering stack of crates. A twenty-three-year-old handyman named Isaac Dripps was told to assemble the unmarked, unnamed parts. He had never seen a locomotive, of course, but he bolted the parts together by trial and error. Nicknamed the *John Bull* because of its English background, the locomotive was ready for its first trial on November 12, 1831.

That day, Dripps sent the *John Bull* roaring through Mile Hollow near Bordentown at thirty miles an hour. Many refused to ride the snorting monster, but a few gained courage after young Madame Caroline Murat of Bordentown, niece of Napoleon Bonaparte, enthusiastically hopped aboard the train.

Horses drew the first cars between Bordentown and South Amboy in January 1833. The *John Bull's* first cross-state trip was in September 1833. As an omen, the locomotive struck a hog that wandered on the track. The hog was beheaded; the *John Bull* landed in a ditch, and a passenger "in his fright turned a summerset out of the window."

The Rage For Railroads

The nation went wild over railroads. Promoters sprang up everywhere, seeking charters in every state, and boasting they would "go west" to the Mississippi River or even to the Pacific Ocean. Railroading was at a fever pitch.

Paterson railroad enthusiasts beat back Morris Canal lobbyists to receive the state's second rail charter on January 21, 1831. They planned to build their Paterson & Hudson River Railroad eastward to Jersey City, conquering the swamps of the meadowland and the broad Passaic and Hackensack rivers.

Another railroad syndicate, the New Jersey Railroad Company, also had its eye on Jersey City. It was chartered on March 7, 1832, despite powerful opposition from backers of both the Morris Canal and the Camden & Amboy Railroad. The railroad promoters promised to limit operations from Jersey City to New Brunswick, via Newark.

Both railroads reached Jersey City, but they allowed a full year for their embankments across the soggy Jersey Meadows to settle sufficiently to permit use of steam locomotives. By 1835, the locomotives steamed across the meadows at thirty-five miles an hour.

The two railroads jointly blasted a cut through the hard rock of Bergen Hill to Jersey City in 1838. A year later, the Camden & Amboy built a straight line from Trenton to New Brunswick and linked with the New Jersey Railroad. Thus, as the 1830s closed, rails joined Camden to Jersey City. Wonder of wonders, a trip between Philadelphia and New York now took only seven hours, including steam ferry trips at either end of the rail line.

Race To The Coal Mines

Two more railroads inched westward through New Jersey as the 1830s closed. Both had the same goal: the rich Pennsylvania coalfields. The towns that lay between tidewater and the mine country were considered inconsequential.

The Elizabethtown & Somerville Railroad, chartered in 1831, did not reach Somerville until January 1, 1842, nearly eleven years after the chartering. The new line celebrated its entrance into Somerville by serving lemonade and cake in the village inn. This railroad was not a champagne and caviar venture.

The snail-like pace of the Elizabethtown & Somerville gave backers of the late-starting Morris & Essex Railroad hope of reaching the coal mines first. The Morris & Essex, begun in January 1835, was the first New Jersey railroad to cut directly across the mountains. Three years passed before the first train steamed into Morristown from Newark on New Year's Day, 1838.

Flushed with success, Morris and Essex promoters slowed down. The rails did not reach Dover until 1848. There the sponsors called their railroad "as substantial as the iron mountains." It took more than seventeen more years to get the line to Phillipsburg. The Elizabethtown & Somerville's name was changed to the Central Railroad of New Jersey in 1849, amid a frenzy of energy. It reached Phillipsburg in July 1852 when passengers rode into town aboard "eight splendid cars, drawn by the gigantic locomotive Pennsylvania and accompanied by Dodsworth's band."

Both of these fledgling railroads soon grew fat on their diet of coal. They also gave rise to a new American phenomenon — the commuter, the person who wanted to "work in the city and live in the country." The first commuters left Morristown as early as 1838, putting up with a six-hour round trip each day for the joys of the country life.

Rails To Farms And Oceanside

It was easy to get money for railroads to the coal fields or for trains that ran between New York City and Philadelphia, but rails to southern New Jersey farm towns were not appealing to financiers. As for tracks to the New Jersey seacoast, who would visit that wasteland, except for a very few of Philadelphia's high living young people?

Thus, southern New Jersey did not get its railroads until the 1850s and 1860s. The first train did not chug into Woodbury until 1858 and into Millville and Glassboro until two years later. Rails finally snaked all the way to Cape May by 1866.

No New Jersey railroad brought greater changes than the Camden & Atlantic, started in 1852 with few prospects. It would serve a few bog iron furnaces and glassworks in the Pine Barrens. The trains might bring out some wood. Perhaps a few farmers would ship vegetables or cranberries.

Closer to seeing the real potential was Dr. Jonathan Pitney, an Absecon supporter. Dr. Pitney believed offshore Absegami (or Absecon) Island, where the railroad would terminate, could become "the El Dorado of the Atlantic Coast."

The Camden & Atlantic promoters met in January 1853 to discuss the Atlantic Ocean terminal. Richard Osborne, the railroad's construction engineer, unrolled a map of the site, emblazoned "in large letters of gold … (with) the words, ATLANTIC CITY." The "city" had only sand dunes and twenty-one eligible voters, but the railroad backers liked the ring of the name. It was approved.

The first train to Atlantic City carried six hundred visitors and the press to an opening party in the still-unfinished United States Hotel on July 1, 1854. Green flies stung the visitors; they were glad to escape back to Camden and Philadelphia at nightfall. Railroad officials speculated in oceanfront land at $17.50 an acre, hoping it might someday be worth $500 an acre. (That land can now bring millions of dollars for an acre.)

Goodbye To Old New Jersey

New Jersey fell into place beside those railroad tracks. Communities rose where none existed before. Villages became towns; towns became cities. Ever-larger factories, using coal to power their steam engines, settled beside the tracks. Raw materials poured in from the West to feed the machines of New Jersey. By 1850, the state was headed for urbanization, pulled along by the "Iron Horse."

The railroads reversed the outward flow of people who had been trekking west across the Delaware River in droves until the 1830s. Farmers had long employed wasteful, unskilled ways of planting and harvesting. As the soil became infertile, the farmers moved on.

The census of 1820 dramatized that. New Jersey's population increased by fewer than 100,000 between 1790 and 1820. New York, in the same period, was up

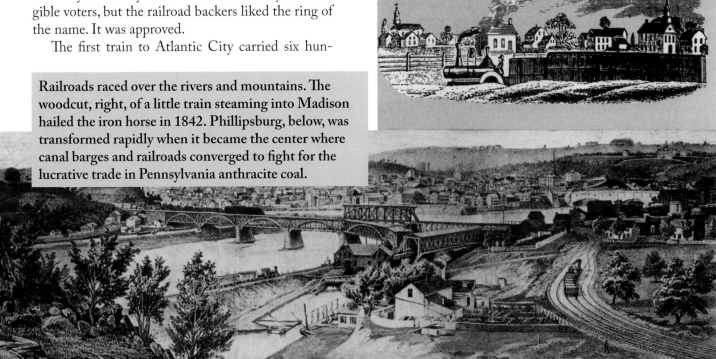

Railroads raced over the rivers and mountains. The woodcut, right, of a little train steaming into Madison hailed the iron horse in 1842. Phillipsburg, below, was transformed rapidly when it became the center where canal barges and railroads converged to fight for the lucrative trade in Pennsylvania anthracite coal.

This was Atlantic City in 1857, three years after the single track railroad was completed from Camden. Prosperity is already evident in a string of new homes built close to the railroad depot.

more than one million people; Pennsylvania was up 600,000. Ohio, not yet a state in 1790, had 581,000 residents in 1820, and Kentucky had 564,000. New Jersey could boast of a mere 277,500 residents.

Thomas Gordon made much of the outward flow of humanity in his *Gazeteer of the State of New Jersey,* written in 1834:

The state has been … constantly sending out swarms. Instead of being distinguished for the growth of numbers within her borders, she is remarkable for the paucity of their increase.

Turnpikes had been abuilding for thirty years. This was the dawn of the canal and railroad eras, although Gordon noted "... the state is, in the aggregate, agricultural."

He could have noted also the times were simple. In 1830, water still turned most factory wheels. A person born on the farm was likely to remain there, unless he could run away from home to become a sailor or be apprenticed to a town craftsman. As for women, they could only dream of marrying out of the drudgery of the farm. It was a dream that seldom came true.

Importing Industrial Skills

New Jersey's farm-minded people could build barns, weave homespun cloth, or make the tools or furniture they needed, but when railroads began expanding markets and making steam engines hum in factories, workers with other skills had to be found.

Paterson's first skilled workers were imported from the British Isles. Many had to smuggle themselves out of England, defying rigid restrictions against skilled workers leaving the land. Eventually, New England became New Jersey's greatest source of nimble fingers and keen minds.

The list of New Englanders transplanted to New Jersey grew longer each year. Almost every town had its share of "Yankee craftsmen." Thomas Rogers came

The Patient Waiter Who Lost

Samuel F.B. Morse, professor of art at New York University, and a young theological student, Alfred Vail, worked overtime in the fall of 1837 in a barn at the Speedwell Iron Works near Morristown. They were hot on the trail of the telegraph, an idea that had been forming in Morse's mind.

Morse had little mechanical skill. He leaned heavily on Vail to make the telegraph practical. Morse also needed desperately the money given the two by Judge Stephen Vail, Alfred's father.

Judge Vail grew impatient as his cronies joked about throwing money away on a "lightning machine." He demanded a public showing. Young Vail strung three miles of copper wire around the barn, perfected the instruments, and devised a code. A demonstration was set for January 6, 1838.

Handing Alfred a slip of paper, Judge Vail said he would be satisfied "if you can send this and Mr. Morse can read it." Vail ticked out the message. Three miles away (as the wire looped), Morse received the ticks. Within seconds the professor handed Judge Vail the message: "A patient waiter is no loser."

Within a month, Alfred Vail and Morse went to Washington to demonstrate their instrument. Already Alfred noted Morse was "inclined to go alone." Vail continued to work, however, discarding Morse's cumbersome code and substituting the dot and dash system still used and erroneously called "The Morse Code."

Morse's fame and fortune rose. Vail returned to Morristown, hoping in vain Morse might share both credits and royalties. When Vail died in 1859 at age fifty-nine, he was ignored, even as Morse's glory became greater. Vail waited patiently — and he lost.

to Paterson from Connecticut to make railroad locomotives. Connecticut's Colt family made Paterson a textile mill town. One of the Colts, Sam, fashioned his first automatic pistol in Paterson. The most ingenious of all the ex-New Englanders, however, was Seth Boyden of Massachusetts.

Boyden arrived in Newark in 1815. He made America's first patent leather in 1819 and produced this nation's first malleable iron in 1826. He worked for some time at improving locomotives and, before his death, had experimented with modern telescopes, simple electrical devices, hair dyes, and even giant strawberries. Boyden had no interest in money. He either gave away or sold, at low prices, all of his inventions.

Others came to New Jersey to make industry hum — Peter Cooper and Abram Hewitt of New York reached Trenton in 1845. Within five years they were operating the nation's largest iron establishment. John Roebling arrived from New York in 1859 to open the Trenton wire rope company that would become the country's famed builder of suspension bridges. (Roebling's spans in later years included the Brooklyn, George Washington, and Golden Gate bridges).

Clay molders chose the Raritan River valley surrounding New Brunswick to make bricks and other clay products. Trenton and Jersey City earned fame for the excellence of their pottery and dishes, using potters who drifted in from other states and other nations.

Newark added brewing to its growing list of industries in 1840. Brewers needed glass bottles; southern New Jersey glassblowers responded so well that by 1845 nearly one-third of the nation's glassworks surrounded Millville. Paper makers thrived in Paterson, Whippany, Millburn, and Trenton. Paterson became known for cotton and silk. New Brunswick made rubber and wallpaper.

Industry was seldom far from a railroad track or a canal bed. The burgeoning factories poured forth an astonishing variety of products for the time — nails, blankets, wagons, wire, shoes, cloth, silk flags, and hundreds of other necessities and luxuries.

Red Bricks And Black Smoke

Canal barges splashing into town and trains roaring across the landscape changed New Jersey forever, by 1860. The powerful lure of industry pulled rising populations within walking distance of the new factories. Urban life had begun, although the word "urban" was never used at that time.

If "urbanization" was used then, it would not have been an unflattering term. Cities were idealized, and they were often places of beauty as well as centers of emerging culture and education. They were also places of power, where bankers and investors gathered to pool money for more industrial growth.

Cities and towns took on a new substantial look. Larger stores, homes, and factories were built of brick. This was especially marked in manufacturing plants, where heavy steam engines required sturdy walls. Cities took on a red hue because of the many brick buildings tucked around the old, tall church spires.

City officials seldom discussed another growing urban phenomenon — the squalid "shanty towns" where most factory workers and day laborers lived, whether it be Newark or Paterson, Jersey City or Camden. Large numbers of Irish, imported to dig the canals, heave up the railroad embankments, and lay the bricks, lived in wooden hovels hastily thrown together to accommodate as many people as possible as cheaply as possible.

Industrialization brought with it the city slums. Americans never before knew such miserable living conditions. True, many farmhouses were little more than shacks, but at least the owners could sense an identification with the open land and the blue sky.

Black smoke belching from the factory chimneys became the sooty sign of prosperity. Artists of the 1840s and 1850s proudly painted the black smoke rising high — in Dover, Newark, Paterson, Bridgeton, Camden, Elizabeth, Jersey City, or any place where factories dotted the skyline. Nothing in those days spread gloom more widely than the absence of smoke, for that meant the factory fires were banked.

The Miseries of Industry

People piling into the cities doubled the state's population between 1830 and 1860 — up from 320,000 to 674,000 in those thirty years. Several towns grew, but Newark remained New Jersey's foremost city, in every way: in money, in transportation, and in urban perplexity.

Factory owners almost always resided as close as possible to their establishments. Many industrialists built homes next door to the plant, ready to leave a warm bed at any hour of the night in case of trouble. Absentee ownership was almost unknown. Workers in turn, lived close to the factory gates.

The days of boom did not last forever, however.

Connecticut-born Sam Colt became a sailor at age 16 and, during long sea voyages, whittled a wooden model of a six-shot pistol he hoped someone might want.

He drifted to Paterson in 1836 and found several New York and New Jersey capitalists willing to put his gun into production. The 22-year-old gun maker began making the Paterson Colt revolver, one of the most famous weapons ever produced. Unfortunately, buyers were few.

Sam found President Andrew Jackson interested, but his term was ending. When he arranged a demonstration for President Van Buren, the revolver sounds caused the President's horses to bolt. Army officials, the real target, denounced the Colt weapons as useless and impractical. Colt had worn out his Washington welcome.

Colt left Paterson in 1842, discouraged and penniless. War with Mexico forced the Army to beg Colt to make his revolver again in 1846. By then, Sam did not have a revolver, much less plans or models. He designed a new weapon and manufactured it in Connecticut.

Sam Colt prospered so in Connecticut he left an estimated $15 million when he died in 1862. Today, one of his original revolvers is worth a small fortune.

Depressions struck periodically, forcing the black smoke out of the chimneys and plunging entire communities into deep gloom bordering on panic.

Factory workers were hurt little at first by the economic setbacks. In Paterson, the "Bull Mill" workers were ex-farm men and women. In the bust of 1796, they merely packed up and returned to plowing. That was generally true as well in the depression that followed the War of 1812.

Depressions were coming at approximate twenty-year periods — in 1816, 1837, and 1857. Then came periods of prosperity: boom and bust, boom and bust; the cycle was fastened on the land.

Each succeeding depression struck the cities with increasing savagery. Most of the workers of 1837 and 1857 had never been farmers; they had no plows to take up again, no barns to tend once more. Now they were indigent laborers shackled to their slums.

Newark suffered badly in 1837. One $30,000 factory that sold at auction for $1,800 typified the collapse. Workmen walked the streets that winter, searching in vain for employment. Many fled westward: the city's population dropped off by more than fifteen percent before 1840. For the first time, the cities had brought misery and suffering.

The Panic of 1857

The boom times came again; 1837 faded into memory and was a generation in the past when prices began to rise in 1854. A few factories slowed down throughout 1855 and early 1856. By October 1856, money was scarce.

Three months later, during the winter of 1857, every industrial town was swept by what became known as the Panic of 1857. Beggars combed city and town streets in search of any small picking. Homeless, penniless people often begged for a night's lodging in a town jail, one of the few warm places open to the paupers.

Once again, Newark was hurt most cruelly of all New Jersey places. So many people were homeless and starving "A Friend of Education" offered a novel, if revolutionary, suggestion in a letter to the *Newark Daily Advertiser* in November 1857. He would close the public schools and "turn the basements into soup establishments and the upper stories into apartments where hundreds may be kept warm."

An *Advertiser* reporter wrote cynically on November 23 of the opening of an emergency relief food store. Apparently well-fed and jolly himself, the reporter declared "a half hour's visit is as good as a play."

The *Advertiser's* man reported Germans were the most numerous in the welfare lines, but "the Irish, for some reason, do not muster as strongly as usual." He noted "a sprinkling of colored people also gives variety to the complexion of the crowd."

Within the store, the reporter heard "a confusion of jargon scarcely equalled since the dispersion at Babel." (This was a snide reference to the number of foreigners on the streets of Newark by 1857.) According to the *Advertiser's* reporter, the doling out of welfare food proceeded "with apparent good humor."

The report did not amuse the poor or the unemployed. A week before, 2,000 of them gathered in a town park to urge employers to provide jobs. The meeting reflected a new attitude on the part of the workers — a feeling they were vital to a city, and fully entitled to share in the good things of life.

Westward The Course Of Jerseyans

Americans moved westward in steady streams after the American Revolution. They climbed the steep slopes of the Allegheny Mountains, trekked across the level ground toward the Mississippi River, crossed the wide Missouri, and streamed across the plains, ever seeking claim to some of the vast open lands that were there for the taking.

New Jerseyans joined the nomads. They left because they had exhausted the rich soils of Salem and Cumberland counties, they could buy land cheaply, they wanted to escape the pressures of an increasingly urban society, or merely because they yearned for adventure.

As they went, they left their marks, naming towns for places they had left. They founded a string of Salems, all the way to Oregon, every one named for Salem, New Jersey. They founded Newarks and Princetons, calling them by names they loved.

Nicholas Longworth of Newark was one of three founders of Cincinnati, Ohio. John Cleves Symmes of Sussex County purchased one million acres of Ohio land. Zebulon Pike of Lamberton (near Trenton) climbed a Colorado peak that is now Pike's Peak. Paul Tulane, Princeton merchant, founded a New Orleans university that bears his name.

Of all New Jersey's "winners of the West," few deserve more to be remembered than the three below.

David Burnet was the son of a distinguished Revolutionary War physician. Born in Newark in 1788, he left as a young man to seek his fortune beyond the Mississippi. Burnet settled in Texas in 1831 and played an active role in the Texas rebellion that led to independence from Mexico.

He was elected the first President of the Republic of Texas, while Texas was still an independent nation.

James Wilson Marshall discovered gold in California and set off the wild "Gold Rush" of 1849. Marshall left Lambertville in 1831 at age 21, drifted to Missouri, and crossed the Rocky Mountains to the Sacramento Valley in California. He opened a lumber business in Colona Valley, California and, one morning in January 1848, discovered a huge nugget of gold near his mill.

Within a year an amazing mob of humanity flowed into California, trying for some of the gold. They drove Marshall off his land, stole his lumber, and seized his diggings. Marshall died nearly broke, leaving an estate of less than $400.

Commodore Robert Field Stockton was born in 1795 to the wealthy Stockton family of Princeton. He joined the US Navy, rose to the rank of Commodore, and in 1846 was put in command of the ship *Congress* and sent west with orders to seize California.

Stockton entered the seacoast village of Los Angeles in August 1846, declared California a territory of the United States, and named himself governor. He returned home and resigned from the Navy in 1850. The California city named Stockton recalls his West Coast deeds.

Workers were fastened in place. Railroads, industry, and cities were here to stay. So were depressions, slums, poverty, and black smoke.

Thoughtful 19th century citizens considered how to improve the lot of humanity. Anyone with a conscience could see large segments of society were being mistreated or ignored — because of color, nationality, lack of skills, unfortunate disabilities, or industrial slowdowns.

The "apparent good humor" of welfare recipients really was not amusing.

American life was due for a change. Strident voices, including for the first time those of a few women, were asking why America could not move more rapidly toward the ideals of the Declaration of Independence and the laws of the Constitution of the United States.

HARPER'S WEEKLY

A JOURNAL OF CIVILIZATION

Vol. II.—No. 56.] NEW YORK, SATURDAY, JANUARY 23, 1858. [Price Five Cents

IN THE BITTER COLD.

Seth Boyden: Uncommercial Inventor

Seth Boyden of Newark, named by Thomas Edison as "one of America's greatest inventors," was not against profits merely because he never kept any for himself. The search for new ideas gave Boyden much more pleasure than watching his bank balance grow. Others could have the profits.

Boyden had no funds, when he reached Newark from Massachusetts in 1815, to market his new machine to slit leather. He made some money and sank it into a search for the secret of patent leather. When he discovered the secret and made America's first patent leather in 1818, he let others take over the business (in time patent leather meant untold millions of dollars in profits — for others).

Now Boyden sought to make easily-worked malleable iron, a product then known only in England. He announced his success on July 4, 1826, the 50th anniversary of the Declaration of Independence. He set up America's first malleable iron factory in Newark in 1826 and was on the way to another possible fortune.

Riches were not in Boyden's plans. He cleared the iron from his mind in 1835 by making a railroad locomotive able to climb the steep grades west of Newark. It was the first such hill-climbing locomotive ever built.

The years rolled on. Boyden made this nation's first daguerrotype and helped Samuel Morse on his telegraph. He

Harper's Weekly, that pridefully called itself "A Journal of Civilization," devoted its entire front page on January 23, 1858 to a bereft young woman out in the snow with her two young children. She was victim of the economic collapse that closed factories, threw people out of work, wrought bankruptcies, and forced Americans to wonder what had gone wrong in the nation.

went to California in 1849, but while there forgot the gold and sought unusual "seeds, trees and curiosities." Gold, even for the digging, was not Boyden's interest.

Boyden worked on a hair dye (it turned his hair black, then purple, then green). He moved to a suburb near Newark and grew strawberries, more than two inches in diameter, highly valued in New York restaurants. Boyden gave the precious plants away to neighbors.

Boyden died in 1870. Newarkers erected a monument to his memory in 1890, depicting Boyden at his anvil, wearing his shop apron. It was said to be the first statue ever dedicated to a workingman.

Nineteenth Century Counties

The old colonial alignment of counties would not do for the 19th century. People complained trips to county seats took far too much time. From those complaints grew eight new counties.

Warren was sliced away from Sussex in 1824. Passaic County was set up in 1837, only after it could be balanced in southern New Jersey the same year by Atlantic. Mercer County was welded together in 1838 from pieces of Hunterdon, Somerset, Middlesex, and Burlington counties.

Hudson became a county in 1840. Camden was carved from Gloucester four years later. It was Gloucester's second major surgery in seven years; Atlantic had also been severed from Gloucester. Ocean was set apart from Monmouth in 1850. Union County, divided from Essex in 1857, was the last county to be formed. The Civil War was approaching; the word "union" was in the air, but Union County people were seeking division, not union.

Two of the new counties were named for Revolutionary War generals: Joseph Warren, killed at Bunker Hill, and Hugh Mercer, fatally wounded at Princeton. Two recognized adjacent rivers: Hudson and Passaic. Ocean and Atlantic looked to the sea. Camden was named for a real estate development, that in turn was named for Charles Pratt, the Earl of Camden and friend of rebellious Americans.

MOTHERS LOOK OUT FOR YOUR CHILDREN!
ARTISANS, MECHANICS, CITIZENS!
When you leave your family in health, must you be hurried home to mourn a
DREADFUL CASUALITY!
PHILADELPHIANS, your RIGHTS are being invaded! regardless of your interests, or the LIVES OF YOUR LITTLE ONES. THE CAMDEN AND AMBOY, with the assistance of other companies, without a Charter, and in VIOLATION OF LAW as decreed by your Courts, are laying a
LOCOMOTIVE RAIL ROAD!
Through your most Beautiful Streets, to the RUIN of your TRADE, annihilation of your RIGHTS, and regardless of your PROSPERITY and COMFORT. Will you permit this! or do you consent to be a
SUBURB OF NEW YORK!!
Rails are now being laid on BROAD STREET to CONNECT the TRENTON RAIL ROAD with the WILMINGTON and BALTIMORE ROAD, under the pretence of constructing a City Passenger Railway from the Navy Yard to Fairmount!!! This is done under the auspices of the CAMDEN AND AMBOY MONOPOLY!
RALLY PEOPLE in the Majesty of your Strength and forbid THIS
OUTRAGE!

Enchantment with steam-powered transportation began to wear thin by the middle of the nineteenth century, particularly after terrible accidents showed how high-handed and arrogant operators of the railroads and steamboat lines could be.

The accident of the Camden and Amboy Railroad (above), on August 29, 1855, killed twenty-one persons and wounded seventy-five others. The wreck focused attention on the fact the line was still a single track after twenty years of high prosperity.

That kind of accident prompted outrage against penny pinching, power-conscious railroad executives. Such outrage was expressed on the broadside (left) that was distributed widely throughout the state. It asked, among other things, whether the populace was willing to let New Jersey become a "suburb of New York."

Camden's worship of its ferryboat connections was given a severe jolt on the night of March 15, 1856 when the ferryboat *New Jersey* caught fire and burned on the Delaware River. The lithograph (right) of the "terrible conflagration and destruction of the steamboat *New Jersey*" brought home to thousands of people the horror of that night when sixty-one persons perished in the flames or in the icy river. The tragedy considerably slowed Camden's growth.

NEW JERSEY.

140

New Jersey Portrait: 1842

John Warner Barber, shown to the right "sketching from nature" (as he described it), is the primary source for recognizing how New Jersey looked on the eve of its transportation and industrial revolution. He traveled across the state in 1842, pencil and portfolio in hand, sketching whatever he saw. Thus, in woodcuts made from his drawings, New Jersey was drawn into place at a dramatic time in its development. Barber sketched everything that caught his fancy — scenic splendors, country towns, railroads, and the beginnings of cities.

Barber was half of a team that put together six "state" books in the 1830s and 1840s. The other half was Henry Howe, who did most of the writing. Both were born in Connecticut, but once they began their travels in 1825 they were seldom home.

Barber and Howe called themselves "compilers — mere camp followers of the great army of authors who combat alone for fame." They bounced across the country in one-horse wagons, or they walked over narrow trails, always seeking the dramatic and the unusual, the bright stuff of history.

New Jersey was the fourth in six "state" books compiled by the fast-moving pair. Connecticut, Massachusetts, and New York came first, and then New Jersey, Virginia, and Ohio. All the books were markedly similar.

They devoted considerable time to the Revolution, and then wove in and out a miscellany of information that ranged from ghost stories, to a list of taxes for tavern drinks, to a report of a nearly-forgotten hurricane.

The New Jersey volume appeared in 1844, two years after Barber made his sketches. The text is rambling and at times confusing; it is neither literature nor history. Barber and Howe did not try to deceive. Their title plainly said the book was a collection of "facts, traditions, biographical sketches, anecdotes, etc." plus "geographical descriptions."

Whatever negative may be said about the writing, the woodcuts cannot be too highly prized. Barber's sketches were drawn just as railroads completed a triumphant link across the center of the state. The centers of such towns as Newark, Elizabeth, Trenton, and other places about to be cities showed the hustle and bustle of population centers on the way to transformation.

Amid the city changes there were town pumps, muddy streets, hay wagons, town markets, and all the other marks of simple villages. Outward, beyond the railroad tracks, Barber sketched canals, winding roads, beaches, courthouses, smoking factories, scenic vistas, and major historic sites.

The crude, stylized woodcuts show evidence of haste, but they tell far better than thousands of words what New Jersey looked like in 1842.

Samples of Barber's woodcuts are shown on the next two pages. The titles, by the compilers, show little originality. The scene below shows Trenton, the state capital, as it appeared from the Pennsylvania side of the river. Rafts floated serenely past the little town that was just beginning to feel its growing pains.

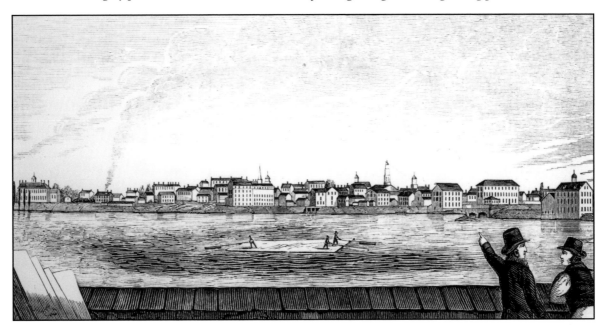

Smoking Skies ...

Southern view in Bridgeton

Northwest view of Millville

Northern view of Dover

Eastern view of Belleville

Emerging Cities ...

Northeast view of New Brunswick

View in the central part of Elizabethtown

Southeast view of Jersey City from New York

View in Broad Street, Newark

Crossroad Hamlets ...

View of Crosswicks from the Bordentown Road

Southwest view of Deckertown

Methodist and Presbyterian Churches, Rockaway

View of Lambertville from New Hope, PA

And County Seats ...

View of the courthouse and church, Hackensack

View of the courthouse, Newton

View of the county buildings, Mays Landing

View of the Village of Cape May Courthouse

143

Chapter Seven - Search for The Good Life

United States		New Jersey
US Bill of Rights 1791		
	1793	Congress meets in Trenton
Lewis & Clark 1804 expedition		
	1807	Women lose right to vote in NJ
	1820-	Underground
Missouri 1830	1860	Railroad for
Compromise		escaping slaves active in NJ
	1836	NJ's first free public school founded
	1844	Dorothea Dix reports on state treatment of insane
Mexican War 1846	1846	Slavery abolished,
begins		but freedom limited
1st women's 1848		
rights convention,	1851	Newark opens
Seneca Falls, NY		state's 1st school
Harriet Beecher 1852		for "colored"
Stowe's *Uncle*	1855	1st teacher-train-
Tom's Cabin is		ing schools open in
published		Trenton, Paterson, and Newark

The United States celebrated the fiftieth anniversary of the Declaration of Independence on July 4, 1826 with full acceptance of a social atmosphere where nearly everyone "knew his place," in New Jersey or anywhere else. Most were resigned to remain forever on whatever rung of the social ladder they had reached.

Old-line family prestige dominated social, political, and economic life. At the top were clergymen, lawyers, and large landholders. Next, considerably below in rank, came storekeepers, craftsmen, and farmers, who in turn felt superior to apprentices and day laborers. Apprentices and laborers, for their part, knew they were at least better off than white paupers.

At the bottom, despised if they were recognized at all, were half-breed Indians and African American slaves. Free blacks had a vague status, although many worked as craftsmen or tradesmen.

In such conditions, as New Jersey historian Francis Bazeley Lee wrote: "There were no sudden changes of fortune . . . any alteration (of society) was an evolution rather than a revolution."

Another revolution was just offstage in 1826. Railroads and canals were about to make fortunes for

◇◇◇◇◇◇◇◇◇◇◇◇◇◇◇◇◇◇◇◇◇

Pursuit Of Happiness

New ideas, new dreams, and new hopes swept the nation as the first half of the 19th century raced by. Railroads and canals sped ideas quickly. New telegraph wires ticked out news and messages across hundreds of miles. The newspapers became bigger and better.

Americans became aware of democracy's potential. New England's intellectuals questioned all thought. President Andrew Jackson's stress on the importance of the "common man" lifted the aspirations of classes long accustomed only to changeless drudgery.

Happiness, whose pursuit had been held up as a right in 1776, became a goal — but happiness was a relative matter.

For ever-increasing numbers, happiness was having their working day in a Paterson mill or Newark factory reduced from fourteen hours to a mere twelve. For others, happiness was striving to reduce the

widening gap between the very many poor and the very few rich.

Those at the top worked less as they benefited from the expanding economy. For the first time, America had a genuine leisure class. It sought happiness in new sports and games and even summer vacations (although Puritan consciences still excused absence from work only to benefit health).

The quest for broader human rights picked up pace. Voices were raised against corruption in government, oppressive working conditions, foul prisons, lack of educational opportunities, the shocking mistreatment of the mentally ill, and the terrible abuses of child labor.

America was simmering. New Jersey, well-established as the crossroads of the East, became a testing ground for nearly every social movement — from the easing of misery to the passion for fun and games.

The Fourth of July in the Country, as this mid-19th century sketch was titled, featured fervent oratory (with few listening), firing a cannon, waving flags, or exchanging gossip. The large cask and the overly happy spectators, however, indicated it was mostly a time for a heavy intake of holiday spirits.

their builders. Industry was about to grow amazingly, bringing to one-time blacksmiths what old line families considered "vulgar wealth." Labor imported to build the railroads, dig the canals, and work in factories, added yet another class: the immigrants.

Old notions of "knowing one's place" were about to be tested by reformers, and in the testing New Jersey would begin evolving a system of public education, an enlightened attitude toward prisoners and the insane, and an increased uneasiness with the clearly undemocratic institution of slavery.

Woman's Place Is Clear

Woman's place in society was clear enough by 1826. She was taught "womanly arts" — cooking, housework, sewing, and fancy needlework. Girls received little formal education, although most were taught some reading and writing (but not much spelling or grammar, as letters of the day prove).

Womanly duties were not really arts. They were hard work. Big, heavy meals had to be cooked and served three times a day. Upper class town ladies might enjoy an iron cook stove, but countrywomen still prepared meals on an open fireplace. Either way, they used wood, for coal was simply a curiosity.

What might have been considered some emancipation from the home, for women, began in mill towns such as Paterson. As increased numbers of mechanics came to town to build and run heavy machinery, their wives and daughters were hired to operate looms in the textile mills.

Harriet Martineau, an Englishwoman who visited this country in 1836, wrote seven jobs were open to women — teaching, needlework, running a boardinghouse, working in the textile mills, setting type for

A woman's place was in the home, and she was busy — cooking on an open fireplace or washing and ironing clothes in a crowded room.

a printer, binding books, and household chores.

Those were jobs for wages: "genteel" and "respectable" employment, no matter how long the hours or poor the pay. Most girls expected to become wives and mothers, infinitely preferable in their minds to what was regarded as the lonely life of a spinster.

Wives of well-to-do merchants or lawyers enjoyed some leisure time, particularly if they could hire some household help. They could look forward to evenings of sewing or knitting and possibly a summer stay in a seaside boarding house. They were not freed from work; they labored in their hot, dim kitchens, for work was considered a virtue.

If, as the saying of the day went, "man works from sun to sun, but woman's work is never done," the lot of a child born into a poor factory-town family was even worse.

Hide The Children

Use of child labor began in New Jersey as early as 1794. That year the manager of the Paterson cotton mill wrote to the owners urging "gentlemen and ladies should never on any pretense" be admitted to the mill. His reason:

It will be impossible to keep the children to their work whilst this is suffered, and the Society [owners of the mill] cannot afford to keep up such an establishment as a Show Shop).

By 1820, thirteen Paterson cotton mills employed

Sons and daughters of factory workers knew little of the supposed joys of childhood, for by age eight many of them were at work in dingy, unsanitary rooms, laboring 13 to 14 hours a day, six days a week.

"between sixty and seventy men, fifty or sixty women, and six hundred children." The survey was by a mill owner, not a reformer. No one saw anything wrong with eight-year-old children working at looms.

Paterson workers charged, in 1835, children worked thirteen and one half hours, six days a week. The employers replied haughtily that children really worked only eleven and one half hours a day.

The irony and tragedy of the long hours were underscored when it was proposed free night schools be opened for Paterson's child workers and cotton mill apprentices. One writer declared:

> *A night school would not benefit the mill hands inasmuch as they could not stand it. It is a well-known fact that the children have to rise ere dawn of day, consume their morning meal by candlelight, and trudge to the mill to commence their labor ere the rising of the sun.*
>
> *At noon a very, short time is allowed them for their dinner, and their labor terminates at what is called 8 o'clock at night, but which is really (by the time they have their frames cleaned) much nearer 9 o'clock.*
>
> *They then take supper and immediately retire to bed in order that they may arise early, in the morning — this being the mode of labor pursued in this and other manufacturing towns.*

Sunday was a day of vitally needed rest and relaxation for child workers. Sunday mornings were devoted to church or Sunday school, where children were taught to read and write along with their Bible lessons.

Leisure On Their Minds

Sunday afternoons were open for simple pleasure and amusement. For the poor working class in towns, pleasure had to be free — leisurely walks on the edge of town for young couples, simple games for little boys and girls, and gossip exchanged by wives over a cup of tea in the kitchen or by men gathered on the village green.

Farm people were luckier than their town cousins. Their work hours were not as rigid or as long, and they could receive pleasure from their harvests. In slack hours, men and boys could slip off to fish, to trap fur-bearing animals, or to hunt birds and rabbits in the upland fields.

Farm women and girls enjoyed the frequent "bees," when families for miles around came together to husk

While their fathers and mothers discussed gossip and farm crops in the kitchen, young people took advantage of a "husking bee" as their prime chance to mingle with the opposite sex.

corn, make quilts, cut grain, or raise a barn frame. The "bee" was the best occasion for young people to meet. It was the best place for men to discuss politics and for women to exchange homemaking ideas.

Funerals were a time for infrequent family gatherings, particularly in the isolated farm areas. There was a morbid interest in death, for it always lurked nearby. Seven- or eight-year old girls often stitched mournful samplers to commemorate someone's death.

Funerals were long and tearful. Families and friends journeyed from so far for the service, a huge

Death brought people together in the 19th century, first for the "death watch" at the bedside, and then for long days and nights of mourning before the deceased finally was buried.

meal, washed down with plenty to drink, enabled nearly-forgotten relatives to see one another again. The socializing also eased the pain of the death by proving once again the strength of family solidarity.

Basically, therefore, those without money — overwhelmingly the greatest number of people — depended on one another for enjoyment and leisure-time pleasure. A small, if growing number of others, however, found that if money could not buy happiness, it could help pass away leisure hours.

Whiling Away The Weary Hours

Some of those with excess time and money spent the hours betting on racehorses at Jersey City and Camden until both tracks were forced to close in 1845. Townspeople in both areas complained bitterly about bookmakers, hoodlums, and drunken crowds for so long that finally their pleas were heeded. The idlers found other pleasures.

The vicious "sport" of "bull baiting" had a phenomenal popularity in Jersey City and Paterson between about 1820 and 1840. The anticipation of seeing a bull torn to pieces by dogs filled a 3,000-seat Jersey City amphitheater every Friday. Spectators cheered lustily at "the sport afforded by bulls, bears, buffaloes, and dogs fighting."

Anyone able to spend Fridays watching such action obviously was not a craftsman, mill worker, or farm hand. Fans of bull baiting, local people insisted, came "mostly from New York."

Amusement parks at Camden spawned protests from both sides of the Delaware River. Philadelphia churchmen complained Sunday morning service bells, instead of calling the young to church, alerted them ferryboats were about to leave for New Jersey, where visitors could "engage in every sort of mischief and dissipation."

Philadelphia's pleasure seekers headed in summertime for the crude floating bathhouses anchored just off Camden's shores. Swimmers undressed in unscreened accommodations, shocking more sedate passengers aboard the ferryboats that passed nearby.

After swimming, the happy Philadelphians frolicked in John Johnson's Vauxhall Gardens, Gottleib Zimmerman's Columbia Gardens, and other beer emporia. All-night reveling prompted the Camden villagers to set up their own town government in 1828, with stiff policing power.

Quiet Fun In Staid Hoboken

Hoboken attracted a quieter crowd to its famed Elysian Fields overlooking the Hudson River. Visitors enjoyed the German beer gardens, not for drunken brawling, but for refreshment after strolling through the gardens.

Thousands of New Yorkers rode the ferryboats to Hoboken every Sunday. Elysian Fields, shaded by stately trees, helped make Hoboken "the playground of the East." Major cricket matches between American and English teams attracted large audiences and won considerable publicity for Hoboken.

The Hoboken cricket grounds earned an important place in sports history, on June 19, 1846, when the world's first organized baseball game was played there. Until that day, when the New York Knickerbockers faced the New York Baseball Club, baseball was only a loosely organized game without rules. On June 19, for the first time, basepaths became ninety feet, three strikes were out, and three outs comprised an inning. All of those are still part of the game.

No questioning of the umpire was permitted, since the participants considered themselves gentlemen. Proof of their social status was the fact they could play baseball on Monday and Thursday afternoons, at a time when Paterson's child cotton makers were beginning the second half of their long day.

Hoboken vacationers included Edgar Allan Poe, Martin Van Buren, William Cullen Bryant, and John Jacob Astor. Summer visitors also loved nearby Bayonne, "The Newport of New York," where many of Gotham's wealthiest families acquired large estates

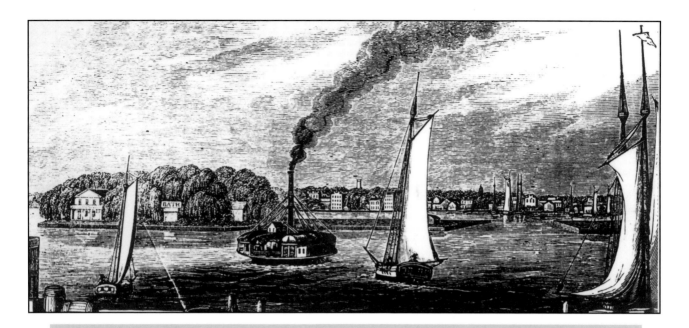

Camden, as seen from Philadelphia in the early 1840s, was emerging from its traditional status as the pleasure resort for Pennsylvanians who wished to escape Philadelphia restrictions. Windmill Island to the left still had bathhouses, but the town's pace was now oriented to railroad and ferry business.

overlooking beautiful (and then sweet-smelling) Newark Bay.

Rest And Relaxation

Wealthy vacationers also discovered New Jersey's mountains and ocean beaches between 1820 and 1850. Schooley's Mountain in Morris County became a widely appreciated "health spa," and Long Branch and Cape May vied strenuously to be the nation's top seaside resort.

The Morristown-Phillipsburg Turnpike, chartered in 1806, pushed the Schooley's Mountain "health" business to prosperity. "The most gay and fashionable company" rode stagecoaches up Schooley's slopes, to stay at the Alpha Hotel, the Heath House, and later, the Dorincourt Hotel.

Schooley's visitors were assured the mountain springs would miraculously cure all aches and pains. Physicians prescribed for wealthy patients the many health-promoting minerals in the springs (including sodium bicarbonate, a good digestive after the heavy hotel meals).

Physicians had praised the healthfulness of Cape May's combination of sun and salt air for many years before Ellis Hughes, owner of the Hotel At-

Organized baseball began on June 19, 1846 at Elysian Fields in Hoboken. Genteel spectators lined the tree-shaded diamond. Note the umpire sat in a chair, well behind the catcher and batter.

Summer vacationers learned to love Cape May between 1800 and 1850, particularly after such luxurious hotels as Congress Hall (above) were built overlooking the wide beach and the rolling ocean. Steamboats regularly plied between Philadelphia and Camden and the Cape, seeking customers with colorful posters. There was no questioning the fun to be found in the surf, whether diving for shells or helping cooperatively fragile females in the waves.

lantic, boldly advertised the Cape's benefits in 1801. Hughes had business (as well as health) on his mind when he inserted his much-quoted advertisement in *The Philadelphia Daily Aurora* on June 30, 1801:

> *The public are respectfully informed that the subscriber has prepared himself for entertaining company who use sea bathing, and he is accommodated with extensive houseroom, with fish, oysters, crabs, and good liquors. Care will be taken of gentlemen's horses.*

A stage left Cooper's Ferry (Camden) every Thursday and made the tortuous trip to Cape May in less than two days. Hughes advertised those who preferred sailing to the resort town "can find vessels almost any time."

Competition From Long Branch

Cape May entertained so many visitors that a sloop started regular service between Philadelphia and the cape town in 1815. Thomas Hughes had just finished his large Congress Hall, much to the disbelief of other villagers. They saw the building as "Tommy's Folly." Hughes responded:

"The day will come when you'll have to cover every square inch here with a silver dollar to get enough land to put up a house!"

Hughes was right. By 1844, the town welcomed "as many as 3,000 in a single summer." Most of them came from Baltimore, Washington, and points south. Visiting southern ladies rocked away the hours on the hotel porches while their husbands gambled in such places as Henry Cleveland's *Blue Pig*. There must have been some daring souls among the generally conservative crowd: the town had to pass a law forbidding nude bathing on the crowded beaches.

Cape May's assertion it was easily the most famous summer resort in the nation was challenged by Long Branch, where summer visitors had boarded since 1788. By 1792, an establishment run by Messrs. Herbert and Chandler advertised "a good stock of liquors and everything necessary for the entertainment of ladies and gentlemen."

Many farmers near the Long Branch waterfront opened their homes to July and August health seekers. Soon hotels rose on the bluff overlooking the rolling Atlantic Ocean. By 1850, Long Branch boasted no place, including Cape May, Saratoga, New York,

Cape May's contention it was America's foremost seaside resort angered Long Branch's boosters. With magnificent hotels lined along their famous bluff and their wide avenue available for late afternoon promenading, Long Branchers could not believe any other resort came even close. The Mansion House (above) was probably the leading hotel along Ocean Drive.

or Newport, Rhode Island, had greater prestige.

Long Branch attracted wide attention for its discreet beach regulations. When a white flag was raised on the beach, only ladies bathed. A red flag permitted only male bathers. On one long-remembered day in 1819, a local prankster hoisted both flags together, "which created some awful squinting and no little confusion."

The Press Becomes A Force

As the nation changed, a variety of newspapers emerged in most parts of the state. The papers were small, poorly printed, and badly edited, but at least they spread information and advertisements.

Editors mainly reported political matters, believing politics was as fascinating to readers as it was to editors. Nineteenth-century journalists, fiercely partisan, made no pretense of presenting both sides of an issue.

The advertising columns told the story of the passing parade in ads for services, fashions, and commodities. Advertisements for the new railroads began to appear in the 1830s and 1840s. Long Branch and Cape May advertised their attractions. Factory man-

agers sought workers and masters sought runaway slaves through newspaper notices.

New Jersey had six weekly newspapers by 1800 and about twenty-five in 1830. The first daily paper, the *Newark Daily Advertiser*, appeared in March 1832. By 1860, the state had fifteen dailies and seventy-five weeklies.

Increasing dispersal of news and information by the newspapers made it possible for many more people to realize not all was right with the world. A public concern was rising about government, education, and the plight of the helpless. Reform was in the wind.

Editors very rarely proposed reform or even change. Letters to the editor, however, often in striking opposition to an editor's viewpoint, gave readers knowledge of social evils. Differing viewpoints, and the fact there *were* differing viewpoints, became clear enough to readers.

Newark proclaimed itself a city when this lithograph was published in 1847. It did have activity along the Passaic River docks, factories were four or five stories tall, and increasing clusters of houses spread outward from the center. Yet, across the river, within sight of the city's tall church spires, cattle grazed in open pasturelands, totally unimpressed by trains speeding to Jersey City.

The Weaknesses of 1776

The deficiencies of New Jersey government, particularly the old State Constitution adopted on July 2, 1776, were aired often in the papers. That hastily drawn constitution did not reflect either sound thought or solid government.

Demands for a new constitution swelled during the 1830s. Conservatives cautioned against complete revision, arguing chaos might result. They were not swayed by arguments that South Carolina, Maryland, Georgia, Vermont, Massachusetts, and Pennsylvania all had radically revised their original constitutions before 1800.

The old New Jersey Constitution had a number of major flaws. The governor's powers were too broad. He could not be impeached, even for the worst misconduct. He was elected by the legislature rather than by the public.

On the other hand, the governor could not appoint his own state aides. His veto could be overridden by a simple majority of the legislature. He had to be re-elected every year, a challenge that permitted legislators to force temperamental governors into line.

A chief weakness was the absence of a judicial branch. The State Senate acted as the state's highest court, and when it met as a kind of "supreme court,"

the governor presided as "chief justice" in everything but name. That enabled those who made the laws to interpret them as well.

Every legislator had to face re-election every year, following the John Adams theory "where annual elections end, tyranny begins." Every office holder became a perpetual candidate, bowing always to whatever political winds flowed across the state.

Worst of all, the original Constitution could not be amended, an incredible oversight on the part of the hasty writers of 1776. The only possible way to reform the state government was to scrap the old document.

Constitution of 1844

Governor William Pennington, a member of the more conservative Whig Party, urged constitutional revision in his 1840 annual message. Three years later, Governor Daniel Haines, a Democrat, endorsed revision. Whigs and Democrats agreed to call a Constitutional Convention.

Sixty delegates opened the convention at Trenton on May 14, 1844. Delegates represented the best in both political parties, and they moved with dignity and purpose. More than six weeks of debate and compromise went by before the new Constitution was ready on June 28.

152

Political leaders, industrialists, farmers, and politicians of every shade of opinion supported the new document. It was approved overwhelmingly on August 13 — by 20,276 to 3,526.

Fewer than 24,000 people voted in the election, however, as clear evidence that New Jersey's voting restrictions kept most people from casting ballots. The new Constitution's chief virtue was the fact it permitted nearly every male to vote. Excluded were paupers, idiots, the insane, criminals, African Americans, and women, all regarded as equally untrustworthy in 1844.

Any white male United States citizen over twenty-one could vote, provided he had lived in New Jersey for one year and had been a resident of any one county for five months. There were no property qualifications; even the ordinary poor (but not the paupers) could vote. This was an advanced kind of democracy, for 1844.

Strengths And Defects

The new Constitution divided government into executive, judicial, and legislative branches. The courts at last were independent, although the governor's power to appoint judges gave him considerable influence in the judiciary.

Governors also were elected, for the first time, directly by the people. A governor would serve for three years, but that improvement was offset by the fact a governor, no matter how worthy, could not succeed himself. He could run for election again after a three-year wait.

Fundamental liberties were ensured for most people by the state Bill of Rights. Basic was the political philosophy "all political power is inherent in the people." Other freedoms included freedom of religion, press, and speech, and fair treatment in the courts. Women, African Americans, and a wide group of other disadvantaged peoples were not included, but for its time the Bill of Rights was progressive.

Passing years would reveal glaring defects in the Constitution. The governor lacked power, for a simple legislative majority still could override his vetoes. Amending the Constitution required difficult and lengthy procedures. Particularly limiting was the provision "no amendment or amendments shall be submitted to the people by the Legislature oftener than once in five years."

The new Constitution proved an unflagging spirit was abroad in the state. Determined people were at work elsewhere, seeking to improve treatment of the weak, the underprivileged, and the exploited.

To Punish And To Reform

Prisons concerned many. The harsh, Puritanical attitudes toward criminals offended those interested in establishing justice fit for a nation two centuries old. Harsh sentences were meted out to a wide variety of people, whose offenses often were as slight as not paying bills because they could not find work.

The prisons to which offenders were sentenced were places of horror. County jails were especially abominable. Murderers, thieves, the insane, and debtors — some whose only crime was being poor — were

all cast into dungeons in courthouse basements. They were herded together like so many animals, regardless of sex, age, the nature of the alleged crime, or proof they had committed a crime.

Humane treatment of prisoners was regarded as a weakness. When New Jersey's first state prison opened in 1799, the motto over the front door told the story:

"Labor, Silence, Penitence … That Those Who Are Feared for Their Crimes May Learn to Fear the Laws and be Useful."

Wardens and guards at the state prison believed in unrelenting punishment. Everyone worked at hard labor. Meals were "corn meal mush and molasses for breakfast and the same for supper; at dinner, soup or salt herring and bread." Water was the only beverage. Silence ruled, except for the sounds of work.

Thoughtful minds sought something better. Burlington County hired Robert Mills, a distinguished Philadelphia architect, to design its new Mt. Holly jail in 1810. His drawings for what he considered an ideal jail were accompanied by a brief of compassion toward those imprisoned.

Mills urged "infants in crime" not be associated with "veterans in wickedness." New prisoners would be bathed and fumigated on admittance. All prisoners would get the same cleansing and fumigating periodically.

Mill's plans for a new "Debtors Jail and Workhouse" were accepted, along with his "advanced" ideas. He created the Burlington prison motto: "Justice Which While It Punishes, Would Endeavor to Reform the Offender."

A "Debtors Jail" in Burlington County was not surprising; people could be jailed merely for owing money. New Jersey did not abolish imprisonment for debt until March 9, 1842. It was much the same in other states; Maine was the first to abolish debtor imprisonment in 1835.

"Hatching Ground For New Crimes"

Increasing concern about prisons forced the New Jersey legislature to investigate the foul state prison in 1829. A study team quickly concluded the place was little more than a "hatching ground for new crimes."

The study team found "gambling, fighting, and other mischief" within the prison. Witnesses told of savage riots within the walls and of discharged prisoners climbing back over the walls, to rob their former guards or to release prisoners. The reason for the evils, the commission wrote, was prisoners are removed "as far as possible from the control of the officers."

John Haviland, a pioneer prison planner, was asked to design a new state prison. His new jail featured light and fresh air. It also centered on Haviland's theory violators could be best aided by solitary confinement.

Every prisoner, according to Haviland, would improve if he were kept always in his cell — for eating, sleeping, working, exercising, and receiving "moral instruction." If a prisoner had to be moved, a hood was placed over his head so other prisoners would not know him or talk with him.

Haviland's system failed. Dr. James B. Coleman, the prison physician, wrote in 1840 the effect on the prisoner was "a diminished force on his organs generally." Dr. Coleman said an inmate's brain could be so seriously affected "when absolute derangement does not take place, its powers are considerably weakened."

Dr. Coleman's attack on the system made no difference; the state could not afford to build another prison. In any case, rising crime rates made solitary confinement unworkable because so many prisoners were being shoved through the iron gates at Trenton the principle of solitary confinement soon became forgotten in the need to find room.

"Inducements For A Horse Thief"

Prison welfare was just one of many concerns. There were other mistreated humans. Surprisingly, reform came most slowly in educating the young. Thus, in 1848, Thomas C. Rogers, a Superintendent of Waterford schools in Camden County could declare:

> *The state penitentiary presents more inducements for a horse thief to seek his subsistence and comfort in its rooms than any common school or academy — founded and supported by the state — offers an aspiring youth a thirst for knowledge.*

New Jersey's backwardness in public education was typical of East Coast practices into the early nineteenth century. It was believed education beyond family training was mainly a church responsibility, a holdover from colonial days.

The church schools gradually became private academies intended to educate the children of the privileged. Thomas Gordon's *Gazetteer* of 1834 listed more than forty such small private academies scat-

These grim gray walls rising over the Delaware and Raritan Canal in Trenton, in 1840, were among the show-places in the state capital. Built in the 1830s to replace an old prison, the prison featured solitary confinement as a "sure way" to make prisoners repent on their crimes. Within less than ten years after the prison was completed, a doctor warned solitary confinement led to a mental instability. By the time this woodcut was made in 1842, rising crime rates sent so many prisoners to Trenton solitary confinement became forgotten in the need for space to house criminals.

The little brick building, above, on Brainerd Street in Mount Holly dates to 1759. It is believed to be New Jersey's oldest school still standing on the original site. Twenty-one men of varied religions including Quakers and Episcopalians bought shares to buy land and build the school. It operated as a paying school until 1815. The Female Benevolent Society operated it for 55 years for those who could not afford to pay.

Mount Holly's boys and girls fared well, but most children of the early 19th century still were taught in crude surroundings, by instructors hired for cheapness rather than ability.

tered throughout the state.

Academies took care of children whose parents had wealth or community prestige. Also assured of some education by state law were "minor slaves, apprentices, and pauper children." Between those destitute and the prosperous were most New Jersey children. Legislators, themselves usually at least modestly well off, ignored the in-betweens.

The Rich Get Richer

The legislature created a state fund of $16,000 in 1816 for the "support of free schools." That small sum was approved despite the powerful opposition of private and church-supported schools. Only obvious need forced the legislature to take its first faltering step toward supporting free education.

State funds were distributed on the basis of state taxes paid by counties. In turn, counties gave funds to towns in proportion to the county taxes paid. Since wealthy areas paid the most taxes, wealthy areas naturally received the most money back. The rich got richer.

Support for free education came from an unexpected source, in 1828, when Professor John Maclean of the College of New Jersey in Princeton called for a "common school" system. His proposal embraced a combination of state aid, local taxes, and a small tuition charge.

A public meeting of "friends of education" in Trenton reported, in 1828, 12,000 New Jersey children between ages five and fifteen were not receiving any kind of schooling.

Children in school were not much better off, the "friends" believed. They lashed out at schoolmasters who were "subject to no inspections or supervision" and school districts that hired teachers with little regard for training or culture. "Moral character" was considered the ultimate credential for a schoolteacher.

The legislature passed the first comprehensive New Jersey school law in 1829, providing education be supported by state funds matched by local money. State subsidies were pitifully small, and in 1830 and 1831 the legislature let private schools share in the fund.

Clara Barton

"Tax Yourselves ... For The Schools"

Governor Pennington bowed to rising pressures. In his annual message of January 1838, he called for "a thorough revision of our common school system." A month later, a distinguished group, including both church leaders and heads of private schools, declared in an "address to the people:"

> *Tax yourselves for the support of the public schools and you will never be in danger of taxation from a foreign power. You will need less taxation for the support of pauperism and the punishment of crime.*
>
> *Look to your schoolhouses. See that they are convenient of access, that they are comfortable; that they are neat and tasteful. Look to the teachers. See that they are taught themselves and apt to teach men that fear God and love their country. See that they are well accommodated, well treated, and well remunerated.*

Bright spots began to appear on the New Jersey education picture. Newark established the state's first free public schools in 1836. Two years later, it opened the state's first public high school (now Barringer High School). Paterson and Jersey City eliminated all school fees by 1848. Still, most New Jersey schools charged tuition until 1871, when a full system of free schools finally was established.

Free Schools, Little Education

Newark led the way in education. Its leadership was largely due to the determined effort of one John Whitehead, who was appointed to the city's school committee in 1845.

Whitehead visited the city schools. He found classes meeting in musty, candle-lit basements or gathered in rooms where the walls were "green with mould." Some classrooms were so crowded children sat on stairways or on the teacher's platform. Some classes were meeting in the open air and were taught by students rather than qualified teachers.

Whitehead approached the City Council, only to be brushed aside by warnings the city needed "an additional supply of water and more policemen" before it could think of improved schools.

Outraged, Whitehead hired a horse-drawn car and took the councilmen on a tour. They saw for the first time the sad condition of the schools. They watched teachers trying to cope with 100 or more children of all ages. The tour shocked the council into action. Immediately after, it unanimously agreed to improve public education.

Three new Newark schools were built in 1846, each costing $4,000. Three more were built in 1851, when a "colored school" (a most progressive move) also was started in the basement of the African Presbyterian Church. By 1854, more than half of Newark's children were in public schools.

"The Cullings Of New England"

Statewide, the situation was so bad that fewer than half of all children between five and sixteen were in schools. Dr. T. F. King, a medical doctor who became the first State Superintendent of Schools in 1846, wrote of school buildings in 1848:

> A merciful man, being merciful to his beast, would not winter his horses in places appropriated at present for district schoolhouses.
>
> Let him travel over our state, in what direction he will, and if he sees a building, some sixteen feet by twenty, with the clapboards off in some places, in others hanging by a single nail, the roof open, the door with one hinge and that a leather one, the windows wanting glass, but abounding in old hats, caps and cloaks, or copy books, he may with tolerable certainty set it down for a country schoolhouse.

If the buildings were bad, teachers were worse. A Monmouth County educator protested in 1850:

> We have to depend on the cullings of New England for teachers rather than educating our own sons and daughters.

Teachers themselves, seeking self-improvement, began meeting for mutual study. About fifty teachers from eight counties met in New Brunswick in 1853 to organize the State Teachers Association, the forerunner of today's New Jersey Education Association.

The Teachers Go To School

The legislature voted $10,000 in 1855 to establish a state normal school ("normal" coming from the French école normale) to prepare teachers for the elementary grades. The New Jersey normal school could be located in any town willing to donate a "suitable location and buildings without expense to the state."

New Brunswick, Trenton, Beverly, Orange, Princeton, Pennington, and other towns competed for the site. The legislature accepted Trenton's offer of free land plus $14,000 to build the normal school. Trenton's school for teachers opened on October 1, 1855, three weeks before textbooks arrived.

Meanwhile, principals in Newark and Paterson opened their own schools, requiring teachers to attend four-hour Saturday morning classes from September to July. Completion of 720 hours of classes qualified teachers for a certificate. They might then aspire to a position such as that of Isaiah Peck, principal of Newark High School. As the state's highest paid teacher in 1855, he received $19.74 a week.

Newark's expenditures for its schools angered some local taxpayers. Thirty-one of them petitioned in 1856 for elimination of the high school because it was "aristocratic." The petition was answered by a letter in the *Newark Daily Advertiser* from someone who signed himself "Father."

Declaring students in the high school were entering trades and becoming clerks and bookkeepers, steps upward on the work and social scale, "Father" concluded:

> The children of the artisan and the laborer share the priceless advantages here afforded those of the cultivated and wealthy; and by the true process of upward levelling stand on the same republican equality.

The Insane And The Odd

As might be expected, no group suffered more than the insane, the odd, the senile, and the mentally disturbed. Society saw only one way to handle these sad people: put them behind bars.

Spurred on by the Medical Society of New Jersey, the legislature, in 1839, appointed a commission to investigate treatment of the mentally ill. The commission found 338 "lunatics" and 538 "idiots" confined to poorhouses or jails, including a twenty-eight-year-old woman who had been in chains in the Gloucester County jail since she was sixteen.

Stressing insanity could be cured in some cases — as had been proved sixty years before in France — the commission urged a modern asylum be built in New Jersey. The economy-minded legislature tabled the report.

That opened the way for Dorothea Dix of Massachusetts. Miss Dix's reputation for intensive research and tart reporting of social evils had earned her the hatred of New England legislators. She arrived in New Jersey in 1843 to study the state's jails and poorhouses, completely indifferent to the fact many politically powerful people despised her.

Miss Dix personally visited nearly every New Jersey place where people were housed because of criminality, poverty, mental illness, or all three. Although hardened by her studies in Massachusetts and Rhode Island, Miss Dix was sickened by the shocking conditions she found in New Jersey.

Chains, Beatings, Nakedness

No area escaped the scathing denunciation of Miss Dix. She told of a Salem County jail without beds and Salem keepers who beat insane inmates with blocks of wood. Burlington County kept its insane in "dreary confined cells, pervaded with foul air." Monmouth had two small cells complete with chains and a straw bed.

Miss Dix found a demented Middlesex County man chained "in a sort of a box" next to a cell where a madman stood naked except for a laced straitjacket. Passaic County's accommodations were "loathsome." Morris County kept its inmates in quarters that were "dark, damp, unfurnished, unwarmed, and unventilated."

Miss Dix finished her tour of the state's institutions in late 1843. She presented her report of New Jersey's shame to the legislature in January 1844, with the recommendation that $150,000 be spent for a new asylum.

The legislators, who considered $16,000 or $20,000 for public education princely sums, were stunned. The first action on the blistering report was a jovial resolution to vote $1,000 "to carry Miss Dix across the Delaware and get her out of the state." She was not amused.

The Massachusetts crusader became a one-woman lobby. She pleaded, argued, berated, and prayed with and for the legislators — and she won. In April 1844, the legislators accompanied her on a triumphant tour of 100 green acres in Ewing Township north of Trenton, where Miss Dix decided the new mental hospital should be built.

Work began on a large sandstone building at Ewing Township, and the first patients were transferred into this, the nation's most modern asylum, in 1848. Miss Dix called the building "my first child." Much later, she moved into an apartment in the asylum where she lived until her death in 1887.

Flaming with determination that all who were sick, old, weak, or deranged must receive humane treatment, Dorothea Dix of Massachusetts swept through New Jersey in 1843 to survey the state's jails, almshouses, and mental asylums. Her appalling report was met at first with indifference, but Miss Dix pressured legislators into voting in, April 1844, for a new mental hospital near Trenton. The first patients were transferred, in 1848, into the new building (below) considered to be the finest mental institution in America at the time.

When Does A Slave Become Free?

Most reformers acknowledged eventually the worst stigma facing the nation was slavery in a "land of the free." After the invention of the cotton gin in 1792 fastened slavery on the South, controversy raged across the nation.

New Jerseyans took a look at African American families in their midst. Some took comfort in the fact increasing numbers of masters had freed slaves, largely because it was expensive to maintain slaves in a state that was taking on an industrial character. All African Americans, slave or free, were expected to "keep their place," as much out of sight as possible.

Antislavery advocates pushed an act through the New Jersey legislature on February 18, 1804 for "the Gradual Abolition of Slavery." Female slaves remained servants bound to their masters for twenty-one years; males were bound until age twenty-five. Every child born of a slave was to be free, but remained a servant of the mother's owner until the mother was twenty-five. If this was abolition, African Americans sensed no difference in their lot.

An 1846 state law finally abolished slavery in New Jersey by making all slaves apprentices. Children born of apprentices were free — yet had to be bound out for service by the local overseer of the poor after reaching six years of age. This, too, was freedom of the most grudging sort.

Some free African Americans made remarkable progress within the limits of the severe obstacles placed in their paths. When Benjamin Thompson Pierson published Newark's first directory in 1835, he found 112 adult African Americans (identified as "coloured" or "col'd"). About twenty owned their homes.

The 1835 Newark directory showed the town's African American population included a teacher, a barber, two blacksmiths, and three carpenters. One, John O'Fake, owned a celebrated oyster and ale house on the town's main street.

Send Them Back To Africa

African Americans chafed under a white rule that even included segregation in the churches, where African Americans were forced to sit in slave balconies. African American leaders resented the fact they were permitted, not invited, to worship at services.

James Still

William Still

James and William Still, born deep in the Pine Barrens of Burlington County, attended schools only on rainy days and faced such prejudice that years later William recalled praying for sunshine to keep him out of school.

Both overcame powerful youthful handicaps — James to become the noted "Black Doctor of the Pines" and William to become the foremost historian of the mysterious Underground Railroad by which slaves escaped to freedom in the North.

James was born in 1812. He had no formal schooling after age eight. Self-taught, he never claimed to be a medical doctor, but he cured sick neighbors. In time, hundreds of people — black and white — were cured by his home-mixed medicines and herbs.

William was the last of twenty-one children in the Still family. Vividly recalling stories of his mother's escape from slavery in Maryland, he vowed to help his people. He found that chance in Philadelphia as clerk of the Pennsylvania Anti-Slavery Society, where his home became a stop on the Underground Railroad. His voluminous, secret records of the "railroad" were published in 1872.

160

Newark's first formal African American church was organized in 1822. Then, in 1831, a group of African American worshipers withdrew from Newark's Old First Church, established when Newark was founded in 1666. Theodore Frelinghuysen aided them in building their own church.

Frelinghuysen undoubtedly was sincere in extending help to African American citizens, but he totally misunderstood their desires and character. Thus, in 1826, when he helped found the American Colonization Society, he believed the Society's aim to resettle African Americans in Africa would be met with enthusiasm.

The "send them back to Africa move" failed completely. Few of this country's African Americans, free or slave, knew as much about Africa as did Frelinghuysen and his earnest followers, who proclaimed themselves "firm and ardent friends of this unhappy race." Africa, to most African Americans, was an unknown land a century or two in their vague family pasts.

Peter Johnson and Henry Drayton, both African American Newarkers, countered by organizing the Antislavery Society in 1834 to protest both slavery and the treatment of freed slaves. They were joined by the Reverend Samuel Cornish, a Newark African American who became known throughout the North for his strong opposition to African colonization.

Only one white church in Newark took a strong position against slavery. That was the Free Presbyterian Church, founded in 1851 in opposition to Protestant churches that collected pew rents. The Free Presbyterians from the start were opposed to slavery, a stand that alienated them from other congregations.

Railroad To The North Star

African Americans already settled within New Jersey had some measure of security. Far less safe here were the thousands of slaves fleeing from bondage on Southern plantations. New Jersey, alone among Northern states, supported the Fugitive Slave Act and offered no opposition when slaves were seized here and carried back to the South. New Jersey lawmen were pledged to arrest and turn fugitives over to their slave hunters.

However, a band of white abolitionists worked secretly and effectively to aid escaping slaves. These were the operators of the mysterious "Underground Railroad," formed before the Civil War to whisk runaway African Americans northward to freedom. The

When Northern whites thought of slavery at all, in the 1850s, they remembered Uncle Tom, the meek hero of Harriet Beecher Stowe's book, *Uncle Tom's Cabin*. The book became a stage play, usually advertised with the drawing shown above. Uncle Tom, for all his woes, escaped the much harsher fate of escaped slaves: the professional hunters who returned slaves to the South. The woodcut below, showing a mother and child being beaten and captured, helped stir Northern sentiment against the Fugitive Slave Act.

"railroad" had no tracks, timetables, or records, but it did have "stations" and "conductors" who routed "bundles" across New Jersey.

Hundreds of former slaves first glimpsed hope and freedom along the lower Delaware River. They looked for yellow and blue signal lights that flickered on the New Jersey side of the river in all kinds of weather. Following the lights, runaways would be met by Quaker sympathizers who kept them until a "shipment" left for the North.

The routes to freedom varied. When fugitive hunters concentrated on the Raritan River landings at New Brunswick, the route circled inland to Jersey City. If Jersey City teemed with Southern agents, the "railroad" sped its passengers through the hills of Morris and Passaic counties, onward to New England or Canada.

Those who aided the slaves, by talk or by deed, were committed to Abraham Lincoln's principle that a nation could not "exist half slave, half free." They probably sensed, too, that soon North and South must come to war over the issue.

The years of controversy over slavery slid away through the 1850s, dwindling down to weeks, and then to days in 1861. The ugliest of conflicts — a civil war — faced America as spring came to the land in 1861.

When war exploded, New Jersey would be torn apart by conflicting interests. Industrialists with large markets in the South opposed war. Abolitionists approved it. Between lay the uncommitted, the great majority.

Choices had to be made: slavery or freedom? Union or division?

Route Of The North Star

The "Underground Railroad" had no locomotives, no cars, no timetables, no tickets — and above all, no public relations department. It operated dangerously, for it existed to break the law by aiding escaped Southern slaves find their way to freedom.

Fleeing slaves used the "railroad" to cross New Jersey between 1820 and the start of the Civil War. Hundreds, perhaps thousands, of runaways were hastened along the road, following the North Star to a new life.

Slaves rode wagons or walked along as many as a dozen routes through New Jersey. If slave chasers gathered at bridges at New Brunswick or Trenton or at the Camden & Amboy ferry terminal in Camden, the railroad swiftly set up alternate escape routes.

Canada became the main goal of most escaped slaves. Runaways streamed northward through Indiana, Ohio, Pennsylvania, New Jersey, and New York. William Still's book The Underground Rail Road *tells the story best.*

Even Still's massive accounting depends largely on word-of-mouth stories that often are shadowy, vague, and possibly inaccurate. No one operating the railroad wished to be caught with written records, for the work was criminal as well as humane.

The most famous "agent" on the route was Harriet Tubman, a short, stout former slave. Mrs. Tubman ventured nineteen times into Delaware and Maryland to lead some 300 slaves to liberty. She worked as a servant in Cape May hotels to earn money for her trips south.

Many Quakers in southern New Jersey helped the escaping slaves. One was Miss Abigail Goodwin of Salem, shown at bottom of opposite page. She gave so much to the movement that she often was more ragged than the runaways who knocked on her door.

The fleeing slaves used any kind of transportation — riding horseback, walking for hundreds of miles, rowing across the broad Delaware River, or boldly taking the ferry with white friends. One of the most famous escapees was nailed in a box and shipped North on a real freight train.

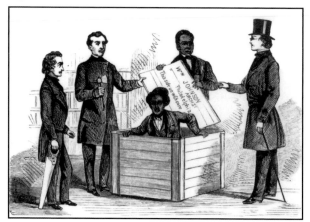

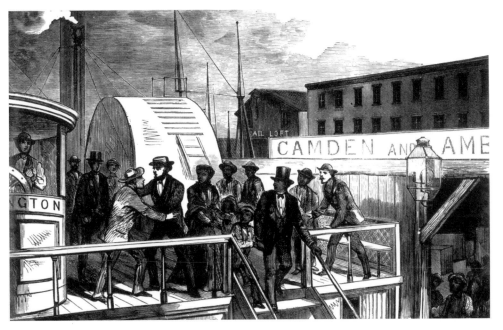

Chapter Eight - Shades of Blue And Gray

United States		New Jersey	
War fever rises	1859	1859	NJ opposes war
Lincoln elected	1860	1860	NJ votes against Lincoln
South bombards Fort Sumter	1861	1861	NJ first state to meet military obligation
		1861	Arrest of Copperhead James Wall creates national stir
Battle of Antietam	1862	1862	Gen. Philip Kearny molds NJ forces; killed in Virginia
Emancipation Proclamation	1863	1863	Democratic legislature passes peace resolution
Union victories at Vicksburg & Gettysburg	1863	1863	NJ and other states violently oppose draft
Sherman's march to Atlanta	1864	1864	Gen. Judson Kilpatrick leads Sherman's assault
Lincoln re-elected	1864	1864	NJ electoral votes go to McClellan
South surrenders to General Grant	1865	1865	Sorrowing crowds watch Lincoln's funeral train

The threat of Civil War distressed many New Jerseyans, and not for fear of bloodshed. Industrialists faced the loss of prime Southern markets. Cape May's hotels catered mainly to Southerners. The College of New Jersey in Princeton was in a quandary, for as many as half its students came from below the Mason-Dixon line.

Southern markets were not to be dismissed lightly. Newark, Trenton, Paterson, and other industrial cities looked southward for much of their annual sales. Large ships sailed regularly for the South, their holds filled with New Jersey products — cheap shoes or clothing for the slaves, and handsome carriages, fine leather saddles, and glittering gold jewelry for the masters.

Bolstering the economic opposition to war was the fact that New Jersey long had been a strong "states' rights" advocate, as had been proved at the Constitutional Convention in 1787. Politicians remembered that, and most argued that slavery was the sole business of Southern states, to be worked out in their fashion and in their time.

The national anti-war sentiments of the Democratic Party were reflected in much of New Jersey,

◇◇◇◇◇◇◇◇◇◇◇◇◇◇◇◇◇◇◇◇◇◇

Dawn Of Civil War

War clouds had been gathering across America for more than forty years. The attempts at compromise between North and South, most notably in 1820 and 1850, had merely postponed the conflict that both areas knew was inevitable unless slavery could be abolished.

Many on both sides of the Mason-Dixon Line argued that slavery was a matter of "states' rights," although slaves were sold and transported across state lines like cattle. Some simplified the issue as industrial North against agricultural South, avoiding the fact that agriculture in the South meant one thing: cotton — requiring more and more slaves.

Just before dawn on April 12, 1861, cannonballs aimed by secession-minded South Carolina gunners tore into the stone walls of Fort Sumter in Charleston harbor. Two days later, defenders of the fort pulled down the United States flag and filed out of the battered stronghold. The Civil War had begun.

New Jersey, perhaps more than any other state, reflected the vital choice that had to be made: should the Union be preserved without slavery, or should slave-holding states be permitted to secede peacefully?

This state seethed with Southern sympathizers on April 12. Despite the antiwar feelings, New Jersey sent into battle considerably more than the numbers of troops demanded by the government.

Off to war went the soldiers, to kill or be killed at places so obscure they didn't even appear in school geography books: Bull Run, Antietam, Sharpsburg, Shiloh, Lookout Mountain, The Wilderness, and scores of other places whose lasting fame would be written in blood.

The issue had been joined: could a nation live half-free, half-slave?

The newly-formed Republican Party hoped that the presence of Freehold lawyer William L. Dayton might solidify New Jersey behind the first national Republican quest for the White House. This 1856 campaign poster showed a bold, clear-eyed John C. Fremont, the Californian whose exploits in conquering the Rocky Mountains and the West were already close to legendary. Balancing the ticket in traditional style had to be a somber, quite conservative Easterner. Together, voters were assured, they would be "The Champions of Freedom." Dayton could not swing the New Jersey electorate to the Republicans; this state instead voted heavily for Democrat James Buchanan.

JNº C. FREMONT.   Wᵐ L. DAYTON.
THE CHAMPIONS OF FREEDOM.

particularly in Essex and Bergen counties. Democrats hated the newly-formed Republican Party, whose leanings against slavery quickly attracted the support of Abolitionists. New Jersey's first Republicans dared not run counter to strong Southern sympathizers. So they campaigned simply as "Opposition" candidates (opposition to the Democrats). Under that vague banner, they hoped to enroll a variety of disgruntled foes of the Democratic Party.

Republicans On The Rise

Republican strength in New Jersey was robust enough by 1856 to make William L. Dayton, a Freehold lawyer, the Vice-Presidential candidate on the national party ticket headed by John C. Fremont of California. Among the Vice-Presidential hopefuls cast aside for Dayton was a gangling young Illinois lawyer named Abraham Lincoln.

Even with a native son Dayton on the Opposition Presidential ticket, New Jersey overwhelmingly supported Democrat James Buchanan. However, on the same ballot, William A. Newell of Allentown was elected as the state's first Republican (or Opposition) governor. New Jersey voters were not against Republicans; they were simply for Buchanan.

Three years later, the Republicans elected Charles S. Olden as governor. Olden, only mildly anti-slavery,

was hopeful that war with the South could be avoided.

National attention focused on a New Jersey Republican, in February 1860, when Congressman William Pennington of Newark was chosen as Speaker of the House of Representatives. The choice was memorable. Wrangling over the selection of a Speaker stalled Congress for fifty-nine days until Pennington was confirmed.

Violence flared in Washington early in 1860 as North and South locked in a bitter conflict over the vital choice of the Speaker of the House of Representatives. Several Congressmen struck one another on the floor of the House during the angry debate, as lampooned in a *Harper's Weekly* cartoon. Republican William Pennington of Newark, right, became a compromise choice after fifty-nine days of acrimonious debate.

Pennington was not even considered in the first stages of the debate. The chasm between North and South widened in the long days of fruitless argument, between December 5, 1859 and February 1, 1860, when Pennington finally was chosen as a compromise.

Congressmen from both sides of the house aisle rose to applaud the choice of the mild, middle-of-the-road Pennington, who sought to soothe tempers by declaring that he had "a natural heart, embracing all parts of our blessed Union."

A few adamant Southerners refused to believe that the New Jersey congressman could lead them impartially. When the vote for Pennington was assured, Representative Hickman of Tennessee rose to shout in angry disbelief: "We've elected a Black Republican!"

"Wide Awakes" and "Hickory Men"

Pennington represented one of the last prospects for bringing North and South together. Then, in the summer of 1860, Abraham Lincoln's nomination for President threw the issue before voters, who had to decide, as Lincoln said, whether the nation could exist with slavery in half its territory.

Every city, every village, every crossroad hamlet, seethed with excitement as the showdown campaign proceeded. The Democrats themselves were so sharply divided about the North-South issue that they put three separate Presidential Democratic nominees on the 1860 ballot: Stephen A. Douglas, John Breckinridge, and John Bell.

Streets and community halls echoed nightly to the sounds of the campaign. Republican "Wide Awakes" and Democratic "Hickory Men" marched under flaming torches and bright banners on the way to hear speeches that often were closer to slander than to truth.

Newspaper editors joined the battle. Papers such as the Newark *Journal,* the Trenton *Daily True American,* the Mount Holly *Herald,* and the Sussex County *New Jersey Herald* assailed Lincoln and all Republican candidates. The Newark *Mercury,* New Brunswick *Fredonian,* and the Toms River *Ocean Emblem* typified the staunchly pro-Republican papers.

Edward N. Fuller, Newark *Journal* editor, arguing editorially that slavery was a matter of "states' rights," expressed astonishment that anyone would wish to upset Newark's booming trade with the South. One unsigned letter in the *Journal* quite likely written by Fuller himself declared:

If Lincoln is elected, many of our journeymen will be compelled to face the rigors of winter and meet the answer everywhere: NO WORK! NO WORK!

Lincoln Loses New Jersey

In this charged atmosphere, the Republicans cautiously ran Lincoln under the Opposition label. The Democrats could not unite under any banner. Many liked Stephen Douglas — the "Little Giant" who stood up to "Big Abe" in the well-known Lincoln-Douglas debates. Others favored John C. Breckinridge for his outright southern sympathies.

In New Jersey, the three Democratic tickets drew a combined total of 62,800 votes; Lincoln received 58,000. The three-way split, however, gave Lincoln four of the state's seven electoral votes. Lincoln's strength lay mainly in southern New Jersey, as shown by the ten counties that he carried — Passaic, Morris, Mercer, Ocean, Burlington, Salem, Gloucester, Atlantic, Cumberland, and Cape May.

Lincoln's mediocre showing in New Jersey meant disaster for many Republican candidates, especially Speaker of the House Pennington. The Newark *Mercury* blamed Pennington's loss on "unprincipled men engaged in the Southern trade." The editor fumed:

> *If they had been slaves themselves, and every morning had been lashed into humility, they could not have worked more heartily to carry out the wishes of their Southern masters.*

Lincoln's New Jersey failure was not unusual; he won only about forty percent of all votes cast nationwide. But the Republicans won enough electoral votes — all from the North — to make him President. The nation was close to war.

"Southern Cause Our Cause"

South Carolina announced, on December 20, 1860, that it had seceded from the Union. Powerful New Jersey editorial and political voices supported the South Carolina move. Leading the way, as usual, was the Newark *Journal*.

Three days after the dramatic South Carolina withdrawal, a *Journal* headline declared, "SOUTHERN CAUSE OUR CAUSE." Editor Fuller thanked the seceding state for saving America from "a worse calamity than disunion abolitionism!"

Fuller's plea that New Jersey join the South was reinforced by others. Commodore Robert F. Stockton

The "Wide Awakes," pro-Lincoln all the way, lit up city streets in flamboyant torchlight parades matched by Democrats who loudly proclaimed themselves to be "Hickory Men."

of Princeton, descended from a signer of the Declaration of Independence and a distinguished naval hero in his own right, told a convention at Trenton in December that New Jersey should "supplicate the North to yield."

Judge David Naar of Trenton predicted that without the South, "New York will be no more than a fishing village and New Jersey but little better." Ex-Governor Rodman Price said that if New Jersey had a choice "she should go with the South from every wise, prudential, and patriotic reason."

Governor Olden urged caution in his annual message of January 1861: "The troubles connected with slavery have in great measure been brought on by a few persons of extreme views in both the North and South." He suggested a peace conference to discuss the issue.

The Last Bid For Peace

Olden led a nine-man New Jersey delegation to a peace conference in Washington, DC on February 4. It was called to discuss a proposal by Kentucky Senator John F. Crittenden that the northern limit of slavery be extended from the southern Missouri boundary to the Pacific Ocean. Crittenden's plan also called for non-interference with slavery in any state where it existed.

The peace conference was probably the last chance to avoid war. New Jersey's delegates strongly favored negotiating with the Confederate states. Commodore Stockton told the conference on February 19: "Peace we must have. The Union can only be preserved by peace."

Frederick T. Frelinghuysen, a Republican who later became an important figure in state government, recognized that the conference was handling a two-edged sword. He pleaded with the South to appreciate what his state was doing:

"New Jersey has voted in this convention against interference with slavery in the territory, present or future, and she is the only Northern State that has cast her vote in favor of your demand."

The peace conference however, had no chance. It disbanded in disagreement, with the New Jersey delegation supporting the Southern bloc. By then, eight states had established the Confederate States of America.

Lincoln Wins New Jersey Hearts

Abraham Lincoln knew that New Jersey was the only Northern state that voted against him. He knew that "peace Democrats" were active in the state and that many editors opposed his solemn vow to keep the Union together whatever the cost. Despite all this, Lincoln deliberately included New Jersey on his journey from Springfield, Illinois to the inauguration.

Lincoln rode the ferry from New York City to Jersey City on February 21. More than 25,000 jubilant people jammed the Jersey City station to greet him. Newark gave Lincoln a reception that the President-elect said exceeded anything he had seen since leaving Springfield.

Every town along the route from Jersey City to Trenton hailed the bearded President-to-be. Cannons boomed. Crowds applauded Lincoln's every word. College students gave him a campus salute as the train went through Princeton. Trenton's streets overflowed with the curious hoping to see the towering sad-faced man as he paused in the capital to address a hostile New Jersey legislature.

The Democratic-controlled Assembly waited for the next President by introducing a series of disagreeable, almost childish resolutions concerning Lincoln's lack of good looks and his ungainly height. The resolutions were tabled, but the atmosphere was decidedly unfriendly when Lincoln appeared.

The new Chief Executive spoke briefly, expressing his hope that "this Union, the Constitution, and the liberties of the people shall he perpetuated." He declared that he had "no malice toward any section." At this, the sullen audience turned respectful. Then Lincoln said:

"The man does not live who is more devoted to

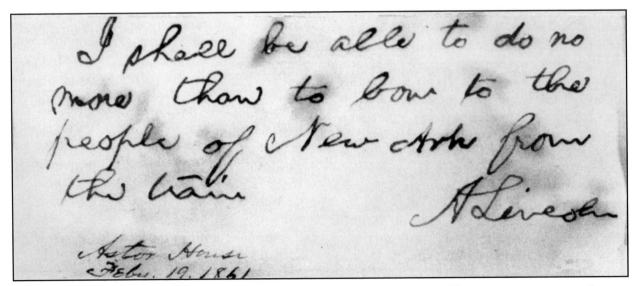

This precious little slip of paper, now owned by The New Jersey Historical Society, was written in the Astor House, New York, two days before Lincoln visited "New Ark" on his way to the White House.

peace than I am. None would do more to preserve it, but it may be necessary to put the foot down firmly."

To Lincoln's amazement, and possibly to its own surprise, as noted by a reporter for the New York *Tribune*, the legislature broke into "cheers so loud and long that for some moments it was impossible to hear Mr. L.'s voice." The President-elect continued: "And if I do my duty, and do right, you will sustain me, will you not?"

The legislators responded loudly, "Yes! Yes! We will!" The man from Illinois had won, temporarily, the good will of New Jersey's lawmakers. He left the legislative halls, crossed the Delaware River, and headed south to be inaugurated.

"The Flag Is Down!"

Telegraph wires that had been cut in South Carolina on April 12 were repaired in time to carry the news that Fort Sumter was under siege. Crowds jammed telegraph offices on April 13, eager for any news from the beleaguered fort. Charles Perrin Smith, a leading Republican and Clerk of the New Jersey Supreme Court, wrote of the drama:

> *Thousands of people gathered in the streets, mournfully discussing the imperfect items and conjecturing as to the result. Suddenly there flashed over the wires, "The Flag is down, and the Fort is in flames!"*
>
> *Then burst forth the long-pent patriotic enthusiasm! The cities suddenly became resplendent with flags! The women and children vied in displaying the National Colors, in badges, rosettes, and in every possible manner. Crowds paraded in the streets, with drums and shouts, visiting the residences of supposed disloyalists and demanding that they show their colors.*

The long wait for war was over. A feeling of release swept the state. Many newspaper editors who had opposed the war softened their attitudes temporarily. Politicians either spoke enthusiastically for the war or kept still. Commodore Stockton, pro-Southern, offered his services to Governor Olden.

Lincoln called for 3,120 volunteers from the state on April 17. Volunteers rushed to sign up; in less than a week more than 10,000 names were on the Army rolls. Hundreds more crossed the rivers to New York City or Philadelphia to enlist, believing that the big city regiments might move into action more quickly. Young enlistees expressed the fear that the war might

end before they could reach the South.

Flags flew everywhere, including divided Princeton, where nearly half the student body streamed to the railroad for the long ride home to don Confederate uniforms. Every town and city from Sussex to Cape May rang with the sounds of a state deliriously at war.

The Issue: The Union's Existence

Governor Olden summoned the legislature into emergency session. He said the issue was the Union's existence "and the place indicated for its determination is the field of battle." The legislature rose to the challenge, authorizing a $2 million war chest.

Financial support flowed in. Private banks loaned the state $451,000. Business leaders of Jersey City outfitted the city's Second Regiment. Flemington raised $5,000 in a one-night rally. John I. Blair of Warren County offered a $20 bonus to the family of every county man who enlisted.

Most of Newark joined in a massive outdoor rally on April 22. That day, New Jersey discovered its first Civil War military leader — Theodore Runyon,

Strung out across Chesapeake Bay, sixteen commandeered ferryboats carry the rag-tag New Jersey army toward Washington, DC. The boats were "sketched on the spot" by an army officer and appeared in *Leslie's* weekly newspaper. Also sketched "live" for *Leslie's* were Brigadier General Theodore Runyon, commander of the New Jersey troops, and the Virginia encampment where the New Jersey Brigade prepared for action. Called "Camp Princeton" by *Leslie's*, the staging area also was known as "Camp Runyon."

a leading Democrat lawyer who frankly admitted at the rally that he had worked the previous fall to keep Lincoln out of the White House. Now he was committed to the Union.

Five days later, Governor Olden named the thirty-eight-year-old Runyon as brigadier general to organize the state's first volunteers. Although Runyon had been active in the local militia, he had never led soldiers in the field. Neither had many others, in the North or South.

Runyon's lack of military experience did not disturb the rag-tag group of volunteers descending on Trenton. They gathered in a holiday spirit, gleefully shouting slogans and boasting of how quickly they would put the "Confeds" to rout. Their assorted, often gaudy, uniforms were as varied and as ill-suited for war as were the men who wore them.

Flintlocks And Yorktown Cannon

The men were at least superior to the arms they would receive. The "weapons" had been rusting away for years in the damp, gloomy State Arsenal, built originally in 1798 as the state prison. Trenton's Company A solemnly marched to the "arsenal" to guard the "weapons," a gesture that would have been hilarious if it had not been so pathetic.

The arms consisted of 11,000 flintlock muskets of Revolutionary War vintage, so old and rusted that sending soldiers equipped with them into battle would have been a greater crime than any ever committed by the arsenal's one-time prison inmates. Also available were three cannons. Two were captured at Yorktown in 1781; the third was seized from the Hessians at the Battle of Trenton.

Not one pound of powder, one bullet, or one cannonball could be found. The rattle of rifle fire in Trenton camps came from troops that brought their own bullets. A special agent raced to New York City to seek powder and bullets, and the state ordered 7,500 of the flintlock muskets converted into more modern weapons.

Happy in their ignorance of actual conditions, the ill-equipped, poorly prepared New Jersey contingent was loaded aboard sixteen hastily converted old steam ferryboats on May 1. The fleet headed for Washington by a water route, since Baltimore had fallen to Confederate sympathizers and had to be bypassed.

All four New Jersey regiments paraded through Washington on May 6. Other states sent some troops earlier, but these Jerseymen represented the first organized, equipped state brigade to reach the national capital.

Despite the official bumbling, the delays, the disappointments, and the deficiencies, New Jersey performed well. On April 15, it had no militia to speak of and no weapons worthy of the name. Now, twenty days later, on May 5, it had fulfilled every obligation before any other state in the North. It was no mean accomplishment.

Fight Before Johnny Quits

The New Jersey troops grumbled when Union officers set them to building fortifications around the capital. These confident recruits wanted to move south. They were sure that the "Johnny Rebs" would surrender once they felt the first sting of Union arms.

This confident, unwarranted attitude was typical, as manifested in Bridgeton a month earlier. Congressman John T. Nixon, representing the Cumberland County area, boasted foolishly before a public audience:

"This rebellion could easily be put down by a few women with broomsticks!"

Three months later, a crowd of beaming officials

Not everyone yearned for a uniform. Army officials punished "Skedaddlers" and drunks by drumming them out of camp in mock ceremony.

New Jersey inevitably became the crossroads for soldiers bound for war action. Above, a regiment of New York volunteers trained at Sandy Hook paraded on board walks stretched on the seaside sand. They wore the "Zouave" uniform, patterned after supposedly glamorous Algerian fighting gear. Below, the Sixth Massachusetts Regiment, in considerably less colorful attire, marched aboard a train in Jersey City in April 1861 to head for Washington.

and their wives and friends rode south out of Washington toward Virginia to watch the North meet the South at Bull Run. Congressman Nixon was among those eager to be in on the expected kill.

About 35,000 raw Union troops surged toward Bull Run on July 21, 1861. They wore almost every color of uniform imaginable — blue, green, red, brown, and gray (the war had not yet become a matter of The Blue and The Gray). The Confederate army of some 30,000 was as equally undisciplined, as colorfully uniformed, and as naive.

By nightfall, the Union army had fled in terror from the bloody fields of Bull Run. New Jersey troops, assigned to rear guard action, were ordered to stop the wild flight with drawn bayonets. Not even bayonets could stem the panic. These Union soldiers learned that Johnny Reb was also determined — and on that July 21, better prepared.

The Confederate soldiers were in no condition or mood to follow the retreating Northerners to Washington. The Battle of Bull Run, begun almost as a schoolyard fistfight, had turned savagely bloody. Both sides were shocked into reality.

Rise Of The Copperheads

Wearied only by trench digging and still strangers to direct enemy fire, the First New Jersey Brigade returned home on July 25, four days after the Battle of Bull Run. Their ninety-day enlistments had expired. Fire bells summoned townspeople everywhere to give the returning troops the kind of welcome accorded victorious heroes.

Bull Run was a sobering jolt, but the zest for war was undiminished. Men continued to go south all summer, in response to an almost casual telegram received from President Lincoln three days after the disaster at Bull Run. The message said that the Union would accept five more New Jersey regiments, "if tendered in reasonable time."

By October 4, the state had eight full regiments camped in or near Washington. These included the Eighth Regiment, composed mainly of re-enlistees from the original group discharged after Bull Run.

The war settled into a stalemate during the summer and fall of 1861, as if the Battle of Bull Run had been a mistaken prelude. The antiwar editors and politicians emerged again to lash out violently at "Lincoln's War," demanding that it be stopped.

Bergen County became the center for peace spokesmen and "Copperheads." (Copperheads were antiwar Democrats who wore in their lapels Indian heads cut from copper pennies and whose enemies likened them to "snakes ready to strike without warning.") Bergen's nearness to New York City, the center of Copperhead sentiment, made the county fertile soil for those opposing the war.

Bergen County was not alone in opposition to the war. A large contingent of young Sussex County men marched off to Canada in March 1862, in the so-called "Skedaddle Army" that fled from service. A year later, a Southern-minded assailant fired a bullet in the Branchville Presbyterian Church at the Rev. G. W. Lloyd, a Union supporter. The shot missed.

Civil Rights In Wartime

New Jersey's loosely-knit Copperheads were troublesome but not effective. They needed a leader and found him, in September 1861, when the federal government suddenly and illegally arrested Colonel James W. Wall of Burlington.

Wall was a highly vocal Peace Democrat. He had been a frequent contributor to newspapers opposing the war, especially the Newark *Journal* and the New

Nothing disturbed pro-war Northerners more than "Copperheads," antiwar Democrats who wore pieces of copper pennies in their lapels to flaunt their Southern sympathies. Cartoons such as this showed the Copperheads as insidious, traitorous "snakes," ready to strike the Union without warning.

York *Daily News*. His arguments, however, were no more inflammatory than the writings of many others, in New Jersey and around the nation.

A United States marshal secretly arrested Wall on September 11 and whisked him away to Fort Lafayette in New York. No reason was offered for the arrest. Nor was any explanation given after his release, on September 24, when he swore allegiance to the United States.

Burlington gave Wall a rousing welcome home on September 27. Indignation at the arrogant treatment of the colonel solidified antiwar and Copperhead sentiment throughout the state. Even loyal war supporters were incensed over the shocking violation of civil rights.

Wall's imprisonment made him a national celebrity. It also was a factor in the crushing defeat of Republicans in the elections of November 1861 and November 1862. The 1861 election swept Democrat Joel Parker into the governor's chair, but he was no comfort to the antiwar strategists. Parker served as a Union major general early in the war and supported the fight against the South.

General Philip Kearny transformed the lackluster First New Jersey Brigade into a respected fighting unit during the summer of 1862. The pencil sketch, top right, shows Kearny's forces fighting in the woods during the Peninsular Campaign of 1862, while below, the Kearny Brigade "turns the fortunes of the day near Charles City, Va., on June 30, 1862" (according to a correspondent for *Leslie's* weekly).

Further divisive news came in the fall of 1862 with President Lincoln's announcement, in September, that he would issue an *Emancipation Proclamation* on January 1, 1863, freeing slaves in southern states.

Copperheads altered their strategy in the autumn of 1862. The war had long ago ceased to be a springtime lark; the casualty lists grew longer. Copperheads carefully used the growing fatalities to support their efforts to end hostilities, hoping for support from those whose relatives were among the dead and wounded.

"Follow Me To Hell"

Twenty-seven New Jersey regiments were in the field by October 1862, including seven regiments of nine-month volunteers. The call for manpower was demonstrated in Cumberland County, where all five sons of Mrs. Martha Cobb of Downe Township were in Company G of the Twenty-fourth Regiment.

New Jersey troops were involved in a widening field of battle in 1862 — up the Virginia peninsula and into battles at Fair Oaks and Yorktown. They were back at Bull Run for a second battle in September and fought across the pasturelands at Antietam in Maryland on September 17 and 18 when 22,500 men on both sides were killed or wounded in two days. Many New Jersey names were among Antietam's 12,500 Northern casualties.

In that summer of 1862, New Jersey found and lost its most incredible battlefield leader, General Philip Kearny, a hard-riding, tough, professional soldier. He was as brilliant a battlefield leader as the North could boast.

Kearny fought the Indians in California, was gallant in the Mexican War (where he lost his left arm), and won honors with French troops in Italy and Algeria. He came home to join the Union army when the war began, only to be shunted aside by the federal government and his native New York.

The Civil War's major railroad story involved the battle-scarred Texas *(above) and the* General *(below). The story of the chase of the two wood-burning locomotives across Georgia has been told and retold many times.*

The episode began on April 12, 1862 when twenty-one Union soldiers, led by James J. Andrews, seized the General *at Marietta, Georgia and headed northward toward Chattanooga at breakneck speed. The plan was to destroy tracks and telegraph wires along the way.*

Confederate soldiers who left the General *for breakfast at Marietta immediately commandeered the* Texas *and raced after Andrews. The Union soldiers abandoned the smoking, battered* General *after sixty-five miles and soon were captured in the nearby woods.*

If a New Jersey war correspondent had been at the scene he could have found an amazing "Jersey angle." The Texas *was finished in Paterson, New Jersey in 1856 by Danforth, Cooke & Co. The* General *was completed the same year by the Rogers Locomotive Works — just down the street from Danforth, Cooke.*

New Jersey commissioned Kearny a brigadier general four days after the rout at Bull Run in July 1861. He transformed the disorganized First New Jersey Brigade into a tightly disciplined force that he proclaimed would "follow me to hell!" His men, for their part, admired their "One-Armed Devil."

Kearny was particularly intrepid in the Peninsular Campaign in Virginia. In the late afternoon of September 1, 1862, he rode his horse into a wild thunderstorm at Chantilly, Virginia to probe enemy lines. An enemy volley killed him in the darkness. If Kearny had lived, there is little question that Lincoln would have named him commander of the Army of the Potomac.

"Strew Your Graves With Flowers"

War was still somewhat of a glorious adventure in the fading days of the summer of 1862, at least to one Newark group. The Thirteenth Regiment was getting ready to leave town when "a delegation of ladies" from the South Baptist Church stopped by on August 26 to give "the boys" a regimental flag they stitched themselves. Their spokesman, the church minister, told the assembled troops:

"Female patriotism still survives. While your regiment is far away from home and loved ones, tender hearts will be praying for your success, and gentle hands will be preparing to wreath your brows with honors, or to strew your graves with flowers."

Less than three weeks later, the ladies could fulfill half their promise. The untrained Newarkers of the Thirteenth suffered heavy losses at Antietam: the female patriots had ample opportunity to "strew your graves with flowers" when the coffins came back to Newark.

Death and crippling wounds came in a variety of ways. The five sons of Mrs. Cobb who left Downe Township in October 1862 were a prime example. One died of typhoid fever at Chain Bridge, Virginia on November 14. Two of his brothers were wounded in late November assaults near Fredericksburg. In all, the Cumberland County regiment lost 160 soldiers outside of Fredericksburg only six weeks after leaving New Jersey.

Return Of The Copperheads

More than 30,000 New Jerseyans were in uniform by the winter of 1863. At home, the Copperheads and Peace Democrats made one more effort to stop

Hell On A Pea Patch

Tradition says Pea Patch Island off Salem County in the Delaware River began when a boatload of peas capsized at the site. Pea vines grew, catching floating weeds and eventually making an island that would become one of the worst blotches on the Northern war record.

Fears that Confederate ships might invade by way of Delaware River prompted sending troops to the island early in the war to man the walls of Fort Delaware. Soon after the island was converted into the most despised and infamous prison camp in the North.

Thousands of Confederate prisoners were herded into the foul, damp fort after the summer of 1862. About 12,500 Southern soldiers were on the little island by August 1863. They were poorly clothed and meagerly fed. (The drawing above shows prisoners fighting for crusts of bread.) Often the river flooded over the island.

Dozens, then scores, then hundreds, of the hapless prisoners died — of malnutrition, disease, neglect, and brutality. In all, about 2,700 succumbed to the dismal hell called Pea Patch Island. Nearly all were rowed ashore to Salem County for burial in Finn's Point cemetery.

In 1912, fifty years after the first prisoners were set on Pea Patch Island, the US Government raised an 85-foot obelisk at Finn Point to commemorate the 2,436 known Southerners who lie in the cemetery as silent warning that war tragedy comes in many ways.

the war. This time they expected the appalling casualty lists and Lincoln's *Emancipation Proclamation* to reinforce their demands.

The peace supporters believed stop-the-war resolutions could be eased through a New Jersey legislature split among Republicans, War Democrats, and Peace Democrats. The division gave the Copperheads a decided voting edge.

Two Bergen County men lead the peace advocates in the legislature, Senator Daniel Holsman and Assemblyman Thomas Dunn English (a poet best remembered for his romantic ballad, *Ben Bolt*). Significantly, the legislature elected Burlington's Colonel Wall to fill an unexpired term in the United States Senate.

Outside of the political ranks, the bitterly antiwar editor Edward Fuller of Newark and Judge David Naar of Trenton were pushing for an end to the hostilities. The chief Copperhead of all was C. Chauncey Burr, ever on the lookout for opportunity and power. Before coming to New Jersey, he had been a clergyman, writer, wife deserter, and bigamist.

Burr spoke heatedly at a Trenton meeting, called on March 4, 1863, to protest proposals to draft Northern soldiers. Yet Burr's scalding words paled beside the cynical statement made by Justice Naar the same day:

"We are cutting our throats for the sake of a few worthless Negroes!"

Comeuppance To "Peace Makers"

Riding what they believed to be a popular wave, New Jersey's antiwar legislators passed peace resolutions in mid-March 1863. The measures opposed emancipation of slaves and called for the federal government to appoint a peace commissioner to meet with the South to end the war. The resolution said "the war was unnecessary in its origin, fraught with horror, and suffering in its continuance."

The horror and suffering were real enough, but the men enduring both were not about to buy the easy peace that seemed so wonderful (and politically sound) in the comfortable legislative chambers of Trenton. Two New Jersey regiments encamped in Virginia took unprecedented action, so directly aimed at the lawmakers that under other circumstances they might have been considered mutinous.

The Eleventh Regiment sent a written resolution to the legislature saying "even the introduction of the so-called Peace Resolution was wicked, weak, and cowardly." It minced no words, asserting that "secret enemies who at home foment disaffection [were as much] traitors as the foe in arms."

The Twenty-fourth Regiment, bloodied and torn at Fredericksburg the November before, assembled to hear Lieutenant William E. Potter say:

"It is a matter of regret and shame that as we endure the perils and sufferings of war ... these traitors at home should be striving to outstrip each other in the haste to throw themselves at the feet of the slave power."

That did it. The Copperhead movement began to shrivel away. Democrats ruled the legislature for the duration, but they were War Democrats. Democratic Governor Joel Parker declared the "absorbing question" now was "how are we to end the war and at the same time preserve the nation?" He had no intention to press for a one-sided peace.

War Gets Close To Home

Meanwhile, the tide of battle was with the South. General Robert E. Lee made his major bid to win the war in the late spring and early summer of 1863. Northern troops fell back steadily before the Southern onslaught. On one day alone, April 30, the First New Jersey Brigade lost sixty-five men killed and 358 wounded in a futile attempt to slow Lee's advance across the Rappahannock River in Virginia.

The Confederate war machine rolled across Maryland and into Pennsylvania toward Gettysburg. Fear began to seep across New Jersey. Governor Parker called for militia volunteers to speed to Pennsylvania's aid. Thousands of recently released soldiers were available, but few of them answered the call.

One Camden County company of volunteers "unaccountably disbanded" when ordered to Harrisburg. A Somerset County town meeting demanded that the militia be kept home for self-defense, "since we have no confidence in the wisdom and ability of the administration to protect the lives and property of the people of the United States."

Despite such fear and opposition, several of the state's militia companies did get as far as Harrisburg, well away from the scene of battle at Gettysburg. It was just as well. The Union regulars, including thousands of New Jerseyans, did not need this reluctant militia. Lee's mighty army was halted and turned back in the savage three-day battle that began on July 1.

Two years of unprecedented slaughter proved that volunteers could not supply enough manpower. Enlistments were falling off in all parts of the nation. President Lincoln finally ordered, on July 13, 1863, troops to be drafted. (The South also was resorting to frequent draft calls to replace its fallen soldiers.)

Cheers Turn Into Protests

The announcement, on July 4, of the victory of Gettysburg brought forth in thanksgiving the bell ringers, the flag wavers, and the churchgoers. Nine days later, announcement of the first draft revealed

The 26th Regiment of NJ Volunteers tried to cross the Rappahannock River in Virginia on June 5, 1862 — two days after their enlistments expired. The regiment lost fifteen men in fifteen minutes. Earlier, on April 30, the 1st NJ Brigade in one day lost sixty-five dead and 358 wounded in another futile crossing.

Leslie's weekly took this dim cartoon view of the young draft dodger telling the draft clerk he was exempt from service because he was sixty-three years old and remembered because "I was born the year George Washington died." Many violently opposed the draft in 1863, surging into the streets to kill and loot in protest. New Jersey sought to fill draft quotas by enticing recruits with colorful posters. If appeals to patriotism failed, those who wanted to avoid war could buy a substitute for $300.

the dangerous rot that underlay the Northern war effort.

Opposition to conscription came from those against the war on any terms or from the cowardly. War had also brought bulging pay envelopes to the North's expanding factories; few cared to leave the safety and luxury of a well-paying job.

Conscription also highlighted a general feeling that this was "a rich man's war and a poor man's fight." The draft law provided that a drafted man could hire a substitute to go in his place. Moreover, anyone could get out of serving merely by paying a $300 fee. Such a law clearly favored the wealthy.

Mobs surged into the streets of New York City on July 13 to protest the draft. After four days and nights of rioting, more than 1,000 people lay dead or wounded. New Jersey's riots were small in comparison, but in Newark a downtown mob threw rocks at the newspaper office of the pro-Lincoln *Mercury*. The angry crowd also showered the home of Provost Marshal E. N. Miller with stones.

New Jersey petitioned the President for permission to meet its quota of 8,783 drafted men by stepping up enlistments. Lincoln agreed, "if the day is not too remote."

Governor Olden promised full enlistment within ninety days. Lincoln insisted on thirty days. By October 25, the state had signed up 4,998 men, far short of its quota but a higher total than any other state achieved by drafting soldiers.

Tall, gaunt, and sad-faced, Abraham Lincoln was a perfect foil for cartoonists during his bid for re-election in 1864. His opponent, former General George B. McClellan of West Orange was short ("a little joke," one cartoonist believed). The two were photographed in an amiable talk in McClellan's tent at Antietam on October 4, 1862, but amiability was gone by November 1864.

Historians have mistakenly perpetuated the fiction that New Jersey acquired all its troops by enlistments. The state did send 6,981 volunteers in response to the March 1864 draft call, but another 3,614 "men and substitutes" were drafted between November 1, 1864 and November 1, 1865.

Bergen County's freeholders offered $300 to each volunteer or draftee. The freeholders explained they were "doing our duty to the government and saving much of our friends and brothers who had no desire to leave their homes and go live a soldier's life or die a soldier's death." It was not even a lukewarm endorsement of the war.

"Little Mac" Downs "Big Abe"

The draft was a major issue in the 1864 election for President. Lincoln faced tough going in New Jersey; the losing campaign of 1860 was still much in mind. His second campaign was much more difficult because the Democratic opponent was former Major General George B. McClellan, whose estate was located on a mountain top in West Orange.

"Little Mac" served the Union Army with distinction in the early years of the war and rose to command the North's most powerful unit, the Army of the Potomac. His career ended when his delay and confusion after the victory at Antietam enabled Lee's army to escape.

Lincoln relieved McClellan of his command after Antietam and ordered him to Trenton "for further orders" that never came. He was available for the Democratic nomination and accepted it eagerly, despite a total lack of experience in public life.

The Democratic platform of 1864 contained a plank that declared the war had been a failure. McClellan strongly repudiated that declaration, but as the party's candidate he had to stand on the platform,

Cornelia's "Sea Of Anguish"

Cornelia Hancock left her little village of Hancock's Bridge, in the Salem County marshes, on July 4, 1863 to head for the terrors of war at Gettysburg. The twenty-three-year-old Quaker was a mere five feet tall and favored with bright blue eyes and silken hair.

When Cornelia reached Philadelphia on July 5, Dorothea Dix, the head recruiting nurse, told her she was "too young and too pretty" to nurse soldiers on a battlefield. Cornelia refused to budge from the train.

When she reached Gettysburg, Cornelia wrote "the need was so great there was no further cavil about age." The Hancock's Bridge girl entered a Gettysburg church being used for a hospital and declared she "seemed to stand breast high in a sea of anguish."

She had no training, no medicine, no supplies, but Cornelia instinctively knew that kindness was most needed by Gettysburg's casualties. She wrote letters home for dying soldiers. She obtained food without a voucher, made sandwiches, and passed them out to soldiers starving on the battlefield. She obtained tobacco for wounded men despite her hatred for smoking.

Late in the summer of 1863, Gettysburg soldiers had a special medal struck for Cornelia, and a song was written in her honor. She went south to continue nursing. After the war, she stayed in the South to devote most of her remaining life to working with freedmen. She returned home to die in Atlantic City at the age of eighty-seven.

offensive planks and all.

"Little Mac" easily downed "Big Abe" in New Jersey, winning by 7,000 votes. McClellan won all the state's seven electoral votes, but his campaign nationally was a failure; he won only two other states. Lincoln was re-elected, despite New Jersey's continuing opposition.

The Army Turns South

McClellan's failure as a general was discussed in the campaign, but he was only one of several commanders who had been unable to move the Northern army. Finally, in March 1864, the President appointed General Ulysses S. Grant to head the Army of the Potomac. Grant turned the columns south, determined to meet the enemy head-on.

The fighting and dying picked up in intensity. Grant drove his army relentlessly through The Wilderness in Virginia and on toward Richmond. Eleven days of the Battle in The Wilderness cost New Jersey the lives of 155 men and left another 671 with disabling wounds. One bloody charge alone cost the Fifteenth New Jersey Regiment 169 killed or wounded out of 270 men.

Simultaneously, General William T. Sherman rammed south and east toward Atlanta. Helping Sherman on the way were two unusual New Jerseyans. General Judson Kilpatrick of Sussex County and Colonel George W. Mindil of Newark.

Kilpatrick was a Sussex farm boy who went to West Point but left the campus to join the cavalry. His men called him "Kill Cavalry" because of his reckless sacrifice of manpower, but he personally risked as much as he demanded.

When Sherman needed a man to lead the way to Atlanta and the sea, he chose Kilpatrick. "He's one hell of a damned fool," Sherman told friends, but that was exactly what Sherman needed to spearhead the daring march through Georgia.

George Mindil took command of New Jersey's Thirty-third Regiment in the summer of 1863. He had been fighting for two years at that point and had been promoted to colonel at age twenty. Mindil outfitted his regiment in the gaudy pantaloons and hats popular with "Zouave" regiments. The young colonel and his New Jersey Zouaves helped take Chattanooga, stormed Atlanta, and marched with Sherman to the Atlantic Ocean.

Mindil came home to Newark in August 1865 wearing the two stars of a major general — still a

Two of New Jersey's foremost Civil War characters came from opposite ends of the state — General Judson Kilpatrick (left) from Sussex County, and Captain Henry W. Sawyer (below) from Cape May. Kilpatrick drove himself and his cavalry unit so mercilessly that he was nicknamed "Kill Cavalry." The pencil drawing above was made as Kilpatrick's cavalry headed out for a raid on Richmond, where the Sussex man showed such reckless daring that General William Sherman personally chose him to help lead the decisive advance on Atlanta.

Sawyer fame came not on a battlefield but in the wretched Libbey (or Libey) Prison in Richmond. Confederate jailers of Sawyer and Captain John M. Flinn (or Flynn) of Indiana chose the Northern pair, on July 6, 1863, to die in retaliation for two Southern captains who had been executed in Texas two weeks before. When Sawyer's wife heard the shocking news, she appealed directly to President Lincoln, who forced the South to stop the execution.

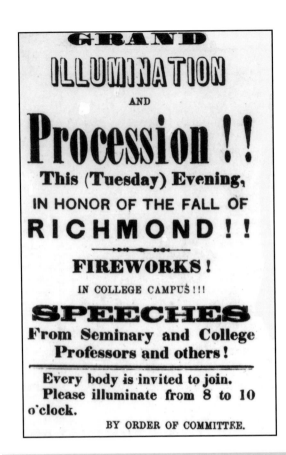

Princeton's original lukewarm attitude toward the war had disappeared by mid-April 1865 when a "grand illumination" and procession were held on the college campus to celebrate Richmond's fall. Half of the college's war dead wore gray uniforms; half wore blue.

month shy of his twenty-second birthday! His Thirty-third Regiment fought in eight major battles, trudged more than 1,700 miles, and paid its way by losing 300 of the 500 original members of the outfit.

"We Saw The End"

Grant forced his weary Army of the Potomac deep into Virginia in the winter of 1865, pounding toward Petersburg and Richmond. On April 2, 1865, a soldier of the Eighth New Jersey Regiment wrote home after his outfit fought its way up a slope overlooking Petersburg:

"We saw *THE END* shining luminously through the battle-smoke!"

It was nearly the end. One week later, the curtain came down for the South when General Lee surrendered to Grant at Appomattox Court House. An officer of the Second New Jersey Brigade recalled the scene:

"Officers and men were perfectly wild. There were greetings and congratulations and cheering. Shoes and hats flew high in the air; speeches were called for loudly and made, but could not be heard, the boys cheering at every sentence."

New Jersey exploded with joy at the news of Lee's surrender. Church bells and factory whistles sounded throughout the day on April 10. Local militia units turned out in uniform to fire cannons. Thousands crowded into halls and churches to offer prayers of thanksgiving.

Then, as the nation anticipated the first peacetime Easter weekend in four years, the telegraph ticked out the awful word that President Lincoln had been shot on Good Friday night in Ford's Theater in Washington. He died the next day, April 15. The state and nation collapsed in a state of deep mourning.

The last sorrowful scene occurred on the morning of April 24 when Lincoln's funeral train passed through New Jersey, taking the President's body home for burial in Illinois. Grief-stricken, bare-headed crowds lined the tracks along the route. Wherever the train stopped, the sounds of sobbing could be heard above the hiss and the steaming of the locomotive.

Lincoln, in death, conquered New Jersey as he had not done in life.

The Cause Is Soon Forgotten

The tired troops limped home, filled with bittersweet memories of distant pastures and hilltops whose names they would remember because young men like themselves, in blue or gray uniforms, turned the ground red with their blood.

New Jersey's list of dead had mounted steadily. The final tally disclosed the dreadful toll: 218 officers and 6,082 enlisted men had died in battle, in prisons, or in makeshift hospitals. They were victims of cannon fire, gunshot wounds, disease, and starvation.

The dead were silent — at Gaines' Mill, Gettysburg, Chantilly, The Wilderness, and Atlanta; at Sharpsburg, Antietam, Crampton's Gap and Fredericksburg. Many died in unnamed fields or orchards. Most went to their graves subscribing to Abraham Lincoln's solemn belief that a nation could not live divided.

There *had* been a cause — abolition of slavery. The political leaders of New Jersey never really accepted that. Governor Parker's annual message in 1865 questioned the Thirteenth Amendment abolishing slavery, just as if there had been no war, no casualties,

Nine days elapsed between Abraham Lincoln's death on April 15 and the passage of his funeral train through New Jersey on the long, sad journey home to Illinois. Newspapers carried a detailed schedule for the special train that left New Brunswick at 7:55 AM and reached Jersey City two hours later. Huge crowds lined the tracks or gathered at depots where the train stopped briefly. By mid-morning, the funeral car was aboard a Jersey Central Railroad barge (above) headed from Jersey City to New York. The President's casket was loaded aboard a black open-sided hearse in many cities and drawn past mourners, as in the lithograph below. So the President was returned to Springfield, Illinois where his path to the White House began.

Black And Blue

Long after the bullets stopped flying, old soldiers remembered their glory days in uniform. Aaron Hush of Franklin Township, was one of nearly 3,000 New Jersey African American soldiers in the Civil War.

The Record of Officers and Men of New Jersey In The Civil War shows that Hush served from February 29, 1864 until August 22, 1865 in the 32nd Regiment of the United States Colored Troops.

President Lincoln's Emancipation Proclamation of January 1, 1863 permitted African American soldiers to enlist, be drafted, or receive bonuses to serve as replacements. The Record lists, by name, rank, and place of service, a total of 2,872 New Jersey African Americans who wore the blue uniform.

New Jersey's African American casualties included 469 dead, about eight percent of the state's slain. Six were buried in the Arlington National Cemetery. Several died in a celebrated charge against a dangerous mine at Petersburg, VA on July 30, 1861.

no cause.

"Restoration of the Union should be the sole consideration for peace," Parker said. He condemned the proposition that slavery must be ended as a condition for the return of the Confederate states. Emancipation, said Parker, should be an issue for southern states to work out for themselves. It was a speech that could have been made in 1860 — or 1820.

The Democratic-run legislature slavishly agreed with Parker. It refused to ratify the Thirteenth Amendment in February 1865.

"Sum Of All Villainies"

This time the politicians misread the mood of the people. Voters in effect endorsed the Thirteenth Amendment by electing Republican Marcus Ward as Governor in November, since he supported it.

Ward did not win because of the Amendment alone. He was also popular with ex-soldiers, having been nicknamed "The Soldier's Friend" for his unceasing wartime efforts on behalf of soldiers and their families.

Ward carried a Republican senate and assembly into office with him. The new legislature approved the Thirteenth Amendment in January 1866. Three-fourths of the states already had ratified the Amendment and it had been the law of the land since the previous December 18.

The legislature adopted a resolution of apology for the obstructionist efforts of the Democrats. It concluded:

"New Jersey is gloriously redeemed in her political and moral history from the disgraceful stigma of being in sympathy, through her legislators, with the sum of all villainies."

Freedom — But Not Too Much

Full freedom still came slowly. The Republican legislature approved the Fourteenth Amendment (protecting the privileges of all citizens and refusing office to those engaged in a rebellion against the country). Within a year, the same Republican legislature refused to amend the state constitution to permit African Americans to vote in New Jersey.

The fickle public turned on the Republicans as soon as Ward's term ended and he could not succeed himself. Conservative Democrats returned to power in the election of 1867 and promptly rescinded New

Jersey's ratification of the Fourteenth Amendment.

Congress, however, refused to honor the New Jersey turnabout. It told the legislature that its action on the Fourteenth Amendment was "disrespectful to the House and scandalous in nature."

Democratic majorities continued to keep New Jersey out of the mainstream of American thought and action. In February 1870, the legislature voted down the Fifteenth Amendment, protecting the rights of all citizens to vote regardless of "race, color, or previous condition of servitude."

The see-saw political struggle continued as Republicans returned to power, on November 1, 1870, and voted approval of the Fifteenth Amendment. Five years later, the state complied with the national law by striking from the New Jersey Constitution the word "white" as a qualification for voting.

New Jersey marched for nearly two decades in war and peace — to the beat of an antiwar, antiblack drum. Now, reluctantly, the state was in step. A New York newspaper editor summed it up. New Jersey, he wrote, "is back in the Union."

The poignancy of a nation divided in Civil War is underscored in these two graves in the Presbyterian cemetery at Springfield. Confederate soldier Elias Bryant Poole lies to the left, under a stone that lists him as a member of the Virginia Light Artillery. His brother, William, to the right, belonged to the Union's 8th NJ Infantry. Elias went south from Springfield as a young man seeking work, enlisted in May 1861, and served throughout the war. Brother William joined the Union forces in August 1864. Both brothers returned to Springfield after the war. Elias died first and was buried in Springfield. When William died, he was first scheduled to be buried in Arlington Cemetery in Virginia. Friends of the pair insisted that the brothers should spend eternity next to one another.

Unit IV

Thirty-six states emerged after the four bloody years of the Civil War. About thirty-five million people inhabited the war-weary nation — with all but about five million east of the Mississippi River. The State of California seemed as distant from New Jersey as Russia.

Westward from the Mississippi, great herds of buffalo still thundered across the Plains; Indians still fought bitterly with the US Cavalry, and gunslinging desperadoes still challenged US marshals in the muddy streets of shabby frontier towns. Alaska had not yet been purchased from Russia. The northwestern border between Canada and the United States was still in dispute.

A transcontinental railroad inched slowly westward from Chicago and eastward from San Francisco in 1865. Four years later, the two lines met at Promontory, Utah; the Atlantic and the Pacific oceans were linked by rails. A hectic half century for a literally united nation had begun.

No state would be altered more dramatically than New Jersey in that half century. Every national surge of transformation in urbanization, in industry, in immigration, in progressive ideology would be mirrored in the state. Its inventors would lead the way in discovery. Its newly-created millionaires would rival those of any area in pomp and circumstance.

People went west all right, by the millions, to plant their roots in the wide open spaces, but more than two million now sought out New Jersey between 1865 and 1915. This was a place where opportunity and promise far outweighed the increasing complexities and problems of the cities.

Life was simple in 1865, even for the very wealthy. There were no electric lights, streetcars, automobiles, or airplanes; no plastics, elevators, tall buildings, typewriters, or telephones; no movies, phonographs, refrigeration, or even a bicycle that could be ridden by anyone except a skilled acrobat.

Streets were muddy and poorly lit, in villages and cities alike. Indoor plumbing was a rarity. City sewer systems were shockingly inadequate. Diseases struck regularly, killing people in large numbers.

In 1915, about ninety-five million people lived in the forty-eight states (Arizona and New Mexico were admitted to the Union in 1912). Gunslingers had vanished from western

The Hectic Half Century

streets. The buffalo was on the way to near-extinction. Indians had been herded together on barren reservations. Industry had grown by 1915 to an extent that could not possibly have been imagined fifty years before. Fortunes were being made in steel, petroleum, telephone, and telegraph companies; in life insurance and banking, and in corporations formed to generate and distribute electricity. Incredible profits poured into the pockets of railroad owners. Automobile makers had begun to ride the millionaire circle.

These people were "different" from the Anglo-Saxons who first came to America and were reaping its rewards. The immigrants were welcomed by industry because they would cut labor costs. They were scorned, however, by most others — for these newcomers from southern and eastern Europe spoke "foreign" languages and perpetuated their "foreign" ways.

Newspapers and magazines boasted by 1890 of America's power and riches. However, amid obvious evidences of wealth, it was all too evident that something was desperately out of kilter in the fabulously rich United States. As the feverish half century neared its end, reformers demanded the rampaging millionaires be checked and the wealth of the nation be shared more equitably among far more people. The hectic half century would end with sweeping improvements in life for most people.

At the close of the period, the nation was heading for a rendezvous with another awesome war. The United States was isolated in 1865. By 1915, its sphere of influence had spread from Panama to the Philippines; from Cuba to China.

In 1865, a war between European or Asian powers would have disturbed few Americans. In 1915, it was a different matter. With American munitions factories employing many thousands and with the new sense of the nation's international status, a major war anywhere inevitably involved the rich, ambitious young republic.

So America would enter World War I. Its men and women would sail for France, some to die in trenches in places whose names they could not even pronounce. An age of innocence would be smashed forever.

United States		New Jersey	
Alaska purchase	1867		
Transcontinental railroad finished	1869	1869	1st football game: Rutgers-Princeton
Panic of 1873	1873	1873	Railroad monopolies end
		1875	NJ permits Blacks to vote
Centennial of Declaration of Independence	1876	1876	Edison opens world's 1st organized research lab at Menlo Park
		1877	Edison invents phonograph
		1879	Edison perfects incandescent lamp
50,155,000 people in US Census	1880	1880	NJ population passes 1,000,000; State declared urban
		1881	Holland (Paterson teacher) launches first practical submarine
		1883	NJ workers get first legal right to strike
American Federation of Labor organized	1886		
Both major parties attack trusts	1888		
Kansas passes first antitrust laws	1889	1889	NJ legalizes trusts
		1891	Edison patents movie camera
		1894	State Federation of Women's Clubs starts
Supreme Court legalizes school segregation	1896		
Spanish American War	1898	1898	NJ troops report to guard coastline
8,000 autos in US	1900		
First airplane flight	1903	1903	Edison makes first movie with plot
Panama Canal started	1904		
Peary reaches North Pole	1909		
Immigration reaches high level	1910	1910	NJ 5th in immigration
		1910	Wilson elected governor
Wilson elected President	1912		
World War I starts	1914	1914	Boom starts in supplying munitions to Europe

Chapter Nine - The Tracks Of Change

United States			New Jersey
13th Amendment abolishes slavery	1865	1865	Clark opens giant thread works in East Newark
Transcontinental railroad finished	1869	1873	Singer hires 3,000 workers in new plant
		1873	General Railroad law ends monopoly
Colorado becomes state	1876	1876	Edison opens Menlo Park laboratory
		1876	Railroad reaches Greenwood Lake
		1877	Edison invents phonograph
		1879	Edison perfects electric light
Population passes 50 million	1880	1880	Population passes 1 million
		1880	Oil pipeline reaches Bayonne
1st trolley in Cleveland	1881	1881	Paterson man perfects submarine
Standard Time starts	1883	1883	NJ man perfects Standard Time zones

The most "American" sound in the late nineteenth century was the drawn out, mournful wail of the train whistle. It rolled across fields and city streets. It warned people off the tracks, made horses skittish at crossings, and called a friendly greeting to farmers in the fields. During the night, the melancholy whistle stirred dreams of faraway places.

Train whistles signalled change. They meant work for most Americans by 1875, for they foretold the approach of a string of ponderous freight cars or a speeding passenger train. As the nation followed the railroad tracks, it prospered.

Railroad locomotives steamed into town hauling raw materials and chugged out with manufactured products to be sold in distant towns and cities. Farmers who once fought the spreading rails now welcomed the trains, for they carried products of fields and orchards to far-flung markets. Seaside and lakeshore resorts boomed when the trains came.

Trains transformed the entire nation, knit states together from coast to coast, and brought readily-seen economic benefits to most people. Wherever railroads went, industry and people followed, seeking both pleasure and profit.

◇◇◇◇◇◇◇◇◇◇◇◇◇◇◇◇◇◇◇

On The Edge Of Tomorrow

Uneasiness filled the nation as America paused in 1876 to celebrate the Centennial of the Declaration of Independence. *Still fresh in memory were reconstruction, economic depression, and political scandals that reached all the way to the White House.*

Southern states showed no inclination to accord freed slaves the equal rights guaranteed by the Constitution. Northern leaders, in turn, showed little desire to agitate the South by enforcing federal laws.

Scandals marred the two terms of President Ulysses S. Grant, the heroic Union war general who became a weak, ineffective president. Unscrupulous manipulations of the stock market ruined thousands of investors and shook confidence in the business world.

The clouds of economic collapse were just clearing away. The Panic of 1873 had been a cruel blow. Factories stood idle. Workers walked the streets hoping for even a few hours work. Several towns were bankrupt or nearly so. Both Elizabeth and Rahway were insolvent. Jersey City was on the brink of collapse.

Now, though, it was 1876 — a time to celebrate.

More than 30,000 state residents rode excursion trains to Philadelphia, on August 24, 1876, to celebrate New Jersey Day at the Centennial Exposition. They were astonished by the mechanical, agricultural, and cultural displays.

Gold Medal winners were everywhere. Still, the Philadelphia show, for all its boasts of being up-to-the-minute, really represented a past that was about to disappear, chiefly because of one person who was not honored at the Exposition. He was Thomas Alva Edison.

That summer Edison opened an "invention factory" (or research laboratory) atop a high hill in Menlo Park, New Jersey. He devoted twelve to fourteen hours a day to his research. There was no time for an Exposition.

Edison, more than any Gold Medal winner at Philadelphia, was hard on the trail of the elusive future. He, more than any other person of his time, would light the way to tomorrow.

New York City was the nation's prime market, and that city's nearest railroad link to the South and West lay on the New Jersey side of the Hudson River. Hudson County shot into prominence as the home of massive railroad yards and the huge docks needed to handle railroad freight. New Jersey's corridor was alive with the greatest volume of traffic in the world.

Industry and railroads needed one another. They became inseparable during the Civil War, and the relationship intensified in the 1870s and 1880s. Both grew sleek and fat by feeding one another.

Railroading became an appealing way of life. Children dreamed of growing up to be a glamorous railroad engineer or a much-traveled conductor on a handsome passenger train. The sound of the whistle made people of all ages yearn to board a train bound outward toward adventure.

Railroads were everywhere available, fastmoving, and, in a way that later generations would envy, almost always on time. They were the very essence of a nation on the move.

Competition In The Middle

New Jersey's corridor between New York City and Philadelphia became the most traveled section in the nation during the Civil War. The old single-track Camden & Amboy Railroad between Jersey City and Camden had to be double tracked to eliminate danger and to speed traffic.

Railroad owners exploited the situation. They boosted rates so high that a wartime Congress intervened to urge that a rival line be built across the state. Powerful Camden & Amboy friends in Congress turned back that threat by pleading "states rights" were being violated.

The Camden & Amboy tightened its grip on the vital corridor in 1867 when it purchased the Delaware & Raritan Canal and the New Jersey Railroad (that since 1840 had carried Camden & Amboy cars into Jersey City). There was no question now that a powerful monopoly held New Jersey transportation in its claws.

Three years later, a Philadelphia syndicate called the National Railway asked the legislature for permission to build a rival line from Trenton to Bound Brook. The new railroad would have connections to Philadelphia and New York. That proposal was halted by Assembly Speaker Leon Abbett's plea that "local pride" would be hurt by a railroad operated by out-of-state interests.

Railroads caught everyone's fancy. The Central Railroad depot lured travelers westward to adventure and opportunity. Plush cars carried the elite between home and work or pleasure in the cities. For many, just meeting a railroader was enough.

President and Mrs. Grant made Long Branch the nation's "summer capital" by visiting in 1869 and returning often during Grant's eight years as President. Contemporary drawings show their comfortable "cottage" and the carriage that Grant used for long afternoon rides. The President could be coaxed into opening a ball (such as this one at the Stetson House in July 1869) but he never enjoyed dancing.

That plea lost its validity in 1872 when the Camden & Amboy monopoly leased all its tracks and buildings to the Pennsylvania Railroad — *for 999 years.* New Jersey railroading was now ruled by "foreign" dictators.

The New York Herald summed up the situation:

"The halo of New Jersey's glory has left her … The Camden and Amboy Road, the pride of the state and the rider of her legislatures, has been ceded to Pennsylvania."

A State "Wild With Joy"

There no longer was an excuse to prevent a rival in the corridor. The New Jersey legislature enacted a "General Railroad Law" in 1873, opening the state to new tracks — especially the long-delayed Trenton-to-Bound Brook line. William Sackett wrote in his book, *Modern Battles of Trenton*, that New Jersey "went wild with joy" in the belief that the law would bring "new prosperity."

The National Railway Company quickly began laying rails between Bound Brook and Trenton. The Pennsylvania Railroad fought a delaying action all the way, both in the courts and with fist fights by

lured hoodlums. Finally, the State Militia had to be summoned, in January 1876, to restrain a Pennsylvania Railroad gang that had blocked the National Railway from laying track at Hopewell.

State Geologist George H. Cook wrote in 1876 that there was "a line of railway within five or six miles of almost every dwelling" in New Jersey. Trackage in the state expanded nearly fifty percent within less than ten years after passage of the General Railroad Law.

Much of the new construction of the 1870s was double tracked and a few sections even had four tracks side by side. Cook reported proudly in 1876 that almost all New Jersey residents could easily travel to Philadelphia or New York "transact business there and return to their homes on the same day."

Railroads To Prosperity

The clouds of depression were lifting by 1876. United States population was soaring. Western lands were opening up. Too many people needed too many products for the factories to be still for long. Railroads led the way back to prosperity. Long lines of coal cars left Pennsylvania mines and followed tracks to New Jersey's coal-hungry factories. Tracks

The ending of the Pennsylvania Railroad monopoly in 1873 opened the New Jersey corridor to competition, but the powerful Pennsylvania owners resisted. They blocked a rival from laying a "frog" (or intersection) where their lines crossed near Hopewell. The resulting "Frog War," sketched by a *NY Illustrated Graphic* artist, called out the State Militia to offset the Pennsylvania R R power.

brought raw materials to the glassworks of Cumberland, Salem, and Gloucester counties. The iron mines of Morris and Sussex counties depended on the railroads to reach unprecedented production.

Farmers learned the value of railroad transportation. So-called "pea train" specials left southern New Jersey regularly, loaded with fresh vegetables for markets 200 miles away. One Burlington County vegetable grower wrote in 1895 that New York was only his third-best market, behind Newark and Boston. He did not even mention nearby Philadelphia.

Railroads turned northwestern Bergen County into "one large strawberry patch." Erie Railroad cars, painted a gleaming white, left every evening from Mahwah, Ramsey, Allendale, and Ridgewood, loaded with strawberries for the New York markets. That sweet red harvest lasted until real estate promoters edged the strawberries aside in the 1890s.

Jersey City became "agricultural" in 1874 when a meat packer built a tremendous stockyard and slaughterhouse at the railroad terminal. The company assured nearby residents that the cattle pens were "open on every side to all the winds of heaven." By 1880, more than 1.5 million beef cattle were being slaughtered annually at the Jersey City "range."

Hudson County stockyards grew smaller after refrigerated railroad cars brought in meat from Chicago's giant slaughterhouses. Jersey City's beef cutters did not vanish entirely, for an expanding Jewish population in New York required Kosher meat. Railroad trains could not import Chicago beef overnight to comply with Rabbinical laws. Cattle were brought live to Jersey City and slaughtered to meet the need.

The Day of Two Noons

William F. Allen of South Orange literally stopped every official clock in the United States at High Noon on November 18, 1883 — a day still known in railroad circles as "The Day of Two Noons." By having the intelligence and the stature to force the clock stoppage from Maine to California, the New Jersey man ended a situation that made train travel chaotic.

Son of a Bordentown railroad man and a railroader himself since he turned sixteen in 1862, Allen was deeply upset by the incredible confusions in railroad "time." Watches and clocks were set by the sun. Thus, when it was High Noon, sun time, in New York City, it was 11:58 AM in Trenton, 11:56 AM in Camden, and so on across the nation.

In large railroad terminals where five or six railroad lines converged, each line usually used the time of its home office. Thus six clocks in a depot would show six different times.

Allen was elected secretary of a General Time Convention convened in 1875 to bring railroad clocks into uniformity from coast to coast. Eight years later the railroads accepted Allen's plan to divide the nation into the now-familiar four zones, with time the same anywhere in each zone.

The proposal was greeted with scorn, fear, and as "contrary to nature," but on that one November day in 1883 all railroad clocks in the nation were stopped simultaneously at High Noon, reset, and restarted. America has ticked in unison ever since.

Railroads inevitably enriched farmers as well as industrialists. Jersey City became a prime marketing focus for agriculturalists whether for the early morning delivery of "downstate peaches" and other products or as the place where Western cattle awaited slaughter in the sprawling riverfront stockyards.

The easy chairs shown in this 1870s woodcut, titled *Express Train to the Sea*, provided ease for wealthy vacationers. The top scene on the opposite page caught the excitement at Long Branch when the afternoon's train crowd raced for wagons that drove them to favorite hotels. Others traveled to Barnegat Light on church-centered activities (center, left). Some stout-hearted adventurers liked to rough it at out-of-the-way places such as Beach Haven. Cape May's genteel ways still won favor, but the Jersey Shore's main excitement was at Atlantic City where in 1870 the nation's first boardwalk had been laid directly on the sand.

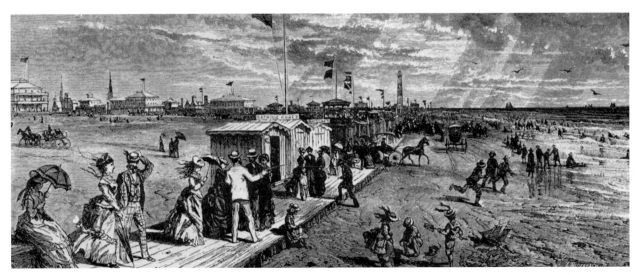

Gold In The Seaside Sands

Changes in industrial patterns and farm marketing might have been anticipated as the result of railroads. Trains also lifted the modest and traditional Jersey Shore entertainment of visitors into a major industry between 1870 and 1900.

The Camden & Atlantic Railroad literally created Atlantic City in 1854. Rival capitalists set out in 1877 to capture some of the seaside business. They laid fifty-four miles of their Narrow Gauge Railroad (so called because of its track width) from Camden to Atlantic City in an astounding ninety-eight days. The competitors cut fares and lured new sand lovers to the beach.

Atlantic City was "Queen of the Coast" by 1900. Its population jumped from a handful of people in 1854 to 28,000 full-time residents. The "Queen's" real estate, nearly valueless in 1854, was estimated to be worth more than $50 million in 1900. Seven hundred thousand visited Atlantic City that year.

Other resorts grew more modestly. Cape May had its own railroad by 1863, but many of its former regulars from Philadelphia and Baltimore had deserted to Atlantic City. Cape May could not live down its reputation as a place of "spinster and dowager habitues. . . fond of whist" (as an unimpressed New York writer noted in the 1870s).

Northward, a railroad reached Tuckerton in 1872 and made Long Beach Island an accessible resort land. The New York and Long Branch Railroad whistled slowly south from New Brunswick between 1875 and 1885, opening the coast between Long Branch and Seaside Park. As many as 103 daily trains, carrying 8,000 visitors, arrived at Asbury Park every day in 1883.

"Enjoy The Shore In Summer"

A new breed of people who could "work in New York and enjoy the Shore in summer" entered the scene in the 1880s. Colonel L. U. Maitby, owner of Sea Girt and Spring Lake hotels, told the railroad if it could run a train from Sea Girt to Jersey City in

Heaven For A Sunday

The railroads and the public came most closely together on Sundays, when packed excursion trains left Jersey City, Hoboken, Newark, Montclair, and other stations to transport thousands of families to a one-day heaven at the North Jersey lakes.

Almost left out of the Sunday trade was the Morris & Essex branch of the Lackawanna Railroad, that permitted no Sunday trains until 1899. By then, most excursioner trade had gone to the Jersey Central, Lehigh Valley, and New York & Greenwood Lake railroads.

Greenwood Lake's attractions prompted an artist from the New York Daily Graphic to sketch the scenes at the top of the opposite page. He depicted the long pier and excursion steamboat near the railroad, the quiet joys of the lakeshore, the hotels, and fishing spots. The Sunday "Greenwood Lake Express" left Jersey City at 10:13 AM and reached the lake at 12:30. The return trip from the lake began at 4:45 PM. That allowed 4 hours and 15 minutes to savor the lake's pleasures.

Lake Hopatcong did not become popular until the 1890s, when the Jersey Central developed a resort at Nolan's Point and provided trains to get urban people there on Sundays. Gustav Kobbé wrote in his *Jersey Central* that many people "concentrated a whole year's holiday into a single day at the lake."

Not all lakes welcomed the pleasure seekers. After the Lackawanna made Cranberry Lake a stop for 1,000 excursioners every Sunday, a lake chronicler noted "old residents were aghast at the hordes unloaded on our erstwhile peaceful shores." The "hordes" flocked anyway to enjoy, among other treats, the unique miniature railroad (below) in Cranberry Lake's amusement park.

New York and Greenwood Lake and Watchung Railways

TIME TABLE

Newark's Roseville Avenue Station (above) was an important junction on the Lackawanna Railroad by 1900. Lines converged here from commuting areas: Montclair and Glen Ridge to the north, and the Oranges, Short Hills, Summit, and Morristown to the west. Elsewhere on the Lackawanna, commuters built houses near the tracks at such places as Wyoming Station (below). Llewellyn Park in Orange (bottom) was an exclusive hillside settlement where wealthy settlers enjoyed country life.

RESIDENCE OF O. D. MUNN ESQ.
LLEWELLYN PARK, ORANGE, N.J.

ninety minutes, he would guarantee 150 Wall Street brokers to ride it daily.

The railroad compromised at two hours for the trip. The 150 brokers accepted the slower time, accommodating other brokers who preferred to get off at Long Branch, Asbury Park, or Ocean Grove.

Families of the brokers and other well-to-do businessmen spent the summers in huge Victorian "cottages" overlooking the rolling ocean. Railroads brought in their servants and their trunks and baggage — enough to hold clothing and supplies for a full season. The wealthy visitors themselves were driven to their resort homes in splendid horse-drawn carriages.

Full-season families were not numerous. Most of the Jersey Shore visitors were laboring people whose only release from work was on Sunday. They patronized one-day Sunday rail excursions to Long Branch, Wildwood, or Atlantic City. Excursion trains left Jersey City, Newark, and Camden soon after dawn and returned after sunset. The round-trip fare was usually $1 — not small in a time when a working man made only about $4 a week.

The excursion trains grew increasingly popular in the 1880s and 1890s. They came to be called "Dollar Specials" or "Shoe Box" Excursions (because lunches were often carried in shoe boxes). In later years, "Fishermen's Specials" left Camden for Wildwood. So many fishing poles stuck out of car windows the trains looked like speeding porcupines.

Lines To The Lakeland

Northern New Jersey's lakeland also attracted railroad-borne vacationers, although in far fewer numbers than the seacoast. After the Civil War, lakeside "camps" (often with tent homes) became common at Budd, Hopatcong, and Greenwood lakes, and Green Pond. By 1880, a few small cottages began to appear.

"Dollar Excursions" also ran to the lakes, especially Lake Hopatcong. Sunday visitors went to Hopatcong from Jersey City or Newark, via High Bridge and Long Valley — a dollar's bargain if only for the ride itself. The favored destination was Nolan's Point on Hopatcong's northern shore.

Gustav Kobbé wrote of the lakeland adventures in his book, *Jersey Central*, published in 1890. Fifty thousand visitors rode to Hopatcong that year. They enjoyed chartered boats, picnics, flying swings, and a dance pavilion. They could also eat a substantial hot lunch for fifty cents at the nearby Hotel Breslin.

Also favored by the excursioners was Greenwood

Lake, reached in 1876 via the New York, Montclair and Greenwood Lake Railroad. Excursion trains from Jersey City to this "Switzerland of the East" made twenty-seven stops along the way.

A round trip between Jersey City and Greenwood Lake required four hours and fifty-four stops and cost a dollar and a half, but the four-hour stay at the lake was temporary heaven even for those who had to work nearly two days to earn the cost of the fare.

Commuters Follow The Rails

Far more important, good railroad transportation encouraged city dwellers to seek the hastily built suburban housing developments that transformed New Jersey pasturelands into towns. Strings of such places sprang up in Union, Morris, Somerset, and Bergen counties between 1870 and 1910, accommodating commuters to Newark and New York.

The towns grew beside the tracks, clinging closely to the Morris & Essex Railroad, out to Morristown and to the Jersey Central across the flatlands to Plainfield and Somerville. Several lines, especially the Erie, coaxed railroad riders toward Upper Montclair and up through Bergen County.

The commuters were usually executives in big city companies who believed they knew far more about town government than noncommuters. By 1910, nearly every town along the railroads was run by gone-all-day, govern-all-night residents whose chief interest in government often lay in keeping local taxes at a minimum.

Railroad executives encouraged commuter towns, even to the extent of buying their own vegetable fields or orchards and dividing the land into home sites. A prime example of a railroader-turned-developer was John Taylor Johnson of Plainfield, president of the Jersey Central Railroad. Under his direction, the Central Land Improvement Company was formed to develop land in Union County.

Commuting came to southern New Jersey much more slowly and really was not important until the 1920s. For one thing, that area's railroad boom did not begin until long after the Civil War. For another, towns south and east of Camden were provincial and self-sufficient, unlikely to attract Philadelphia executives.

Philadelphia's commuter exodus went westward along the Pennsylvania Railroad to found a string of towns that became famed as "The Main Line." Southern New Jersey simply was not fashionable and

SCENE AT THE LAST BERGEN FIELDS SALE.

WHERE IS BERGEN FIELDS?

BERGEN FIELDS is situated on the main line of the West Shore Railroad, 45 minutes from New York.

Every Lot is beautifully situated, elevated and sloping, and all of them are high and dry, and close to the depot.

WHAT HAS BERGEN FIELDS?

Bergen Fields has 22 trains daily (10 on Sunday). Commutation 10 cents. It has Churches, Public and Private Schools, good Stores, Building and Loan Associations, Masonic and Benevolent Associations; also Village Improvement and Protective Associations, all near by. TERMS: $10 a Lot down on day of sale.

few of the wealthy set cared to take a long ferry trip and train ride to such a place.

Fresh Air In The Mountains

Commuting appealed especially to those who felt "mountain air" was a curative, easing the pain of the tired feeling at the end of a busy day in a city office. This induced swelling numbers of businessmen to patronize the Morris & Essex Railroad (later known as the Delaware, Lackawanna & Western, or just "The Lackawanna").

The trackage of the M. & E. (The Lackawanna) snaked its way in sweeping curves through the Oranges, Millburn, and Short Hills up to Summit; then moved westward through Chatham, Madison, and Morristown.

Service on the Lackawanna was far superior to that on most American railroads. Special treatment was afforded the top-level executives, and so many of them lived in Madison, Convent, and Morristown the railroad started its famed "Morristown Banker's Express" in 1883. The train and its own crew were reserved for the privileged few who could afford the extra fare.

The Banker's Express became one of the most esteemed trains in railroad history. The deluxe train steamed out of Morristown every morning, *promptly* at 8:23 o'clock, and stopped only twice on the speedy run to Hoboken. The schedule was reversed in the afternoon, starting from Hoboken at 4:15. The plush train had the right-of-way over everything on the line.

Counting the ferryboat ride across the Hudson River, Banker's Express riders could get from

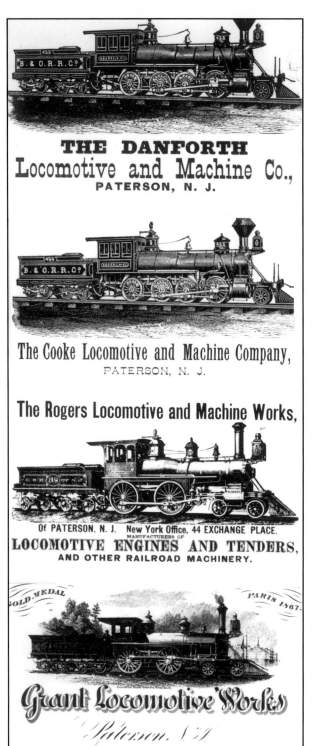

THE DANFORTH
Locomotive and Machine Co.,
PATERSON, N. J.

The Cooke Locomotive and Machine Company,
PATERSON, N. J.

The Rogers Locomotive and Machine Works,
Of PATERSON, N. J. New York Office, 44 EXCHANGE PLACE.
MANUFACTURERS OF
LOCOMOTIVE ENGINES AND TENDERS,
AND OTHER RAILROAD MACHINERY.

GOLD MEDAL   PARIS 1867.

Grant Locomotive Works
Paterson, N. J.

Business cards of four major companies told the world Rogers, Grant, Danforth, and Cooke made Paterson a leading locomotive building center. Not mentioned was the fact that none of the factories had a railroad spur. The "iron horses" had to be towed through town by real horses before being set on main line tracks.

Morristown to New York in fifty minutes. Anyone who could stroll into his Wall Street office well after 9 AM and saunter out soon after 3 PM could aspire to ride the Banker's Express — if he could afford it.

"Mecca Of Suburban Dwellers"

Just after the Civil War, the Erie Railroad began printing its Bergen County timetables on the front pages of local newspapers, with predictions the county would become "the future garden spot of New Jersey." It already was a garden spot because of its farms, but the promoters meant houses, not cabbages or strawberries.

The Erie's prediction in the 1870s that Bergen would become "the mecca of thousands of suburban dwellers" was realized. A stream of "outside folks" poured into the area, lured by such Erie propaganda as this:

> *Lose no time in selecting your property. Do not fail to provide for keeping poultry and a cow, nor for the culture of fruit, vegetables and flowers, and you will live in your Suburban Home to an honored and ripe old age and see your children, and your children's children, rise up and call you blessed.*

The railroad promoters had plenty of shrewd local help between 1860 and 1885. J. Wyman Jones began promoting sales of his 625 acres of farmland at Englewood. William Walter Phelps, who moved to Teaneck in 1865, set up a land company in Closter that within thirteen years owned 4,000 acres. Phelps built thirty miles of local roads and planted more than a half million trees.

As the railroad lines spread up the Bergen County valleys, developers prepared fancy property maps with fancy new town names to match. One developer built a station in a wide open field near Schraalenburgh and named it, quite simply, "Bergen Fields." Soon a town arose (now called Bergenfield).

Bergen's new towns and villages lost their distinctive old Dutch or Indian names. The Bergen County Historical Society sought in 1872 to prevent "the old historic names of the county from being blotted out by namby-pamby sentimental 'Ridges,' 'Woods,' and 'Parks.'" That failed. Gone were such wonderful old Bergen town names as Boiling Springs, English Neighbourhood, Weerimus, Red Mills, and Schraalenburgh.

The Spurs To Industry

There could be no mistaking how railroads had changed industry in New Jersey. By 1885, railroad-fed industry had locked New Jersey in a powerful embrace.

New Jersey was not rich in natural resources: some iron, clay, and glass sand, and that was about all. Without the railroads, New Jersey might have remained a pastoral landscape to keep New York and Philadelphia apart.

Wherever the railroads went, industry followed. Coal-powered steam engines freed factory workers from the need to be near water power. Industry could locate wherever a rail spur could replenish coal piles and stocks of raw materials.

Industrial architecture underwent transformation. New steam-driven factories rose three or four stories tall. They usually were of brick rather than wood in order to support heavy machinery. The skies above were blackened by smoke from the towering stacks, as evidence that coal fires were turning the wheels.

Little New Jersey was fourth smallest among the thirty-eight states in 1880. Significantly, it was fifth largest in manufacturing. The state's role was clearly cast, and industrialists were transferring in from other states to be near the big markets and the railroad tracks.

Old industries expanded steadily — jewelry, leather, and beer in Newark; rubber in Passaic, New Brunswick, and Trenton; clay products in Trenton,

Clark Thread Company's mill dominated the Passaic River waterfront after completion in 1866. Thousands of workers, mostly women, turned out millions of yards of Clark's "O.N.T." (Our New Thread) monthly.

It was easy to pass the old man by as he shuffled along Camden's streets, in the 1880s, in shabby gray clothes and floppy hat.

Yet those who recognized the old man as Walt Whitman knew he was world-acclaimed for his poetry, probably better known in France or Japan than in New Jersey.

Born in Huntington, Long Island in 1820, Whitman became a drifting newspaperman before he was 20. He worked for at least 10 newspapers before being named editor of the Brooklyn Eagle in 1848.

Whitman immediately sported the fine clothes of a successful editor, but his work did not match his appearance. He was fired, wandered again, let his graying beard grow, and began wearing gray suits. He published 12 poems in 1855 in the first edition of his ultimately famed Leaves Of Grass. *Critics damned Whitman as much for his free life style as for his poetry.*

Ever experimenting, Whitman sought to portray nature and to denounce Americans for their inability to make the dream of American freedom ring true. He was only moderately accepted as a poet in this country when he came to Camden in 1872.

The Camden period was productive and satisfying. Whitman revised Leaves Of Grass *for five new editions between 1876 and 1892 and wrote his loosely-autobiographical work,* Specimen Days and Collect *in 1882-83.*

Whitman bought a house on Mickle Street in 1884. It was gray, matching his clothes. He liked being called "The Good Gray Poet," and he continued to write even after suffering a paralyzing stroke.

Facing death in 1892, Whitman chose his own burial plot in Camden's Harleigh Cemetery. When the poet died in 1892 at age 72, friends buried him beneath the epitaph he wrote himself: "For that of me which is to die."

It was a fitting memorial. By 1892 Whitman knew his poetry would long outlive his mortal remains.

Sayreville, and Perth Amboy; locomotives and silk in Paterson; textiles and handkerchiefs in Passaic.

Cumberland, Salem, and Gloucester counties were a national center of glass manufacture. Morris, Mercer, Passaic, and Essex had important iron and steel works. Nearly every town of more than 10,000 population had clothing factories.

Keeping A Nation In Stitches

Most factories remained small, employing fewer than fifty persons, but an age of industrial goliaths was under way. Two were so big, in 1876, each had a special "day" at the Philadelphia Centennial Exposition, and each hired entire railroad trains to carry their thousands of employees to the fair.

The two giants were the Clark Thread Company of East Newark and the Singer Sewing Machine Company of Elizabethport. Both gave evidence American women were stitching and sewing with a zeal that would have astonished, or dismayed, their hard-working grandmothers.

George and William Clark came from Scotland to East Newark in 1865 to make spools of thread, just the right size for a sewing basket. Those little spools led to big business. The Clarks expanded twice in fifteen years, until by 1881 they employed 2,000 persons (mostly women and girls).

In 1873, Isaac Singer consolidated his several small, scattered sewing machine factories into a tremendous $3 million plant in Elizabethport. His huge factory ran completely with steam, at a time when about half of New Jersey's factories still used water-power. Four thousand employees worked in the Elizabethport plant.

The Singer factory turned out two million sewing machines annually as early as 1879. Many went into slum apartments in Newark, Jersey City, Paterson, and other cities where immigrant families worked feverishly to get an economic foothold in America.

Some immigrant families operated eight to ten machines in a single room, stitching clothing on contract. Everyone worked in such families, even the smallest child who could operate a treadle. Such operations were quickly — and properly — called "sweat shops."

The Age Of The Practical Man

One of the wonders of the age was the crude tele-

Wherever the railroads ran in the 1880s, industry was sure to follow — whether in the country, to serve Morris County's Bartley Machine Shop, or in the city, to supply the Currier machine works in Newark's busy factory section. Tracks ran through the Camden Iron Works to the Delaware River waterfront, and railroads linked the Salamander Works in Woodbridge with the far-flung markets for its ceramic products. The huge Trenton Iron Company sent iron beams out by train, and the Clayton Glass Works in Gloucester County was tied to rail spurs. The Paterson Iron Company interchanged prosperity with the nearby railroad, for many of its products went directly to supply railroading needs. Railroads, smoke, and prosperity: that was the story.

John Philip Holland, wearing rimless glasses and a derby, looked more like the Paterson schoolteacher he had been than a famed inventor when he posed in the 1890s in one of his early submarines.

phone Alexander Graham Bell was hoping might win some small attention at Philadelphia's Centennial Exposition. Visitors were intrigued by Bell's device, but considered it merely a "toy." The Exposition failed to reflect fully a new age that was dawning.

Within two decades after the Exposition, incredible things would come into being. Bell's "toy" would intensify communication. A submarine would revolutionize warfare. Electricity, plastics, petroleum, and the movies would change society forever. And, wonder of wonders, buggies would be driven by motors.

Each invention unleashed new industrial spinoffs. New Jersey's strategic location at the center of things insured a share of that industrial spurt. More important, the state had more than its share of inventors.

In New Jersey, a typesetter would perfect the first plastic, a minister would make the first flexible photographic film, and a schoolteacher would invent the first workable submarine. Above all, a one-time telegraph operator would perfect electricity, the phonograph, and the movies all in New Jersey.

A typesetter, a minister, a schoolteacher, a telegraph operator; none of them was trained in mathematical or scientific theory. They were practical,

trial-and-error men. They typified a new breed of inventor in the period of 1875 to 1900, for this was the age of the practical man.

There was a constant search for new, durable materials to replace diminishing supplies of natural substances. Persons who made such discoveries were assured wealth and fame, if they could capitalize on their ideas.

Phelan & Collander Company of New York, makers of pool tables and supplies, unwittingly introduced the plastics age. When diminishing elephant herds could not supply enough ivory tusks for the balls needed in pool parlors in the 1860s, the firm offered $10,000 for an ivory substitute.

John Wesley Hyatt, a young Albany, New York typesetter, accepted the challenge. Working in the kitchen of his unenthusiastic landlady, Hyatt accidentally combined pryoxylin (basically highly flammable nitrocellulose) with camphor.

Using heat and pressure, Hyatt and a fellow printer, James Brown, created a synthetic substance they called "Celluloid." It was the world's first commercially successful plastic.

Hyatt envisioned uses for Celluloid far beyond pool balls. He sought financial backing to permit him to open a new five-story factory in Newark in 1873.

Hyatt soon expanded to three more buildings. His company made dental plates, knife handles, piano keys, harness ornaments, and Celluloid collars and cuffs. The last-named were attached to shirts to make laundering easier: the collars and cuffs could be wiped clean with a damp cloth.

The ingenious Hyatt and an aide named Charles Burroughs made the first injection molding machinery in 1878. The Hyatt machine could turn out molded buttons, buckles, shaving brush handles, and combs. Injection molding is still used in major plastics industries around the world.

Another inventive mind found a use for Celluloid that Hyatt had overlooked. The Rev. Hannibal Goodwin, a Newark minister, hoped that sheets of Celluloid could be used to replace glass slides of Bible scenes his Sunday school children were always breaking.

Working in the attic of his parsonage, Goodwin invented flexible film in 1887. His attic discovery laid the base for all of today's huge production of photographic and movie film. The minister did not prosper. He died long before drawn-out court suits earned his widow both confirmation of Goodwin's discovery and a large cash settlement.

A Weapon To "End War"

John Philip Holland, who taught at St. John's Parochial School in Paterson, yearned to construct a ship that could travel long distances under water. Born in Ireland in 1841, he taught school there and began experiments with an underwater ship, or submarine.

Underwater craft, experimented with as early as the American Revolution, posed two challenges. The first was to stay deep under the surface without a fresh air intake. The second was to get back to the surface. Holland emigrated to Paterson in 1873.

Three years later, he closed the lid on a fourteen-foot craft and took it to the bottom of the Passaic River. Seconds later, the schoolteacher surfaced. His submarine remained at the bottom. What went down, Holland discovered, did not necessarily come up.

The US Navy refused to look at Holland's scheme in 1875, with good reason. It was not a success. An Irish group, the Fenian Society, agreed to supply funds to further Holland's research. Rumor had it the Fenians intended to use submarines to blow the British Navy out of the ocean.

Holland launched the thirty-one-foot *Fenian Ram* in 1881. The Ram went down sixty feet off Staten Island and stayed on the bottom for a full hour before surfacing with its three crewmen alive and joyous.

The US Navy asked Holland to submit further plans in 1888. Seven years later, it offered him a contract, and then changed his plans so much the Navy submarine was a complete failure. Infuriated, Holland privately built his own craft and launched it successfully in 1898. His submarine fired a torpedo from beneath the water.

Holland believed his invention had made war so horrible to contemplate that no sane nation ever again would declare war against another. Nevertheless, the US Navy bought his ship in 1900 and commissioned him to make several others.

Holland's hope the submarine might be an instrument for peace proved fleeting. Soon the powerful nations of the world would be using his Paterson-perfected invention to make sea warfare lethal beyond imagination.

A Man To Change The World

As John Holland tinkered with his submarine, a young telegraph operator named Thomas Alva Edison came to Newark in 1871. He would make New Jersey his home for the remaining sixty-one years of his life.

Edison's story is familiar. Born in Ohio in 1847, he left school in the fourth grade when his teachers agreed Tom was "addled" and slow. He drifted throughout much of his young life, became a telegraph operator and, in 1870, developed an improved stock ticker.

He sold the ticker for $40,000 and came to Newark to make telegraph equipment. By 1874, Edison had also invented the quadruplex telegraph, enabling one wire to handle four messages simultaneously. He then created an automatic telegraph system to multiply telegraphic speed nearly thirty times. Edison's company was soon the world's largest maker of telegraph instruments.

Edison found riches in Newark, but the restless inventor wasn't satisfied with money. He turned his factory over to his superintendent in 1876 and bought a site atop a hill in Menlo Park. There, Edison announced, he would build a "brain factory" — the world's first organized research center.

The hilltop was covered with wild strawberries, an

Menlo Park was known world-wide by January 1880 when a *Leslie's* artist sketched the tiny village. Edison's laboratory (far right) already produced electrical power to light the village.

Edison's youth impressed those who saw him demonstrate his phonograph in 1878. He was just 30 when he invented the machine to record and reproduce sound.

unexpected bonus, but Edison bought the site because of its location between New York and Philadelphia. Just down the hill in New Brunswick, Pennsylvania railroad trains could be boarded to speed a man and his inventions toward either city.

"Mary Had A Little Lamb"

Edison built a two-story wooden building at Menlo Park and installed machinery and scientific equipment. He surrounded himself with a bright young team: John Ott, a wonderfully skilled mechanic; John Batchelor, an able mechanical draftsman; John Kreusi, a master craftsman who could make anything; and Francis R. Upton, a mathematician and physicist.

Telegraphy was the first order of business at Menlo Park. Trying to record telegraphic messages in 1877, Edison found he could reproduce sounds on a piece of wax paper attached to a revolving cylinder. He was certain he could reproduce the human voice.

Edison directed Kreusi to build a machine designed to roll tinfoil under a needle on a sensitive diaphragm. During the summer of 1877, Edison turned the crank of the crude little machine, reciting "Mary had a little lamb" as he cranked. Edison reset the needle and re-cranked the machine. There, squeaky but clear, was Edison's voice and "Mary had a little lamb."

"I was never taken so aback in my life." Edison wrote. "Everybody was astonished. I was always afraid of things that worked the first time."

Edison personally demonstrated the phonograph, as he called it, before Congress and President Rutherford B. Hayes. Thousands journeyed to Menlo Park to listen to the scratchy little "talking machine."

Visitors suspected trickery. One morning, noted Methodist Bishop John Vincent came to see the phonograph. He was openly skeptical and Edison offered to record the bishop's voice. Edison later wrote:

"He commenced to recite Biblical names with intense rapidity. On reproducing it, he said, 'I am satisfied, now. There isn't a man in the United States who could recite those names with the same rapidity.'"

"Only The Rich Can Burn Candles"

Edison and his aides put the phonograph aside for ten years. The team was hot on the trail of a practical system of electric lighting. Speed was crucial; many others around the world also were actively seeking a cheap, practical way to use electricity.

Edison did not *invent* the electric lamp, nor did he invent electric *power*, but he achieved his announced goal of making electrical light "so cheap that only the rich will be able to burn candles."

The key to the practical use of electricity was the lamp, and the key to the lamp was finding an inexpensive filament that would last for many hours. Edison used many filaments, even trying hairs from Kreusi's beard. Early in the fall of 1879, he began experimenting with pieces of cotton thread.

The thread had to be carbonized by extremely careful and controlled burning, and then placed in a bulb from which all air had been drawn by a vacuum pump. Finally, on Sunday, October 19, 1879, Edison turned on a lamp with a carbonized thread filament.

The cotton filament glowed brightly. It continued to burn for forty hours, through the darkness for two nights. On October 21, Edison turned up the current to see how brightly the lamp could burn. It expired in a dazzle of brightness.

Edison cautioned against premature optimism, but Edison's backers promoted a full-page article in the *New York Herald* on December 21 to announce the new light. The startled Menlo Park team read there would be a "public demonstration" on New Year's Eve.

This news was greeted by ridicule from resentful rivals and cautious scientists. The Menlo Park researchers ignored the controversy and worked tirelessly for the New Year's Eve event the *Herald* article had made necessary.

When the promised night arrived, visitors swarmed in the street outside the laboratory, marveling at the lamps that brightened both the outside street and the inside laboratory. Visitors left convinced, and in the manner of holiday crowds in any period they stole eight of the precious lamps as souvenirs.

Making Electricity Practical

The stolen lamps were not useful to the thieves. No electrical system existed to light a bulb, stolen or otherwise, except at Menlo Park. Edison's challenge was to make electricity available to the masses.

Edison and his associates pressed on, ignoring newspaper reports and court fights from competitors. The team had to make everything: generators, sockets, lamp bases, meters, switches, and a practical way to transmit the current from generators to houses and businesses.

Large-scale public use of incandescent lights started in September 1882 when the Edison Company completed the Pearl Street generating station in New York City. Current flowed through underground wires to light nearby stores and homes.

Pleased with the dramatic impact of the Pearl Street station and its power to light 5,000 lamps, Edison next sought to prove electricity could be practical in a small town of scattered homes. He chose Roselle, New Jersey, and the villagers there eagerly cooperated in 1883 when he offered to wire their homes free and to give them light bulbs.

Edison's fame tended to overshadow others, particularly Edward Weston of Newark, who set up the nation's first commercial dynamo in an abandoned Newark synagogue in 1877. He used the dynamo to light one carbon arc street light on a main intersection in the city.

Carbon arc lights gave plenty of illumination, but were far too garish and dangerous for indoor use. They continued in popularity for outside use through the 1880s. In 1883, Weston provided four strings of his carbon arc lamps to light the new Brooklyn Bridge.

Weston's inventive genius nearly rivaled that of Edison's. By 1884, his patents covered the spectrum of the electrical field from motors and generators to underground cables, batteries, switches, and fuses.

Weston then turned his interest to making precision instruments to measure electrical current. He later won enduring fame by inventing the photoelectric cell.

A self-taught electrical genius, Edward Weston developed a reliable dynamo by age 21. Six years later, he opened America's first generating station (right) to run machines and to light carbon arc lamps. His greatest contributions were in electrical measurement. His greatest invention was the photoelectric cell (or "electric eye").

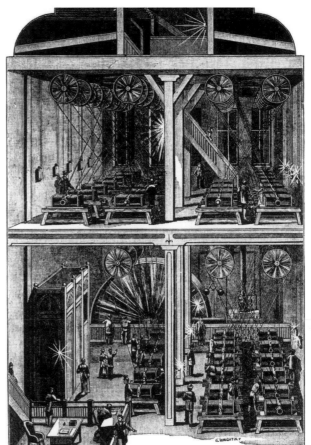

Movie Capital Of The World

The above scene is from The Great Train Robbery, *filmed totally in New Jersey in 1903. Said to be the first movie with a plot, it featured several things that would become traditional movie fare: violence, crime, bloodshed, and a chase, all in a "Western" setting.*

Edwin S. Porter made the film for Thomas Edison's company in West Orange. By 1903, Edison was the fore-most name in motion pictures; extravagant claims were made he had invented this new art form that would profoundly influence 20th century life.

Edison did not invent motion pictures; many others had been trying to capture movement on film before his team of inventors took up the problem in 1888. Much of the work in perfecting movies was done by an Edison assistant named William L. K. Dickson.

The world's first motion picture "studio," built in West Orange in 1893, was a large tar paper-covered building, nicknamed "The Black Maria." The big structure could be moved on rollers so filming could take advantage of maximum sunlight.

Other filmmakers entered the field after 1900, with New York City backers providing financial support. Working with limited funds, moviemakers turned to New Jersey for its varied outdoor backgrounds — mountains, woodlands, lakes, fields, brooks, and small towns.

Thus, by 1910, New Jersey had become the movie capital of the world. Several filmmakers built large studios at Fort Lee, only a ferryboat trip away from New York City, where actors and actresses (and company owners) preferred to live.

The nearby Palisades was especially used for shooting rugged adventure stories. Many movies were made on or near that cliff, featuring such stars as Pearl White, Mary Pickford, Harold Lloyd, Douglas Fairbanks, and others famed in the 1920s.

After World War I, moviemakers shifted their studios to Hollywood, California to take advantage of more days of sunshine. Efforts to revive filming in New Jersey have been made recently, for the variety is still here.

Power Beyond All Imagination

Edison, however, was the name on everyone's lips, and he was the force that made electricity both useful and inexpensive. No single man of science before (and perhaps since) so completely revolutionized the world. Later, his phonograph and movie cameras transformed entertainment, but his chief contribution to mankind was the harnessing of a power beyond all imagination.

Electrical power emerged slowly. Installations were extremely costly, chiefly because of the skyrocketing cost of copper. The industrial census of 1890 for New Jersey showed only 706 horsepower derived from electricity — about one-third of one percent of all power needed to run New Jersey's factories.

Still in the future was an electrified world when factories could move away from railroad sidings because they no longer required coal for steam engines; when small electrical motors would replace dangerous flapping belts in industrial plants; when tremendous power could be summoned merely by the flick of a switch.

Also far in the future were days of crisis when great areas of the state would be paralyzed if summer hurricanes or winter sleet storms felled electrical wires and shut off taken-for-granted power. Only at such times would the incredible influence of electricity on everyday life be realized.

Oil For The Lamps Of New York

As Edison worked toward production of a new energy source, others, unaware of the coming of electricity, battled in New Jersey to control the distribution of petroleum, another emerging energy source. When petroleum producers realized the greatest market in the world for their fuel was New York City, only a narrow river away, they fought to control Bayonne real estate.

Petroleum was discovered in Pennsylvania in 1859 and, by 1875, was being refined into kerosene, the prime fuel for household and store lamps. Most of the kerosene lamps in the United States were in or near bustling, thriving New York.

Prentice Oil Company established the East Coast's first oil refinery at Bayonne in 1875. It imported Pennsylvania petroleum in railroad tank cars. Close by, Bayonne's fine beaches along Newark Bay were so unspoiled that in summertime the town proudly called itself "The Newport of New York."

Bayonne's bayshore retained some of its early charm in 1890, when Gustav Kobbé sketched this scene (left), but drastic change was imminent. Gangs of workers snaked pipelines eastward to bring Pennsylvania crude oil to Standard Oil and Tidewater refineries in Bayonne. By the mid-1880s, Standard's plant (below) refined millions of gallons of kerosene annually.

Now, however, dark black smoke and soot swirled over the once-lovely beachfront. The noxious smoke came from huge fires lit by Prentice to dispose of objectionable residues — especially gasoline, for which there was no use in 1875.

Competition came in 1877 when John D. Rockefeller's Standard Oil Company of Cleveland, Ohio built another refinery in Bayonne. A few months later, Rockefeller bought out Prentice's twenty employees and 600-barrels-a-day capacity. Standard Oil was prepared to ship kerosene around the world.

War For Bayonne's Waterfront

Meanwhile, in Pennsylvania, a little firm called Tidewater Oil Company also eyed the Bayonne waterfront. When the railroads refused to carry Tidewater petroleum in competition with Standard Oil, the company began to build a 288-mile-long pipeline over the Allegheny Mountains, through the lesser hills of New Jersey, and under Newark Bay to Bayonne.

John D. Rockefeller appreciated Tidewater's plans. His company immediately started laying its own pipeline from its gushers in Pennsylvania, 400 miles away. The last mile proved the most difficult to conquer. Bayonne's mayor vetoed a resolution permitting Standard to lay pipe through Bayonne's 30th Street.

In retaliation, Standard backed a rival candidate for mayor in the next election. He won, and Rockefeller's company received the permit.

Standard's pipeline brought oil into Bayonne in 1880, as Tidewater patiently inched its way toward the waterfront, finally reached in 1888. The two Bayonne oil companies settled into competition; there were enough nearby kerosene lamps for both. By 1899, the rivals were refining more than 8.6 million barrels of petroleum products (mostly kerosene) a year.

Outbound tankers carried Bayonne-refined oil to the world in steel holds. At home, kerosene stoves became popular for winter warmth or as a summer substitute for the kitchen coal stove. Factory owners began lubricating steam engines and other machinery with petroleum lubricating oils instead of old-fashioned whale sperm or lard oils.

By 1895, vacationers had fled Bayonne. That was considered a small economic loss compared to the taxes paid by the refiners. As for the oil men, they had only one problem: what to do with the exasperating waste fluid called gasoline. In the 1890s, who needed gasoline?

On The Edge Of Tomorrow

The 20th century was approaching. Every turn of

a century inspires predictions of plenty and forecasts of doom. As the countdown began on the 1800s, a few visionaries dared to predict the so-called Victorian Era (named for England's Queen Victoria) would soon be swept away.

Old moral values were being tested by the changing times. Tastes in music and styles in clothing were evolving. Demands for entertainment were increasing. Taller buildings were rising at a pace that would pick up as electric elevators improved.

And even as city planners beautified "downtown," the slums grew worse. Increased urbanization brought problems of water pollution. Streets were littered with refuse and manure. Disease was rampant in crowded areas.

Despite the slums, the teeming dirty streets, and the wretched pollution, people flocked more than ever into the cities. Some came from the farms — young men and women hoping city life might provide a way up the economic ladder. Entire families of immigrants swarmed in from foreign lands, certain that America's streets were paved with gold.

The Victorian Age was dying. Those who benefited from its gaudy, money-conscious, moralistic aura hoped it might never end. The great masses of people — the poor, the uneducated, the exploited — feared it might last forever.

A kerosene stove was the height of luxury for housewives in the late 19th century. A "New Perfecto" three-burner was a goal for any homemaker who cooked on a woodburning stove in summertime.

John I. Blair owned more than 2 million acres of western land, traveled 40,000 miles each year, controlled 60 railroads, and piled up $60 million. It all began at age 18 when he opened a grocery store, in 1820, at Gravel Hill in Warren County. Gravel Hill changed its name to Blairstown in 1839, with Blair already headed for fame. After the Civil War, he began building railroads west of the Mississippi River. In time, he controlled 2,000 miles of track and was called the "Railroad King of the West."

Other New Jerseyans followed golden trails in the 19th century. Lewis and George Green of Woodbury grew rich on patent medicines. Lewis, the father, began making a medicine for dyspepsia called "Green's August Flower." By 1870, he had amassed a half million dollars.

George Green, a Civil War surgeon, enlarged the business by advertising extensively. The millions distributed *Green's Atlas and Almanac* annually. The 1883 cover showed the Green complex in Woodbury.

Trenton's Roebling family became the nation's foremost builder of suspension bridges after John A. Roebling suspended a railroad bridge over the Niagara River in 1849. Twenty years later, he died while making a survey for the Brooklyn Bridge.

George Washington Roebling, John's son, finished the Brooklyn Bridge in 1883, watching progress on the spectacular span from a nearby window after he was stricken with illness during construction. The Roebling firm in modern years built both the George Washington and Golden Gate bridges.

James H. Birch made more than 70 types of horse-drawn carriages in his Burlington factory, but his place in history rests on his "Oriental jinrickshas." The first Birch 'ricksha appeared in the early 1880s. By 1918, when the factory closed, practically every Far Eastern 'ricksha bore the label, "Made in Burlington, New Jersey, U.S.A."

Chapter Ten - Urbanizing The Garden State

United States			New Jersey
Typewriter invented	1867		
Farmers organize	1867		
National Grange			
		1871	Stevens Tech opens in Hoboken
		1872	Newark bans segregation in schools
		1873	1st immigrants reach Vineland
		1875	Prudential Insurance Co. founded
Flood of immigrants begins	1880	1880	State called urban by Census Bureau
		1885	Newark Tech opens
Statue of Liberty dedicated	1886		
Oklahoma Territory opens	1889	1889	State's 1st trolley runs in Atlantic City
1st national use of secret ballot	1892	1892	Newark starts water system
Bureau of Immigration created	1894		
Oil discovered in Texas	1901		
		1910	NJ 5th in immigrants

Ex-Attorney General Abram Browning of Camden revived an old saying before a "New Jersey Day" crowd at Philadelphia's Centennial Exposition, in August 1876, by declaring that once the state was called "a beer barrel, with all the live beer running into Philadelphia and New York."

Browning admitted that in the past many of New Jersey's most ambitious young people headed across the state borders to seek opportunity. Times had changed, he said, boastfully:

"The reverse is true now. They [the cities] are paying us back … Their wealth and refinement are fast building rival cities on our shores; and ornamenting our hills and valleys, with palatial residences and sloping lawns."

Four years later, the 1880 Census showed New Jersey's population was growing. It edged over the one million mark for the first time (that same year the United States population topped fifty million). New Jersey's census takers found exactly 1,130,892 people between High Point and Cape May.

The total really was not startling. Seventeen other states had higher populations, including such farm or

Birth of the Urban Frontier

Americans of the 1890s longed to believe free land frontiers still awaited those with courage to tackle them. The truth was, however, by 1890 increasing numbers of people were locked into rapidly growing, teeming cities.

Historian Frederick Jackson Turner led those who credited America's wide open spaces with creating sturdy individualism in the mountains and across the plains. In a celebrated essay written in 1893, however, Turner admitted the old frontier land opportunities had all but disappeared.

A new and greater challenge was emerging. Major cities were rising, creating problems of overcrowding, pollution, and poverty. A different kind of frontier was opening.

United States population skyrocketed between 1860 and 1915 — from thirty-one million in 1860 to ninety-two million in 1915. The people who flocked into the cities came mainly from two ranks — those dissatisfied with

American farm life, and those sick of Europe's endless wars and brutal persecutions.

Twenty-three million European immigrants who came to the United States between 1860 and 1910 had yearned for frontier land, too. They settled instead for city slums or migrant farm labor camps.

So, the historians said, there were no longer any major frontiers by 1890. If frontiers are measured only in terms of Indians to repel, wild beasts to slay, and wood lots to clear, they were right.

Yet, in facing the dangers, desperations, and uncertainties of the wildly growing cities, the newcomers of the 1890s were displaying a bravery as great as that of the mountaineers, homesteaders, and cowboys so beloved by those who wrote of the "Wild West."

The urban frontier, with its urban pioneers, had been born.

Urbanization was speeding into New Jersey by 1880, evidenced by steam freighters and steam ferries in the harbors, a faster pace on the streets, and taller buildings that challenged stately church spires in the old towns. Jersey City's waterfront was filled with shipping; its sky with smoke (top left). Elizabeth (top right) was still resisting city status, but Camden (below) welcomed the river traffic. New Brunswick's major structures (bottom) were churches, although the train chugging northward foretold an urban future. Downtown Newark (right) appeared slow-paced beneath the First Church steeple, but horse-drawn carriages, wagons, and streetcars crowded streets of the state's largest city.

mountain states as Alabama, Mississippi, Missouri, Tennessee, and Kentucky. Browning's anecdote about people "fleeing" from New York and Pennsylvania to settle in New Jersey was more boast than truth. New York State had more than five million people in 1880 and Pennsylvania well over four million.

Significantly, the Census Bureau listed New Jersey as "urban" for the first time in 1880: more than half (fifty-four percent) of the residents lived in towns or cities. Newark led with 136,508 people, closely followed by Jersey City's 120,722.

The "urban" designation also was questionable. Only five of 270 New Jersey towns had populations exceeding 30,000. Fourteen of the twenty-one counties had no communities with as many as 9,000 residents.

Nevertheless, the trend from farm to urban life was fully under way. Young people from agricultural areas were heading for the cities to seek work, education, advancement, and pleasure.

Farming At The Crossroads

New Jersey agriculture was nearing a key turning point in 1880. The railroads that were building the cities were also opening markets for New Jersey farmers in cities as far as 200 miles away. Every new city dweller was a potential customer.

On the other hand, railroads also were intensifying competition from farm areas in other states. The invention of refrigerated railroad cars permitted farmers in distant states to compete vigorously for the rich markets in Philadelphia and New York City.

Farmers close to New York and Philadelphia faced a tough decision that could not even have been imagined in 1865: should they sell their acres to the industries and home developments that were pushing out into their pasturelands? Demand had driven land prices upward. By 1880, an acre of New Jersey land averaged $90, four times the national average. Near the cities, prices were far higher.

Happy songs and legends depicted farmers and their families as cheerful, independent, and hard-working from sunup to sundown. Dudley W. Adams, master of the National Grange (the nation's leading farm organization), dwelled on the hard work and destroyed the myth of happiness in a memorable talk in 1872:

> We have heard enough, ten times enough, about the hardened hand of honest toil, the supreme glory of the sweating brow, and how magnificent is the suit of coarse homespun which covers a form bent with overwork.
>
> To toil like slaves, raise fat steers, cultivate broad acres, pile up treasures of barns and land and herds — and at the same time bow and starve the God-like form, harden the hands, dwarf the immortal mind, and alienate the children from the homestead — is a damning disgrace to any man and should stamp him as worse than a brute.

Angry at low crop prices and huge government grants of Western lands to railroads, farmers fought for status through the National Grange. Started in the Midwest in 1867, the movement reached New Jersey in 1873. This scene in a typical Grange hall appeared in *Leslie's* weekly in January 1874.

The Barnum & Bailey Greatest Show on Earth

THE MEERS SISTERS.

MARIE and OUIKA

EUROPE'S GREATEST LADY EQUESTRIENNES

SECURED AT A SALARY OF $100 PER DAY.

THE WORLD'S GRANDEST LARGEST. BEST. AMUSEMENT INSTITUTION.

The arrival of the Barnum & Bailey Circus was the biggest event that could happen in a town or city as the 19th century turned into the 20th. Posters lauded troupes of "lady equestriennes," paid the then-unbelievable sum of $100 per day. Every diversion — weddings, church socials, harvest home suppers, band concerts, or baseball games — helped ease the heavy burden of earning a living.

"Opening A Thousand Fields"

Rural sons and daughters could be excused for deserting the farms for city life, Adams declared. Young people were not "less virtuous" than farm children of old, said Adams, but "they are wiser." The railroads, he pointed out, "opened a thousand fields for their ambitious daring."

Certainly there was little room for ambition or daring in the farm areas of 1880. Farmers struggled just to keep even with problems of soil, weather, and markets. There was never hope for vacations away from the cows or chickens. There were no pensions at the end of a long life of plowing, no way to finance an unexpected disaster.

Farmers generally knew very little of the outside world except what they read in farm journals, their local weekly newspaper, or the Sears, Roebuck catalogue. The Sears "Wish Book" only made them yearn for places where dreams might come true.

Local news, gossip, and farming ideas were traded at the general store in the center of every farm village. Farmers and their families bought nearly everything in that store — from pickles to shoes, from horseshoe nails to salted mackerel.

The typical farm center featured the store, a church, a blacksmith shop, and a shabby, wooden one-room school where children learned the "Three R's" (Reading, 'Riting, 'Rithmetic). Graduation from the eighth grade was a major achievement in rural areas in 1890; most children left school before the third or fourth grade to labor as unpaid hands on the family farm.

Only the village blacksmith shop or the local gristmill, operated by a waterwheel, seemed industrial. The miller, the smithy, and the store owner were the most prosperous people in any farm area. Yet they were only a shade better off than the impoverished farmers with whom they dealt.

The Reality Of The City

Farm boys and girls who left the fields and farm kitchens for city life soon found their dreams were harshly restricted by urban realities: constant noise, dirty streets, crowds, and low wages.

Most of the farm boys and girls found work in cluttered, poorly-lit, and badly ventilated factory buildings where they shivered in the winter and found it nearly impossible to breath in the summer. Most of them boarded in slum apartments (or tenements),

Artists and poets imagined America's nineteenth century farmers to be robust, cheerful outdoorsmen, tackling the problems of soil and weather with spirit and love of nature. In truth, many young men and women in New Jersey and elsewhere in the East fled from rural areas to seek higher pay and a less confining life.

sometimes sleeping three or four to a room.

Unskilled men and women earned $4 to $6 weekly, with women at the lower end of the scale. New hands in the textile mills often received as little as seventy-five cents a week as they "learned." It was a hard life, but few returned to the farm. There were opportunities to be found in the cities. Young men might learn a craft or trade and earn $12 to $15 a week as skilled workers. Young women might find a job as a maid or cook in a mansion or sell clothing or hats in fashionable shops.

There was at least a visible way upward in the cities, and there was fun that made farm life incomparably dull. Robert G. Athearn summed up some of the city appeal in his American Heritage volume, *The Gilded Age:*

> *They had joys denied to their country cousins. The circus came more often, and for those who liked them, there were museums and libraries. And City streets offered more interesting sights — crowds, fights, fallen horses, new buildings going up — than anything in a country town.*

The Chance To Learn

Cities also offered working people the chance to get an education. By 1890, nearly 3,500 pupils attended night classes in Newark. Trenton operated an evening school since 1864, although it was reported Trenton's early night classes were "marred by the invasion of hoodlums and rowdies."

Technological advances increased demands for skilled young people. Newark's Board of Trade campaigned in 1883 for a $5,000 grant to establish a technical school to train mechanics. One of the earliest backers of the school was Edward Weston, the brilliant young Newark inventor whose work in electricity already had made him famous.

Newark Technical School opened in 1885 and heeded the Newark *Sunday Call's* warning not to place the school on "too high a plane." Forty-six young men entered the first class, meeting three hours nightly for three to five years before graduating. The school's first day students entered in 1897. Newark Technical Institute prospered (and has now become the New

Jersey Institute of Technology).

Stevens Institute of Technology also rose from the need for new skills. It opened on a much grander scale at Hoboken, in 1871, as the first school of mechanical engineering in the United States. The Institute was handsomely endowed by the Stevens family whose pioneering in railroad planning had built up personal fortunes.

Machine technology offered opportunity for young men. Young women of the late 19th century found for their part that two expanding, important (and "nice") city careers were open to them — typing and teaching.

"Something For The Women"

C. L. Sholes, a Wisconsin printer, gave women the chance to break away from textile machines and domestic service by perfecting a typewriter in 1867. By 1890, sales of the machine skyrocketed. Sholes said modestly, "I feel that I have done something for the women who have always worked so hard."

Advertisements began suggesting the wonderful things that could befall a lady who was introduced to a typing machine. One Remington ad in the *Nation*, for December 16, 1875, also stressed social significance:

"No invention has opened for women so broad and easy an avenue to profitable and suitable employment as the 'Type Writer'. It merits the careful consideration of all thoughtful and charitable persons interested in the subject of work for women."

It was coyly suggested that typing in an office gave young women a chance to meet and marry a "clean-cut" office type. This possibility especially came true in Newark's Prudential Insurance Company, the state's first large-scale employer of women office workers.

Founded in 1875 to provide cheap life insurance to workingmen, the Prudential became a huge success in less than fifteen years. The company opened an imposing ten-story gray stone office building in downtown Newark in 1892.

Every room in the Prudential's castle-like structure was lighted by electricity. Elevators reached every floor. Every room had a telephone, and hundreds of typewriters sounded the message of continuing prosperity. Young women employees were nearly everywhere. Through the years, the "Pru" became well known as the unofficial matchmaker, where boy met girl and where, for more than fifty years, girl had to

Newark Technical School (or Institute) required a home less than thirty feet wide when it opened in 1885 in response to the city's mushrooming need for young men with advanced technical training. Forty-six students squeezed into this building nightly in the first year, and most of them kept attending for three to five years needed for graduation. The Institute's first day students entered in 1897. It was renamed the Newark College of Engineering, a name that was changed to the New Jersey Institute of Technology in recognition of the school's state-wide contributions.

Invention of the typewriter, in 1867, gave women the first real chance to forsake drudging farm or factory work to find "nice" employment in offices such as the Prudential Insurance Co., whose new building (right) opened in 1892. The "Pru" became a major employer of women in its clerical departments.

quit her job after the wedding ceremony.

"Love, Affection, And Kindness"

Until the Civil War, male teachers outnumbered females two to one. In 1861, however, as the number of females increased rapidly, State Superintendent of Schools William Ricord saw the need to reassure the state legislature:

"Females, as instructors, are quite as desirable as males... The notion that women cannot govern [control the class] is overwhelmingly refuted by the experience of all ages. They were made to govern ... by love, by affection, by kindness."

That tender sentiment expressed, Ricord became practical: "Schoolmistresses at $200 a year can, without much hesitation, be selected in preference to $300 schoolmasters."

Young women teachers increased in numbers un-

til, by 1866, Principal John S. Hart of the Trenton Normal School bemoaned the lack of male applicants for teacher training: "We are educating almost none of that sex."

A social change had been wrought. By 1900, most elementary grade teachers were women. However, high school male teachers far outnumbered women, and virtually all school principals were men.

Male or female, teachers liked the city — where higher pay and better cultural advantages could be found. By 1900, Jersey City was paying its high school teachers $3,000 a year, a splendid salary for the period.

With women finding broadened city opportunities thanks to typing and teaching, and males finding expanding chances to move up in city business and industry, the places at the bottom had to be filled. Someone had to do the back-breaking, tedious, menial work in the factories and on the farms. America

Trenton Normal School, started in 1855 in rented quarters, moved on March 17, 1856 into this "admirably adapted" new building, just down the street from the State Capitol.

opened its arms, as never before, to immigrants. At first, many of them turned to rural areas.

"Advantages Offered To Settlers"

Right after the Civil War, immigrants from Germany and Sweden poured into Jersey City on the way West. They rode the Erie's flat-bottomed ferryboat to the Hudson waterfront, boarded the "emigrant" trains, and rode the wooden cars to Wisconsin, Minnesota, Missouri, and on to California. New Jersey decided to keep some here.

Charles K. Landis, who founded Vineland in 1862, believed Europeans would help his venture prosper, although he wanted his "inner city" to be populated by culture-loving New Englanders. Italian settlers were invited to test their celebrated green thumbs against the sandy soil surrounding the town.

The first Italian farmers reached Vineland in 1873. By 1881, a visitor noted "they raise good crops and are well pleased with their new homes." Entire families — fathers, mothers, and toddling children — amazed the inner city people by working together in the fields.

Other New Jersey farm areas needed such workers. Governor George B. McClellan asked the state legislature in 1879 to send propaganda to Europe to praise the state's soil, taxes, and work opportunities, "so they may perceive the advantages offered to settlers."

A year later, a state broadside circulated through Europe declared: "Why should the immigrant go to Minnesota, where the climate is like Sweden, when he can secure a home in the southern part of New

Oasis In The Pines

Charles K. Landis, 28-year-old Philadelphian, amazed natives in the Pine Barrens in August 1861 by announcing he would build a city in this forsaken Cumberland County wilderness. Landis predicted within ten years his "Vineland" would flourish along a main street 100 feet wide, running in a straight line for two miles. He bought 16,000 acres of woodland for $7 an acre and he intended to make his investment pay.

Landis put local axmen to work hewing out streets. As he assessed the value of his forty-eight square miles of property, the young planner ruefully admitted the soil was thin, the trees stunted, and skilled local workers were not to be found. The main asset was the Glassboro to Millville railroad that cut through the tract.

Despite the deficiencies, Landis set high standards for the width of the streets, types of homes, and land use. Every new buyer pledged to build a home according to specifications, plant trees, and till the soil.

A mile-square inner city was planned for industrialists, businessmen, and artisans. Outside that core would be farms and orchards to supply food.

Landis advertised his land in New York newspapers and sent circulars to southern Europe, hoping to attract some of the increasing numbers of immigrants to Vineland. The first buyer arrived in October 1861 and paid cash for ten acres in the heart of the "city."

New Englanders, especially liking the idea of a central city, were the first heavy purchasers. Soon Italian immigrants arrived to try their hand at turning the sandy soil into rich gardens.

By 1868, when the woodcut below was made, Vineland was well on its way toward matching the grand promises Landis made only seven years before.

Because of his "eminent qualifications and distinguished success," Augustus Scarlett received the impressive First Grade State Certificate from the State Normal School at Trenton in 1881 (below).

Scarlett was one of the few male teachers of his time. The available certified males usually taught on the secondary level — but there were few New Jersey high schools when Scarlett graduated.

Most teaching was by females in small, under-equipped, poorly-heated one-room rural schools. The teacher was not well trained and her pupils were not all as loving as those shown in the engraving on the right. Teaching was hard, frustrating, underpaid work.

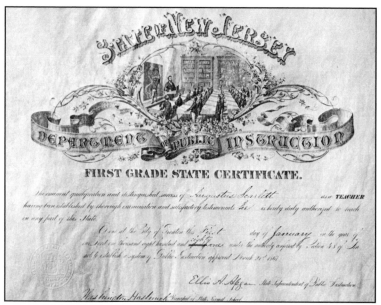

Jersey, where the climate is more like the south of France or the shores of the Mediterranean?"

Village In Woodbine's Forest

That invitation was aimed directly at farmers. Soon the Italians were joined by Polish and Russian Jews, most of whom had been poor dirt farmers in their native lands. The bustle of city life was certain to bewilder them.

The Hebrew Immigrant Society believed southern New Jersey's inexpensive land offered an ideal solu-

tion. The Society planned villages to combine agriculture with small apparel factories. The first was started at Alliance in Salem County in 1881 and soon was followed by others in nearby Norma, Brotmanville, Rosenhayn, and Carmel.

The most notable of the farm-plus-factory Jewish colonies was founded at Woodbine in 1891 with the backing of the Baron de Hirsch Fund, set up by a wealthy French banker to help European Jews. A primitive, roadless section in the pine forests of northwestern Cape May County was acquired for $50,000. It was given the poetic name of Woodbine.

Within a year, South Russian Jews cleared 650 acres of farm land and built more than twelve miles of roads through the property. A dozen small factories were erected and furnished.

Professor Hersch L. Sabsovich, Woodbine's director, insisted young people be trained in agricultural science. His school taught more than 100 young students annually. Three years after the town's founding, one of Woodbine's students, Jacob Goodale Lipman, entered Rutgers College. Seventeen years later, Dr. Lipman became director of the Rutgers Experiment Station. He was named first dean of the College of Agriculture in 1915.

If the $50,000 from the de Hirsch Fund achieved nothing more than finding and preparing Jacob Lipman, it was money well invested. Lipman's pioneering studies in soil science helped change farming methods dramatically throughout the world.

Types.

Making a clearing for a future home.

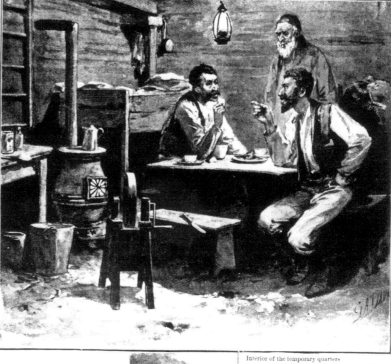

Interior of the temporary quarters

New arrivals.

School—Learning the English language.

Woodbine excited so much interest within less than a year of its founding that *Leslie's* sent an artist to sketch the Cape May colony for the issue of April 7, 1892. Miss Davis, the artist, found "about sixty-three families in the settlement, averaging about five persons to each family." She was initially upset by the "solitary station" on the railroad, but her enthusiasm grew as she walked through the vigorous Hebrew colony.

A Pedestal For Ms. Liberty

Fireworks flared, orators shouted, and bands played, on October 28, 1886, when the Statue of Liberty was dedicated. No band played more proudly than the Butler Silver Cornet Band, personally invited by the committee that arranged for the statue to be erected on Bedloe's Island just off Jersey City.

The committee chairman was Richard Butler, president of the Butler Hard Rubber Co., whose name was given to the Morris County town in 1881. Richard Butler became interested in the Statue of Liberty after France announced, in 1867, it was building the monument to American-Franco friendship.

Butler founded the American committee to build a proper pedestal for Miss Liberty, but in 1884 he admitted the committee had no money to complete the base for the 151-foot-tall statue already completed in France. Joseph Pulitzer, fiery editor of the N.Y. World, *unleashed a series of editorials that shamed this nation into raising funds.*

After Miss Liberty was formally in place on October 28, 1886, the Butler Silver Cornet Band returned home to the town named for the man who put Miss Liberty on a pedestal. The band musicians were often reminded of the statue, since Bartholdi Street in Butler was named for Frederick Bartholdi, Miss Liberty sculptor.

"Yearning To Breathe Free"

The trickle of immigrants, such as those headed for Woodbine or Alliance, quickened into a flood after industry began to welcome the hard-working newcomers. More than twenty million immigrants came to the United States between 1880 and 1920. About 517,000 — one in forty settled in New Jersey.

This state ranked fifth in the total number of immigrants in 1910, trailing only New York, Pennsylvania, Illinois, and Massachusetts. New Jersey was first in concentration of immigrants.

Immigrants came for various reasons. Italian peasants fled from impoverished soil. Russian Jews left their German-occupied land because of demands all children be taught German and because their sons were forced into German, Russian, and Austrian armies.

America was the Land of Promise, a notion promoted by the agents and brochures of the steamship lines. As Louis Adamic wrote, the immigrants had one shining dream:

> *In America, one could make pots of money in a short time, acquire immense holdings, wear a white collar, and have polish on one's boots like a gospod (one of the gentry) and eat white bread, soup, and meat on weekdays as well as on Sundays, even if one were but an ordinary workman to begin with.*

The Statue of Liberty, a stone's throw from Jersey City, became the symbol of American liberties. Poetess Emma Lazarus wrote eloquently of the statue and of a nation that called out:

> Give me your tired, your poor,
> Your huddled masses yearning to breathe free
> The wretched refuse of your teeming shore.
> Send these, the homeless, tempest-tossed to me,
> I lift my lamp beside the golden door!

Waves of people from Italy, Poland, Austria, Hungary, and Russia swept through the golden door in the 1890s. For a time, America welcomed them. There was ample land, industrialists wanted more cheap labor, and the growing factories absorbed the successive tides of immigration.

"Men Of The Meaner Sort"

Many Americans, forgetting their own immigrant heritage, ignored the spirit of Emma Lazarus's poetry. They dwelled instead on the line that described immigrants as "the wretched refuse of your teeming shores."

Woodrow Wilson, president of Princeton University and later hailed as a liberal, wrote a typical appraisal of the "new" immigrants in his *A History of the American People*, published in 1902:

> Now there came multitudes of men of the lowest class from the south of Italy and men of the meaner sort out of Hungary and Poland, men out of ranks where there was neither skill nor energy nor any initiative of quick intelligence.
>
> And they came in numbers which increased from year to year, as if the countries of the south of Europe were disburdening themselves of the more sordid and hapless elements of their population, the men whose standards of life and work were such as American workmen never dreamed of heretofore.

These people with the darker complexions, the richly seasoned foods, and the strenuous dances and games neither read nor accepted Wilson's stern disapproval of them. They flocked into any city that needed their strong arms and their willingness to work for low wages.

Clay Pits, Factories, And Mines

Industrialists around Perth Amboy and New Brunswick sent to immigrant centers for Hungarians and Poles to labor in the clay pits. Madison, Morristown, Summit, and other wealthy areas sought Italians to work in greenhouses or to keep estate gardens in trim.

Poles gathered in Bayonne to work in the oil refin-

Immigrants at Castle Garden crowded aboard the *Erie Eisenbahn* (Railroad) barge to head for Erie piers in Jersey City. Barge sides told of Erie destinations as far west as San Francisco. New arrivals on "emigrant trains" out of Jersey City dozed, read, or sat in dazed silence as they rolled across America.

eries. Wharton and Franklin companies summoned Hungarians for the mills and mines. Passaic factory owners hired Slovaks to tend the looms in their woolen mills and handkerchief factories.

Immigrants undertook anything that promised a few dollars. Russian Jews opened little shops in towns and cities, and then broadened their merchandising market by hiking through the countryside peddling wares from pushcarts or from packs on their backs.

Italians worked wonders with the sandy soil near Vineland and Hammonton. The rich black soil near Great Meadows in Warren County delighted Poles, who made the one-time swamp green with onions and lettuce. Poles, Russians, Hungarians, Slovaks, and Italians aided Manville in its industrial boom. Greek boys shined shoes in every major city.

American industry absorbed most of those immigrants, using them as another raw material to keep factories and mills operating at high speed. The growing cities turned to them to dig the ditches, pave the streets, carry the bricks, lay the railroad tracks, and unload ships in the harbors.

Labor For "Half Nothing"

Inevitably this "new" kind of foreigner irritated the descendants of foreigners who arrived earlier. These newcomers came from European farms, uneducated, unskilled, and unused to the ways of their neighbors.

The one-time farmers were hopelessly lost in the cities. A 1911 study of 47,000 New Jersey immigrants showed only 7,300 had any kind of skill. Between thirty and fifty percent of them, depending on the country of origin, were illiterate even in their native languages.

Foreigners angered "old line" factory workers, who believed they lost, or might lose, their jobs to the intruders. Terence V. Powderly, Grand Master Workman of the New Jersey Knights of Labor, reflected that fear in 1892:

> *Corporate greed is alone responsible for the sweeping tide of immigration now flowing in upon us ... The corporation reaps the benefits of the immigrants' presence by having its labor performed for half nothing; the poor immigrant lives but twenty-four hours ahead of the poor house, the man he replaces becomes a tramp.*

Actually, the great influx of unskilled labor had the effect of pushing English-speaking, Anglo-Saxon workers upward to managerial and clerical jobs, to positions on the police force and the fire department, to delivery routes and clerking jobs in the Post Office, and to roles as foremen over the Italians, Poles, and Hungarians who paved the streets.

Employers claimed they would much prefer to hire "native Americans," but one manufacturer noted in 1914:

> *You cannot secure the services of native-born persons to work in the mills, as the general feeling is abroad that native-born persons should be the bosses or should work in an office or some superior position, but not mill work.*

Little Italy, Little Hungary

Every city had its "Little Dublin," "Little Italy," "Little Hungary," "Little Slovakia." Passaic, for example, grew from 6,500 in 1880 to 54,700 in 1910. Most of the 48,000 new inhabitants were from the

Labor and "old line" Americans hated immigrants. The 1880s cartoon (above) portrayed "foreigners" as strikebreakers hired to harm American workers. The other cartoon, from *Leslie's* in 1888, lampooned Uncle Sam as being wooed by greedy newcomers.

plains of Slovakia and Hungary or the Carpathian Mountains.

Emily Greene Balch of Wellesley College wrote idyllically in 1910 of *Our Slavic Fellow Citizens:*

> *From a purely aesthetic view, no one need wish to see a prettier sight than a Passaic handkerchief factory full of Polish girls in kerchiefs of pale yellow and other soft colors, the afternoon sun slanting across the fine stuff on which they are working.*

Miss Batch also gave a truer, and less pleasant, picture of immigrant life when she wrote of the Slovak:

> *The immigrant sees less of America than we think. He comes over with Slovaks, goes to a Slovak boarding house, a Slovak store, a Slovak saloon, and a Slovak bank. His boss is likely a Slovak. He deals with Americans only as the streetcar conductor shouts, "What do you want, John?" or when boys stone his children and call them "Hunkies."*

John S. Merzbacher wrote a book, *Trenton's Foreign Colonies*, in 1908, describing the streets of South Trenton as a "place where the American language is scarcely heard." Trenton then had 6,000 Hungarians, 5,000 Poles, 4,000 Russian Jews, 3,000 Slavs, and,

according to Merzbacher, "Trenton surely has Italy transplanted."

Merzbacher dwelled on the happiness of the city's immigrant populations, each clustered in its own section. In Little Italy, however, he contrasted the crowded Trenton tenements with the farm huts the Italians left "near the tranquil waters of the Adriatic." He surmised many had been happier in their homeland.

"Robbed Of Their Assets"

The foreigners suffered at the hands of every kind of swindler and exploiter. The New Jersey Commission of Immigration summed up the situation in a searing report published in 1914. It focused attention on Hoboken and Jersey City, where four of the largest steamship companies were located.

Confused immigrants came down the gangplanks to face a horde of hustlers out to cheat them in any way possible. Law enforcers looked the other way as porters, cab drivers, and immigration officials fleeced the newcomers. The commission report said:

> *The sum total of their [immigrants'] assets when they enter the country, are, first, a good*

223

physique; second, an average of $50 in money; and third, hope ... Many however, are robbed of their last two assets [money and hope] before they have passed beyond a New Jersey terminal.

Once past the waterfront, the immigrant faced nearly as much danger from his own national group as he did from strangers. Sometimes fourteen or fifteen people lived in three rooms that an earlier immigrant had rented for eight or nine dollars, and then sublet to each boarder for a dollar and half per month, plus two dollars weekly apiece for cooking privileges.

"Foreign Banks" organized by shrewd swindlers often robbed unwary fellow immigrants. For every authorized immigrant bank, the Commission of Immigration reported six operated without license. In Jersey City alone there were several illegal immigrant "banks" in 1911 — and not one authorized bank to serve the foreign groups.

The list of those out to keep the immigrants in subjection went on and on — justices of the peace, land swindlers, employment agencies, and padrones.

Padrones (leaders of Italian groups or families) herded workers out of the cities every spring and summer to work on southern New Jersey farms. The padrone contracted directly with the farmer and paid his workers as little as possible.

The padrone supplied "housing." On one farm, the Commission of Immigration counted nineteen families living in one wooden shack — each family occupying a space six feet by eight feet, where they cooked, socialized, and slept.

The Commission concluded ironically, however, the exploited workers of the padrone might have been worse off in the cities. The farms "were probably more healthy than tenements," the Commission believed, and a family might save $150 to $200 to take back to the city at the end of the summer.

Help In Becoming American

The aliens endured the fleecing, the exploitation, the hard work, the miserable housing, the taunts, and the cruelty of those who wrote them off as "men of the meaner sort." They accepted all of these as part of the price of becoming an American. It was better than the despair and suffering they and their families knew in Europe

Help was on the way. The Commission report of 1914 turned the glare of publicity on the swindlers. Leaders in foreign communities worked to make the banks honest. Tightened factory laws protected both

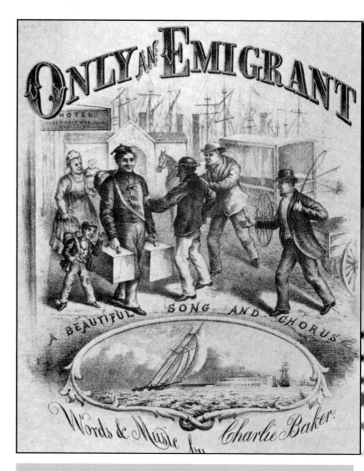

The "beautiful song and chorus" of *Only An Emigrant*, published in 1879, might well have had its cover drawn on the Hudson River waterfront. The happy, eager newcomers and their families were met at the dock by cab drivers, promoters, and other hustlers and schemers. A 1911 immigration report said new arrivals were robbed of "money and hope" on the New Jersey docks.

immigrant and "American" workers. Many groups, including the DAR, the YWCA, the YMCA, and local women's clubs, helped form the Americanization classes where immigrants learned English.

Settlement houses or "Neighborhood Houses" in many towns lent a helping hand to immigrants. Day nurseries run by dedicated, often wealthy women aided working alien mothers and their children. The strong influence of the Catholic Church or the synagogues helped keep the majority of immigrants within the law.

Roman Catholic priests and nuns worked strenuously to educate the young Italians, Poles, and Hungarians in their parish schools. Second generation "foreigners" also began to demand, and get, better public education for their children.

The Public Library Commission of New Jersey started, in 1911, to study ways of supplying books in foreign languages. John Cotton Dana, director of the

Newark Library, did not wait for a study; he put foreign-language books on his shelves, and then advertised in six languages that his library had them.

World War I hastened the process of assimilation: foreigners who enlisted in the army could become naturalized citizens quickly. Once naturalized, they could vote. That was important. The Irish and Anglo-Saxon ward leaders sought out the voting Italians, Hungarians, Poles, Russian Jews, and others and even permitted a few to run for minor offices. Votes, by any nationality, counted.

The smoldering animosities continued, but they would lessen. The "new" foreigners were being assimilated by 1910, as had the Germans, the Irish, and others before them.

The Forgotten "Native Born"

Foes of immigration took pride in being "Native Born Americans," charging that their rights and privileges were threatened by the new arrivals. These enemies of foreigners also managed to ignore the rights of one group of native-born — African Americans.

New Jersey's African American population was not large. In 1880, there were 38,853 in the state, about three percent of the population. In 1910, that total increased to 89,760, still only slightly more then three percent of the total population.

James M. Baxter came to Newark in 1864 to head the "Colored School." He fought until his death in 1909 to gain equal opportunity for African American students.

African American citizens had won the legal right to vote by passage of the 15th Amendment to the United States Constitution in 1870 (although New Jersey did not eliminate "white" as a voting qualification until 1875). Since African Americans did not constitute a major threat or strength at the polls, neither political party paid them any heed.

Factory owners and labor loaders displayed an open hostility toward African Americans. A 1903 report by the State Bureau of Labor and Industries on *The Negro in Manufacturing and Mechanical Industries* studied 398 manufacturing establishments. Eighty-three reported using African American labor, but 292 employed none at all. The factories that employed African Americans showed only 963 out of 38,400 employees. Of that handful, eighty percent were common laborers, stablemen, or wagon drivers.

Labor unions fought against minority workers. Only fifty-four African Americans were members of New Jersey trade unions in 1903, one-third of them barbers. The African American union membership also included seven carpenters, seven steam engineers, five rubber workers, and three musicians.

New Jersey had even fallen behind the South. The 1903 report emphasized that the capacity of African Americans to become artisans "is not a new proposition, but a fact well known all over the South where many hundreds of the race are now employed at skilled industries."

"Necessary To Highest Interests"

The Bureau of Labor and Industries worried over the implications of anti-African American sentiment in a free society:

> *So important is this subject [the employment of African Americans] that a general conviction is growing everywhere in the nation, that a careful study of conditions and needs of the Negro population, a study absolutely removed from race prejudice and partisan bias, is necessary to the highest interests of both Negroes and whites.*

Conditions were not improved by the idealistic report. The rising complaint of immigrant leaders that their people were "last hired, first fired," was not the cry of African Americans. They knew they stood behind even immigrants.

Scaling that wall of prejudice was difficult. One African American who fought unceasingly was James Baxter, a Newark school teacher who was

This was the total of high school graduates in Newark in 1899 when that city led the state in providing educational advantages. Girls dressed in ruffles and bows outnumbered the slick-haired boys by about three to two. The city's only African American graduate that year (upper left) was J. LeRoy Baxter, son of Newark's noted "Colored School" principal. A study of Newark's schools in 1909 showed that seventy-two percent of all the city's pupils left school before the eighth grade. Most children left in the fifth grade, when they reached the legal age for dropping out of classes, to work.

determined that his people at least have a chance to get an education.

Newark voted to desegregate its public schools in 1872, but the "Colored School" of pre-Civil War days lingered on. It used the same textbooks as other schools, but the course of study was poor. The lowest salaries in the school system went to Colored School teachers.

Baxter came to Newark in 1864 as a 19-year-old teacher in the Colored School. He stiffened his fight for equality, in the 1870s, when he urged a talented African American student named Irene Pataquam to enter Newark High School. One opponent of Miss Pataquam's admittance warned that "if the high school is opened to Ethiopians, all schools will be opened to them."

Miss Pataquam won her fight, and by 1908 about 1,000 African American children attended formerly "white" schools. Baxter began his forty-fifth, and last, year of teaching in 1908, still in the Colored School, supervising about 150 students. All five of Baxter's own children graduated from Newark High School, attended college, and pursued professional careers.

Locked Into A Constant Struggle

Education was not a matter of great concern for most families, African American or white, in urban areas. A Russel Sage Foundation study of Newark schools in 1909 found that seventy-two percent of all the city's children left school before the eighth grade.

The highest dropout year was the fifth grade, when children became old enough to work in the city factories. The Sage Foundation summed up the situation simply: children left school early because their families needed whatever they might earn as full-time workers.

Urban living for most — native-born, foreign born, African American, or white — was a constant struggle to stay alive and optimistic in the face of low pay, poor living conditions, and lack of official political or industrial concern. Still the people poured in.

New Jersey's population rose to 2,537,167 in 1910, a leap of nearly 1.5 million people in thirty years. Half of all the state's people lived in three counties: Essex, Hudson, and Passaic. Newark, the largest city,

Proposals for tapping the upper Passaic River watershed to give Newark clean water in the 1880s prompted opponents to hang Mayor Joseph Haynes in effigy. Haynes persisted, and in August 1891, when *Harper's Weekly* visited the watershed, work was far along at Oak Ridge Reservoir, and part of the twenty-one-mile-long pipeline to Newark was in place. Passaic County water reached Newark in January 1892.

had 347,469 residents, followed by Jersey City with 267,779, Paterson with 125,600, and Trenton with 96,915.

The influx of people compounded major problems: pollution of water supplies, antiquated sewers, miserable streets, incredible traffic tie-ups, crowded and antiquated schools, and soaring tax rates. As urbanization swept New Jersey into the 20th century, enlightened city leaders fought to make their communities livable.

"Injury To Our Reputation"

Newark's Board of Trade surveyed the city's haphazard system of sewers in 1883. It warned:

> Stagnant water and filth raise the death rate, and all this, besides distress and sorrow, means injury to our reputation as a healthful city, and inflicts damage and loss of property interests and many times over the cost of applying the remedy.

The city poured millions of dollars into sewer construction. By 1910, Newark had 310 miles of sewer lines, nearly ten times the 1880 total. Even that failed to clean up the Passaic River that flowed through the city. Paterson, Passaic, and other upriver towns still poured their sewage into the stream. Industrialists in Newark continued to pump factory waste into the

river.

Newark and seven other towns in the Passaic River watershed started a joint sewer system in 1889, an early recognition that regional control of the watershed was necessary. Newark paid most of the cost, but it did so willingly, since it also suffered the most from the vilely polluted water.

Traditionally, Newarkers drank water from the foul Passaic or from tainted underground wells. Traditionally, too, Newark suffered annual outbreaks of typhoid fever and dysentery. Joseph Haynes, a Newark school teacher who was elected mayor in 1883, was determined to eliminate the dangerous condition.

Haynes forced through the City Council a measure to spend $6 million to get water from three reservoirs in the mountains of Passaic County. Twenty-one miles of forty-eight-inch steel pipe would bring the water to Newark.

Opponents rallied against Haynes. He was vilified in public and hanged in effigy outside City Hall, but he ignored the opposition. Passaic County water began flowing from Newark faucets in January 1892. Within one year, deaths from typhoid fever dropped seventy percent!

Farewell To Horse Cars

Movement of inner city populations became easier in the late 1880s when electric streetcars appeared. They were called "trolleys" because of the long poll, or trolley, that ran from the top of the car to overhead electric lines and brought power to the streetcar engines.

New Jersey's first electric streetcars operated in Atlantic City on April 24, 1889. Free rides had to be offered to persuade passengers to climb aboard on opening day. Intertown service began in the summer of 1890 when the Passaic, Garfield & Clifton Railway ran a three-car electric street train to link the towns.

Some towns and cities retained their horsedrawn cars. Paterson boasted in 1890 that "it is extremely doubtful whether there is a city in the country in which more money is spent on horse railroads." It was a questionable honor.

Newark saw its first streetcar on October 4, 1890, amid widespread fears that riders might be electrocuted. Woodbury spokesmen condemned the trolley in 1893 as a "road to hell" because it sped people to gambling dens in Gloucester. Montclair opposed a trolley franchise for fear it might make the town "a dumping ground for Dutch picnics and sick-baby excursions."

Trolley lines did not spread the population widely. They served rather to increase urbanization in the areas where it had always been. Except for a long run to Lake Hopatcong, a run from Phillipsburg to Port Murray, and a line from Vineland to Bivalve, nearly all New Jersey trolley tracks were in the heavily populated corridor between Bergen and Camden counties.

Trolleys gave the urban masses a mobility they had never known. They first rode the streetcars to picnic areas and resorts out of town. Then people began moving out permanently to the edges of the cities and into adjacent towns. Trolleys soon made it difficult to tell where Newark ended and East Orange began.

A Chugging In The Distance

Francis Bazley Lee completed in 1902 a monumental, well-written four-volume history of the state, *New Jersey As A Colony And As A State*. As an on-the-scene observer, he wrote in his last chapter:

> But the nineteenth century brought many changes to the state, converting a population distinctly affected by rural influences into one whose life was largely urban.
>
> In other words, in 1800, scarcely two percent of the people of Near Jersey lived under city influence; in 1900 eighty percent of the population of the state resided in great municipalities or were in daily communication with Philadelphia or New York.

Lee did not even mention the problems of urbanization. He made no mention of immigrants. He never mentioned filthy rivers, miserable streets, or unsightly states. He praised the stimulating effects of industrialization on the state's economy, but made no mention of low wages or dangerous working conditions.

Commentary on social conditions was not the mode of the day. Thus Lee failed to mention two major events already well under way. One was a faint chugging that could be heard in the distance: the horseless carriage. The other was a wind of social reform that was sweeping through urban America. Perhaps Lee did not even sense the latter, for it was a subtle wind.

Urbanization gone wild might be a proper caption for this photograph. It was taken in 1914, looking down on Newark's Mulberry Street in the heart of the city. Trolley cars inched along the cobblestone street, with motormen exchanging vituperative shouts and threats with drivers of horse-drawn carts and wagons. If automobiles were important, there was little evidence of the fact on this day. The photograph offers a striking contrast to nostalgic recollections of days when cities supposedly were neat and clean and life was simpler.

Morristown had nearly everything that a millionaire could desire after the Civil War: healthful air, tree-covered hills, a notable heritage, plentiful land, and, most important, a reliable railroad to carry rich commuters between the canyon of Wall Street and the hills of Morris County.

By 1874, Morristown was called "favorable in comparison with Newport." By 1890, a full-fledged, if self-appointed, "royalty" ruled the mountains between Far Hills and Summit, with Morristown as the hub.

Those were days of easy money, piled up in railroad ventures, banking, market speculations, insurance sales, and merchandising. Very few government regulations interfered with business transactions. Consumer protection was non-existent. There was no income tax. Money begot more money; millionaires were hard pressed to spend it all.

Nearly a hundred millionaires lived in or near Morristown by 1890. One source identified ninety-two persons each worth $1 million or more. Heading the list were Hamilton McKay Twombly, who had made millions in sulphur mines, and his wife, the former Florence Vanderbilt, the best-loved granddaughter of Commodore Cornelius Vanderbilt. The Commodore made his money in railroad speculations, but his title was earned in early boating ventures.

Between them, the Twomblys possessed about $70 million. Trailing them were fourteen Morristown-area tycoons each worth at least $10 million, fourteen more with upwards of $2 million, and forty-nine who admitted only the basic $1

million to qualify for the regal set.

The Twomblys knew how to get rid of money. They built a hundred-room mansion just east of Morristown, paying a reputed $2 million or more to recreate the Hampton Court Palace that stood in England.

Carrying out their royal notions, the Twomblys outfitted all their staff in expensive maroon uniforms. It was town gossip that the couple paid their chef $25,000 annually. Garage mechanics were not paid well, but it was deemed an honor to work on the fifteen Twombly automobiles (including five Rolls Royces) all painted in Twombly maroon.

Parties at the Twombly estate paid homage to old royal traditions of public showiness. One "barn dance" in 1891 required $6,000 just for electric lights. The 900-acre Twombly estate was called Florham (for Florence and Hamilton), and in 1899 the couple induced the little village of Afton, where they paid most of the taxes, to change its name to Florham Park.

Once each year the neighbors, most of whom could never aspire to make $6,000 in three years of hard labor, were invited to tour the premises. They gaped at the grounds and, if lucky, peered in through heavy drapes at the expensive furnishings in the drawing room (above).

The millionaires took themselves intensely seriously. They claimed to live "simple lives" in their little "cottages" of thirty rooms or so. A few were frankly ostentatious, building their homes (as did the Twomblys) in

Millionaires

imitation of British castles. One went so far as to have his castle exactly duplicate one in England, stone by stone.

Weekends and long summer vacations were times of high pleasure. Always topping the social list was the annual horse show, when glistening carriages, drawn by matched teams of four horses, rolled through the gates of the opulent Higgins estate (above). Note that "tailgating" began then; witness the "picnic" in the picture to the left. The outdoor lunch needed a formally-dressed butler to clean up, of course.

Chinks appeared in the millionaire solidarity. One serious split came in 1894 after local women founded the Morris County Golf Club, shown below in a painting by the celebrated artist, A. B. Frost, who lived nearby. This was the nation's first country club run by women, but by 1896 men had taken control.

The royal dreams ended. Some of the Morristown millionaires were named in a national insurance scandal in 1907. World War I brought a cessation of excessive partying, the income tax was started, and depression came. Morristown's millionaire dream world faded into history.

Chapter Eleven - A State In Ferment

United States		New Jersey	
		1883	NJ workers get 1st legal right to strike
American Federation of Labor organized	1886		
Kansas bans trusts	1889	1889	NJ legislature authorizes trusts
Basketball invented in Springfield, MA	1891	1891	Cyclists prod state to improve roads
		1892	Standard Oil incorporates in NJ
Colorado grants female suffrage	1893	1893	Infamous "Jockey Legislature" convenes
Labor Day made holiday	1894	1894	NJ State Federation of Women's Clubs starts; saves Palisades
Supreme Court legalizes school segregation	1896	1896	Jersey City gets reform mayor
US goes on gold standard	1900	1900	Glass companies end company stores in NJ
1st auto trip across US	1903		
		1906	Wilson warns autos spread "socialistic feeling"
NAACP founded	1909		
Boy Scouts founded	1910	1910	Wilson elected governor; inaugurates reforms
Wilson elected President	1912		

Historians have labeled the 1890s the "Gay Nineties," in recognition of the high mood of merriment that embraced city and village alike. Others call the period the "molting nineties," for old ways were being shed for new.

The 1890s were, in hindsight, the midway years. The nation in 1890 was exactly midway between the fading nightmares of the Civil War and the unimaginable horrors that World War I would bring. So it was an age of innocence, an era of self-indulgence.

Rich and poor alike sought pleasure, both in their own fashion. The rich frolicked on huge estates near Morristown or in palatial summer homes overlooking the Jersey Shore. The poor played baseball, strolled in the city parks, rode bicycles over country roads, or took one-day excursions to Lake Hopatcong or Atlantic City.

By 1890, every village, town, and city had baseball fever. Teams of doctors, lawyers, firemen, factory workers, college students, and neighborhood boys played whenever they could. That meant twilight games after supper, games on Saturday afternoons and

◇◇◇◇◇◇◇◇◇◇◇◇◇◇◇◇◇◇◇◇◇◇

The Quality Of Life

America bubbled with energy, excitement, and confusion as the nineteenth century eased into the twentieth. There were problems aplenty, but many sought to forget their cares in sports and games, in dreams and entertainment, and in theaters and amusement parks.

It was a time of romantic fancy — of gushy greeting cards, sentimental family gatherings, and supper tables that groaned under calorie-filled meals. It was a time when Horatio Alger heroes "rose to the top" through "pluck and luck," a time to toast the economic wonders of a nation that stretched from the Atlantic to the Pacific.

It was, as well, a time to recognize that in the midst of pleasure and plenty, far too many people suffered. Far too few made it, despite Alger's success stories.

A surge of reform swept the nation. The progressive movement grew stronger and bolder. Young politicians joined

older leaders to attack cynical cooperation between big money interests and corrupt legislators. A few independent newspaper editors backed the cause.

Women joined the fray, to become the irresistible force that pushed the progressive movement to ultimate success. They could not vote; they fought instead with intelligence, emotion, courage, and without obligation to any political party.

Progressives battled for conservation of natural resources, decent labor laws, better schools, and an end to unfair business practices. They demanded humane prisons, aid for unfortunate women and children, and a check on reckless politicians.

The period from 1885 to 1915 has been called the Progressive Era — when people found the resolution to fight injustice and moral decay in a nation that had grown careless about human rights.

Gibson girls (and the males who looked at them) immediately identified the upper class of the 1890s and early 1900s. Patrician, gorgeous, flirtatious, and openly snobbish, the girls drawn by Charles Dana Gibson dominated magazines — whether playing cards, attending the horse show, sunbathing, or making a man's head spin. It was also the Gingerbread Age, thanks to an improved bandsaw (left) that cut the ornate wooden decorations (called gingerbread) on Victorian buildings, such as those (below) sketched in the 1880s at Cape May.

Tension gripped combatants on the rough pasture in New Brunswick, on November 6, 1869, when Rutgers and Princeton played the nation's first organized collegiate football game. Artist W. M. Boyd (Rutgers '32) visualized the scene in his painting (right). Each team had twenty-five players; the game was played with a round ball. Rutgers won 6-4. Football caught on quickly. When Princeton played the Orange A.C. at Tuxedo, NY on October 11, 1890 (below), the game was a society event for a select gathering of polite spectators. Princeton, Yale, and Harvard soon controlled the game; for decades the "Big Three" competition topped all football rivalries. Not even driving rain stopped the 1891 Yale-Princeton fray.

on Sundays, if local laws permitted. Many industries, such as Thomas Edison's factory in West Orange, hired college stars to bolster employee teams.

Newspapers gave increasing attention to baseball heroes. Fans argued year-round about the relative merits of Big League stars that most of them would never see. Village teams played regularly before crowds that often far outnumbered the total local population.

Baseball was the "national pastime," but a brash challenger was born in New Brunswick in 1869 when Rutgers and Princeton played the first intercollegiate football game. The sport caught on so quickly that by 1900 a college game could attract thousands of spectators. When Yale played Princeton, the roads between Morristown and Princeton were clogged with horse-drawn carriages headed for what was known as *the* game.

Baseball and football were "American." Immigrants introduced other sports. Teams of Englishmen played cricket in Newark, Hoboken, and Gibbsboro. Soccer attracted big crowds in Kearny and Harrison, where Scots congregated. German and Slovak gymnasts competed in Newark, Passaic, Hoboken, and many other towns. Immigrants everywhere danced so strenuously as to leave trained athletes breathless.

The Craze For Cycling

Action was the key to enjoyment. No sport surpassed cycling in giving the masses both exercise and enjoyment between 1890 and 1910. Getting "wheels" — bicycling wheels — was as important to young Americans of 1890 as getting automobile wheels would be to their great-great-grandchildren.

Cycling gained popularity when the old "high wheeler" bike was replaced by a rubber-tired, low-slung "safety" bicycle with equal-sized wheels. Riding an old high wheeler was a challenging, risky balancing act limited to the very few daring enough

to try. Anyone could learn to ride a safety bike in a few minutes. Apparently nearly everyone learned.

Young people poured out onto country roads, pedaling as far as their legs could take them. When muddy, rutted thoroughfares limited their sport, cyclists pressured the state legislature in 1891 into appropriating $75,000 for road building. New Jersey was one of the first to make better roads a state concern.

The Cape May Bicycle Road Improvement Association could not wait for the slow-acting legislature. It spent thousands of dollars of its own money to build bike paths from Millville to Cape May. Cyclists raced shoreward causing Cape May to set a bicycle speed limit of eight miles an hour.

Some of the invading female cyclists horrified the staid matrons of Cape May. The ladies formed an Anti-Bicycle Club to warn fast-riding, bloomer-clad out-of-town girls that in Cape May at least there were still some who maintained standards of modesty.

The women bike riders struck back in letters to the county newspaper. They scoffed at the old-fashioned "Antis" who "affected wasp-waists, high necks, and trailing skirts." A well-known Cape May physician endorsed the loose costumes of the liberated cyclists by writing that "corsets fill more graves than whiskey."

The Two-Faced Mask

Rich America at play fascinated newspaper and magazine editors. Fashionable readership demanded and got the face of the happiness that wealth could bring. Sunday papers featured "rotogravure" sections

Not one smile showed on the faces of the Essex County cyclers shown above; cycling on the old high-wheeled cycles was a serious business meant only for those with nerve and delicate balance. Then the "safety" two-wheeler changed everything, particularly for women. They could pedal practically anywhere with a freedom that few women had ever known.

to reveal the life styles of the nation's trendsetters.

Rotogravure pages showed slim-waisted (corseted), wealthy young females in discreet sports activity. Croquet and lawn bowling offered them the major chance to compete in genteel sport. Some socialite women played lawn tennis with their Ivy League gentlemen friends (a well-bred Princeton or Yale man without his suit of "tennis flannels" was unthinkable).

Morristown's millionaires received flattering attention in the Newark and New York newspapers. Their annual horse show was a glittering affair. Formal dances, debutante balls, and church weddings that united large fortunes sent photographers and society writers flocking to Morristown.

The times were relatively happy, both for rich and poor, because it was an uncomplicated age. There was an air of prosperity; more people were working than ever before. Yet the nation wore the two-faced mask of happiness and tragedy that is the mark of the theater.

America's long, bittersweet sleep was ending. The staid, pleasure-seeking "Victorian Age" was tottering; it would collapse under the grim guns of World War I. Two major factors were transforming America: the automobile and a sweeping new sense of social responsibility.

"A Picture Of Arrogance"

The faint sound of the automobile already was heard by 1900. Young men of money or mechanical inclination — sometimes both — became enchanted

Sports played an increasing part of the lives of those who could find the time. There was variety — ranging from autumn's lonely hunters (above) staked out in a duck blind along the Jersey Shore to the tingling stimulus of the toboggan slide at the Essex Club's Winter Carnival on Orange Mountain.

Eagerly awaited were regular regattas on the Passaic River or on the Hudson, where the "Grand Regatta" (top, opposite page) was held in Hoboken. Female activities were necessarily limited, but a real swinger could try her hand (and show her ankle) in croquet.

Ocean bathing was an acceptable sport and, apparently, so was girl-watching. When artist Winslow Homer sketched well-clad beauties on the bluff at Long Branch, he especially saw the slim lines of his models as they braced against sea breezes. Skaters on outdoor ponds included boys in knee pants, business men in conservative garb, and girls in daringly short skirts.

"The Passing of the Horse"

The "passing of the horse" was a matter of opinion. Noted cartoonist Homer Davenport was certain in 1899 that anything able to "run all day" with "no oats, no hay," and "no tender feet" was sure to stay. He titled his opinionated cartoon "The Passing of the Horse." James Birch of Burlington, one of the nation's foremost makers of carriages, saw the "passing" differently in his 1907 catalogue. Birch's message was clear enough, if highly colored by his business hopes. Totally undecided about the auto's future were the motorists negotiating New Jersey roads in the early days of the twentieth century.

with the horseless carriage. Two sons of wealthy families, Thomas Edison Jr. of West Orange and Edward Hewitt of Ringwood, bought steam-powered "locomobiles" on the same day in 1899. The locomobiles were considered dangerous: New Jersey law required that a man with a flag walk a hundred yards ahead of any steam vehicle on the roads.

In time, the nation would abandon its bicycles for automobiles, but the change would not be rapid. A man making $4 to $6 a week in 1900 had about as much hope of owning an automobile as he had of swimming the English Channel.

Enough rich New Jersey families bought automobiles by 1905 to arouse anger against motorists. Preachers spoke against "speed-mad" drivers. Newspaper editorials warned against automobiles. Farmers forced into ditches by motorcars swore to fight.

Woodrow Wilson, the president of Princeton University, told the North Carolina Society in 1906, "nothing has spread socialistic feeling in this country more than the automobile." He explained:

"To the countryman they [automobiles] are a picture of the arrogance of wealth, with all its independence and carelessness."

Blaming the automobile for "socialistic feeling" was much too easy. Far more vital forces were sweeping the land. They were called variously socialism, progressivism, radicalism, muckraking (and usually all four by entrenched forces opposing change).

Attacks On Special Interests

The reformers were as diversified as the evils they preached against. Reform groups ranged from women's clubs and conservation groups to an occasional independent newspaper and a few millionaires with disturbed consciences; from labor leaders and educators to anti-saloon societies and socialists.

No single idea could possibly have united them all. However, underlying the concern of most groups was the tight grip that large corporations and other special interest groups had on politicians.

Industry's gigantic spurt between 1865 and 1900 bestowed many obvious benefits: increased employment, better and cheaper products, and some sharing of tax burdens. It also brought pressing new problems: increasing pollution, the collapse of many small businesses, and the increasingly impersonal relationship between owners and workers.

Nothing stirred business foes more than the formation of powerful national industrial "trusts" or monopolies — sugar trust, leather trust, petroleum trust, etc. Such monopolies could control prices, rig shortages, and grind under all opposition.

Both major political parties attacked the evils of the big business monopolies in 1888. The Republican platform in that Presidential election year opposed "combinations of capital, organized as trusts or otherwise." The Democratic platform declared that trusts betrayed "the interests of the people."

New Jersey's Open Arms

Kansas adopted the nation's first anti-trust law in 1889. Other states quickly followed, until trusts were legal only in New Jersey, Delaware, and West Virginia. New Jersey legislators strengthened the power of the trust by authorizing "holding corporations" in 1889.

Any firm with a "home office" in New Jersey was permitted to hold stock in other companies, contrary to national policy. Hundreds of national companies promptly established "home offices" in the state. One building in Jersey City had 1,500 "home office" signs on its very wide doors. The Corporations held mock "annual meetings" in those offices, and then returned to their real home bases to do as they pleased.

Standard Oil Company set up a New Jersey trust to pull together companies from coast to coast. When the United States Supreme Court dissolved that trust in 1892, the powerful oilmen merely reincorporated under conveniently revised New Jersey corporation laws.

New Jersey's cynical action prompted Lincoln Steffens, a leading reform writer of the day, to observe that the state was "in the business of selling not

Thomas Nast, satirical cartoonist who lived in Morristown and drew for *Harper's Weekly*, put his pen to the Statue of Liberty in 1889. He had her raise her torch to "the Home of the Trusts and the Land of the Plutocrats" while she wore the patches of big business combines.

only indulgences, but absolution."

The state was ridiculed throughout the nation. It appeared in a widely circulated cartoon, calling "come to mother" as it welcomed trusts banned nearly everywhere else.

Why did New Jersey openly ignore the nationwide anti-trust sentiment? Steffens said the state's role as the East Coast's leading railroad area made it subservient to big business. New Jersey lawmakers had been responsive to railroad lobbyists for half a century.

The main reason probably was the temptation of easy money. Corporation fees were set low — twenty cents on each $100 of company capitalization — but mass production of corporate charters produced very high income. It became a painless way to balance the New Jersey state budget.

The Plight Of Labor

Legislative cooperation with corporation owners was not matched by any concern for labor. Owners once worked side by side with workers; now they disappeared into distant front offices, surrounded by

The Fearsome Pen

Thomas Nast, who lived in Morristown from 1871 until his death in 1902, sketched his political and his business foes with such savagery that he wielded the most feared pen in America. Nast's powerful cartoons appeared regularly in Harper's Weekly, *hacking impartially into Democrats and Republicans alike. Scheming politicians hated Thomas Nast; his audience loved him.*

Born in Germany in 1840, Nast came to this country in 1854 and by age 15 was an artist for Leslie's Weekly. *He won his first national fame for vivid battlefield and campground drawings during the Civil War.*

Nast is best remembered for creating the symbols for both major political parties. His concept of Democrats as donkeys first appeared in 1871. Initially he showed Republicans as horses, but in 1874 he created the Republican elephant in a cartoon directed against President Grant's hopes for a third term. The cartoon that first featured the elephant (along with the donkey) appears below. It depicts a timid elephant running in panic while the donkey, disguised as a lion, brayed that Grant would be another Caesar if he could. Nast aimed his cartoons at corrupt political leaders, particularly Boss Tweed of New York City.

Each Christmas, Nast put aside his bitter political cartoons and drew fat, jolly Santa Clauses, thus popularizing another well-known image.

boards of directors. It became increasingly difficult for workers to bring their grievances to the attention of management.

Workers in New Jersey lacked even the legal right to organize until 1883. Until then, employees could be jailed for conspiracy if they assembled "for the purpose of changing conditions of employment." The 1883 law granted labor the right "to enter into any combination for organizing, leaving, or entering into the employment of others."

The plight of the working people can be illustrated in three industries widely separated in geography and product: pottery making in Trenton, brewing in Newark, and glassblowing in the pine forests of South Jersey.

Trenton's pottery makers walked off their jobs in the bitterly cold winter of 1877-78 to protest a wage cut. They returned after a long holdout, asserting they were "beaten rather than convinced."

The potters struck again in the winter and spring of 1883-84. The action earned them an eight percent wage *cut*. An 1890-91 strike ended with another decrease in wages. The pottery balance sheet showed three long strikes and three wage cuts.

Brewery workers walked off their jobs at Newark, Elizabeth, Paterson, and New Brunswick in 1886. One study declared that beer makers "were always working except when asleep." Their workday began at 5 AM and lasted fourteen to eighteen hours, plus six to eight hours on Sundays. Their pay was $20 to $25 a month: *five to seven cents an hour.*

The brewers won their strike; brewing was too prosperous for the plants to remain closed long. The brewer's day was cut to ten hours, wages climbed thirty to fifty percent, and Sunday work was discontinued.

Slaves In Glass Houses

South Jersey's glassmakers were the most forlorn of all. Wages were miserably low; but worse, workers were forced to buy everything at inflated prices in company-owned stores. An 1899 report showed 3,000 glass company pay envelopes that contained not one penny of cash because of such company deductions as "rent," "store," and vague charges listed as "also."

Glass workers were unofficial slaves, since company store debts made the jobs an unrelieved burden. Each month families owed a bit more to the company store. Leaving the job could mean prison.

Boys were forced at age seven or eight to join their fathers and grandfathers to help pay debts that rose

A Paterson labor paper (upper left) cynically viewed labor's treatment by capitalists "before and after" election. Labor had reason to complain; the shiny interior of a Newark brewery with its fat brewmaster was a front for wretched working conditions. By 1900, however, working men marched in Labor Day parades.

with each passing week. The boys were officially called "apprentices," but most of them learned little except that work forced them into debt. By the time they were men, they owed money to the company through no fault of theirs.

Three desperation strikes in 1886, 1893, and 1899 won the glass workers nothing against the all-powerful glass companies. South Jersey legislators friendly to the company owners killed every action aimed at curbing the evident evil of company stores.

Finally, on August 15, 1900, manufacturers and glass blowers agreed to end the company stores. It was a small victory — hours were just as long, wages just as poor, and working conditions just as wretched — but at least the store was no longer an anvil around a sinking worker's neck.

Contempt For The People

Legislative obedience to corporations, railroads, glass companies, and money interests of any kind was an acknowledged New Jersey tradition. In 1893, however, the legislators finally outdid themselves in their contempt for people they supposedly represented.

The 1893 Assembly was nicknamed the "Jockey Legislature." The Assembly Speaker was Thomas Flynn of Passaic, whose work outside the legislative halls was as a "starter" of racehorses at Billy Thompson's

notorious racetrack in Gloucester. Billy himself sat in the Assembly, surrounded by lawmakers mainly interested in protecting their own schemes.

William Edgar Sackett, author of the lively, informative, *Modern Battles of Trenton,* wrote: "Everything that was venal or corrupt or offensive in the management of public affairs was largely reflected in the Legislature."

A few lawmakers opposed the racetrack gang. Thomas F. Lane, Democratic Assemblyman from Union County, demanded a public hearing on 1893 bills to legalize gambling. Speaker Flynn contemptuously responded that those opposing the legislation were "old women and dominies."

Lane retorted that Flynn's remarks were an "insult to the honest mothers and sisters and daughters of the Commonwealth." He added: "The Speaker will remember that the hand that rocks the cradle rules the world!"

Ignoring both Lane and the "cradle rockers," the legislature rushed through a series of racetrack bills. Governor George T. Werts vetoed the measures, but the track supporters easily overrode him.

The legislative "horse lovers" were in the stretch, and they lost. Five thousand angry citizens forcibly took over the Assembly chambers on Washington's Birthday in 1893 when ministers, priests, lawyers, and others orated against the race track interests.

Billy Thompson's Gloucester City hotel deserved the widespread raves it won for its famed planked shad, but the owner's main interest was his race course. As a State Assemblyman, Billy and others in the infamous "Jockey Legislature" of 1893 inspired statewide anger by their strong pro-gambling laws.

The next November, the racetrack Democrats were swept out of Trenton. Three years later, John Griggs became the first Republican governor in twenty-seven years. The people of New Jersey had expressed themselves: the state did not belong to the gamblers.

Rocking The Cradle

Assembly Speaker Flynn's sneering assault on protesters as "old women" and Assemblyman Lane's defense that "the hand that rocks the cradle rules the world" signified the subordinate role of women in the nineteenth century society.

One "cradle rocker" long had been nationally known. She was Lucy Stone (Mrs. Lucy Blackwell) of Orange who refused, in 1858, to pay town taxes unless she could vote. When she insisted that she was a victim of "taxation without representation," the tax collector sold her household furnishings, including her baby's cradle.

Women leaders recognized in time that strength lay in organization. New Jersey's first women's club was formed in Orange in 1872. The town where Lucy Stone lost her cradle would become a center of organized female activity.

The Orange club appeared meek enough on the surface. It quietly debated such innocent-sounding subjects as "Do the women of the middle and upper classes do their share of work in the world?" Such a subject could not alarm any political leader.

Beneath the silken exterior, however, the Orange club was taking a tough look at its town. Members carefully studied the public schools and in 1876 submitted to the town a detailed, critical report on classroom heat and ventilation. That alerted males to the fact that women's clubs were more than harmless excuses for afternoon teas.

Thirty-six clubs organized as the New Jersey State Federation of Women's Clubs in 1894. They represented the best-educated, most energetic women of the day. The Jersey City Women's Club, for example, included New Jersey's first woman lawyer, a physician, a college vice-president, the principal in the city's manual training school, and other distinguished citizens. Few clubs, male or female, had such an array

America also had its "upstairs" and "downstairs," but downstairs Americans roared with laughter as a maid mimicked the "lady of the house." The lady, meanwhile, probably sensing the disrespect, also was growing bored with duties as wife and mother. She sought a challenge: she found it in public service.

of talent.

Jennie Cunningham Croly, the national women's club historian, wrote in 1898 that the clubs were "part of the great educational movement which is sweeping like a tidal wave over the country." She saw the clubs as "not the mere banding together for social and economic purpose, like the clubs of men," but as a "purely altruistic and democratic activity."

Saving The Palisades

Since they had no political obligations, women were not afraid to dispute legislators on unpopular issues. The State Federation found its first great public battleground in 1894 when it opened a fight to save the beautifully rugged Palisades overlooking the Hudson River in Bergen and Hudson counties.

Contractors had blasted away at the Palisades for several years, crushing the magnificent cliff into trap rock for road building. The state legislature assured protestors that nothing could be done about it.

The State Federation refused to accept that. Mrs. Margaret Yardley of Orange, the Federation president, led 300 club members to Trenton when the legislature met in March 1896.

The women's meeting was blandly called "Literary Day." Any legislator who listened knew that the destruction of the Palisades, not poetry, was the matter under discussion. Mrs. Yardley candidly agreed that "Literary Day" was a move "to show women's organized strength to the legislators on the Palisades question."

Unrelenting Federation pressure forced the legislature to create a Palisades study commission in 1899. Miss Elizabeth Vermilye of Englewood and Miss Cecelia Gaines of Jersey City, both Federation members, served on the study group.

New York State adopted legislation to create an Interstate Park Commission in 1900. Lobbyists for the trap rock interests held up a companion bill in the New Jersey legislature for weeks, while the blasting continued at the cliff. The lobbyists finally caved in before the Federation. The Palisades Interstate Park Commission was established in 1900.

New Jersey women had saved the Palisades. They won national acclaim for their achievement in defeating, without funds or political power, the well-financed forces of destruction. Yet neither New

Cast into place when lava from an ancient volcano cooled, the Palisades amazed and charmed visitors from the time of the explorers. Henry Hudson's mate wrote of the rocky eminence in 1609, and the columnar-like cliffs reminded colonists of the palisades of a fort. Artists sought constantly to capture the beauty as in the engraving above, made in 1837, or that to the left, made in 1874. Shortly after the 1874 view was made, road builders began heavy blasting in the Palisades. Vigorous action by New Jersey women's clubs saved the area from destruction.

York nor New Jersey found room for even one woman among the ten commissioners appointed to control the Palisades. Woman's day was yet to come.

"Boys Above Bottles"

Federation women did not sulk over the slight, for they were skirmishing on a hundred other fronts. A historian of the women's club movement wrote that after 1902 women began to "make a mark all over the state." More accurately, women had become an unleashed fury.

Their aims were those of most progressives: greater opportunity and greater protection for greater numbers of people. The Federation investigations reached everywhere, even deep into the Pine Barrens where they found glassmakers were working boys eight to ten years old through the night.

Abolish that night labor, the Federation demanded of legislators, "thus placing our State with those that favor boys above bottles." Again the power of

TO THE WOMAN IN THE HOME

How can a mother rest content with this—

When such conditions exist as this?

There are thousands of children working in sweat-shops like the one in the picture. There are thousands of children working in mines and mills and factories. Thousands more are being wronged and cheated by Society in countless ways.

IS NOT THIS **YOUR** BUSINESS?

Sharp contrasts between America's extremely rich and its woefully poor disturbed women's groups. This National American Woman Suffrage Association poster bluntly urged women to be concerned.

enraged women prevailed. A law was passed to abolish night work for boys in glass factories.

Clubwomen were now under full sail. They advocated home economics courses in the schools, urged establishment of kindergartens, and argued for laws to protect women factory workers. They battled to eliminate the billboards that lined the railroad rights-of-way, and insisted on laws to control factory smoke.

Every time a legislator paused to listen, he heard the voices of women: demanding improved sanitation, civil service reform, child-labor laws, tuberculosis control, slaughter-house inspection, and clean railroad stations.

Education was much on women's minds. They stumped for better pay for better-trained teachers, compulsory school attendance, special instruction for

handicapped children, and well-built, well-equipped schools. They campaigned for a state college for women, but they did not forget those in trouble — they also demanded a modern state reformatory for women.

New Jersey had never seen the like of these zealous, fiery women. They fought on without expectations of personal reward or political favor. They were neither liberal nor conservative, Republican nor Democratic. Many were wealthy, eager to champion those without money or friends.

Children, Prisons, College

Several of the causes had major impact. Mrs. Emily E. Williamson of Elizabeth, State Federation president from 1898 to 1900, concentrated on prison reform and child welfare.

As secretary of the State Charities Aid Association, Mrs. Williamson conspired with a young associate, Frances Day, to enter the Hudson County Almshouse in 1897-98 as a supposed inmate. Miss Day stayed for two months, and then emerged to write a scathing report that rocked the state.

Miss Day told of exploitation and mistreatment of children in the almshouse. The report helped to shame the state into forming the State Board of Children's Guardians, whose original purpose was to place children in foster homes rather than in public institutions. The board later expanded its aims to include broad protection for children.

Prison reform spurred Mrs. Caroline B. Alexander of Jersey City into action. She pushed for a modern, separate women's prison. This was realized in 1910 when the New Jersey Reformatory for Women was started on what was described as "a picturesque and salubrious site" at Clinton.

Other women stepped to the fore. Mrs. Stewart Hartshorn of Short Hills sought improved conditions for women factory workers. Miss Mary McKeen of Morristown distinguished herself as a dedicated worker for conservation causes. Mrs. Henry H. Dawson of Newark threw herself into the long struggle for better public schools.

College education for women was the beacon for Mrs. Mabel Smith Douglass of Jersey City. Disturbed because only the College of St. Elizabeth in Convent and Centenary College in Hackettstown offered women a New Jersey college education, Mrs. Douglass stumped the state between 1912 and 1918 in support of the New Jersey College for Women. She became the first dean when the college opened in 1918. (Appropriately, it was renamed Douglass College in 1955).

Miss Lakey And Pure Food

Miss Alice Lakey of the Cranford Village Improvement Association found her cause in 1902 when Dr. Harvey Washington Wiley, nationally known chief chemist of the Department of Agriculture in Washington, spoke to her club. Cranford was another stop in Dr. Wiley's relentless battle against the food and drink trusts.

Alice Lakey's horror and indignation grew as Dr. Wiley told the Improvement Association of the harm that befell people from the uncontrolled injection of chemicals into food, drink, liquor, and patent

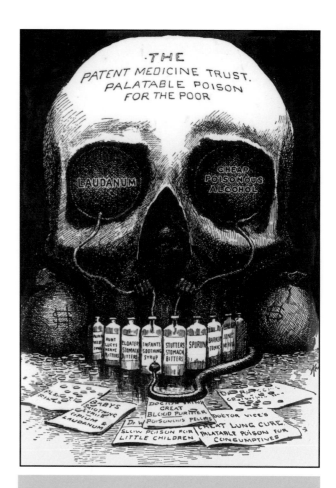

Patent medicines offering "miracle cures" for everything from headaches to flat feet were blasted in this cartoon in *Collier's Magazine* for June 3, 1905. The artist focused attention on the dangers of nostrums that often were merely thinly-disguised alcohol.

medicines.

Approaching Dr. Wiley after the meeting, Miss Lakey volunteered her services. She promised to help persuade the State Federation of Women's Clubs, the National Federation, and the National Consumers' League to back the doctor's crusade.

Miss Lakey lectured before women's clubs up and down the state and across the nation. Often she encountered suspicion and uneasiness. Usually she stirred strenuous action.

Congressmen, canners, packers, and the liquor trusts could not hold back the angered public. President Theodore Roosevelt and other Congressmen joined the few lawmakers who had fought for the cause. The Pure Food bill became law on June 20, 1906.

Mark Sullivan wrote in *Our Times* of Miss Lakey and her crusade:

Miss Lakey was moved by one of the most dynamic of forces, the indignation of a woman against evils practiced, as the adulterations of food partly was, for profit at the expense and happiness of children.

Sullivan believed that clubwomen, "by the pressure they brought on Congress — without votes, without ever thinking they needed votes — did a work greater than anything that women accomplished or attempted in the eight years after women got the suffrage in 1919."

Fagan Makes His Mark

Democratic and Republican leaders tried to downplay the progressives. Both parties especially opposed every effort to reform voting methods (including the introduction of secret ballots) or any other movement that threatened the iron grip they held on every level of government.

"The system," however, was about to crumble. A young Jersey City undertaker named Mark M. Fagan would lead the demolition.

Fagan recognized in 1896 that his city's outrageous slums must be cleaned up. Republicans permitted him to run that year for the Hudson County Board of Freeholders, possibly in the belief that his chance of winning in the overwhelmingly Democratic district was negligible.

Fagan campaigned strenuously in the tenement areas, where Italian residents loved the hardworking, sincere young Irishman. Fagan won an upset victory, and four years later he was elected mayor of Jersey City.

The Republican leaders at first welcomed this youthful newcomer with such remarkable vote appeal in a Democratic area. Fagan soon disappointed the bosses. He demanded better schools, the elimination of foul sewers, a new building to replace the city's leaky, old, vermin-infested hospital; better parks, and public concerts.

Fagan then took on the railroads, New Jersey's most sacred cow. He decided that the railroads must pay an increased share of the city's taxes. That was logical; some thirty percent of the city's land was railroad-owned. All railroad taxes (which were modest) went to the state.

The mayor promised during the 1903 campaign to carry his fight for local taxation of railroads to Trenton. He won handily, and carried out his promise, only to have the Republican-dominated legislature ignore him. Fagan sent off a wrathful open letter to Republican Governor Franklin Murphy.

Fagan charged, "the Republican legislature is controlled by the railroad, trolley, and water corporations, and the interests of the people are being betrayed. As a member of the Republican party, I deplore its subservience to corporate greed and injustice."

Copies of Fagan's letter were sent to the newspapers. The newspaper publicity proved to be far better than the appeals to Trenton. Jersey City's share of railroad taxes jumped seventy percent in one year.

Republican bosses decided that this Jersey City upstart must go. The party abandoned him in 1905, but Fagan won his third straight term as mayor and carried twelve Hudson Republicans with him into the State Assembly.

A "New Idea" In Orange

An even stronger progressive force was building in Essex County. It started when young Orange Republicans, including wealthy Alden Freeman and brilliant lawyer Frank Sommer, opposed a local trolley franchise that was to be granted "forever." Their chief foe was the county's Republican boss, aging Carl Lentz, a one-armed Civil War veteran, who bragged that he preferred "to crush opposition rather than face it."

Alerted to Lentz's "official" party policy, the Orange group widened its interest in county affairs. Lentz's party regulars loftily dismissed the "new idea" of the Orange group and so gave the insurgents a name. When the Newark *Evening News* backed the "New Idea," it became a valid force.

By 1904, the "New Idea" had found its leader: handsome, aristocratic, and wealthy Everett Colby. Lentz backed Colby when he won election to the Assembly in 1902. He withdrew the support, however, when Colby defied party instructions and voted as he saw fit.

Colby won enough Assembly respect by 1905 to try for the post of Speaker. Lentz foiled that move, but he could not quiet Colby. Progressive votes swept Colby into the State Senate in 1905. With Fagan in Hudson County and Colby in Essex County, the New Idea rode high.

Even the staunchest old-line conservatives began to spout progressive theories. Acceptance by the bosses of liberal policies weakened the need for the New Idea, and when Colby declined to run for Governor in 1907, the movement lost momentum.

Both Fagan and Colby lost bids for re-election,

Woman Of The World

Driving from Trenton to New York was hazardous enough in 1909 when cars were poor and there were no service stations or road maps — so Harriet White Fisher of Trenton decided to drive around the world.

No one had ever traveled around the earth by automobile, but Mrs. Fisher was accustomed to success. She was only in her early twenties when her husband died in 1903, but she took over his Trenton business — making blacksmith anvils — and prospered.

Mrs. Fisher prepared for a long trip, installing extra gasoline and oil tanks on her forty-horsepower Locomobile. She allowed space for a chauffeur, mechanic, cook, and personal maid. Mrs. Fisher was courageous, but not about to give up comfort.

The car was shipped to Paris on July 17, 1909. Mrs. Fisher drove to Italy, shipped the car to Bombay, and drove the Locomobile 2,300 miles across India, at times following mountain trails 20,000 feet above sea level.

After visits to Ceylon (where her car was in the above photo) and Japan, Mrs. Fisher set out for San Francisco by boat on May 27, 1910. She then drove across the United States, reaching Trenton on August 17, exactly thirteen months after leaving New York. The time was a far cry from the fictional eighty days of Jules Verne's novel. Mrs. Fisher explained that she wanted to "drive" around the world, not "race" around it.

defeated by liberal young Democrats who advanced the same philosophies. Even at its demise the New Idea had won.

Honor In High Places

Often overlooked in studies of the progressive era is the fact that New Jersey had several excellent Republican governors between 1896 and 1910. They built traditions in the governor's office that later served Woodrow Wilson well.

Politicians and State House workers were shaken when Franklin Murphy, millionaire Newark varnish maker, became governor in 1902. He demanded that every state employee show up for work on time (as Murphy did). He removed state funds from politically favored banks and reinvested the money in savings accounts that bore interest. (That earned $60,000 in the first year.)

Many things caught Murphy's attention. He fought for state aid to clean up the filthy Passaic River. He backed a law to make school boards independent of political control, with power to ask local governments for money. That insured — for the first time in many towns — that teachers received their salaries regularly.

Murphy sought election reform. A 1903 law endorsed by the governor set up a system of voter registration and provided for the use of official ballots and official ballot boxes. Until then, local officials fashioned their own ballots and often made do with cigar boxes or cardboard cartons on Election Day.

Protecting The Children

Nothing irked Murphy more than reports of mistreatment of thousands of children in New Jersey factories.

Murphy knew (as did anyone who cared to find out) that the cigar makers hired children for two dollars a week to perform work for which men were paid eight dollars. Owners of South Jersey's glass works did not bother to deny that their boys living away from home learned drunkenness at an early age — often before the age of ten.

When Consumers League Secretary Helen Marot tried to investigate child labor in a Paterson mill in 1901, she was turned away. The mill owner said that so many children worked in the factory that Miss Marot could only "disturb" them at their benches and looms.

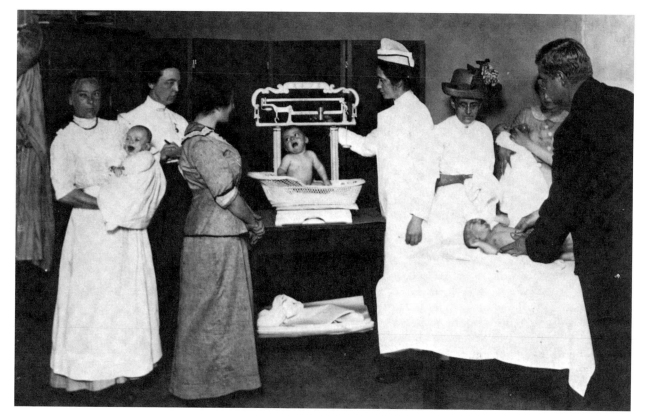

New Jersey doctors and nurses fought increasingly, after 1900, to improve health standards, particularly in the cities. The needs of immigrant families prompted civic-minded doctors to open public clinics, such as this "Baby Keep Well" station in Newark. (Dr. Henry L. Coit, who originated this clinic, works in the foreground.) Elsewhere, medical leaders opened or expanded hospitals, experimented with improved techniques of surgery and pre-natal care, and used improved drugs and surgical dressings. As a consequence, Newark's death rate, highest in the nation in 1890 among cities with more than 100,000 population, dropped to sixth lowest in 1910.

Murphy had an answer — and the power. He forced the state factory inspector, a former Salem County state senator, to resign. He sent his personal secretary into Passaic County textile mills to investigate. Within six weeks, Murphy had proof of more than 200 violations of child-labor.

Lobbyists for the textile mills, glass works, and other factories attempted to delay legislation to correct the abuses. Murphy forced his reforms through the legislature and signed them into law. Children under fourteen thereafter could work only in stores, on streets, or on farms.

Heavy penalties were set for violations. The law also provided for a staff of thirteen investigators, including two women, and made employers — not the children — responsible for proving a child's age.

Fort Conquered By Guardians

Just before Woodrow Wilson made his spectacular entrance into politics, Republican Governor John Franklin Fort tried in vain to introduce many of the reforms that later won Wilson lavish praise.

Fort entered office in 1908 with a public statement of his hopes. He wanted a strong law to control public utilities. He proposed abolishing county tax boards that he believed favored railroads. He advocated a civil service law. He asked for power to remove any official found guilty of wrongdoing.

The governor urged that New Jersey stop water from being diverted to neighbor states. He asked for deepening of the inland waterway along the Jersey Shore and proposed an ocean highway to help lure visitors to the shore resorts.

Dismayed by Fort's liberal notions, the Republican bosses closed ranks against him. They set up a committee in 1909 to "assist" party lawmakers. This Board of Guardians hemmed in Fort to make certain that his dreams would not interrupt New Jersey's deep sleep.

The Republican guardians urged economy, although Fort could point to figures that proved New Jersey's growth: population up to 2.5 million in 1910, manufacturing more than doubled in the decade af-

Thomas Woodrow Wilson, who doffed his hat when he posed (above, right) with a few others in his Princeton Class of 1879, became the university's most distinguished graduate. He returned to teach at Princeton College (above) and was a noted historian when the campus name was changed to Princeton University in 1896. When Wilson became Princeton's president in 1902, he urged that the university be dedicated to national service. He left Princeton to win election as Governor of New Jersey in 1910. In that office, he appeared solemn and stiff atop a horse in reviewing the State Guard. Wilson's unflinching reforms as governor won him such attention that national artists caricatured him in 1912. By then he was well on his way to the White House.

ter 1900, taxable property up three times in value in the same period.

Fort warned, "Our state is growing fast. It must spend more." Since Fort was not eligible under the State Constitution to succeed himself, many of the reforms were still on the drawing board when his term ended.

Woodrow Wilson was elected governor, in November 1910, by 49,000 votes over his Republican opponent. Wilson's victory was a repudiation of boss-ridden, penny-pinching corrupt politics in Trenton. Fort agreed. After hearing the election returns, he wrote:

My only regret is that the legislation I advised was not enacted, and I believe that the result of the election evidenced that the people joined me in that regret. They have forcibly expressed their opinion.

Indebted To No One

Wilson had no experience in public office. He won the governorship because of his brilliance, grace, and charm. He owed no political debts to anyone.

Virginia-born Thomas Woodrow Wilson graduated from Princeton in 1879, returned to become a professor, and then was elected university president in 1902. His biographer, Arthur Link, declared Wilson took a "backward college" and "transformed it almost overnight into one of the leading educational laboratories in the nation."

Wilson encountered trouble on the campus, after 1906, when he tried to abolish as undemocratic the university's revered social eating clubs. He failed to win his point; the clubs survived. Alumni who favored the old system hated Wilson for his viewpoint.

Three years later, Wilson and Professor Andrew West quarreled openly over the location of a proposed graduate school. Wilson wanted it on the old campus. West favored a location on a golf course about a mile from the main campus. A multimillion-dollar gift from a Massachusetts donor to create the graduate school settled the issue by stipulating that the school be built on the golf course.

Rumors filtered across campus that the university president might resign, and it was clear that many among both alumni and trustees would have been delighted.

Losing the graduate school fight presented the tempting possibility that Wilson might turn to politics. His nationwide reputation as a scholar, writer, and speaker stirred talk of national office — at least the US Senate, or possibly the Presidency.

First, A Stop In Trenton

James Smith Jr., Democratic boss of Essex County, tried in vain to get Wilson to run for the US Senate in 1907. Smith saw the proper Princetonian as a fine candidate and, in 1910, rammed Wilson's name through a disgruntled anti-boss Democratic convention. This won him the nomination for Governor.

Wilson stepped before a sullen, unconvinced audience in the Taylor Opera House in Trenton to accept the party nomination. He was, to this point, only Smith's man. The audience changed its mood as Wilson spoke and finally cheered his declaration that he was pledged to no one.

The candidate promised a vigorous campaign, based on the party's progressive platform. An eyewitness said that Wilson's "earnest eloquence moved some of his more emotional and less sober audience to tears."

Once a cool conservative in economic and political philosophies, Wilson, according to Arthur Link, had moved by 1910 "from the right of center to center." He accepted reform, and party regulars found him acceptable. Liberals were charmed by his grace and wit.

Wilson was swept into office, along with a Democratic Assembly and a Senate narrowly held by the Republicans. Wilson had a mandate for change.

When the Democratic Party bosses called to request their usual, expected patronage, the new governor rebuffed them coolly. He owed them nothing. He gave them nothing.

Wilson's fight against business and industrial trusts, begun in New Jersey, continued after he became President. This 1913 cartoon from the *New York World* had him reading a "death warrant" to unscrupulous financiers.

Wilson fully intended to lead without outside interference or "suggestions" from the bosses. A few days after taking over the governor's office, he wrote he saw himself as "the representative of the common people against those who have been preying upon them."

The new power gave Wilson what he saw as "a sort of solemnity that I am sure will not wear off." He declared: "I do not see how a man in such a position could possibly be afraid of anything except failing to do his honorable duty and set all temptations (if they be disguised enough to be temptations) contemptuously to one side."

Wilson set four basic goals: major election reforms, an act to curb corrupt political acts, a strong public utilities commission, and a workmen's compensation act that would protect working people properly.

Four For New Jersey

Under the new election laws, male citizens finally had a genuine voice in the polling booths. They could vote in primary elections to choose party candidates and delegates to Presidential conventions. Official ballots became a matter of law rather than the whim of local political clubs. Newspapers across the nation hailed the election law as "a death blow to party bosses."

Fraud, the hallmark of New Jersey politics for many decades, was placed under direct fire by the corrupt-practices act, the second Wilson reform. Ample evidence of the need to control cheating by both parties quickly surfaced.

In 1911, in Democratic Newark, sample ballots were sent to "registered" voters. About 11,000 were returned undeliverable; those phantom "voters" in the previous elections did not exist. In Republican-bossed Atlantic County, an investigation in the same year showed eighty percent of all votes cast were fraudulent.

The public utilities law, the third major change, created a three-man board of public utilities commissioners. Most important, the new board had sharp teeth. It could evaluate public utility property and fix "just and reasonable" rates. At last the word "public" shared equal billing with "utilities."

The fourth Wilson measure was the workmen's compensation law, enacted over the opposition of industry and business. The Newark *News* campaigned for the new law, calling the old one "the most ancient and unjust of any employers' liability laws in the country."

Wilson received bipartisan support for the workmen's compensation law. Senator Walter E. Edge of Atlantic County (who later was twice elected governor) wrote the new statute that abolished the old principle that workers assumed all personal risks. Instead, employers were made responsible for injuries sustained in their factories.

Eye On The White House

Wilson grew restive. His eye clearly was on the White House, and he was often out of New Jersey in his second year as governor. The Republican-dominated legislature criticized his long speaking tours in 1912. Wilson replied tartly, "no important matter of business has been allowed to fall in arrears in my office."

The times were made for Wilson. Theodore Roosevelt broke with the Republic Party in 1912 and ran for President with the independent Progressive ("Bull Moose") Party. William Howard Taft, the Republican choice for President, showed progressive leanings, but he lacked crowd appeal.

With the Republicans so badly splintered, the Democrats should have had an easy march into the White House, but they argued among themselves over a wide range of political ideology, from conservative thought to progressivism. Badly splintered, they met in Baltimore in the summer of 1912 to choose a candidate.

After wearying debate, the delegates compromised on Wilson on the forty-sixth ballot. His progressive views endeared him to many Democrats. Southerners liked him because of his Virginia birth and his promise not to press for new federal powers.

With three major candidates in the 1912 campaign, the voting was split, giving the Democrats the victory. Wilson received 6,296,547 votes to 4,188,571 to Roosevelt and 3,486,720 for Taft. New Jersey gave Wilson all of its Electoral College votes, but only about thirty-eight percent of the popular vote.

Return Of The Bosses

Wilson stepped up his pace in Trenton while awaiting his inauguration. He remained in the governor's office until four days before departing for Washington to be sworn in as President.

During his last days as governor, Wilson persuaded the legislature to pass seven laws abolishing most of the privileges of giant trusts. The seven anti-trust statutes became known as the "Seven Sisters Acts" of 1913.

The Seven Sisters arrived much too late. Other states, envious of New Jersey's success in attracting the "home offices" of new corporations and gaining tax ratables, eased their corporation laws. The profitable trust business merely transferred elsewhere, and all of the Seven Sisters laws were repealed by 1920.

The bosses quickly regained their old power after Wilson left for Washington. New faces appeared among them, particularly that of young Democrat Frank Hague of Jersey City. In time, Hague would become the most powerful boss in New Jersey history.

Ironically, Hague gained his first chance at power as the result of a Wilson-inspired reform to create new forms of local government. Hague won election as a Jersey City commissioner and was off and running on a political career that would ultimately stamp him as one of the most potent — perhaps *the* most potent — political bosses that the nation ever would know.

Machine politics was fully back in the saddle by 1915, discouraging those who fought so hard and so

long to drive it out. Revived bosses, however, had a nagging headache. All over the land women demanded the right to vote.

Don't Let Females Vote

Women had pressed for full voting privileges for more than a half century. Lucy Stone of Orange founded the New Jersey Suffrage League in 1866, three years before the National Suffrage League was organized. Miss Stone also headed the national group.

Slowly the movement gathered strength. By 1915, women were ready for a showdown with New Jersey's political bosses. James Nugent of Newark, one of the state's top Democratic Party leaders, summoned all bosses of both parties to Asbury Park in 1915. He piously warned them of the chaos that surely would follow if females won the right to enter the voting booth.

A special election on equal suffrage was set for October 19, 1915. Women leaders worked feverishly. More than 2,000 meetings were held around the state, with more than 1,000 street meetings in Newark alone.

Progressivism faced its most serious challenge when women pressed determinedly for the right to vote. Males looked on with mixed skepticism and cynicism (above) as Newark women posed beside a llama to win newspaper attention in 1915. Morristown women traveled in a fancy Ford, with brass radiator, to call attention to the suffrage election in October 1915.

Democratic boss James Nugent, lampooned in a 1919 Newark *News* cartoon, jovially led opponents of female suffrage. Voting was a serious goal, however, for Morristown socialite Mrs. Alison Hopkins, shown in newspaper photo (above, right) with two other suffrage leaders in a Virginia prison where they spent thirty days after a Washington demonstration. Mrs. Hopkins is in the center of the three inmates.

Women speakers endured taunts, threats, obscenities, and thrown vegetables. They fought on.

County bosses in Passaic and Atlantic enlisted eagerly in Nugent's war against women. Party leaders in rural Hunterdon County warned farmers that suffrage was "a notion of the Wild West."

The day before the special election, Nugent issued an open letter that alleged an "exhaustive survey" (his own) showed that whenever females voted, "freak laws" came into being. Nugent wrote:

> *New Jersey citizens through all history have stood for fidelity on contracts, the preservation of personal integrity of the courts, stability of government, and above all, the purity, privacy, and loving unity of the home.*

All these rights and privileges would be lost if women voted, said Nugent solemnly. Some of the state's editors, even those who opposed women's votes, must have choked over that statement, but they didn't

gag enough to keep them from printing Nugent's urgent appeal to vote against the women.

"Five Dimes For A Vote"

Nugent recognized (although he refrained from writing it) the greatest losers might be the political machines if women "voted wrong." The bosses passed the word that the amendment must be defeated at all costs.

The "cost" varied from county to county. Votes were bought openly, with Newark's going rate set at "five dimes for votes against suffrage."

Opposition to female voting was not limited to machine politicians, as many suffragists insisted. The State Federation of Labor opposed women's voting, as did several Catholic bishops. Newark's Protestant Episcopal bishop said that even discussion of the matter was "disruptive of family life." The State

Federation of Women's Clubs, so active in other progressive measures, felt the proposal had a divisive effect on club members.

The women could not match the dimes, the dollars, or the votes of the bosses on Election Day. The equal voting proposal went down to a ringing defeat in an all-male election: 184,390 to 133,282. The bosses hailed the result as the "wisdom of the electorate."

Woman's suffrage, however, would come to New Jersey in time, for it was undoubtedly the most logical of all the progressive ideas that swept across New Jersey between 1880 and 1915.

Women had to postpone temporarily their drive for equality. Gathering strength across the Atlantic Ocean was a far greater threat to the liberties of all people. Europe was again at war.

In October 1915, World War I was still only a matter of newspaper headlines in this country. President Wilson was beginning to shape his campaign for re-election on the vow to "keep us out of war." The United States had long boasted of its intention never to meddle in foreign wars. This time, the nation would be forced to take a new look at its boast.

"Why We Oppose Votes For Men"

1. *Because man's place is in the army.*

2. *Because no really manly man wants to settle any question otherwise than by fighting about it.*

3. *Because if men should adopt peaceable methods women will no longer look up to them.*

4. *Because men will lose their charm if they step out of their natural sphere and interest themselves in other matters than feats of arms, uniforms and drums.*

5. *Because men are too emotional to vote. Their conduct at baseball games and political conventions shows this, while their innate tendency to appeal to force renders them particularly unfit for the task of government.*

Cynical male arguments about "women's place," "feminine charm," and "erratic female emotions" were thrown back at them in satiric words written in 1915 by Alice Duer Miller, the noted American novelist and poet who lived part of her life in Morristown.

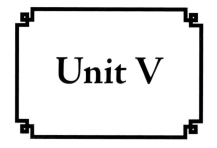

of Frederick William the First: "When one in this world wants to do something with the pen he does not do it unless supported by the strength of the sword."

The United States editors consigned that to the inside pages. It seemed to them nothing but an empty boast.

Those words of Kaiser Wilhelm would come back to haunt the twentieth century. So would the automobile that 1900 editors also did not think had much future, with some reason: there were only 8,000 of them in the United States in 1900.

Disease ran wild. Childbirth was extremely hazardous to both mother and child. Little children died by the thousands each year in epidemics of whooping cough, scarlet fever, and diphtheria. Yellow fever, typhoid fever, and infantile paralysis struck regularly.

There were no "miracle drugs." Doctors and hospitals were closer to the seventeenth century than to the twentieth in drugs, in techniques, in cleanliness. The average life expectancy was a mere forty-nine years.

Few families had electricity in their homes as the century began. Bathtubs and inside toilets were virtually unknown outside of the cities, the fashionable summer resorts, or the millionaire estates. Two-week vacations with pay and forty-hour work weeks were unknown for working people. A weekly salary of $10 was considered a princely income.

Ten dollars went a long way. Sugar was four cents a pound, eggs fourteen cents a dozen, and butter twenty-five cents a pound. A turkey dinner cost as little as twenty cents. Gingham was five cents a yard and a quality man's suit could be bought for $10.

Only about one male in twenty-five went to college; most students left school well before the eight grade. Females were seldom educated beyond eight grade and then mainly for typing or schoolteaching. A woman lawyer or doctor was a rarity; a woman politician was unknown.

Few people in 1900 ventured more than thirty miles from their home in all their lifetimes. Twenty-five miles an hour was a breathtaking speed.

The first sun of the new twentieth century beamed down on a nation of forty-five states on January 1, 1900. Only 75 million people lived in all the land. A mere 117 towns in the nation had populations exceeding 25,000. Only three cities had more than one million residents: New York, Philadelphia, and Chicago.

Newspapers on Monday, January 1 boasted of the progress the United States had made and tried to predict the future, as editors always do when a new century begins.

If the editors really had possessed an ability to see the future that New Year's Day they would have paid more heed to what Wilhelm II, Kaiser of Germany, told his nation on January 1, 1900:

The first day of the new century sees our army — in other words, our people — in arms, gathered around their standards, kneeling before the Lord of Hosts …

I hope to he enabled, with a firm trust in the guidance of God, to prove the truth of the saying

Footsteps To A World Entwined

Early in the twentieth century, John Holland thought his invention of the submarine would render war so horrible mankind would finally end war forever. He, of course, was only partly right — it did make war more horrendous, but it didn't stop it.

A few decades later, Albert Einstein thought his scientific discovery that led to the atomic bomb would also end war. It did end World War II, but mankind found a way to continue war in new ways: the cold war and various skirmishes throughout the world with new war rules — no atomic bombs allowed.

The fear was still there, however. Many of the baby boomer generation honestly believed the world would end in nuclear destruction before they had a chance to grow up!

When the 70s rolled in, children still lived in fear. Did it reassure them to hear that their parents had shared the same fears, and that passage of time rendered those fears unfounded? Maybe, for some, it did.

The twenty-first century dawned with relative calm. The world had averted the Y2K computer disaster. The relatively peaceful atmosphere in most of the world belied the brewing storm that led to the 9/11 terrorist attacks on US soil. The United States that had hesitated to participate in both world wars, charged into aggressive assault.

New Jerseyans, as always, were right in the thick of it. Many of them mourned family members lost in the World Trade Center collapse. Many went off to war in Iraq and Afghanistan. Those that remained argued about whether we should have waited for world support and if Iraq was really a threat.

One thing, however, was very clear; the United States (and New Jersey) had to find its place in a different world, a world that maybe would finally have to learn to work *together*.

United States			New Jersey
Spanish-American War starts	1898	1898	State mobilizes for war
World War I starts	1914	1914	NJ factories hum
		1916	Black Tom depot explodes
US enters war	1917	1917	Hoboken major embarkation pt.
Word War I ends	1918	1918	Casualty lists grow
18th Amend. prohibits alcohol	1919	1919	Rum runners appear
19th Amend: women suffrage	1920	1920	Legislature approves 19th Amend.
"Roaring Twenties" start	1920	1920	State is major bootlegging area
		1921	Port of NY - bi-state agency
Great Depression begins	1929		
		1930	Bergen Co. funds relief work
		1933	Federal funds start 6 jr. colleges
WPA begins	1936	1936	100,000 New J'ns work for WPA
World War II begins	1939	1939	NJ factories busy
		1942	Camp Kilmer opens
World War II ends	1945	1945	300,000 war workers lose jobs
"Transistor Age" begins	1947	1947	Transistor perf'd at Murray Hill
		1947	New State Constitution
1st hydrogen bomb exploded	1952	1952	Dr. Selman Waksman of Rutgers
Supreme court orders school desegregation	1954		discovers streptomycin
US sends man into space	1961		
		1962	Port of Elizabeth opens
President Kennedy killed	1963		
US troops in Vietnam combat	1965		
		1966	Sales tax enacted
Riots disrupt major cities	1967	1967	Riots in Newark, Plainfield
M L King assassinated	1968		
1st man on moon	1969	1969	Edwin Aldrin of NJ
Arabs cut off oil supplies	1973		second on moon
Viking lands on Mars	1976	1976	Supreme Court mandates "thorough and efficient education"
		1976	Income tax started
		1976	Casino gambling approved
		1978	Pinelands 1st Nat. Reserve
Arabs cut back oil supplies	1979	1979	Price of gasoline rises to
Americans taken hostage in Iran	1979		more than $1/gal
Pres. Carter negotiates release of hostages	1981		
Ronald Reagan President	1982		
		1983	NJ Transit begins train & bus commuter lines
		1987	Mandatory recycling begins
Berlin Wall comes down	1989		
Persian Gulf War	1991	1991	NJ-orig'd weapons used in war
		1994	1st woman NJ Gov. takes office
9/11 Terrorist Attacks on World Trade Center & Pentagon	2001	2001	NJ commuters die in attack
War on Terrorism	2001		
		2002	Former NJ Gov. T. Kean heads comm. to investigate 9/11 attacks

257

Chapter Twelve - The Clouds Of War

United States			New Jersey
Battleship Maine sunk; war with Spain	1898	1898	Three New Brunswick men die on Maine
		1910	State's cities expand
World War I starts in Europe	1914	1914	Allied orders to New Jersey factories
Wilson re-elected on peace platform	1916	1916	Wilson campaigns from West Long Branch
US enters war	1917	1917	State is major training and shipping center
Prohibition begins	1919		
Women granted suffrage	1920	1920	NJ last to ratify Prohibition
League of Nations starts without US	1920		
150th anniversary of Declaration of Independence	1926	1926	Delaware River Bridge at Camden opens
		1926	State approves $300 million for highways
Lindbergh solo trans-Atlantic flight	1927	1927	Lindbergh uses engine made in Paterson
1st talking movie	1927	1927	Holland Tunnel opens
Ford replaces Model T with the Model A	1928	1928	Newark Airport started

Telegraph tickers clacked out shocking news on February 16, 1898: the American battleship *Maine* had been blown up in the harbor at Havana, Cuba. That day the United States took its first giant stride into world affairs.

New Brunswick had particular reason for shock and anger. Three of its young men were among the 266 who died in the sunken *Maine*. It was small consolation that Cuba's tearful Spanish rulers apologized the next day.

War with Spain long had been promoted openly and intensively by so-called "yellow journalists," particularly in the New York *World* and the New York *Journal*. Both exploited wretched social conditions in Cuba to sell papers.

No conclusive evidence was found that Spain had plotted the destruction of the *Maine,* but the nation seemed itching for a fight. Congress declared war on Spain on April 21, 1898.

War held the promise of excitement and adventure. No one under the age of forty-five personally remembered the awesome bloodshed of the Civil

◇◇◇◇◇◇◇◇◇◇◇◇◇◇◇◇◇◇◇◇

The End Of Innocence

A Trenton store advertised, on January 1, 1900, a daring new skirt for ice-skating: "Short enough to avoid entanglement with skates." It made sense, but defied standards of the day, for most women still wore skirts that dragged in the muddy streets or tangled with ice skates.

It was a time of innocence. City promoters boasted everything was "up to date." Poets sang of flowered fields and of proud blacksmiths who fashioned horseshoes under "a spreading chestnut tree." Manners were rigid; morals were stern. War was viewed as romantic, even "bully" in the mind of Theodore Roosevelt.

Then, in 1917, the United States entered World War I.

Young men streamed forth to enlist. Young women worked at jobs that had never been considered proper for females. Trainloads of African American workers from the South came north to fill industrial jobs in New Jersey and elsewhere. Salaries soared.

Innocence became a wartime casualty. There was no way,

a popular song of the day said of soldiers, to "keep 'em down on the farm, after they've seen Paree [Paris]."

People went on a wild spending spree after peace was declared in 1918. The economy stumbled temporarily early in the 1920s, and then zoomed to new heights. Anyone who could earn, beg, borrow, or misappropriate funds rushed to get in the seemingly endless boom.

A new sense of freedom swept the nation. Women won the right to vote in 1920. They bobbed their hair, threw away their corsets, wore short skirts, and danced the Charleston.

Prohibition seemed to make Americans go wild for alcohol. The country staggered on a long, self-indulgent binge, confident the pleasure-seeking, money-mad climate of the "Roaring Twenties" would never end. The roaring ended in 1929, in a collapse that quickly sobered the nation.

War, boom, bust: the twentieth century was underway.

War. When President William McKinley asked for 125,000 volunteers on April 23, more than half a million young men stormed recruiting stations.

"Remember The Maine"

The United States took pride in its noninterference in European matters, tied to a determination no world power could interfere in the American hemisphere. The presence of Spain in Cuba posed a threat, no matter how mild.

Emotional readiness masked the incredible fact that only 18,000 poorly-equipped, poorly trained regulars were in the United States Army, scattered around the nation. However, the Navy was powerful.

Commodore George Dewey demonstrated the naval supremacy a week after the declaration of war when he silently sailed an American fleet into Manila harbor on Sunday morning, May 1. Dewey's sailors attacked the Spanish armada shouting, "Remember the Maine!" Before the day ended, the Spanish suffered total defeat. Dewey did not lose even one sailor, much less a ship.

The United States erupted in celebration. Schools closed for "Dewey Day" on May 7. Morristown's joy,

The Monroe Doctrine, in reverse, troubled "Dame Europa" in a cartoon (above) published in *Punch* in August 1898. Uncle Sam's meddling in Spain's Cuban affairs did not trouble volunteers mobilized in Newark (below) after war was declared.

259

Sting of Death

Clara Louise Maass of East Orange, honored in this US stamp issued in August 1976, went wherever duty called. Duty summoned her to Cuba in October 1900, and it called her to death in August 1901, at age twenty-five. She died in experiments to prove mosquitoes spread dreaded Yellow Fever.

Clara Maass knew little except poverty after she was born in Newark in 1876. She quit school at age fifteen to work seven days a week in the Newark Orphan Asylum, sending her meager earnings home to help support eight younger sisters and brothers.

Clara went to school to become a nurse at Newark German Hospital in 1893, graduated in 1895, and became the hospital's head nurse in 1898 at age twenty-one. When the Spanish-American War began, she enrolled as a nurse and served in Florida.

Major William C. Gorgas (who later built the Panama Canal) asked Miss Maass to join him in Cuba, in October 1900, for a series of Yellow Fever experiments. Gorgas believed the fever was spread by filth; Dr. Carlos Finlay, a Cuban, suspected the mosquito.

There was only one way to test the Finlay theory: have humans bitten by infected mosquitoes. Clara Maass volunteered, along with six Spanish immigrants. All became ill, and two of the Spaniards died.

Miss Maass recovered and volunteered again. This time the mosquito bite was deadly. She died August 24 — the only American and the only woman to die in the tests.

---

as noted in the *Chronicle,* was typical:

> *Immediately upon the appearance of the* Chronicle's *thrilling message of victory, our patriotic mayor ordered the big flag to be floated from the lofty staff upon the green. The streets were filled with old and young, men and maidens. . . singing the songs so dear to us all.*

Watch On The Jersey Shore

Dewey's triumph did not ease fears the Spanish forces would invade the United States. Government signal stations were set up along the Jersey Shore to warn of Spanish vessels that might approach with an invasion force. Mines were placed in Delaware Bay.

No Spanish ships ever came; the press had grossly exaggerated Spain's military strength. By July, the signal stations were closed, the mines taken up, and bathing beaches were as busy as ever.

The war ended less than four months after it began, to the chagrin of most of the 5,501 New Jersey men in uniform. Few of them ever saw Cuba. Most spent their war careers fighting insects in camps at Sea Girt, New Jersey or Jacksonville, Florida. Forty New Jerseyans died, mainly from typhoid fever contracted in Florida's murky swamps.

Peace brought the short-term soldiers home to welcomes as enthusiastic as if they had stormed Havana itself. No homecoming topped that at New Brunswick on February 13, 1899. Defying a blizzard, townspeople met the incoming train at 3 AM and marched their heroes to a reception in Zimmerman's Hall.

Prospects Of A Golden Age

The Spanish-American War ushered in another era of prosperity. There was money aplenty. It was beginning to show in the cities, where editors dreamed America's golden age had come.

Newark was the state's prime showcase. A succession of reform mayors tapped the Passaic hills for clean water, worked to clean up the foul Passaic River, and spent money to pave most streets. By 1910, the center of Newark was well worth a trolley ride to see.

The new sixteen-story home office of the Firemen's Insurance Company towered over everything at Newark's Broad and Market Streets. This first New Jersey "skyscraper" looked even taller than it really was, for it was built on very limited ground space.

Powerful teams of handsome horses pulled colorful beer wagons over Newark's stone streets. Sleek carriages slid through the traffic, carrying financial barons to their offices. Other horse-drawn carriages took well-dressed ladies on genteel shopping expeditions. Some of the town's best-known people cycled to work, including the director of the city library.

Automobiles were beginning to make an impression. New Jersey's first automobile show opened in Newark on Washington's Birthday, 1908. More than

John B. Smith: An Unstung Hero

Pictured to the right is Dr. John B. Smith, Rutgers professor, as he appeared to a New Brunswick Times *cartoonist in 1910. The cartoon was meant as a tribute to the greatest general ever known in the war on mosquitoes. Time has made Smith one of history's unsung heroes; he would have much preferred to be unstung.*

Born in 1858 and educated to be a lawyer, Smith became a self-taught entomologist and joined the faculty of the Rutgers College of Agriculture in 1890. Each summer he hated the awesome mosquito invasion; by 1901 he was ready to fight the little stingers, that in those days literally darkened walls, floors, roofs, and streets.

Ridicule swept over Smith, who proposed ditches to drain meadows where the insects bred. The State Legislature gave him $1,000 in 1902, an amount that was more a slap at Smith than at the mosquitoes. He began draining soggy salt marshes near Newark and along the Jersey Shore, simultaneously begging local boards of health to force businesses and private citizens to drain inland pools of water where mosquitoes deposited larvae.

By 1910, Smith's ditches had worked miracles and local towns were cooperating. He died in 1912, nine days before Governor Wilson signed a law creating county mosquito commissions that are still the basis for the continuing anti-mosquito war. Smith did not eliminate the sting, but he found a way to lessen the impact.

Red Bank's Broad Street just before World War I included much from the past — a horse trough, horse-drawn wagons, skirts that swept the dirt street — and much that was "modern," including an electric trolley car and an automobile.

8,000 curious people wandered among the expensive, shiny, brass-trimmed runabouts and touring cars.

The Spark Of War

Other towns and cities boasted of their own growth, although none dreamed of challenging Newark's social, financial, and industrial supremacy. Elizabeth and Newark both began planning for 250th anniversaries (Elizabeth in 1915, Newark a year later). Jersey City, oldest of all, had quietly observed its 250th birthday in 1910.

Meanwhile, across the Atlantic, Germany's Kaiser itched for the chance to unleash his vaunted army, if not against France, then against Russia. Both, in turn, hated Germany. Europe was a powder keg, awaiting only a spark to set it off.

The spark flew on June 28, 1914, in a little town called Sarajevo in Bosnia. That day, in that obscure place, an obscure Serb shot and killed the heir to the Austrian throne. The powder keg was aflame.

Mighty Austria-Hungary promptly declared war on tiny Serbia on July 28. Six days later, Germany declared war on Russia and France. Europe exploded into a war that would kill more than eight million people in four years.

The state's big newspapers carried brief stories on the June 28 murder in Bosnia, but few gave it any prominence. New Jerseyans in hundreds of outlying towns served only by weeklies never heard of the incident at the time.

The President of the United States, Princeton's Woodrow Wilson, urged Americans to be "impartial in thought as well as action" as the war began. The usually belligerent Theodore Roosevelt agreed: "We must remain entirely neutral." The outlook was for a short war, three months at most.

Dividends From "Neutrality"

America's munitions makers interpreted neutrality broadly. They "impartially" favored England, Russia, and France, for those nations at first ruled the Atlantic Ocean shipping lanes.

Passaic County's textile plants wove woolens for French and English blankets and uniforms. Singer Sewing Machine Company in Elizabeth turned out intricate parts for French arms. Middlesex County copper plants stepped up production. Oil refineries in Bayonne and Bayway vowed to float the Allies to victory on "a sea of oil."

Explosives shot New Jersey to the fore. Long-established explosives makers at Kenvil, Haskell, Pompton Lakes, and Parlin all added new products. By the end of 1914, Russia was testing shells at a new range in Lakehurst.

DuPont opened a giant new powder plant at Carney's Point in the Salem County marshes along the Delaware River. New factories at Lyndhurst and Morgan quickly began making shrapnel and shells. A tremendous munitions depot, known as "Black Tom,"

made Jersey City the center for shipping munitions to Europe.

Picatinny Arsenal, a United States Army installation north of Dover, expanded production to include everything from .30-caliber bullets to sixteen-inch shells. The US Army was not at war; Picatinny's activity stretched "neutrality" as far as it could go.

Explosives were a DuPont specialty. By the end of 1916, its factories in Haskell, Pompton Lakes, Parlin, Carney's Point, and Repaupo had more than tripled the company's production over June 1914.

Seldom were so much powder and shell making jammed into such a limited region. Inevitably, New Jersey came to know a wartime boom had more than one meaning.

The Price of Munitions

Minor accidental blasts at Haskell, Pompton Lakes, and Repaupo served as warning the cost of making munitions could be high. The first horror came on July 30, 1916 at 2:08 AM when Jersey City's Black Tom depot exploded.

Set in the most densely populated section of America, the Black Tom depot had a potential for destruction beyond imagination. When the blast came, shrapnel from the Jersey City piers splattered the Statue of Liberty and the Hudson County shoreline. Flaming barges filled with exploding shells floated loose in New York harbor.

By morning, nearly $40 million in damage was done over a twenty-five-mile radius. Amazingly, only three persons died.

Lyndhurst's turn was next. Residents there protested in 1915 against construction of a new plant to make $83 million in shrapnel and shells for the Russian army. The company sought to calm fears by taking out a $100,000 insurance policy.

A small fire broke out in Building 30 at Kingsland, on January 11, 1917, prompting workers to flee. A newspaper account later told of panicky, wild-eyed employees tearing through a barbed wire fence "like so many cattle in a stampede."

Minutes later, the first blast struck. A half million exploding shells kept the area under siege for the next twelve hours. Miraculously, there were no fatalities. Later, damages were set at $16.7 million — 167 times the "insurance policy" of the munitions makers.

German saboteurs were suspected in the explosions, but four weeks after the Black Tom explosion, the courts found four officials of the Jersey City plant

Europe's war made New Jersey munitions factories hum, creating swollen payrolls and danger; seldom had so much powder been jammed into such a small region. Then, on July 30, 1916, the Black Tom munitions depot (above) exploded at Jersey City, spreading terror throughout North Jersey. Less than six months later, on January 11, 1917, a huge shrapnel and shell factory at Lyndhurst blew up, emblazoning the sky with the look of war. The two blasts caused nearly $60 million dollars in damage.

guilty of "criminal and gross negligence." (In 1939, in the heated passion of another war, a government commission found Germany guilty of both the Black Tom and Kingsland blasts).

Shadows Over Shadow Lawn

Suspicions of sabotage at Black Tom and Kingsland heightened sentiment against Germany. Intervention in the European war became almost inevitable, particularly after a German submarine sank the unprotected British ship *Lusitania* on May 7, 1915, taking 1,198 lives including 128 Americans.

German sympathizers in the Hudson County social halls toned down their belligerent support of the Fatherland, except to point out that Germany took out an advertisement in *The New York Times* to warn Americans not to board the *Lusitania*.

President Wilson urged calm. Three days after the sinking, he termed the United States "too proud to fight." He campaigned for re-election in 1916 on the slogan, "he kept us out of war."

Wilson seldom ventured from Shadow Lawn in West Long Branch, his summer White House, during the 1916 campaign. He ignored inflamed voices, particularly that of ex-President Theodore Roosevelt, who shouted:

"There should be shadows enough at Shadow Lawn! Shadows of men, women, and children who have risen from the ooze of the ocean bottom and from graves in foreign lands; the shadows of the helpless whom Mr. Wilson did not dare protect lest he might have to face danger!"

The President went to bed on election night believing he had lost the election to Charles Evans Hughes. Three days later, a final tally showed Wilson won by the slender margin of 277 electoral votes to 254. That was not a mandate either to fight or to remain neutral.

Directly beneath the Cunard announcement of the sailing of the *Lusitania*, the German Embassy warned — on the day of departure, May 1, 1915 — travelers went aboard at their own risk. Sinking of the *Lusitania* on May 7 caused Teddy Roosevelt to explode with war fervor (as depicted in a 1915 cartoon) and prompted another artist to express a violent opinion that President Wilson had lost his backbone.

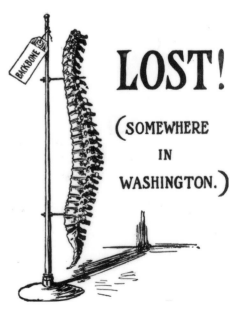

Conducting his 1916 campaign mainly from the summer White House in West Long Branch, President Wilson voted at Princeton on Election Day and went to bed believing he had lost. He was named victor three days later.

Farm Workers Ride North

The pleasant jingle of foreign dollars helped encourage neutrality. Skilled workers earned from $60 to $80 a week, a fabulous wage for the time. Laborers demanded at least $4 a day. Many male clerical workers quit jobs to take up the temporarily profitable career of laborer.

Labor was scarce. Immigration had dwindled to a trickle. Employers looked to the South, encouraging African American farm workers to ride trains north to work as laborers. Early in 1917, the Newark Board of Health estimated there were nearly 30,000 African American residents in town, up from about 11,000 in 1911.

Industry desperately needed this new source of personnel for jobs traditionally assigned to Italians, Irish, Poles, and Hungarians. Industry's interest in the African American workers did not extend beyond quitting time. A 1917 Newark report declared:

> *No white landlord seems to want this class of tenant at all, especially in any modern house. . . At the same time the white landlords take the opportunity of extorting high rents for miserable shacks, cellars and basements, some of those renting for $15 or $16 a month.*

Profiteers forced families "from one undesirable place to another." The Newark report concluded, "it has been our observation that when these people are given a better class of dwelling their habits of living and cleanliness are improved."

The report hoped Newark had "some capitalists who are willing to meet this great emergency by providing the money to build modern colored apartments." No such investors materialized.

"War Without Hate"

Germany grew increasingly arrogant. In January 1917, it warned unlimited submarine warfare would begin on February 1. German-Americans put away Fatherland flags after German submarines sank three United States ships in March. War was now certain.

Wilson called for "war without hate" on April 2. Four days later, throngs of Easter Saturday shoppers learned Congress had declared war on Germany. The next day, most clergymen used strongly warlike themes for their Easter sermons.

The United States was ready for war only in spirit and the ability to make munitions. Everything else had to be done: raise an army, establish training camps, gather supplies, and locate ships to carry soldiers and arms to Europe.

The Regular Army had only about 25,000 soldiers who could be spared for Europe. Military leaders hoped that the passion for war would fill the ranks of an all-volunteer army. They were right, at first.

Three months after the declaration of war, New

Jersey sent 9,285 National Guard troops to Sea Girt to begin preparing for combat. Villagers and city people turned out in the July heat to cheer their young Guardsmen headed off to battle Germany.

Camden loaded its Guardsmen aboard a special train. Many of the new soldiers fainted in the oppressive heat. As the train left the station, however, grinning faces showed above signs chalked on the cars: "Battery B off to give the Kaiser hell!"

The Honor Of Being Drafted

Enlistments failed to fill the ranks. President Wilson reluctantly asked Congress to draft soldiers. After prolonged debate that stressed the wild anti-draft riots during the Civil War, Congress reluctantly passed a draft law on May 18. It set June 5 as the day for all men between the ages of twenty-one and thirty-one to register for military duty.

Public proclamations, combined with a skillful national propaganda program, preceded Registration Day. It was declared a legal holiday. Church bells sounded at dawn. By 7 AM long lines had formed outside registration halls. Some registrants waited more than three hours to sign up.

More than 300,000 New Jersey men registered that day — miners from Dover and Franklin, fishermen from the Jersey Shore, factory workers from Newark; "Pineys" from the South Jersey woodland, farmers from the slopes of Sussex and Warren; sweet potato growers from Gloucester County, oystermen from Bivalve; bank clerks, shoemakers, and silk spinners from the cities.

Never before had Americans been so willing to be drafted. Eventually 762,000 New Jerseyans registered in a series of drafts (the age limits were extended to include all from 18 to 45). About one in ten was drafted.

Cheered by pretty girls and lectured to by talkative politicians, the first draftees headed for camp in September. Farmhands and laborers rubbed shoulders with bank officials and socialites in a truly democratic army.

Camping In New Jersey

Hastily summoned carpenters, plumbers, electricians, and many a farmhand-turned carpenter built the training camps. They built *Dix* in the forests of Burlington, *Wissahickon* close to Cape May City, *Merritt* at Cresskill, *Vail* at Little Silver, and several others. By war's end, New Jersey had sixteen military bases.

The Army bought 6,800 acres in the Pine Barrens, in May 1917, and built Camp Dix from scratch. Workers nailed together 200-man barracks in ten hours. Soldiers housed in the drafty, leaky, yellow-pine quarters never doubted that haste had been more important than skill.

Within a year, Camp Dix could handle 70,000 recruits. More than 1,600 buildings on the property included stables for 7,000 horses and mules. Soldiers trained across the sandy area, learning to shoot and to crawl under barbed wire. At night, they laughed away idle hours in social "huts" built and staffed by the Red Cross, the YMCA, and the Knights of Columbus.

In May 1917, Wrightstown, just outside the main gate of Camp Dix, had forty-two houses, a run-down

Amid fears that antidraft riots might occur, as they had during the Civil War, the government told men to register or face prison. There were no riots; men lined up eagerly to register or to volunteer, as in a Newark center (above). Then, when the soldier-laden trains pulled out of Jersey City, Camden, Newark, Trenton, and other places, cheering crowds said goodbye.

hotel, a gristmill, two general stores, three blacksmith shops, a barbershop, a hay press, and 250 residents. By December, thousands of soldiers stalked the narrow village streets, seeking any kind of amusement.

Nearby, in a still tinier place called Pointville, soldiers found hot dogs, ice cream, and other amusements ("not all innocent," one soldier wrote). Relatives and friends who came to see their soldiers were put up in crude woodland shacks, complete with outside toilets.

The State Department of Health eventually monitored a five-mile-wide zone completely around the camp, enforcing rigid health rules in ten towns and a score of villages.

"Hoboken, Here We Come"

The most-used, least-remembered army base in New Jersey was Camp Merritt in Cresskill. It was completed, in October 1917, as a place to process troops just before shipping them to Europe.

Merritt was the last stop for briefings, equipment checks, and sick calls. Nearly 600,000 men left the Cresskill camp for overseas duty. On a given day, as many as 40,000 men passed through. This was neither the time nor the place for joy; quiet soldiers left Merritt whispering the camp slogan: "Hoboken, here we come."

Secret Service agents swept into strongly pro-German Hoboken on April 6. They seized the North German Lloyd and Hamburg American docks as well as ships that included the luxurious *Vaterland*. German crews sabotaged their ships' engine rooms, idling the vessels for months.

Military control never relaxed in Hoboken. Soldiers guarded the piers, closed the saloons, and patrolled the city neighborhoods to watch for German sympathizers. Hoboken became a city of marching, sailings, weeping, and romance. Chaplains performed as many as forty marriages daily.

All military ship movements on the East Coast (except those at Newport News, Virginia) were controlled from Hoboken. Forty percent of all soldiers sent to Europe cleared directly through the one-time German-American town.

The Eastward Tide Begins

The first convoy of fourteen soldier-laden vessels weighed anchor at Hoboken on June 14, bound for France. Aboard were 11,991 Regular Army officers and men, a few nurses, and 103 "casual civilians." That first departure was described in a little book titled **With the Army in Hoboken:**

> *Along River street, where the old bock beer signs of the German occupation still marked the Deutsch gardens and Kursaals, tramped the men of San Antonio and Rio Grande.*
>
> *So silently and efficiently was the work done that few of the millions across the water knew that the eastward tide of American soldiers had begun…*
>
> *Perhaps along the Staten Island shore commuters wondered as the big gray ships slipped through The Narrows to the sea. Perhaps next morning the offshore fishing boats drew up their nets to watch the great convoy with attending destroyers come over the western rim of the sea.*
>
> *But back in the city none knew of their going. The six millions in New York little guessed that the job of breaking the Kaiser's Army had begun in Hoboken.*

Breaking the Kaiser's back needed more than sailings from Hoboken. The effort needed weapons. New Jersey's industrial prowess came to fullest flower.

New Jersey Goes Over The Top

Soldiers in France quickly learned that "over the

O-ver there, o-ver there, Send the word, send the word o-ver there,

Soldiers sang boastfully once they got "over there" (in the words of George M. Cohan's famed song), the Kaiser would be sorry. First they had to endure the training camps, particularly that sandy wasteland called Camp Dix in the Burlington pine woodland. Within a year after it was started from scratch, Camp Dix could handle 70,000 recruits.

Soldiers drew equipment and rifles at Dix, and then went out to try out such things as the new wonder called wireless transmission, run in the field by hand-cranked generators.

Training rigors were bad enough. Once the day's work was over, soldiers faced difficulty finding what the army called "wholesome recreation." Army-approved (and posed) photographs showed well-mannered soldiers taking books out of the camp library or reading calmly under an American flag while supposedly enjoying a piano player at the camp YMCA.

Away from camp (according to official understanding), the soldiers and sailors heard more piano music or listened to a gramophone in dignified surroundings. If they were lucky, there might be a dance in town, such as the one photographed at the National Service League in Newark. Obviously everyone enjoyed that party.

After the relaxation, the recruits made their way back to the big, cheerless, drafty barracks, that had been thrown together by poorly-trained builders. On Saturday mornings (below) every window was festooned with mattresses and blankets, hung out to help rid bedding of unwanted bugs or lice. It was enough to make soldiers yearn for the guns and muddy trenches of France.

Over There, Over Here

top" meant leaving the trenches to face German machine-gun bullets. At home, over the top meant exceeding governmental quotas for industrial output.

Middlesex County refined more than half of the nation's wartime copper. Thousands of New Jersey factories made blankets, tents, sweaters, uniforms, tools, harnesses, machines, telephone equipment, automobiles, wire, shoes, signaling equipment, and packaged foods. Above all, the state turned out the real stuff of war: explosives and ships.

Early calls from the Allies for powder and shells prepared the United States. Seventy-five percent of the nation's shell-loading capacity was in New Jersey, mostly in Middlesex County. By 1918, DuPont and the Hercules Company boosted their output of smokeless powder within New Jersey 1,500 times above the 1914 level.

Bethlehem Steel built an exceptional new shell-loading plant on the edge of Mays Landing. More than 6,500 employees — about four times the normal population of Mays Landing — worked in the plant. Shells were tested off the beach just north of Cape May City. The workers were housed in a government-built town called Belcoville.

"A Bridge Of Ships"

Shipbuilding increased astonishingly on both sides of the state. New York Shipbuilding Company, established at Camden in 1899, smoothly slid from peace-time to wartime operations.

The Navy ordered thirty destroyers from "New York Ship" (as the yard was known) between July and December 1917. The yard's finest performance was the building of sixteen transports, each more than 500 feet long, for the "bridge of ships" that carried soldiers to France.

Across state, in Newark Bay's marshlands, ship-builders in Kearny and Newark set up emergency ship-building activities. Nearby, Bethlehem Steel turned out more than thirty cargo ships, tankers, and ocean tugs in a remodeled old Elizabethport yard.

Newark's Submarine Boat Company started and finished 118 freighters in less than eighteen months. Thanks to that company, Newark led American cities in shipbuilding tonnage in 1919. The same year, New Jersey led the nation in total shipbuilding value: $238 million to Pennsylvania's $237 million.

Federal Shipbuilding Company, a subsidiary of US Steel, built an extensive permanent plant at Kearny. The permanency was in contrast to Submarine's

Transport Service girls saluted General John J. Pershing, leader of the American forces, as he walked toward a transport on Hoboken docks. Below, part of the 50th Infantry marched through Hoboken.
(Photos from Hoboken Public Library.)

Thousands of women gave up traditional "female" jobs for the first time in their lives and found war work in factories or on farms. The opposite page catches the nature of their labors. Some made explosives, including the women (upper left) making blasting caps at DuPont Pompton Lakes Plant. "Breaks" in another of DuPont state ordinance plants featured exercise rather than coffee. At Newark, women were tested to determine their aptitude as telegraph operators. Workers at Hercules plant in Parlin (bottom) posed on the company porch at lunch time (note the pantaloon styles). In Newark, parading women summed up the effort: they were "The Girls Behind The Men Behind The Guns."

The message of this 1918 poster was clear: Americans had to conserve everything or face a bleak winter.

temporary facilities at Port Newark. Federal made thirty steel freighters.

Birth Of The Aces

Overseas, daring young men donned helmets, scarves, and goggles to soar aloft in flimsy airplanes that introduced the art of aerial warfare. Newspapers and magazines featured glamorous accounts of these reckless young "aces" in their flying machines. Three New Jersey companies began making airplanes.

Aeromarine Plane and Motor Corporation in Keyport started making allied seaplanes in 1914. Soon Aeromarine covered 65 acres and needed sixteen buildings for its work.

Standard Aero Corporation, backed by Japanese money, hired seventy-five people at a new Plainfield airplane plant in 1916. Standard Aero enlarged its Plainfield plant, and then expanded into a former automobile plant in Linden.

By war's end, the Japanese-American plane makers employed 6,500 people to make seventeen dif-ferent kinds of aircraft at Plainfield and Linden. Its most famous fighting planes were the Italian *Caproni* and the English *Handley-Page*. Standard made 1,033 planes before Armistice grounded the aces.

The only air-minded company that survived the war was Wright-Martin Aircraft Corporation of New Brunswick, merged in 1916 with the nearby Simplex Automobile Company, makers of one of America's all-time classic automobiles.

Wright-Martin built 450 of its famed eight-cylinder, 140-horsepower *Hispano-Suiza* (Spanish-Swiss) engines in 1916. Orders of $2 million in 1917 grew to $50 million in 1918; the warplane was here to stay. When peace came, Wright-Martin had plans to finish as many as 1,000 engines a day.

Silk Shirts And Shortages

Money was plentiful wherever war-fueled industries flourished. Every boomtown also suffered serious complications in housing, health, transportation, amusement, and crime. Conditions in one-time farm areas such as Mays Landing or Salem County were like those in the old gold mining camps of California.

The symbol of wealth became the expensive silk shirt. Paterson mills frantically turned out the "prosperity shirts" to meet the desires of thousands of men who might not even have owned a cotton "Sunday shirt" before the war.

Along with the luxuries came privation. As the war progressed, the nation faced serious shortages of everything, from sugar to coal, from razor blades to wheat.

An unparalleled shortage of coal in the winter of 1917-18 coincided with one of the worst winters in years. People begged, borrowed, or stole the precious fuel. Starting on January 21, every Monday was designated as "heatless." Soon, "lightless" nights were ordered to save fuel.

Most New Jersey towns and cities set up areas where coal could be purchased a bushel at a time, if the buyer could show a ration card. Families huddled together in one room to save coal. Sugar was short and so was meat. People wearied of "sweetless, heatless, wheatless, and meatless" days.

Worse, the ugly reality of war was close. Booming guns could be heard off the Jersey Shore, as submarine warfare was waged within earshot of American soil. Newspapers carried the lists of dead and wounded along with reports of battles won. Hoboken began to receive the caskets of New Jersey's casualties.

War soon lost its glamour. Hoboken's docks, once filled with the laughter and boasts of soldiers outward bound, now witnessed solemn vigils (top) for the dead who never would laugh again. Wounded men (above) at Lakewood Convalescent Hospital were grim, and smiles were forced on the faces of one-legged soldiers greeted by Governor Edge at Colonia Hospital. War was no longer a game.

It Is Over, Over There

Vowing they sought total victory and singing they would not come back "'til it's over, over there," American soldiers joined the French and English at the front during the winter and spring of 1918. The Kaiser's legions retreated, stubbornly but steadily.

Newspapers carried accounts of battles in places that soon would be household names: Argonne Forest, Saint-Miheil, Belleau Wood, and Armentieres. It was difficult to single out New Jersey soldiers, for they had been merged into larger units. Only special dispatchers of letters to hometown newspapers linked individuals with the distant war.

Camden's National Guardsmen who marched off in July 1917 "to give the Kaiser hell" became part of the celebrated "Blue and Gray" 29th Division. New Jersey's 1917 draftees fought with the noted 78th "Rainbow" Division. Eventually, about 150,000 New Jerseyans served in the armed forces.

Fighting ended in France at 11 AM on November 11, 1918. Word flashed across New Jersey at 2:45 AM the next day, touching off a wild celebration. By 5 AM everyone was wide-awake. By 8 AM, Newark streets were so jammed with celebrants traffic could not move.

Governor Edge, hunting rabbits in Hunterdon County, put down his gun and hastened to the steps of the courthouse in Flemington, where a crowd of 10,000 danced in the streets. The governor promised the howling mob "soon all Jerseymen will be home," but 3,836 Jerseymen never came home. For those

It was over! The late editions of the state's daily newspapers carried the joyous news the Kaiser surrendered at 11 AM on November 11, 1918. Crowds danced and sang in every city and every village, waving American flags and posing for photographers. The draft was canceled. Soldiers began returning from Camp Dix. Finally, in the spring of 1919, the tough, battle-scarred veterans marched home.

dead, the lights would dim and voices would cease at 11 AM each year on Armistice Day, November 11.

"Safe For Democracy"

Happiness stayed at a high level for months. Each returning detachment of soldiers brought celebration in the streets of Hoboken and again to the cities where the homecoming soldiers marched in long lines. More than a half million people turned out in Newark, on May 20, 1919, to welcome home the 113th Regiment, nicknamed "Newark's Own."

War always ends in promises, Governor Edge told the New Jerseyans: "They fought our battles of war for us. Now let us fight their battles of peace for them."

Those battles of peace would emerge — in unemployment, in the ugliness of Prohibition, and eventually in a cruel depression. The high ideals of a war fought to make the world "safe for democracy" (Wil-

son's words) would falter as a peacetime population forgot what the war had been about.

Returning soldiers bragged of their adventures in Paris (or "Paree"). The miners, the Pineys, the fishermen, the bank clerks, and all the rest would never again be the same. Even within the strict discipline of the armed services they had enjoyed new freedoms.

Young women in jobs once regarded as "strictly male" wanted part of the new freedom. If they could work in shipyards in Camden or help build airplane motors in New Brunswick, they wanted more liberty. As one symbol, young women working in the war time factories discarded the restrictive corsets and petticoats once regarded as the confining, covering marks of "a lady."

Free spirits were curbed drastically when New Jersey's industrial output fell more than a billion dollars between 1919 and 1921. Unemployment punctured the dreams of the nation and its young.

Matters Of Liberty

A steadily rising population intensified the jobless situation. The state reached the "three million plateau" in 1920 (actually 3.1 million — up one million since 1900).

The "native white" population — those "one hundred percent Americans" often praised by Theodore Roosevelt and others — had become a minority in New Jersey. About sixty percent of the people were all or part "foreigner." For the first time, the African American population was significant, totaling 117,000.

The winter of 1920 brought the nation face to face with two matters of liberty: the Eighteenth and Nineteenth Amendments to the United States Constitution.

Just before 1 AM on February 10, the New Jersey legislature approved the Nineteenth Amendment to give women the right to vote. The legislative approval was not enthusiastic, but it was enough.

The women who packed the Assembly erupted in a noisy demonstration, pounding one another and waving purple, white, and gold banners. Amid the pandemonium, Mrs. Robert Paterson Finley of Camden, who was called the "Betsy Ross of Suffrage," calmly sewed another gold star on the freedom flag she kept to symbolize the national march toward female voting.

The next morning, Democratic Governor Edward I. Edwards expressed pleasure that "one of my first pledges to the people of New Jersey has been carried out."

The Governor that morning, as on most mornings, also was working even harder on another pledge: to keep New Jersey "as wet as the Atlantic Ocean." The pledge was an open defiance of the Eighteenth Amendment — the law that forbade alcoholic beverages in the United States.

The Rise Of Rum Row

Politicians of both parties ignored the fact that Prohibition became law on January 16, 1920. Breaking the law had become bipartisan.

The Republican-dominated legislature eventually and reluctantly made New Jersey the forty-sixth and last — state to ratify Prohibition. Rhode Island and Connecticut never ratified the law that most states had no intention of enforcing.

New Jersey soon became the heart of "Rum Row"

between Long Island and Cape May. Large fleets of fishing vessels and schooners laden with illegal liquor from Canada or the Caribbean anchored off the Jersey Shore, loading the liquor into a variety of small craft, including rowboats.

The "rum runners" took the cargo inland at night and disappeared into the dark inlets and back bays. Sympathetic bridge tenders raised the spans for the liquor fleet and lowered them against pursuers.

Bootlegging probably was New Jersey's major "industry" in the early 1920s. One operation, controlled by a powerful shortwave radio atop the Atlantic Highlands, imported 10,000 illegal cases of liquor a week, valued at between $50 and $100 a case — an import of $35 million annually.

"And In-flu-enza"

The chills and fever were nothing, said those who claimed they had no fear of influenza in September 1918. Why be afraid of "old-fashioned grippe?" Jokers sang:

I had a little bird named "Enza;"
I opened the window and in-flu-enza.

That was in September. Within a month, the scoffers were turning pale — and some were dead. This was not the grippe, nor was it like anything ever known before (or since) in the entire world. Before the terrorizing "flu" epidemic subsided, it killed twenty million people in the world, more than half a million Americans, and more than 17,000 in New Jersey (five times the number of New Jerseyans killed in battle).

How, or where, the epidemic of "Spanish Influenza" began probably never will be known. In late August 1918, the disease broke out at Camp Dix; between September 22 and October 21 the quarantined camp's weekly death totals were between seventy and one hundred soldiers.

The epidemic spread nationwide by mid-October. At least 300,000 New Jersey cases were reported in the last three months of 1918. Possibly at least that many more recovered without reporting to a doctor.

The death rate increased to five and six times the average in October. Newark alone reported seventy-nine deaths on one day, October 26. Teams of horses plowed trenches in cities and the dead were buried in rows.

Looking back after the flu epidemic ended, the State Department of Health wrote in 1919: "No city, town, or hamlet escaped its ravages; the hillsides of every community are dotted with newly-made graves."

Since the liquor was cut to about one-third original alcoholic strength for retail sale, the estimated net of the Atlantic Highlands operation totaled more than $100 million a year! Every inlet along the Jersey Shore had its own local operation to augment the Highlands supply.

The Lawless Payroll

No one ever knew for sure how many thrived off the lawless "payroll." Money flowed to the bootleggers, their bodyguards and paid killers, a small army of truck drivers, and those needed to load, unload, and dispense the alcohol.

Also on the bootleg "take" was a large secret flotilla of Jersey Shore fishermen who found cases of scotch or rum a far better "catch" than a boatload of bluefish or cod.

Every town of any size had "speakeasies" where the illegal alcohol was sold by the expensive glass. Their payrolls included entertainers, bartenders, waitresses and waiters, kitchen help, and guards to keep undesirables (the law) off the premises.

Many profited handsomely from the under-the-table bribes: crooked politicians, cynical judges, corrupt policemen, agreeable jurors, and others paid to prevent punishment on the rare chance that anyone might be arrested and brought to trial on bootlegging charges.

With so much at stake financially, law enforcers seldom tried to find evidence of lawbreakers. That laxity spawned worse crimes.

The Roaring Ugliness

More than 325 people died in New Jersey's bootleg wars between 1920 and 1934. The killings were not as publicized as the more celebrated gangland massacres in New York City or Chicago, but the victims were just as dead.

Most of the suddenly deceased were gangsters, but the innocent suffered as well. A Passaic baker was killed in 1928 for complaining about bootleggers. A year later, a caretaker on the Morrow estate in Englewood accidentally found a still. Three men gunned him down with no questions asked.

The state's most spectacular Prohibition case offered clear proof of the cynicism of the law enforcers. The case began to unfold on October 16, 1929 when a Prohibition agent led a raid on an old mansion atop the Atlantic Highlands.

The raiders found a powerful shortwave radio station in the house. The cellar contained an arsenal of submachine guns, automatic rifles, revolvers, and ammunition. Sixteen men in the mansion denied any knowledge of the unusual furnishings. The house obviously was the key to the huge Highlands bootlegging empire.

Trial for the sixteen was delayed until June 1931. Forty-three other defendants were added. During the proceedings, the Prohibition agents and the prosecutors seemed more on trial than their gangster foes. All of the fifty-nine defendants were found innocent.

New Jersey's fifteen chief Prohibition agents earned reputations for dedication to duty, but they satisfied no one. Head Agent Adrian G. Chamberlain smashed illicit breweries and speakeasies at the rate of fifteen a day during 1925 (4,982 in one year). He was pushed out of office — because the Anti-Saloon League branded him as "too lax."

National Prohibition Administrator James M. Doran could write in 1929: "We regard New Jersey as one of the hardest spots to handle in the entire country." Newspapers, magazines, and the movies have glorified the ugly speakeasies and the ruthless gangsters. People with money and power encouraged the lawlessness. In the long run, the people most hurt by Prohibition were poor working people who once enjoyed inexpensive neighborhood saloons. The glittering, sleazy, overpriced speakeasies were beyond their means.

People At Work

Regardless of what they did after dark, most people worked by day. The post-war recession was over by 1925, and New Jersey stood sixth nationally

Life magazine in 1918 imagined the Devil gloating that prohibition would drive people to drink, legal or not. The Devil was right. Many clamored for "membership" cards in dingy speakeasies that satisfied illegal cravings. Federal agents smashed bottled liquor and beer in the Jersey Meadows, but they fought a losing cause. Offshore, a well-financed bootleg "navy" poured in new supplies of alcohol on ships such as the *Atalanta* of Perth Amboy. It was a time of new freedoms, manifested by John Held's flippant flapper and her casual boyfriend in the coon-skin coat. Prohibition proved so evil that by the late 1920s many groups, such as the Morristown women shown on the opposite page, were urging repeal.

in the value of its manufactured products. More than 8,000 plants produced goods worth $3.5 billion in 1925, about the same as in the wildly inflated days of war production.

Industrial diversity was the key. Petroleum refining at Bayway and Bayonne and copper refining in Middlesex County topped the list. Together, oil and copper mounted to one-seventh of the state's industrial output.

Chemicals had become big business, highlighted by the spectacular new DuPont chemicals plant at Deepwater in Salem County. Makers of the chemicals also thrived beside the Passaic and Raritan Rivers, along the Arthur Kill, and along the Hudson County waterfront.

Paterson, resting on an old reputation as the nation's first planned industrial city, was the major blemish on the bright picture. By 1920, two-thirds of Paterson's families depended on silk manufacture. A drop in demand that year threw 30,000 people out of work.

Other silk centers in the nation began converting looms in the 1920s to handle a new synthetic fiber called rayon. Paterson clung to its silk looms. By 1934, there were 47,000 rayon looms in the United States. Paterson had none; the gamble on silk amounted to economic suicide.

Paterson well understood the cycles of boom and bust. It had boomed and collapsed, successively, in past decades on cotton, locomotives, and now silk. The first sounds of another boom could be heard by 1925 in a small old mill, where the Wright Aeronautical Company made airplane engines. Wright left its huge World War I plant in New Brunswick for the smaller Paterson facility. Soon Paterson would soar on Wright engines.

Boosting The Cities

Newark, Jersey City, Elizabeth, Trenton, and Camden all were in their days of glory. They teemed with workers during the day. At night, downtown movie houses, restaurants, and speakeasies prospered. On Saturdays, department stores were jammed with shoppers who rode trolley cars in from the surrounding suburbs.

Cities were in the midst of intense self-praise. Newark proudly acclaimed its skyscrapers — the twenty-one-story Military Park Building finished in 1926, New Jersey Bell's twenty-story home office completed in 1928, the thirty-four-story Raymond-Commerce Building finished in 1930, and the thirty-five-story National Newark Building ready in 1931.

Trenton's pride lay in the new fourteen-story Trenton Trust Building and the tall, handsome new Stacy-Trent Hotel. The city erected what it claimed was the world's largest electrical municipal sign on a Delaware River bridge: *Trenton Makes, The World Takes.*

Elizabeth, Camden, and Jersey City had not yet joined the skyscraper age, but they were proud of new fireproof hotels, multi-story bank buildings, and palatial new movie houses. Camden called itself "The Biggest Little City in the World," a boast that Elizabeth and Jersey City boosters disputed.

Newark's leaders directed their attention to the once-shunned marshlands on the eastern edge of the city. The city's seaport, started in 1915, slowly advanced. Then, on April 1, 1928, the aviation age really began for New Jersey.

On that April Fool's Day, trucks began dumping garbage and ashes into the Newark marshes. The bogs and smoking garbage dumps made way for Newark Airport. The next year, commercial planes made 4,000 passenger trips from the field. Two years later, with 120 daily trips in and out, Newark proclaimed it had "the busiest airport in the world."

Prosperity On Wheels

Horse-drawn vehicles still crowded city streets when World War I ended in 1918, but within five years gasoline engines supplied most of the horsepower. If the Twenties ever really roared, it was because the automobile emerged from curiosity to necessity.

By 1923, buses hauled an average of 200,000 passengers into and through Newark daily. Twenty-two trolley lines averaged 330,000 passengers a day. Three years later, a twelve-hour traffic check of automobiles in the center of Newark led a New York survey firm to label the junction of Broad and Market Streets "the busiest traffic center in the world."

In half a day, the check showed 2,644 trolleys and 33,810 gas-powered vehicles passed the center of Newark. The horse was not completely gone; 124 horse-powered vehicles struggled through the automobile fumes.

The increasing numbers of people and products passing through the northeastern part of New Jersey troubled far-sighted leaders. In 1921, New York and New Jersey established the bi-state Port of New York Authority. Its clear mission was to coordinate railroad transportation and terminal facilities in the two states.

The new Port Authority tried to meet the need, but powerful, profit-hungry railroad officials ignored the new agency. Automobiles, not trains, became the chief emphasis of the Port Authority.

New Jersey's long-time reputation as a place to cross on the way to elsewhere became more deeply ingrained. Both ends of the cross-state corridor stirred with bridge and tunnel construction to hasten automobiles between Philadelphia and New York City.

Across, Over, And Under

President Calvin Coolidge dedicated the new Delaware River Bridge between Delaware and Camden in 1926, in time for the Philadelphia Sesquicentennial Exposition marking the 150th anniversary of the Declaration of Independence.

Two agencies, one in New York and one in New Jersey, completed the Holland Tunnel under the Hudson River in 1917. By the time the Port of New York Authority acquired the tunnel in 1931, more than twelve million fifty-cent tolls were being paid annually.

New bridges spanned creeks and rivers everywhere. In 1928, the Port Authority dedicated two new spans to Staten Island, the Goethals Bridge at Elizabeth and the Outerbridge Crossing at Perth Amboy. The Bayonne Bridge between Bayonne and Staten Island was finished in 1931.

Within the state, long spans were built without help from the flood of silver half dollars flowing into Port Authority tollbooths. The Pulaski Skyway rose 145 feet above the soggy, garbage-filled meadows be-

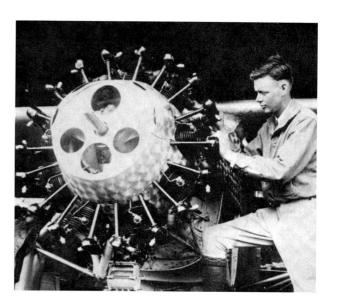

Whirlwind over the Atlantic

Tall, skinny Captain Charles A. Lindbergh had powerful reason for hoping on May 20, 1927 that Paterson's mechanics were first-rate. That morning, his flimsy Spirit of St. Louis was poised on the runway at Roosevelt Field on Long Island, heavily overloaded with the gasoline required to take Lindy and his "Spirit" across the Atlantic Ocean to Paris.

At 7:52 AM, Lindbergh revved up the best engine the nation could make: a J-5 Whirlwind (shown here with Lindy), made by Paterson's Wright Aeronautical Company. The Whirlwind lifted the plane over low electric wires at Roosevelt Field and kept running for the 33 hours needed to fly 3,610 miles to Paris.

Aviation emerged from adolescence with that daring solo flight. Wright rode Lindy's Whirlwind to fame and fortune of its own. Orders from around the world forced the Paterson Company to expand within one year to seven times its pre-Lindbergh size.

Newark Airport, started on April Fool's Day, 1928, was still a muddy joke on September 21, 1928 when the above photograph was shot. Two years later (below), Newark claimed to be the "world's busiest airport" and lined up staff, passengers, and planes near the terminal to show how far aviation had come.

tween Newark and Jersey City. The Victory Bridge across the Raritan at Perth Amboy sped automobile traffic to the Jersey Shore.

No span surpassed the George Washington Bridge, completed in 1931 to join Bergen County and upper New York City. Curving cables held the graceful, 3500-foot-long span high above the Hudson River. Six lanes of automobile and truck traffic poured over the bridge.

The new tunnel and the bridges totally changed the movement of vehicles throughout northeastern New Jersey. In 1926, 13.5 million vehicles crossed the Hudson River all aboard one of the numerous ferryboats plying between New Jersey and New York City. Six years later, an *additional* 15 million vehicles crossed the river each year via the tunnel or bridges. The ferries were doomed.

Within the state, the legislature unfolded a master highway plan in 1926. It provided for $300 million to be spent over a twelve-year period. That plan would give New Jersey a nation-wide reputation for good highways in the mid-1930s.

The Old Order Changes

The nineteenth century was a distant memory by 1930. A few Civil War veterans survived in 1929, but their very advanced ages and oft-repeated tales gave them a low profile except when they rode in Memorial Day parades.

Everything was changing in 1930. Old landmarks were being leveled to make way for new highways or city skyscapers. Both the Morris Canal and the Delaware & Raritan Canal were near extinction.

Cars waiting at the Holland Tunnel entrance on Labor Day weekend in 1931 (top left) proved the auto was here to stay. Elsewhere, the Camden-Philadelphia Bridge (top right) opened in 1926; Goethals Bridge to Staten Island was dedicated in 1928 (above); George Washington Bridge towers rose in 1929 (right); by 1930 the Victory Bridge at South Amboy (below) was an answer to Shore-bound traffic jams.

The Morris Canal was officially abandoned in 1924 after years of nonuse. The Public Service Company created a trolley line in the canal bed in Newark, and then made the route a subway by paving over the bed with Raymond Boulevard.

At Lake Hopatcong, the old Morris Canal property became a state park. Elsewhere, the canal was replaced by roads or became a ditch filled with stagnant, mosquito-breeding water.

Passing years treated the D & R Canal slightly more kindly. After the last boat passed through in 1934, control of the canal passed from the Pennsylvania Railroad to the state. The active days of New Jersey's two big canals had ended.

Fortunately, a new generation saw value in the Delaware & Raritan Canal as a source of water or as a possible park. Also, the coming of the depression made impractical a scheme to convert the canal bed to a highway, except in Trenton. The D & R Canal lives on, not in its old grandeur, but at least as a reminder of by-gone canal days.

Beyond The Concrete

Motorists who left the city streets on weekend drives along the back roads found an amazing New Jersey that contradicted the state's reputation as nothing but a strip of concrete between New York and Philadelphia.

Beyond the corridor were teams of oxen plodding over winding dirt roads. Horse-drawn plows sliced through rich soil. Dusty, unpaved roads were the mark of the northern "back country," sandy trails the pattern of rural southern New Jersey. Splendid old courthouses still shone in rural counties. Mighty oak trees towered above Salem, Basking Ridge, and Crosswicks, offering leafy beauty and cool shade.

Long stretches of sandy oceanfront beach beckoned those who liked solitude by the sea. In 1935, there were stretches of New Jersey beachfront where tents could be pitched directly beside the rolling ocean.

Automobiles rolled toward Asbury Park or Atlantic City on Saturdays and Sundays, but in 1925 a trip to the Shore called for careful planning. Extra tires had to be mounted on the car running board and a can of emergency gasoline was stored in the trunk. Service stations were few and far between on the narrow, rutted roads.

Behind the handsome pastoral scenes so loved by city motorists lay rural drudgery. Many farmers still worked their fields with horse-drawn machinery. Gathering hay, cutting wood, and cleaning the barns or chicken coops were tough, back-breaking jobs done mainly by hand.

Thousands of families (including many city people)

Blueberry Lady Of The Pines

Elizabeth White was born at Whitesbog, deep in the Pine Barrens, in 1872. She died there in 1954, still working at perfecting swamp huckleberries into the rich blueberries that have made New Jersey one of the tops among all states in harvesting cultivated blueberries.

Miss White's father grew cranberries, and at first Elizabeth worked in the cranberry bogs, too. Then, in December 1910, Miss White read of US Department of Agriculture experiments with blueberries. The next spring, she began sending New Jersey blueberry seedlings to Washington, DC scientists.

She drove constantly through the deep Pine Barrens, seeking new varieties and encouraging natives to bring her unusual wild blueberry plants. She carefully credited the finders, using their names to identify new varieties.

Miss White's plantation shipped the nation's first commercial, cultivated blueberries in 1916. She celebrated her 80th birthday in 1952, still actively seeking new varieties.

Indeed, in New Jersey, the blueberry might well be called the "Whiteberry" to honor its greatest devotee.

had neither bathtubs nor toilets in the home. Kitchen pumps for water were common. Many farm families had no electricity. Telephone service was erratic. Hundreds of one-room schools served the backcountry, and the 1930 census showed the state still had 130,000 illiterates.

However, most of the state's political and business leaders lived a far different existence. Factories roared as never before. Business was marvelous. Prosperity became the theme song of a harmonious community of business, politics, and the press.

The year 1929 boomed along. Dreams grew ever rosier. Republicans, swept into national power because of golden promises, predicted the prosperity would never end.

It was comforting to fantasize that this nation, grown so fat and so rich that it could afford even the immorality of Prohibition's racketeers, could only get fatter and richer. The American dream was in full glory in 1929.

Soon, too soon, a new day would dawn and the alarm that shocked America awake on that day would reverberate around the world. The alarm tolled a dreaded word: Depression.

Atlantic City's "Miss America" pageant began in 1921, when eight "Beauty Maids" — as the promoters called them — paraded on the beach (right) along with enough local maids recruited to form an impressive line. The first Miss America was 16-year-old Margaret Gorman of Washington, DC who posed (top) with the other contestants. Miss Gorman, second from the left, daringly rolled down black stockings to expose dimpled knees. Later the eight appeared in formal dress, with Miss Gorman to the left. Only two of the contestants posed hatless in public.

Chapter Thirteeen - Through A Glass, Darkly

United States			New Jersey
		1926	Depression hits Shore
Stock Market crashes	1929		
		1930	Bergen provides relief work
Roosevelt inaugurated; promises "new deal"	1933	1933	"Holiday" closes banks
		1933	Breweries reopen
		1935	State colleges offer 1st 4-year course
WPA creates employment	1936	1936	WPA workers undertake ambitious projects
World War II starts in Europe	1939	1939	State is "Arsenal of Democracy"
US enters war	1941	1941	New Jersyans rush to enlist
War rationing begins	1942	1942	Volunteers run local ration boards
		1942	Camp Kilmer opens
US uses atom bomb; war ends	1945	1945	Most of state's 560,501 service personnel return
United Nations founded	1945	1945	Unemployment serious
Marshall Plan aids Europe	1947	1947	New State Constitution
Truman re-elected President	1948	1948	State's National Guard integrated

When Franklin Delano Roosevelt took the oath of office as the nation's thirty-second President on March 4, 1933, his right hand lay on the Bible passage that begins, "For now we see through a glass, darkly…"

Deep shadows of fear and uncertainty shrouded millions of families caught in the Great Depression. They waited for Roosevelt to fulfill campaign promises of a "new deal" for the American people.

Warnings of economic trouble had appeared ever since 1925. Farmers along the dirt roads of Sussex and Warren or Cumberland and Gloucester counties long knew the rosy economy was gray along the rural edges. Their income stayed low throughout the 1920s, even as costs of fertilizers and feed rose higher and higher.

The New Jersey Shore offered another vivid warning sign in 1926. Completion of the Delaware River Bridge between Camden and Philadelphia that year touched off a "Gold Coast" boom. Seaside property values soared. Handsome brick hotels and expensive boardwalks rose beside the ocean.

Before 1926 ended, wildly inflated real estate

◇◇◇◇◇◇◇◇◇◇◇◇◇◇◇◇◇◇◇◇

The Great Depression

America knew depressions before. Factories banked their furnaces and bankrupt stores closed in 1837, 1857, 1893, and again in 1907. Jobless workers roamed the streets. Relief agencies served the hungry.

The depression, however, that began when Wall Street collapsed in October 1929, was the Great Depression — with a capital G and a Capital D.

At least 16 million persons were known to be unemployed in 1933, and the total was probably higher. Industry collapsed, and areas heavily reliant on manufacturing, such as New Jersey, felt the blows most severely.

Bitterness against the Republican Party grew. That could be expected since Republican Herbert Hoover, running for President in 1928, had assured Americans the good times would continue.

In retaliation, voters swept Franklin Delano Roosevelt into the White House in 1932. He took office in March 1933,

proclaiming in his inaugural address "the only thing we have to fear is fear itself."

Many new Roosevelt-inspired governmental "alphabet" agencies sprang into being to help the jobless and the poor: The WPA (Works Progress Administration), CCC (Civilian Conservation Corps), FHA (Federal Housing Authority), and so on by the hundreds.

Government spending stimulated private industry some, but despite billions of federal dollars poured into the economy, bad times persisted throughout the 1930s.

Then Germany's armies trampled across Europe again. Demands for munitions gave the unhealthy American economy a transfusion of energy. Men and women returned to work.

It was like "old times" again, especially when the United States entered the war in 1941. Factories boomed. The Great Depression was blasted away by the guns of Europe.

Depression's touch was everywhere — in the cities, on the farms, and beside the long-prosperous Jersey Shore. A newspaper photographer portrayed one hopeless mill family (above), in the late 1920s, seated in the kitchen of their slum flat in Passaic. A kerosene lamp provided their only light, a loaf of dry bread was their only sustenance. They really had not far to fall, for they always had been poor, unlike the promoters who completed their 10-story Brigantine Hotel (left) in 1927, just in time to be engulfed by the panic following Wall Street's failure in 1929. Effects of the economic paralysis struck large, wealthy farmers with stunning effect. Those who had been scratching a tough living from the rocky north-western hills (below) went right on scratching a tough living from the rocky terrain. Farmers were a bit luckier than most; their cows gave milk, their pigs provided meat for the winter, and their vegetable gardens provided ample food in summer. They did suffer, too, though; few escaped the Great Depression.

Tradition says the term "Bear Market" began when a trader sold a bear's skin before having the bear. Thus, in 1929, the "bear" gripped the stock market as traders sold what they often did not own to buyers who didn't investigate. Speculating investors frantically clung to the ticker tape, only to plunge in October 1929.

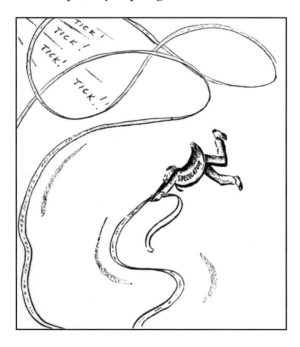

prices collapsed along the entire shore. A piece of property in Sea Isle City, bought for $75,000 early in 1926, sold for $750 within the same year. Some of the new brick hotels had more vacancies than reservations. The seashore gold turned a tarnished green.

A slight business decline in 1927 led to the layoff of several hundred people in Newark factories. By the late summer of 1929, about 1,200 Newark families were on relief. Those warnings were as easily dismissed as the Jersey Shore troubles.

Black Thursday, Terrifying Tuesday

Trouble signs went unheeded. America was drunk with the heady notion it was a land where everyone could get rich. The pot of gold at the end of the rainbow was Wall Street.

Speculation in stocks hypnotized people at most economic levels — bankers, industrialists, farmers, bank clerks, grocers, and even housewives. When novelist F. Scott Fitzgerald went from Princeton to New York for a haircut in the late 1920s, he found his favorite barber had quit work after piling up $500,000 in stock profits.

Areas close to New York City had a high proportion of speculators. Stocks of New Jersey companies were big gainers. During 1928, Wright Aeronautical of Paterson rose from $69 to $289 a share. Radio Corporation of America, with large factories near Camden, rose from $85 to $420 in the same twelve months.

Then came Thursday, October 24, to be known forever as "Black Thursday." That day the market took a nosedive. Stocks plunged twenty-five to thirty points. The following Tuesday, nicknamed "Terrifying Tuesday," was even worse.

Wall Street was smashed. Banks failed. Industry began to close its doors. Idle workers could buy nothing, so production dropped. More workers lost jobs. A vicious cycle was spinning. The Great Depression had begun.

The Skid To Disaster

The dark days grew darker; America was on a greased skid to disaster. Factories lay idle, with makers of motors, metals, and machinery hurt first. Middlesex County's copper refineries banked their fires. Camden's shipyards became ghostly dry docks. Iron mines near Dover and Ringwood closed their pits.

Newark's highly diversified industries were not hit

Any kind of work was eagerly sought in 1930, regardless of the pay. More than 5,600 willing applicants showed up in November 1930 when Bergen County offered emergency jobs to 1,000 unemployed men. The pay was three dollars for seven hours work. This small gang, seemingly with more men than work, felled trees to build a rough pathway up a steep hillside through Bergen woodland.

simultaneously, but by the middle of 1930 more than 7,500 of the city's families were on relief. Textile mills in Paterson and Passaic closed.

Relief rolls grew longer in Morris and Somerset counties, where millionaires closed estates and laid off hundreds of chauffeurs, maids, cooks, and gardeners. Small contractors, exclusive dress shops, and fancy grocery stores went out of business when the millionaires put away their thinning wallets.

Carpenters, plumbers, masons, and other skilled construction hands found little work, for building had ceased. Only petroleum refining and food processing continued at high levels for a time. People would drive and eat, come what may.

Bergen County was the first to take remedial action. In November 1930, it paid unemployed men three dollars to work seven hours on county roads. More than 5,600 eagerly sought the hard, low-paying

labor. Bergen could hire only one thousand. Bayonne, Newark, and Trenton soon introduced similar "make work" programs.

The economy plummeted. The average annual personal income in New Jersey in 1929 was $839. That dipped to $479 in 1932. A year later, it was $433, about $8 a week.

Washington's Republican administration created the Emergency Relief Administration (ERA) in late 1931. Thirty thousand New Jerseyans worked on ERA payrolls.

Top ERA wages in urban counties allowed skilled workers $27 a week and unskilled $20. Rural counties paid $23 for skilled help and $18 for unskilled.

The wages allowed no room for high living. On July 19, 1933, ERA awarded a bonus of five cents an hour for "spending money," believing that such luxury would "help sustain self-respect."

Out in the Jersey Meadows, between Newark and Jersey City, the unemployed built rough little tin shacks for shelter while they tried to grow vegetables in the muckland. They called their settlement "Hooverville," and the name was not meant as a tribute to the President of the United States — on whom they blamed the nation's troubles. Depositors (right) waiting outside the Hobart Trust Company in Passaic were painfully aware that their deposits inside might be lost forever. This bank was closed late in 1929 by the State Banking Department. The well-dressed men and women waiting on the sidewalk reasonably might have once identified themselves as Hoover supporters, but the deepening financial woes were weaning away even that endorsement.

Fear Stalks The Land

Hundreds of thousands of New Jerseyans were unemployed as 1932 slipped into 1933. Government relief offered weekly food allowances of a dollar a person, to a maximum of eight dollars for a family. Anxiety filled nearly every home.

The Great Depression was deepening when Franklin Delano Roosevelt was inaugurated as President on March 4, 1933. A crisis atmosphere enveloped the ceremony, much like the feeling in wartime. Indeed, this was a war against plunging American living standards.

Breadlines coiled around whole city blocks. Men shuffled in the lines, ashamed, beaten, yet defiant. Men and women sold apples on corners, for a few pennies profit a day. Unemployed young men (and a few young women) roamed the country, hitchhiking or "hopping freights" in the hope that a distant state might offer some opportunity.

Banks were in severe trouble. In February 1933,

the rate of withdrawals shot up from five million dollars daily to fifteen million. Depositors were often on the edge of panic and many banks folded in the face of the wholesale withdrawals.

Roosevelt declared a "Bank Holiday" on his inauguration day to give banks the breather they needed to survive. The "holiday" brought a severe shortage of cash. Paterson banks and merchants pooled their coins during the emergency to set up a "change bank" at City Hall. Newark bankers printed nearly $40 million in emergency scrip (temporary money).

However, many banks never reopened. Between 1928 and 1933, more than 140 New Jersey banks went out of business, taking with them in their collapse the savings of thousands of people.

Hard-hit Atlantic City saw twenty-nine banks fail. Ironically, the resort dedicated its famed high-domed Convention Hall, on May 31, 1929, to mark the city's seventy-fifth anniversary. It would be fifteen years before the great facility would be used to any extent.

Education For Idle Hours

Particularly hard hit were young people. High school graduates found work nearly impossible to get. Young applicants for full-time jobs were laughed at, since older, experienced people literally begged for work.

Unemployment encouraged many to stay in high school longer (dropouts in ninth or tenth grades were common before 1930). Some returned for post-graduate courses. In 1932, high school enrollment soared by fifteen percent, due to the difficulty in finding work in the "outside world."

These conditions caused a major overhauling of the state's six "normal schools," or teacher training schools. All normal schools had two-year courses until 1929, when three-year courses began. Then, in 1935, courses were extended to four years, chiefly to accommodate the idle.

There was little point in leaving a teacher's college even after four years. Education budgets kept slipping, despite increasing enrollments. Average teacher salaries dropped to $1,821 a year in 1934. Often teachers were paid in scrip, that they were likely to sell at a loss to get needed cash.

High school graduates who aimlessly walked the streets or set up pins in bowling alleys at five cents a game were offered a strong lifeline in the fall of 1933. That year the Emergency Relief Administration opened junior colleges in six New Jersey towns and cities.

More than 2,500 young men and women flocked to the ERA junior colleges in the first year. Classes met evenings in high schools, usually on top floors of old buildings amid the smells of the chemistry labs. Faculty members — many with PhD degrees — taught the classes and were glad to get the salary of $14 a week.

Some taxpayer groups protested the ERA colleges were "government waste." Most educators believed

Dressed in surplus army uniforms, young men lined up outside a tent at Camp Dix to draw supplies from an army tent. The year was 1933, and these New Jerseyans were among the many men between the ages of 17 and 23 who eagerly enrolled in the newly-formed Civilian Conservation Corps (CCC). They were housed, fed, uniformed, paid a small monthly wage, and sent into parks and forests across the United States to rebuild old recreation facilities or to create new campsites, picnic areas, and hiking trails.

the colleges were sound. The students thought them wonderful. Hundreds of young men and women later transferred the "emergency" credits to four-year colleges and universities.

Leaning On Their Shovels

Favorite targets of newspaper editors, cartoonists, and taxpayer groups were men and women employed by the Works Progress Administration (WPA). More than 100,000 New Jersey men and women became WPA workers, starting in 1936.

Letters-to-the-editor columns were filled with indignant charges that WPA employees were paid for merely leaning on their shovels. Editorial writers found the alleged shovel leaners fair game for their typewriters.

The WPA employees did draw checks — desperately needed checks — but charges they did nothing in return were grossly exaggerated. The WPA workers could point to their accomplishments:

• They demolished the old Newark post office and turned thirty-one acres of Haddon Heights swampland into a park. They reconstructed the old Bradley Beach boardwalk and built jetties and a new boardwalk in Cape May City. They planned and constructed an old age home in Cumberland County.

• They converted the bed of the old Delaware and Raritan Canal in Trenton into a base for a highway through town, built Roosevelt Stadium in Jersey City, constructed the Bacharach Home for infantile paralysis victims in Atlantic City, and built a Greek amphitheater at Montclair State College.

• They repaired Atlantic City's old water mains, restored the Grover Cleveland House in Caldwell, and built Speedwell Park in Morristown. Before 1941, they rebuilt rundown facilities at Fort Dix, Lakehurst, Fort Monmouth, and elsewhere.

• WPA workers also improved county parks, dug mosquito drainage ditches through the state's murky marshes, installed sewer systems in many towns, constructed public schools, and built post offices. They built more than 6,000 miles of streets and highways, constructed or repaired 660 bridges, and built or improved more than 4,000 culverts under highways.

It Was Not All Soup Kitchens

Hopelessness gradually gave way to hope as the "New Deal" rolled along. Some brightness began to edge back into life.

Fear gripped America in the winter of 1933. More than 13 million men and women were unemployed. Towns faced bankruptcy, people roamed the streets looking for work, and starving people ate from garbage pails in the cities.

Scenes such as those on the following pages were common in every New Jersey city. The American Legion collected food and clothing for the desperately poor, piling their contributions in boxes beside the street outside a Newark theater (top).

Eager crowds lined up outside government offices that offered emergency relief work (center left). Out in the Jersey Meadows near Jersey City, jobless men dug vegetable gardens (center right) in the swampland muck. Note the little girl, a true daughter of the depression, watching her father as he worked.

Workers employed by the WPA (Works Progress Administration) picked up bricks in the old Morris Canal bed in Newark (bottom left) — one of the hundreds of WPA projects undertaken throughout the state. On Newark's Prince Street (bottom right), a mixture of clothes (including long underwear), vegetables, and household goods provided bargains for street shoppers.

The new President, Franklin Delano Roosevelt, waged vigorous war on the fear, starting a series of work programs to get wages flowing again. By the end of 1934, when more than 20 million Americans received government aid, Roosevelt started the WPA to employ 33 million. The jobless welcomed the WPA joyfully, but many, including newspaper cartoonists (who held on to their jobs), lambasted the "make work" project (as demonstrated below).

All They Had To Fear ...

One special day was April 7, 1933 when breweries could legally make and sell beer, the first step in the repeal of the Prohibition Amendment (full repeal came on November 19, 1933). The April beer was 3.2 percent alcohol; the phrase "near beer" was appropriate.

Prohibition's repeal permitted the state's brewers and winemakers to operate legally. That meant more jobs and a boost to prosperity, except among the bootleggers and racketeers who enjoyed Prohibition.

Salaries continued low, but that was offset by twenty-five cent admissions to movies, full-course dinners for fifty cents (genuine feasts for one dollar), gasoline for ten to twelve cents a gallon, and food budgets for newlyweds of $8 or $9 a week.

A new car could be bought for $800 in 1939, and a handsome apartment could be leased for thirty-five dollars a month. A day at the Jersey Shore or at Lake Hopatcong cost little more than a few gallons of gasoline. Attendance at state and county parks soared, and the parks were in good condition, thanks to the government-sponsored Civilian Conservation Corps.

If all else failed, there was Monopoly. The game featured Atlantic City place names and it took hours to play fully. That mattered little; people had time enough to play during the Depression.

"Storm Troopers" At Andover

The headlines fed by Depression woes diminished as newspapers increasingly featured a German named Adolf Hitler and, to a lesser extent, a large-jawed Italian named Benito Mussolini. At first, there was almost as much editorial praise as damnation for the two dictators who steadily moved the world toward another war.

Anything that relieved the depression blues was welcome: the movies, the radio, parlor games, and the "Big Name Bands" that appeared regularly at Frank Dailey's Meadowbrook in Cedar Grove, Jenkinson's Pavilion in Point Pleasant, or the Wigwam at Budd Lake.

Miss America seemed a genuine princess, risen from the masses to royal stature. Bette Cooper of Hackettstown changed the image in 1938. Entering the pageant on a dare, Bette was astonished when she won (opposite page). She turned her back on the crown and returned the next week to Hackettstown's Centenary College. This Cinderella preferred being "the girl next door" (a mark of virtue in those times).

People cheered nearly anything, but voices were especially raised when the first beer rolled from a Hudson County brewery after repeal of Prohibition in 1933 (opposite page, top right).

Everything unusual attracted crowds, particularly the air shows at Lakehurst. The giant hanger was always filled with blimps and dirigibles. That fascination ended in May 1937 when the *Hindenburg*, a German dirigible, exploded and burned at Lakehurst, ending an era of ocean-crossing dirigibles.

Radio was the key to entertainment — and to education — for classes often were tuned in to "worthwhile" programs (lower right). Millions faithfully listened at night to Burns and Allen, Jack Benny, Bob Hope, and, of course, the Big Bands. Performers rose rapidly in popularity — but none more rapidly than Hoboken's Frank Sinatra, indisputable king of depression entertainers.

Chasing Away Depression Blues

Rare is the person in the English-speaking world who has not tried at least once to own the most precious paper holdings known to game players: Park Place and the Boardwalk. Given those, victory is close at hand in Monopoly, the most popular parlor pastime ever invented.

At the point where Park Place and the Boardwalk intersect in Atlantic City, a plaque honors the memory of Charles B. Darrow of Germantown, Pennsylvania, the radiator repairman who invented Monopoly in 1930.

Darrow drew his game on a sheet of linoleum. All but one of the game's "properties" were named for places in Atlantic City (Marvin Gardens is in Margate). Street names, said Darrow, were "in gratitude for pleasant vacations" spent in the seaside city.

Parker Brothers began marketing Monopoly in 1935 and has sold more than 200 million sets worldwide. More than five billion little green houses have been "built."

Monopoly retains a fascination for new generations. In 1973, when Atlantic City proposed changing the names of Baltic Avenue and Mediterranean Avenue (to Fairmont and Melrose), thousands of complaints poured in from Monopoly players around the world. The city backed down; Baltic and Mediterranean live on.

Rumors of Hitler's systematic, fiendish elimination of Jews ultimately seeped into the newspapers. Many readers including many political, business, and church leaders doubted the stories of these German atrocities. They could not believe a national leader would condemn an entire race to extinction.

Hitler supporters, calling themselves "Friends of New Germany," rallied in Newark on October 16, 1933 to hear leaders blame "Communists, Jews, and Roman Catholics" for the Depression. The meeting ended in wild disorder when a rock-throwing group attacked the "Friends." More than two hundred police were needed to quell the fighting.

The Friends changed their name to the German American Bund (League) in 1936. They bought a 250-acre sanctuary at Andover in Sussex County and built Camp Nordland as the headquarters for a campaign in support of Hitler's idea of a "master race" composed of White Protestant Anglo-Saxons.

As many as eight thousand poured into Camp Nordland on weekends for "picnics." Brown-shirted young men, looking as much as possible like German Storm Troopers, marched in goose step across the Andover ground. The stiff-arm salutes and the roaring shouts of "Heil Hitler" left no doubt as to the Bund allegiance.

In The Name Of Free Speech

An American "Fuehrer" named Fritz Kuhn spoke often at the Bund rallies. He glowingly described Germany's "greatness" and Adolf Hitler's "infinite wisdom." Followers from New Jersey and New York cheered at Kuhn's glorification of Germany's Third Reich. Jeers greeted every mention of President Roosevelt's name.

Kuhn lost face in 1939 when he was charged with embezzling Bund funds. His successor, Gerhard W. Kuhnze of Union City, was even uglier in his attacks on Roosevelt and the Jews. In a May Day, 1939 speech at Camp Nordland, Kuhnze called on labor unions to "make America a white man's Christian country again." He called Hitler "the prophet of labor."

Legal attempts to stop the Bund's activities were stymied by American traditions that even offensive free speech must be permitted. Many state legislators, as well as the American Civil Liberties Union, argued that because a majority disagreed with the Bund's views was not justification for outlawing the group.

By the late 1930s, the fervor of the Bundist orators was more than matched by the bitter feeling of refugees who had fled to America from nations where the boots of Hitler's troopers were grinding

Sailing northward from Havana to New York in early September 1934, the 508-foot-long luxury cruise liner *Morro Castle* seemed as snug as a floating grand hotel despite the wild storm outside. When fire started on September 5, the ship's captain showed confusion; no radio message was sent for hours after flames were discovered. Many passengers leaped into the stormy sea to escape the inferno; others died on the red-hot decks. By the time the smoking ship lodged on a sand bank in Asbury Park, 134 passengers had died. The hulk was a bizarre tourist attraction until towed away the next spring.

liberty into the dust.

Slovak colonies throughout the state cried out in anguish over the fall of Czechoslovakia in 1938. Polish-Americans wept in the streets of Newark and other cities when Hitler's legions goose stepped into Poland on September 1, 1939.

Poland was one goose step too many. Hitler's unprovoked assault on that country broke the fragile dam that had been holding back World War II. England and France declared war on Germany and sentiment in America began to run heavily against Hitler and Mussolini. The Bund limped along at Andover until late 1940, broken by the war.

Arsenal Of Democracy

Europe's war made New Jersey factories hum again to fill orders from England, France, and other Allied nations. The last vestiges of the Great Depression evaporated with the arrival of the war contracts.

The explosives makers near Kenvil and Dover added new shifts. Iron mines were reopened in Morris and Passaic counties. DuPont's several New Jersey powder mills resumed full operation. Copper began to flow from Middlesex County refineries. Gasoline makers in Union County raced to feed the Allied war machine. Camden's shipyards rumbled with retooling activity.

New Jersey became a genuine "arsenal of democracy" (President Roosevelt's term). This state could provide radios, automobiles, ships, ammunition, uniforms, chemicals, airplane engines, machines, food, gasoline, copper, and hundreds of other things. Those were the materials on which war could thrive.

By the end of 1939, a total of 433,000 men and women labored in the state's industries, the highest total since World War I. The rhythm picked up as France, Belgium, and the Netherlands fell to Hitler. Great Britain teetered on the edge of disaster.

Although President Roosevelt vowed in a campaign address in 1940, "your boys are not going to be sent into any wars," American troops were getting ready. New Jersey's National Guard left for training camp in the summer of 1940 in a preparedness move.

The first peacetime draft in American history followed in October 1940.

Draftees began leaving before Christmas, 1940. The "citizen soldiers" used broomsticks for "guns" and Jeeps for "tanks." Training was unreal, as if rookies peeling potatoes at Fort Dix or getting blistered feet in Texas camp had no relationship with "Europe's War." It was treated more as a joke than a reality.

Between June 1940 and June 1941, New Jersey received nine percent of all prime allied war contracts, topped only by California and New York. People were at work and wages were high. The mood was bright and light as the first snow dusted New Jersey fields in December.

"A Day To Live In Infamy"

Christmas shoppers jammed the stores in the first week of December 1941. Full pocketbooks stepped up competition for scarce goods. Surely Christmas, 1941 would be the happiest holiday in twenty years.

Newspaper headlines gave no reason to feel insecure. Smiling Japanese diplomats met with friendly Washington officials all that first week of December. The war in Europe seemed at a stalemate. Readers of Sunday newspapers on December 7 were more concerned with advertised bargains than with the war.

Most New Jerseyans went to church as usual on December 7, ate hearty Sunday dinners, and settled down to doze or to listen to the Giants football game on the radio.

Far to the west in Hawaii, the dawn of December 7 broke over Pearl Harbor at about the time Sunday services ended in New Jersey. Four young Newarkers, Archie Callahan, Jr., Nicholas Runiak, Raymond J. Kerrigan, and Louis Schleifer — all in military service in Hawaii — dozed peacefully. The smiling faces in Washington left the military relaxed.

Incredibly, Japanese fighter planes and bombers swept in over Pearl Harbor at dawn. Great battleships struck by bombs burst into flames and sank within minutes. The stricken battleship *Oklahoma* rolled over in the harbor and lay with her keel skyward.

Archie Callahan, a 19-year-old mess attendant

Flying the Nazi swastika along with the American flag, German-American Bundists paraded boldly at their Bund camp in Andover during the 1930s. They goose-stepped before admiring crowds, giving the Nazi salute in imitation of Hitler and his German soldiers. Children joined parents in the audience to hear attacks on labor, Jews, and President Roosevelt — along with high praise for Hitler and his Nazi troopers.

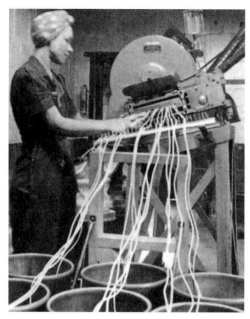

New Jersey munitions plants hummed, making powder at Picatinny Arsenal near Dover (above) and elsewhere. Inevitably, disaster struck. Hercules Powder Company, expanding mightily at Kenvil, was destroyed by a blast on September 13, 1940. Fifty-two persons died; hundreds more were injured.

aboard the *Oklahoma,* was dead in the battleship's hull. Nearby, Raymond Kerrigan was killed aboard the *Vestal,* and Nicholas Runiak's life ended on the *Arizona.* Louis Schleifer, a PFC in the Air Corps, was gunned down on the Hickam Field runway as he fired at the Japanese planes with a pistol.

Back home, the radio account of the football game droned on. Suddenly, the announcer screamed bewildering words: "Pearl Harbor … sneak attack … Japan … emergency." America was at war!

The next day, President Roosevelt described the attack on Pearl Harbor as "a day that will live in infamy." Congress immediately seconded his call for all-out war. There really had been no way for the United States to remain neutral. The actions of Germany, Italy, and now Japan, all ran counter to American philosophies.

The Holiday Mood of War

Even as the President spoke, long lines of young men stood eagerly outside military recruiting services around the state and nation. They laughed and joked in the eerie holiday mood that pervades a nation once war has been declared.

Newspapers spread pictures of the recruiting activities across the front pages. The would-be warriors, not yet in uniform, boasted to reporters of their intentions to "hit Hitler" or "jolt the Japs." It all seemed so easy, so much fun.

Before the war's end, the total of those enlisted (214,949) and those drafted (345,552) added up to 560,501 New Jerseyans in uniform. About 10,000 were women, whose services were actively encouraged by the military for the first time.

Nearly every family was touched by the enlistments or draft quotas since about one-eighth of the state's total population served in uniform. Weddings rose sharply and, inevitably, so did the birth rate.

Americans lived on news from places whose names they scarcely realized existed. New Jersey fighters went ashore in North Africa in November 1942, landed in France on "D-Day" in June 1944, and fought across the Pacific Ocean at Manila, Midway, Guadalcanal, Iwo Jima, and Okinawa.

The best known New Jersey outfit was the 102nd Cavalry Group. Made up initially of members of the fashionable Essex Troop of Essex County, the 102nd

Two pictures shot at Newark within minutes proved high compliance during a statewide test blackout on May 26, 1941. Black-outs became necessary as lights silhouetted ships for German submarines off the Jersey Shore. Dozens of ships were torpedoed, including the sinking Standard Oil tanker pictured here. Only two of the tanker's 43 crewmembers survived.

young people dead on rocky Pacific islands, in Egypt, in France, Germany, or Italy; dead in training camp accidents, in the sinkings of oil tankers and aircraft carriers, or in the jungles of Burma.

The final count showed that 13,172 New Jerseyans died. That statistic was recorded in gold stars in lonely windows and perpetuated on bronze markers in town squares and village greens.

Above And Beyond

There is no way to portray the sacrifices of all those who died, but seventeen New Jersey fighting men won the Congressional Medal of Honor for services "above and beyond the call of duty." These heroes rose for brief moments above the millions who endured the mud and blood of war. Only seven of them survived their exploits.

Marine Sergeant John Basilone of Raritan became New Jersey's most famous Medal of Honor recipient. The son of immigrant parents, he enlisted in the Marines and won his medal in a savage machine gun duel with the Japanese at Guadalcanal.

Government officials brought Sergeant Johnny home and paraded him across the nation to sell war bonds as "The Hero of Guadalcanal." Upset by this experience, Basilone insisted on a return to active duty.

was expanded by draftees and other replacements. It arrived in England in October 1942 — the first American cavalry unit to reach Europe.

Riding tanks instead of horses, parts of the 102nd Cavalry spearheaded an invasion of southern France in 1944. Other units splashed ashore at Omaha Beach in the "D-Day" attack in June 1944. The 102nd eventually rode its tanks through France, Germany, and as far as Czechoslovakia. More than 300 of the proud unit died on distant European fields.

The joy of war ebbed and ended abruptly when the casualties began to pile up. The lists told constantly of

John Basilone never came home again. He died among the marines who waded ashore at Iwo Jima in February 1945. A bronze statue memorializes him in his hometown, and a highway bridge over the Raritan River bears his name.

Another New Jersey Medal of Honor winner whose name is preserved was Air Force Captain Thomas G. McGuire of Ridgewood. As a fighter pilot, he ranked second only to his commander, Major Richard Bong, as the outstanding Pacific War ace.

McGuire shot down thirty-eight Japanese planes before he was killed in 1944 trying to aid a fellow pilot being pursued by an enemy fighter. McGuire Air Force Base in the Pine Barrens was dedicated in his name in 1949.

The Build-Up State

As the military streamed toward Europe, New Jersey again became the "build-up" state, serving as the leading embarkation point for the big push against Germany.

More than 1.3 million draftees experienced their first weaning from civilian life at Fort Dix. The sandy army reservation in the Pine Barrens would be the only memory most of those citizen soldiers would have of New Jersey.

Camp Kilmer in Middlesex County was hastily thrown together on open pasturelands acquired by the army in 1942. The 2,328-acre tract near New Brunswick cost $23 million. On that open farmland grew an amazing complex of buildings, each painted in a variety of colors as camouflage against potential enemy air attack (a very real fear in 1942).

"Top secret" was Kilmer's watchword. Few knew in July 1942 that the camp's first contingent — a corps of Army nurses — had shipped out for England. Eventually, two million men and women passed through Camp Kilmer on the way across the Atlantic. By June 1945, Kilmer sent 100,000 person overseas every month. An entire division could be processed in a few hours.

Hudson County's railroad terminals, yards, and shipping piers were packed with soldiers coming and going on trains. Hudson's dock workers each week sent hundreds of thousands of tons of war supplies to the European theater of war.

Most "hush hush" was the seventeen-mile-square Earle Naval Ammunition Depot in Monmouth County, the Navy's principal East Coast storage and shipping point. After it began shipping in 1943, the

Fort Dix (Camp Dix of World War I) started soldiers toward the front. Every recruit faced the needle — for blood samples or for shots. Out in the field (below), weary privates sought "sack time" (rest) at every break. "War" at Dix (bottom) was too often a matter of "policing" the already neat grounds.

Atlantic City played host to the armed services. Forty-seven hotels became barracks or training centers, and the huge Convention Hall was taken over by the Air Force. These pictures depict boardwalk and beach in wartime — women soldiers marching and singing, a parade of servicemen in front of Convention Hall, mock warfare on the beach known previously only for fun, and an artillery group on the alert against invasion.

depot averaged 128,000 tons of overseas shipments every month.

At times, Earle stored more than enough explosives to blow all of New Jersey and New York City off the face of the earth. Fortunately, Earle's output all went to Europe, except for one destroyer escort that exploded at the pier, killing seven and wounding 165.

Behind The Men Behind The Guns

Slogans became a mark of World War II. Two of them cited workers in war plants as "the men behind the men behind the guns" or as "Rosie the Riveter," in tribute to the thousands of women in war work.

New Jersey lived up to the slogans. More than one million state workers made every conceivable type of war commodity: ships, airplanes, motors, explosives, radar, uniforms, radios, food, and a thousand other things designed to pound the enemy "on land, on the seas, and in the air."

New Jersey again proved its ability to make ships beside the Delaware River and Newark Bay. New York Shipbuilding Corporation's yard in Camden slid ships down the giant ways nearly every day, ranging from small craft for beach landings to enormous aircraft carriers, a new vessel of warfare.

The Camden yard delivered $217 million worth of new ships between March 1942 and March 1943. Its workers built twenty-nine of America's biggest fighting ships — cruisers, battleships, and carriers.

Across the state, Newark Bay was aglow with the sights and sounds of shipbuilding. Federal Shipyard at Kearny, stumbling along on a standby basis since World War I, now came alive again. Thirty-two thousand people worked around the clock at Kearny. Another 20,000 were on day and night shifts at an auxiliary yard in Port Newark.

Six months after Pearl Harbor, Federal's 50,000 workers astonished the shipbuilding world by launching four destroyers and four auxiliary vessels in one day! By 1943, the Federal facilities were building faster than any other American shipyard, delivering a ship every four and a half working days.

Eventually, Federal made nearly one-fourth of all United States destroyers. It cut destroyer completion time from a normal eighteen months to an incredible five months between laying of the keel and the shakedown cruise.

At the same time, Paterson's Curtiss-Wright kept American fighting planes in the air. The company added more than 40,000 men and women to its payroll, spread them out in a hodgepodge of old Paterson mills, and produced engines at a dizzying pace.

Curtiss-Wright delivered 139,000 airplane engines between 1940 and 1945, far more than any other American engine maker. Nearby in Caldwell, Curtiss-Wright made 146,000 propellors, about one-fifth of the entire United States production.

Paterson-made engines took General Jimmy Doolittle's B-25 plane over Tokyo for his daring daylight raid on April 18, 1942. They also powered the B-29 bomber, the *Enola Gay*, that dropped the first atom bomb on Hiroshima, Japan.

The Home Front Survives

World War II tested those who stayed at home. These included older people who worked without pay for the rationing boards and draft boards. Volunteers patrolled lonely, dark streets at night to help in case of an air raid. They manned lonely aircraft spotting stations on high hillsides night after night, in every kind of weather. The fact that enemy airplanes never came did not lessen their dedication.

Rationing of scarce materials was inevitable. Automobile tires were rationed in January 1942, followed by restrictions on gasoline, fuel oil, sugar, meat, and butter.

People at first lined up at local rationing offices for rationing stamps. In June 1943, the Newark headquarters of the Office of Price Administration mailed out fifty-four tons of ration books to eligible New Jerseyans. Thirteen thousand volunteer high school teachers and students took care of the mailing.

Most people behaved well in the face of extreme temptations. There were some chiselers and hoarders and a few outright criminals trafficking in counterfeit ration stamps. Most adults had sons, daughters, or other relatives in uniform; complying with the rationing laws seemed to them only a minimal responsibility.

Volunteer agencies gathered food, clothing, and money for war victims. New Jerseyans responded to drives to aid the Finns, British, Poles, and others who were directly taking the cruel blows of the war. As an example, three thousand field-type kerosene stoves were sent early in 1942 to Russian front-line hospitals and refugee camps.

After October 1942, Newark became headquarters for the Office of Dependency Benefits (ODB), the federal agency responsible for mailing out checks to

Women workers prepared fighter planes for shipment from Newark Airport to Europe. More than 40,000 planes, mostly fighters, were flown into the airport from Port Newark for shipment to England or France.

The "home front" boomed. Federal Shipyard at Port Newark (top, opposite page) was called "Insomniac Shipyard" because it was busy 24 hours a day, seven days a week, turning out destroyer escorts. Federal had 32,000 employees at Kearny and 20,000 at Port Newark in 1943.

At the opposite end of the state, in Cumberland County, Stowman Yard in Dorchester (center left) made a succession of smaller fighting ships. Stowman's big neighbor up the Delaware River, New York Ship Corporation at Camden, earned a stellar reputation for its tremendous production. New York Ship's 38,000 employees made big vessels — battleships, cruisers, and aircraft carriers.

Everywhere, regardless of age or occupation, the civilian effort increased. One major sign of the war effort was the gas ration card, issued to every automobile driver in the nation. Each coupon could buy three gallons; the possessor of the card shown here never used ten of the coupons.

Food was short in supply and high in price. It became necessary as well as patriotic to dig and plant "Victory Gardens." Each wartime spring meant crowds gathered around counters vying for the scarce seeds that promised rich harvests — and the promised harvests came true for some of the gardeners.

dependents of servicemen. ODB took over a new twenty-story office built by the Prudential Insurance Company. More than 10,000 employees each month mailed out more than a half billion dollars to eight million dependents.

The government benefits office hired without discrimination. About one-fourth of all employees were African American, in jobs from supervisors to clerks. For the first time on a major scale, New Jersey African American employees could prove themselves capable of any kind of work.

Women also won the chance, in most industries, to prove they could perform a wide variety of jobs once reserved only for males. "Rosie The Riveter" symbolized women at work on "men's jobs" — riveting, welding, repairing machines, and doing other tough, dirty work.

The Bombs Of August

The Allied forces moved eastward across Europe,

slowly grinding Hitler's war machine to pieces. Victory over Germany eventually came on May 7, 1945. Heavy rains dampened the celebration, but more important, it was not yet time for full joy. The war still occupied millions of Americans in another part of the world.

United States forces had moved westward across the Pacific Ocean, island by island, through 1944 and 1945. The Japanese resisted stubbornly and, on VE Day (Victory in Europe), the island-hopping campaign was exacting a dreadful toll in American lives. The invasion of Japan seemed destined to kill hundreds of thousands more sailors, soldiers, and marines.

Finally, on August 6, 1945, a B-29 bomber named the *Enola Gay* droned westward toward Japan, carrying the first atom bomb. Over Hiroshima, the plane dropped the missile, whose incredible destructive power was not known even to the bomber's pilot.

Downward plummeted the untested weapon, bursting with a heat and force unknown before in all history. As the *Enola Gay* veered back to its home airport, Hiroshima lay in ruin, with 60,000 dead, 100,000 injured, and 200,000 homeless. Three days later, Nagasaki perished under another A-bomb.

Japan asked for peace terms on August 14. Word of the action reached New Jersey at 1:49 AM. By 3 AM, groups of celebrants were forming in every town and city. By 8 PM, city streets were so clogged that traffic was halted for hours.

Celebrating crowds went wild, snake-dancing through the streets. Girls kissed every serviceman in sight, and the servicemen kissed back. Fathers, mothers, sisters, and wives of servicemen alternately wept and cheered. When the noise and fun ran its course, many went to churches to attend hastily arranged morning services of thanksgiving.

The war was over. Also over for most was the romantic notion, of December 7, 1941, that war was "glamorous." The atom bombs exploded over Japan showed mankind had achieved a "sophistication" to kill beyond the most horrible of nightmares. Those bombs brought the world into the atomic age, for better or for worse.

Home To Shape A Peace

In time, the soldiers came home. More than three million soldiers passed through Camp Kilmer on the way back to civilian life. Another two million men and women were discharged at Fort Dix. Nearly half

of all American Armed Forces personnel thus received their last taste of the military in New Jersey.

Both the returning veterans and the war workers faced a world vastly different from the one they knew in 1940. More than 2.5 million New Jersey lives had been altered: a half million by military service and two million by war work in factories or other war-connected tasks within the state.

The war-bloated economy began to deflate as early as October 1943. By October 1945, some 300,000 war plant workers had lost their jobs. The unemployment was doubly felt, for paychecks had doubled in size — up from an average of twenty-six dollars a week in 1939 to fifty-two dollars a week in 1944.

New Jersey And The Atom Bomb

At 8:14 AM on August 5, 1945, Hiroshima was a busy, thriving city. At 8:15 AM, 81 percent of Hiroshima ceased to exist. In that one dreadful minute, the atom bomb that ended World War II also changed the world forever.

Many people from many lands contributed to the making of the atom bomb, but few regions were more vital to the splitting of the atom than New Jersey.

Hitler's crazed hatred of Jews lost him Albert Einstein, often called the "Father of the Atomic Bomb." Einstein, who had proclaimed the existence of atomic energy before 1915, was lecturing in the United States in 1933 when the Nazis stripped him of his citizenship because he was a Jew. Einstein became director of the School of Mathematics at the Institute for Advanced Study in Princeton and continued his studies of energy there.

Two Westinghouse Lamp scientists at Bloomfield developed pellets of pure uranium in 1922 while seeking a new lamp filament. Twenty years later, Westinghouse produced quantities of the needed uranium.

At Princeton University, Professor Hugh Stott Taylor and his associates developed so-called "heavy water" containing the heavy hydrogen needed for the bomb.

Columbia University professor Dr. Enrico Fermi, a top figure in the making of the bomb, lived in Leonia.

Flying as copilot in the plane that dropped the bomb on Hiroshima was Captain Robert A. Lewis of Ridgefield Park.

Later, Dr. H. D. Smyth, head of Princeton University's physics department, wrote the official A-bomb report for the Atomic Energy Commission.

There was talk of depression, even though employment in 1945 was half again as high as in 1939. Many of those who lost jobs were wives of servicemen. They were willing to give up their positions, at least temporarily, although the kitchen would never again be the same to a former welder or airplane builder.

What saved the economy was the tremendous potential in the production and sale of peacetime goods. There were shortages everywhere in automobiles, tires, refrigerators, furniture, toasters, houses, and a thousand and one other items. The wartime crop of babies created a demand for everything from diapers to schoolbooks, from baby carriages to family station wagons.

Peace was not going to be easy to manage. Women were employed in numbers never before known. Many a husband-and-wife working team enjoyed new-found prosperity, even as many sociologists and psychologists feared their growing families were being neglected.

Demands and expectations were high. The twentieth century was nearly at the mid-point. The second half would make the first half seem almost as distant as the days of ancient Greece and Rome.

Horse and Buggy Constitution

Yet as New Jersey neared the second half of the century, its government crept along on a state constitution straight out of the horse and buggy days. It dated back to 1844 — before gold was discovered in California, when only twenty-six states were in the Union, when California and Texas were still ruled by Mexico.

Both political parties had fiercely resisted changes in the old constitution for 103 years, fearful anything new might curb their power in Trenton.

A few amendments were pushed through in 1875, including removal of the word "white" from voting

Jersey City marchers, who paraded through the streets in May 1938, proclaimed that "Reds" would never take over their town. Mayor Frank Hague encouraged such demonstrations. He also proclaimed "I am the law," prompting a cartoon that showed him as the Angel Gabriel calling dead voters to vote. Hague foes charged that names on cemetery stones were on city voting rolls, awaiting a call from "The Boss" to appear at the polls.

qualifications and a requirement that all New Jersey children must receive "a thorough and efficient education."

Political leaders especially feared any changes in the legislature, where a handful of Republican state senators from southern New Jersey's farm and seashore counties long had unofficially ruled the state. They cooperated, when necessary, with Jersey City's political boss, Democratic Mayor Frank Hague.

Reapportionment of the state legislature to give proper representation to urban areas of the state was discussed — and rejected — as early as 1874. That matter was seldom discussed openly in political circles, despite New Jersey's emergence as an urban, industrialized state.

Democratic Governor Charles Edison and Republican Governor Walter Edge both sought to modernize the constitution during their World War II terms. A coalition of Republican senators and the Hague Democratic machine fought back every effort, appealing piously that the document must not be changed "while the boys are away."

Now "the boys" were back, grown into men. Unable to stem the demands for a new constitution after the war, the political leaders permitted voters to decide whether a Constitutional Convention should convene at Rutgers University in June 1947. Voters approved overwhelmingly.

"A Great Work Is Expected"

A shadow over the convention at the start was the tender subject of reform to give city areas adequate representation. The shadow was pushed aside; any change in the makeup of the state legislature was ruled off limits for the convention. The subject would rise again, but not at Rutgers in 1947.

Republican Governor Alfred E. Driscoll, who placed his prestige behind the vote for the convention, rose in the Rutgers gymnasium on June 12 to address the delegates. He saw this as the most important gathering in the state in at least a century, and he spoke bluntly:

> It is only fair to say that a great work is expected of you. While this state has lived under the same constitution for over a century, its people, their life, and work have undergone the effects of a Civil War, of two world wars, and of industrial and social revolutions since our present constitution was adopted in 1844.

The delegates worked harmoniously and effectively through that long, hot summer. By fall they had streamlined one of the nation's oldest and wordiest constitutions into one of the shortest and fairest documents in the nation. Voters gave hearty approval to the new constitution in November 1947.

The new document strengthened government at every level. The governor won strong powers and could serve two consecutive four-year terms rather than one three-year term. Senators would serve four years instead of three and Assemblymen two years instead of one. The longer terms, it was argued, would lead to experience, independence, and better state government.

Courts were streamlined. The State Supreme Court became truly the top court in New Jersey, and the Chief Justice headed the entire court system. A bewildering, inefficient maze of county courts, based on ancient English law, was cut to one court in each county.

Rutgers President Robert E. Clothier, Convention president, said of the new court system: "The interests of judges and lawyers, important as they are, have been subordinated to the interests of the litigants."

Equality Before The Law

Framers of the 1947 constitution foresaw a movement toward equality that soon would stir passions across the nation. In 1844, the constitution only forbade discrimination because of "religious principles." The 1947 document also removed race, color, sex, and national origin as legal excuses for discrimination.

Many inside the political family pleaded for caution in enforcing the antidiscrimination clause. Governor Driscoll ignored their suggestions. He ordered that all schools be desegregated — and to the surprise of many, that included schools in such "northern" towns as Asbury Park and Princeton, where "colored" schools had continued in the midst of wealth and privilege.

Equally impressively, State National Guard officers were ordered to accept African American enlistees immediately. Warned by aides that national Department of the Army policy continued to call for segregated units, Driscoll demanded state law be followed.

The governor met opposition, even open defiance, from State Guard leaders. As late as January 28, 1948, the state commander issued an order prohibiting enlistment of African Americans in white units. Driscoll promptly rescinded the order.

Governor Driscoll's dramatic and unswerving stand

for integration of the New Jersey National Guard had nationwide repercussions. New Jersey became the first state to desegregate its armed forces, despite unmistakable insinuations from top US Army sources federal funds would be cut off.

Within a month, the United States Army backed down. New Jersey's success in combating segregation led other states to desegregate state units. Integration at every level in the United States armed forces inevitably followed.

Driscoll's full support of a new constitution, plus his courageous defense of its Bill of Rights, earned him re-election in 1949 as the first governor to succeed himself in 105 years. (Prior to the 1844 constitution, governors could succeed themselves for an unlimited number of one-year terms.)

New Jersey government was finally into the twentieth century, and just in time, for the century was nearly half gone.

"... And Now, A Message From Your Sponsor"

An expensive toy called television meant nothing to the general public in 1945. It was an unusual luxury, suited only for rich men's dens or for taverns able to afford the high cost of a set.

Television had been emerging for twenty years by 1945. The nation's first television "program" was broadcast, in April 1927, from the Bell Laboratories in Whippany to the company's New York offices. It featured a comic and a pretty girl singer, as might be expected.

Work by the Whippany engineers, RCA scientists in Camden, and TV pioneer Allen B. DuMont of Upper Montclair made television a fully-operable, if costly, medium by 1939.

That year, New Jersey-made TV equipment was featured at the World's Fair in New York. Buyers were few, partially because there were no regularly scheduled TV shows. There were only about 7,000 sets in the nation when Pearl Harbor was bombed in 1941.

War's end heightened enthusiasm for TV, but it was still more a matter of laboratory enthusiasm than public acceptance. There were only seven TV stations in 1946, and in May 1947 there were only about 44,000 TV sets in the United States — more than 75 percent of those in homes close to New York City and its three TV channels.

The nation's advertisers at first were very reluctant to interrupt TV programs with the now-familiar "message from your sponsor." When NBC issued its first advertising rate card in June 1941, it asked $120 for a full hour of prime time between 6 and 11 PM (when stations went off the air). These days, a 30-second ad on a special, such as the Super Bowl game, can cost more than two million dollars.

New York City dominated the medium from the start. It had six channels, with a seventh — Channel 13 — in Newark, New Jersey. By 1955, TV was becoming big time. Regular programs were scheduled and networks began to fight for the growing pot of advertising gold.

Channel 13 was sold in the early 1960s to New York educational interests for $6.5 million. New Jersey became one of only two states (the other was Delaware) without a commercial TV station within its borders. Channel 13 quickly focused on New York, so even in "educational" channels New Jersey was virtually off the air.

Chapter Fourteen - Survival In An Urban Land

United States			New Jersey
		1947	Transistor invented
		1947	GI Bill encourages suburbia
Korean War begins	1950		
US has 1st hydrogen bomb	1951	1951	Voters approve State College expansion
		1953	Turnpike finished; Parkway started
Russia explodes H-bomb	1955		
Russia launches Sputnik into space	1957	1957	Schools stress math and science
		1960	Erie and Lackawanna railroads merge
Peace Corps established	1961		
President Kennedy killed	1963		
Civil Rights Act	1964	1964	New Jersey turns 300
US troops build up in Vietnam	1965		
Race riots in several US cities	1967	1967	Newark, Plainfield hit by riots
US out of Vietnam	1975		
Bicentennial of Declaration of Independence	1976	1976	Study exposes plight of city

The Quiet Revolution

Sussex County had more cows than people. Cape May County residents virtually hibernated between Labor Day and the Fourth of July. Cumberland County vegetable fields stretched beyond distant horizons. Ocean County chickens produced millions of eggs annually. In nearly every county, many thousands of boys and girls still studied in one-room schools.

It was 1945. Peace had come. New Jersey waited for the veterans to come home.

Occasionally a political realist or a newspaper pundit warned postwar needs would be overwhelming, but in 1945 New Jersey's rural-thinking legislature adopted a stringent $80 million budget. A year later, in the midst of intense readjustment, state budget needs "soared" to $131 million, horrifying the New Jersey Taxpayers Association.

Every city in America was in trouble. The littered streets, the abandoned stores, the closed movie houses, and the deteriorating housing areas told the story clearly and starkly. Newark was the example usually cited, even in national stories, and the example often depicted on TV.

Ten years after savage riots rocked Newark, however, the city had ample reason to be optimistic. The evidences of decay and obsolescence could not be hidden, but Newark could look beyond the boarded-up storefronts and cite solid reasons for believing the city was not dead. No transportation area in the world was more impressive than the eastern edge of Newark. Here, within a few hundred acres, was an international airport, one of the nation's greatest seaports, major railroad lines, and superhighways.

Jobs are essential if cities are to be revived. Newark downtown was still national headquarters for the Prudential and Mutual Benefit insurance companies.

Public Service and NJ Bell Telephone Company had state headquarters in the city. Newark was the state's most important financial center. Hundreds of major industries were in place.

Newark was becoming a vital center of higher education. Its health statistics had improved dramatically. The crime rate had decreased. Schools were reported improved.

Problems persisted — big problems — but the optimism bubbled forth. Newark in 1977 seemed closer to revival than most of the cities in America (including New York).

In much of New Jersey little had changed because there had been a World War. In Sussex, 90,000 cows grazed on in sylvan settings. H. P. Lance's store at Annendale in Hunterdon County was a "shopping center" in itself in 1946, selling everything from gasoline to groceries (with apples at 75 cents a bushel). Cape May's wooden Victorian hotels continued to attract a rocking-chair crowd.

The average New Jerseyan cared little about state budgets. The state had no broad-based taxes, specifically no income or sales taxes. Since most people rented their living quarters, few of them had to pay local property taxes.

Not many young people had high expectations; fewer than ten percent of them expected to attend college. When they dreamed, they thought of marriage, a small rented apartment, children whose futures might be slightly better, a good radio for week-night entertainment, Saturday night at the movies, and possibly a small car. (The day of the two-car family had not yet dawned.) Such a cycle of life was familiar, understandable, and attainable.

Tarnish On the Golden Age

New Jersey's "Big Six" — Newark, Jersey City, Paterson, Elizabeth, Trenton, and Camden — boasted of a "golden age." Cities were stable, safe, lived in, and sought out for shopping, pleasure, and work. Most New Jerseyans lived in cities or within ten to fifteen miles of downtown.

A golden age? Perhaps. Yet, in the manner of "golden ages" throughout all history, tarnish could be detected everywhere within the state, if anyone looked closely. Few looked, for the heady feeling of peace made the entire world seem to sparkle. Heady feelings quickly evaporated if someone sought an apartment — so scarce that crowds of hopefuls vied to pay any exorbitant rent. Apartment owners could

The pent-up demand for automobiles ran into stumbling blocks as 1945 turned into 1946. On February 1, 1946, a severe shortage of materials halted the Ford assembly line at Edgewater. It was just as well; roads could not handle more volume. No better example could be cited than the intersection of Routes 1 and 9 at the traffic circle near Newark, as it appeared during the war. Shorebound drivers knew the agonies of bumper-to-bumper delays every weekend. This snarled line on the bridge over Cheesquake Creek on Route 35 was normal in the summer of 1952.

exercise every kind of discrimination, from prejudices of color, creed, or nationality to barring children, pets, and the elderly.

Every civilian commodity was scarce in 1945: clothing, food, automobiles. The scarcity of automobiles was just as well; every highway suffered cruelly from the twin ravages of depression and war. Route 1, the state's premier road, derived its sinister nickname: "The Deathtrap." (It could have applied equally to Routes 22, 130, 206, 17, or 4 — other "major" roads.)

Cities luxuriated in past glories, ignoring the expanding slums and the festering political corruption that infected them. Crowded railroad stations, filled with men and women headed for jobs in the city businesses, fed the misconception that railroads would never fade.

Incredibly, in the light of later developments, more than one hundred million railroad passenger tickets were sold in New Jersey each year in the 1940s. Keen ears could hear the increasing roar of trucks that drained away the railroad's profit margins, pounding over roads paid for by public taxation. Railroads headed for bankruptcy.

The tarnish-touched school systems fit more for 1900 than for 1950. In 1939, New Jersey had 320 one-room and 225 two-room schoolhouses. Most were still in place in 1945. Many schools in central and southern New Jersey continued segregation, not only in rural areas; Princeton, home of the famed university, had a segregated system.

Nearly all high school buildings dated back to the 1920s or earlier. In postwar New Jersey, there seemed little need for expansion. Enrollment peaked at 205,787 in 1940, and then declined steadily until it reached a low of 157,728 in 1951.

Rutgers, a "state university" in name only, claimed an enrollment of 9,000 students, but in 1945 only 750 full-time students attended the Men's College (Rutgers' very heart) in New Brunswick. Six small state teachers colleges staggered toward collapse. Every private college or university in the state faced uncertain futures. Veterans did not care particularly; college educations ranked near the bottom of their priority.

Enter The GI Bill

Life was predictable, unchanging, and unpromising. Then national legislation, the "GI Bill," entered the scene. That legislation affected American life as profoundly as anything in all peacetime history, opening doors that had been closed for centuries to all but the most privileged.

The legislation, officially titled The Servicemen's Readjustment Act, was set up by Congress in 1944 and immediately nicknamed the "GI Bill of Rights." (Enlisted men and women were GIs because uniforms, weapons, food, pay, and allowances were all "government issued." Hence, postwar privileges were "GI" too.)

The GI Bill created such basic hallmarks of security as low-cost insurance and hospitalization for veterans. Most important, *for the first time in the nation's history* (and perhaps in all world history), the GI Bill gave millions of young Americans the opportunity to own homes and to attend college.

Spurred by low-interest mortgages, guaranteed by the government, millions of GIs across the nation rushed to buy the "rose-covered cottages" that long

had been the stuff of song writers' melodies. The GI home loans spawned a phenomenon called "suburbia" that would, in time, drain the cities.

Suburbia was a ring of housing developments clustered outward from every city. The developments became nearly solidly white; African American veterans found banks unwilling to endorse a home purchase in suburbia, even with federal underwriting. That never-mentioned segregation drew white populations out of the cities.

Fields and orchards in Bergen, Essex, Morris, Mercer, and Camden counties yielded to new streets and row-on-row of look-alike new houses. The cottages were not rose-covered, lawns frequently were mud flats, septic tanks often overflowed, and scarcely a tree provided shade. Yet, even with hasty construction, unimaginative architecture, and uninspired landscaping, these "GI homes" were far superior to anything ever within reach of masses of people.

Starting prices for 1945 and 1946 GI homes were as low as $4,500 for a four- or five-room house on a small lot. The veterans and their spouses rode out to suburbia and loved the inexpensive houses rising in onetime pastures. Farms became villages almost overnight, villages became towns, and towns became cities.

Bergen County, long the dormitory for people who wanted to work in New York, but yearned as well for "the country life," doubled in population between 1945 and 1970. Two traditional farm areas — Woodbridge and Clifton — emerged as New Jersey's seventh and eighth largest cities in 1970. Rural Hamilton Township rose to ninth in population. Cherry Hill became a crowded outpost of Camden before realizing what happened.

Storming The Campuses

The veterans, including many of the new homeowners, also amazed educators by swarming to college programs underwritten by the GI Bill. When colleges started the fall semester in 1946, veterans besieged the campus gates.

Traditional educators viewed the hordes of invading GIs with alarm, tinged with distaste. Until 1945, higher education was reserved for a very limited number of people, most of them in the 18- to 20-year old bracket and from homes with middle and upper class incomes.

The GI scholars, in sharp contrasts, ranged in age from about twenty-two to forty-five. Many had been

Suburbia began slowly, appearing first as neat little houses on neat little lots on neat little streets, such as in the development near Ridgewood (above). Then it boomed as in Willingboro (top right). Eventually suburbia was a maze of buildings such as these in Wayne Township (right).

out of school for ten years or longer. Most were the first members of their families to seek any education beyond high school.

Those ex-servicemen and women upset every hallowed college tradition. They were mature, serious, intelligent, and determined to get an education. They were outspoken and demanding if professors coasted on old reputations or old lecture notes. They proved, for the first time, masses of young Americans could absorb higher education if given the chance.

Every campus felt the stunning impact. Seton Hall University enrolled four thousand veterans annually between 1946 and 1950. Fairleigh Dickinson University, founded as a junior college in 1941, had a veteran-swollen enrollment of 8,000 by 1950. Rutgers University was swamped with applications from ex-servicemen and women.

A decade of depression and five years of war left the colleges and universities totally unprepared for the onslaught. Few college buildings were less than twenty years old. Faculties were decimated by low wartime enrollments. Years of low budgets left campuses unkempt. Laboratories were better geared for soil analysis than for a scientific world that had felt the atom bomb.

College For Everyone

The passion for college opportunities was not matched by taxpayer enthusiasm for public higher education. New Jersey voters underscored that reluctance in 1948 by soundly rejecting a $50 million bond issue designed to transform the six state teachers colleges and Rutgers into modern institutions.

Amazingly, in view of the tremendous pressures for college seats, the state's leading taxpayer groups proposed, in 1950, the way to meet the mounting problem was to close teachers colleges in Newark, Paterson, and Jersey City. Only Montclair, Glassboro, and Trenton would remain.

The six state colleges then had only one function: to train elementary and high school teachers. Each campus was inadequate in ways that ranged from old buildings to mediocre faculties. New Jersey voters finally got the message and, in November 1951, approved a $15 million bond issue to start rebuilding all six of the campuses. It was the first significant financial boost in public higher education in New Jersey history.

Roots Of A State University

Rutgers, omitted from the 1951 bond vote, faced mountainous problems. Established in 1766 by the Dutch Reformed Church, Rutgers had partially "gone public" in 1864 by accepting federal funds to add a mechanical and agricultural college. The legislature officially made Rutgers "The State University of New Jersey" in 1917, but neglected to vote funds to match the grandiose name.

For its part, Rutgers hurt itself in its appeal for state help. It cherished the prestigious title of State University, but had little intention of abandoning the old privileges of a private institution. It only hesitantly amended its charter in 1920 to eliminate a 154-year-old provision the university must be a member of the Dutch Reformed Church.

The legislature, in 1945, reaffirmed the Rutgers status as the official state university, but only after winning a greater state voice on the university board of trustees. The legislators also allocated $1.4 million to Rutgers, far less than actually needed, but far better than anything previously given. Compromise took a tenuous hold; the allocations would rise steadily.

Rutgers enrollment tripled between 1940 and 1947, soaring the university into the nation's top twenty in enrollment. Spreading out of New Brunswick to become a real state university, Rutgers acquired the former University of Newark in 1946 and the College of South Jersey in Camden in 1949. The onetime poor-but-proud "cow college" by 1969 had become a five-campus state university. (Douglass College became part of the university in 1919 and Livingston College was opened on the former Camp Kilmer grounds in 1969.)

Albert Einstein: A Gentle Genius

The basic facts of Albert Einstein's amazing genius can be easily found, if not easily comprehended, in any encyclopedia. His famed theory of relativity, announced in 1915, set him far above most intellectuals in all of history and earned him the Nobel Prize for physics in 1921.

Equally amazing was the gentle human being who was fated to become a familiar figure on Princeton's streets.

By then, world honors had poured in on Einstein. Yet, simply because Einstein was a Jew, Adolph Hitler and his Nazis stripped the physicist of his property and his citizenship in 1933. Einstein was in the United States at the time. Soon after, he joined the faculty at the Institute for Advanced Study in Princeton.

His brilliance continued, yet the scientist's neighbors loved him most for his simplicity. Einstein gave no sign he was known throughout the world. He always walked between his home and the Institute, usually clothed in an old sweatshirt and baggy pants. His shaggy white hair flowed uncut and uncombed above his wrinkled, weathered face.

Einstein was forgetful in "worldly" matters. Once he put a $1500 check from the Rockefeller Foundation in a book as a bookmark — then lost the book. He refused to clutter his mind with the nonessentials. The aging scientist cheerfully greeted neighbors, from the youngest to the oldest, the least bright to the best educated. He carried his fame easily. He also won love, and that pleased him.

When Einstein died in 1955 at age 76, it was said fewer people attended his last rites than attended his birth. He insisted there be no fuss — no funeral, no grave, no marker, no shrine. Albert Einstein wanted and needed only one monument: his work.

New Jersey's diversified industry and research facilities provided broadening opportunity for college graduates. The state was represented in about 95 percent of all manufacturing categories in 1952 and had the highest concentration of research labs in the entire nation. A degree holder might seek work in industry, such as at the Gloucester County oil refinery (above), or in research, as at the Squibb lab at New Brunswick.

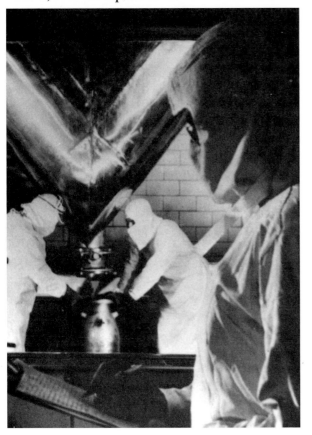

From Here To There

The race to the suburbs accelerated in the 1950s, but most of those enticed out to "the country" in Middlesex, Morris, and Bergen counties still worked in offices and factories clustered in or near the cities. Each day more automobiles entered the highways and traffic jams grew worse.

Compounding the traffic problem was the booming economy and the resulting high wage that enabled most suburban families to buy a second car. New housing developments usually were distant from established shopping areas, schools, and playgrounds. Since there usually were no pavements along dangerously busy roads, mothers drove children to school, Little League practice, and after-school clubs.

Isolated shopping centers, called malls and surrounded by acres of parking lots, started a meteoric growth in the 1950s. Huge new merchandising plazas vied for customers, all arriving by automobile. Two huge New Jersey shopping centers that attracted national attention in the 1960s were built at Cherry Hill and Paramus. Those two would be prototypes for dozens more throughout the state and the nation.

On summer weekends, drivers inched toward the Jersey Shore or North Jersey lakes along antiquated highways. Increasing numbers of trucks each day jammed the highways between New York and Philadelphia. Roads became hopelessly clogged. The "superhighways" of the 1920s and 1930s became the concrete nightmares of the early 1950s.

Governor Alfred Driscoll struggled to solve the glut of automobiles and trucks. His omnipresent stumbling block was the extremely tight state budget. When he began his second term as governor in 1950, the total state spending was only about $160 million annually. There was no way to build needed thoroughfares with traditional funding. Driscoll pushed through two major Bond issues to construct the New Jersey Turnpike and the Garden State Parkway.

Rapidity, Beauty, And Safety

The first New Jersey Turnpike contracts were approved in 1950. Simultaneously, the new Delaware Memorial Bridge was being built across the Delaware River near Wilmington. By 1952, the Turnpike linked US Route 46, near the George Washington Bridge, with the bridge across the Delaware. The trip from New York to Wilmington that once took most of a day now lasted two-and-one-half hours. South

Hundreds of millions of dollars in state-backed bonds dramatically rebuilt New Jersey's public colleges and universities between 1950 and 1970. The Rutgers campus at Newark (top) expanded constantly within sight of the city skyline. At the Kean estate in Union, ground was broken in April 1956 for a totally-new Newark State College (now Kean University). The Douglass College library (above) was representative of the scores of new structures built on state campuses.

Jersey now had a direct link to southern and western markets, augmented when the Atlantic City Expressway opened in 1962.

The Garden State Parkway, completed from Cape May to Paramus in July 1955, delighted shore-bound motorists. They could move rapidly toward the sun and surf on a highway hailed nationally for both its scenic beauty and its record of safety. The Parkway was extended to the New York Thruway by 1957.

Instantaneous success came to the two toll highways. More than one million vehicles traveled the Turnpike weekly by 1962. Annual revenues on the Garden State Parkway soared from $9 million in 1955 to $22 million in 1961. Plans to widen both highways were carried out, year after year.

The public loved those new roads, happily following them outward, buying homes in new developments, and extending the distances they must drive to work each day. Middlesex, Monmouth, and Ocean counties became the new suburbia. All experienced the severe growing pains faced earlier in northern New Jersey.

Ocean County, fastest growing county in the state, experienced a sevenfold growth between 1950 and 1976. Much of the growth was in homes for older, retired people seeking, in the euphemism of real estate developers, "leisure villages" in or near Toms River and Lakewood.

Unprecedented woes overwhelmed scores of onetime villages in the path of the highways. Sewer plants

Signs of the fading past in the 1950s were the wooden covered bridge at Columbia near Delaware Water Gap and the traffic-clogged street of Newark after any major night-time event. A disastrous flood washed away the bridge in 1955. Newark's decline as an after-dark entertainment center served to ease the traffic jams.

were needed to replace backyard septic tanks. Town water supplies were insufficient. Streets had to be widened to handle increased local traffic. Schools were inadequate.

Police and fire departments had to be doubled, tripled, or sometimes enlarged ten times. Municipal offices had to be expanded and re-expanded to keep up with the demands for local services.

People who moved from the cities to "the country" expected the same services they received in the century-old cities. That cost money. Taxes went up and up. Suburbia became a monstrous headache, no matter how much boosters boasted of economic growth.

War Babies And The Schools

A "baby boom" (as newspapers called it) spread across the nation. Between 1940 and 1950 the state's birth total jumped nearly thirty percent. By 1950 the first of the so-called "war babies" entered kindergarten.

The highway mode of the 1950s was set by completion of the New Jersey Turnpike and the Garden State Parkway. The Turnpike crossed the Hackensack Meadows (above, top) on its long way across the state to the twin spans of the Delaware Memorial Bridge in Salem County (above). The Parkway in Ocean County was quiet — at first — but motorists soon fought for space as they raced toward the Jersey Shore.

Fifty-two passengers flew out of Newark Airport at 3:02 PM on December 16, 1951, headed for Miami. Seven minutes later, all of them, plus a crew of four, were dead when their plane crashed into a residential area of Elizabeth.

One month and six days later, on January 22, 1952, a plane inbound for Newark Airport disappeared from the control tower radar screen at 3:45 PM. It flew low over Elizabeth homes and slammed into a house near the high school. This time twenty passengers and three crewmembers were joined in death by six persons trapped in buildings set on fire by the crash.

Now eighty-five were dead; a "once-in-a-lifetime"

tragedy had become twice-in-five-weeks catastrophes. Then, on February 11, shortly after midnight, a plane took off from Newark, bound for Miami. It crashed at 12:21 AM and burned in the streets of Elizabeth (the photo above pictured the remains of the plane). Three crewmembers and twenty-five passengers died, but a stewardess and thirty-four passengers miraculously survived when the plane sheared in two.

With three wrecks in fifty-seven days, 117 dead, houses burned, and Elizabeth residents terrorized, the airport was closed until November 1952. Soon after, jet-powered planes replaced the older propeller-driven planes.

Schools were not ready for them.

Schools everywhere — in cities, in towns, in villages — were too small, too distant, or too old-fashioned. Every municipality in 1950 faced dire shortages of teachers, books, supplies, playground space, and money.

After ten years of depression and war, the condition of most school systems approximated 1900 rather than 1950. Sparsely-settled Hunterdon County still had thirty-two one-room schoolhouses in 1945, and the county's several small rural high schools were a throwback to education before World War I. Schools in agricultural South Jersey were as bad or worse.

Conditions were desperate in most cities. Newark had experienced little school construction after 1912; all but one of its seven high schools were built before World War I. Forty-five of the city's sixty-five

elementary grade schools were built before 1919.

With public education in such a shambles, the state legislature appointed an emergency School Aid Commission, in 1950, to seek solutions. Two years later, the Commission warned chaos was imminent unless more state funds could be found for public education. That warning would return, again and again, year after year, to haunt New Jersey politicians.

The 1952 report also warned inequitable distribution of state funds increasingly shortchanged city children.

Anything For Education

New Jersey public school enrollment skyrocketed from 758,000 in 1954 to 1,260,000 in 1964. Even though towns raised more than a billion dollars in local taxes for school construction in that period, nearly ten percent of the state's pupils, in 1964, still attended school on split sessions or in a substandard classroom.

Education experienced a demoralizing shock, on October 4, 1957, when a stunned United States learned the Soviet Union had zoomed a satellite, called *Sputnik*, into outer space. Frantic at being so clearly beaten by Russia, most American politicians looked for a scapegoat and blamed public schools for not teaching subjects for a space age. In an effect to "catch up," the federal government granted huge sums of money for science and mathematics.

The space race provided the competition and urgency Americans understood, particularly when the national economy was at a peak. Schools enjoyed high popularity, at least until the zooming tax bills came in. New school buildings became sources of local pride. Teacher salaries rose rapidly. New Jersey's expenditure per pupil rose to the second highest in the nation, in 1964, with nearly all of the cost paid for by local property taxes. The state ranked 45th in state aid to education.

When Newark opened its new Barringer High School in 1964, the cost of $7 million set a state record. Elsewhere, in rural and suburban areas, forty-eight new regional high schools were built between 1950 and 1964, consolidating small high schools into major school complexes. Regional high schools provided rallying points for local pride and gave suburbia ample classrooms, gymnasiums, libraries, and auditorium facilities.

Productivity At The Crossroads

Mounting property tax bills prompted many suburban towns and crossroads villages to woo industry. Brochures extolled the advantages of the open fields, the uncluttered roads, and the fresh air.

Industrialists were eager to desert the cities. They accepted suburbia's invitations, fleeing city problems (for which they were mainly responsible) as many of their workers had done before them. Farmers pushed the price of their vegetable patches upward. By 1980, industries paid $50,000 to $70,000 or more for an acre of suburban or rural land zoned for industrial use.

Industry spread grandly across the former farmlands. Architect's dreams became industrial palaces, landscaped for a "campus look." These "country" workplaces had no bus or train links; highways provided the only tie to employees' homes.

Industry became common in areas where it had not appeared before 1950 — in rural sections of Morris and Somerset counties, in Warren and Hunterdon, and outlying parts of Bergen, Passaic, and Union counties. The New Jersey Turnpike provoked a radical industrial spurt in the Delaware River valley south of Trenton. South Jersey promoters constantly stressed how industry could flower on land once set aside for asparagus shoots, tomato vines, and apple orchards.

Hunterdon County's not enviable reputation as the leader in one-room schools evoked nostalgia in 1945 when photographer Harry Dorer of the *Newark Sunday Call* visited one of them. Kindergarten children mingled with eighth graders outside the school. Inside, a stove provided pupils with all the heat needed in winter.

The Race For Space

Russia beat the United States into outer space in 1957, triggering a race for space that picked up pace in the 1960s. Russia's initial success did not totally surprise United States scientists, but media and political dismay mounted across the nation.

New Jersey researchers made the basic contribution to all space exploration, for without the transistor — invented by a three-man team in Bell Laboratories at Murray Hill — all space travel would have been impossible.

Other scientists kept New Jersey in the forefront of the Space Age. Miniaturization of electronics components was pioneered especially at Bell Laboratories, RCA, and IT&T facilities in New Jersey. Reaction Motors (Thiokol), then of Denville, conducted much of the original research in necessary rocket fuels.

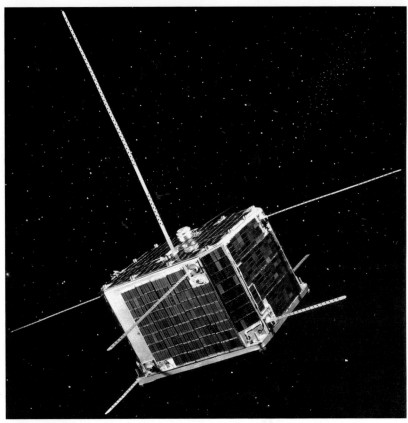

IT&T researchers in Nutley made the satellite (shown above), a space machine designed to yield accurate measurements of the earth. RCA scientists made Tiros, the first weather satellite. Bell researchers perfected the Telestar (below), the forerunner for modern satellites.

Bell Telephone Laboratories in Murray Hill, one of the world's great research facilities, was opened in 1942. By 1953, when this photograph was taken, the laboratory covered nearly a half million square feet of floor space and employed 3,500 persons. Many electronics advances were made here, most particularly the transistor. The laboratories set a tone for suburban industrial development spreading lawns, large parking lots, and university-like buildings, all set in a splendid rural environment.

The Power Of Gasoline

The wedding of industry and the former farmlands enjoyed a long, blissful honeymoon. Gasoline was plentiful and cheap, automobiles were within the economic reach of every worker, asphalt parking lots could be expanded and re-expanded to fit evermore automobiles turning into the lots.

Industry's move to the country accelerated dependence on automobiles. The Port of New York Authority all but abandoned its interest in movement of people by trains, fixing instead its attention on automobiles, buses, and airplanes. Gasoline had powerful lobbyists.

The federal government also made the automobile its star. It tackled highway stagnation by launching a massive Interstate Highway program in the middle of 1950s. Several sections were allocated to New Jersey, including Interstate Routes 78, 80, 95, 195, 275, and 287.

Few states had more problems building these highways than New Jersey. Route 80 was finished nearly coast to coast before a connecting link through Warren County's mountains was paved from Budd Lake to Delaware Water Gap. It took more than thirty-five years to finish Routes 295 and 287!

Interstate routes were finished rapidly through wide-open, farmland areas, where they were needed least. The portion of Interstate 295 in southwestern New Jersey, as an instance, was completed first in Salem and Gloucester counties, closely paralleling the New Jersey Turnpike in an area of least use. Burlington and Mercer needed the highway, but Interstate 295 was long delayed in those counties.

The romance with concrete continued. Interstate Highway 80, finally completed through northern New Jersey between the George Washington Bridge and Warren County, had traffic three lanes wide in almost unbroken streams every morning and evening at peak rush hours in the 1980s.

Supposedly, the Interstate system handled twenty percent of all automobile and truck traffic in the state. Eventually, that traffic left the wide Interstates and poured into single lane roads or local streets. Then, at traffic lights in local towns, the automobiles piled up in long lines, morning and night, idling away gasoline and time. An accident at rush hour could stall traffic for three to five hours.

"The City Is Following Us!"

Endless lines of slow-moving traffic proved beyond doubt that both individuals and industries had, indeed, "moved to the country." By 1976, people began to question if the price was too high.

The *New York Times* documented one case — Montvale, in Bergen County. Montvale's campaign to attract new ratables was successful — too successful. A wide variety of business and industry headquarters moved to town, all welcomed as top-notch taxpayers. Their employees' incoming automobiles severely strained Montvale's roads. The *Times* quoted the local planning board's chairman (who had worked hard to acquire the new taxpayers) as saying, "My God, the city is following us right out here!"

To The Brink Of Bankruptcy

The automobile and highways became both economic boons and environmental scourges. Their rise to preeminence plunged New Jersey's railroads and bus lines into near ruin. Both were in extremely serious trouble as the 1950s waned. Their poor health grew worse.

Railroads in 1945 were nearly as powerful as they had been in 1900, when railroading was at its zenith. Hundreds of thousands of daily commuters still rode trains to Newark, New York, Elizabeth, Paterson, Camden, Philadelphia, and other centers of commerce and industry. More than eighty percent of all freight originating in the New York metropolitan area in 1945 was cleared in and out of giant freight yards in Essex, Bergen, and Hudson counties.

The powerful Pennsylvania Railroad sped its heralded trains across the center of the state; scarcely five minutes passed at any time in the day or night without a Pennsylvania passenger or freight train roaring past, towed by modern electric or diesel locomotives. No tracks in the nation were busier than the Pennsylvania line between Newark and Trenton.

Elsewhere, the West Jersey and Seashore Railroad

Death Of A Shipyard

It had been the biggest shipyard in the world, made more than 500 vessels, was a mighty force in winning World War II, and made the world's first nuclear-powered vessel of any kind. Yet New York Shipbuilding Corporation died in 1967. The reasons likely never will be known.

New York Ship started at Camden in 1899, after first hoping to build on Staten Island (hence the name). Its first vessel was a freighter. In 1906 the yard built the cruiser **Washington** *for the Navy, that would become the Camden firm's best customer.*

World War I shot New York Ship into world leadership. Battleships and cruisers slid down its ways and sailed to distant battles. World War II brought renewed vitality; the yard's aircraft carriers were nicknamed the "Sun-setters" (for sinking Japan's "Rising Sun").

The Navy cancelled seventy-five contracts in 1946, but the company appeared very much alive. It built the first nuclear ship, the Savannah *(shown above), in the late 1950s.*

New York Ship's gross business exceeded $100 million in 1958 and 1959. Despite good profits in 1965 and 1966, the company owners shocked Camden in 1967 by announcing that New York Ship would shut its ways forever.

Interstate highways crept across the state in the 1960s.
A construction foremen (upper right) studied blueprints for the ramp where Route 287 and 78 would link at Pluckemin. Route 78 (upper left) was then just a long, wide path through Warren Township woods.
The hard rock of the Orange Mountains (above) challenged the builders of Route 280.
In time the graceful circles of the interchanges, such as that on Route 78 at Bloomsbury (below), were ready.

dominated southern New Jersey, racing its trains to Atlantic City, Cape May, and other points through all the southern counties. Northern New Jersey's Lackawanna Railroad was hailed as one of the finest commuter facilities in the nation. Its rival, the Erie, while occasionally damned for its failures, provided excellent commuting and freight services for Bergen and Passaic counties.

Wherever rails did not reach, veteran travelers usually relied on dependable bus service. The buses had more leeway than the trains, but they also followed rigidly-set routes between where people lived and where they worked or shopped. People from Bloomfield normally rode a bus to Newark; people from Haddonfield rode buses into Camden. It was cheap, rapid, sensible, and practical — in 1950.

Suburbia's new homes, industries, and shopping centers completely shattered the old transportation patterns. Neither buses nor trains served the new industries or shopping centers; a new "country" factory might have 1,000 employees coming from 350 scattered locations, some of them commuting fifty to sixty or more miles a day. Increasing numbers of people also abandoned the trains and buses to drive into the cities, hoping to be liberated from "regimentation."

Decreasing numbers of passengers and falling freight consignments forced bus lines and railroads to the brink of bankruptcy by 1960. The United States, aspiring to walk a man on the moon, ignored the challenge of moving millions of earthbound earth people rapidly and inexpensively.

The once-proud Pennsylvania merged with New York Central Railroad in 1964, and the result was a tragic example of how mismanagement could bring a once-mighty railroad to ruin. In 1969, Penn Central stock sold for $80; two years later it was nearly worthless.

Falling revenues forced the Erie and Lackawanna railroads to merge in 1960. The merger did not end or lessen the problems. Train cancellations and archaic rolling stock eventually plagued the Erie-Lackawanna to the point of financial collapse and bankruptcy.

So it went everywhere with rapid transit. The State of New Jersey began underwriting many bus lines in the 1960s. Bankrupt railroads were merged in the 1970s into federal government operations. The passenger service was known as Amtrak, and the freight service was called Conrail.

There were a few bright spots in rapid transit. The New Jersey legislature finally forced the Port of New York Authority to assume more responsibility for rail movements as well as for the bus service that the Port Authority encouraged by building its massive bus terminal at 8th Avenue and 40th Street in New York. More than 250,000 daily passengers rode in and out of the bus terminal by 1980.

The Authority took over the worn-out dirty Hudson & Manhattan Railroad in 1962 and, in time, started to run modern air-conditioned cars between Newark, Jersey City, and New York. The new system was called PATH, an acronym for Port Authority TransHudson.

Downstate, the Delaware River Port Authority pioneered a fully-automated rail system between Lindenwold in Camden County and Camden, and then on across the Benjamin Franklin Bridge to downtown Philadelphia. The system began operation in the middle 1960s, using trains fully automated to start and stop, pick up speed, or slow down, with an operator standing by only in case the mechanized controls failed. Even ticket purchases were automated.

Hope For A City

As the highways lured people and industry to suburbia, New Jersey cities slid downward toward disaster. All of them began to decline during the late 1930s, but the booming economy of World War II masked the nature and extent of the decay. After the war, industrialists and storeowners whispered plans to flee. Every move out meant another stab for a city. The wounds were visible as early as 1950, but the illusion of prosperity lingered.

Newark had a radiant burst of hope, in December 1954, when the Mutual Benefit Life Insurance Company announced it would build a new $10 million, twenty-story headquarters in downtown Newark, the city's first major construction in twenty-five years. Newspaper headlines jubilantly lauded the company's decision not to desert the city, proclaiming Mutual Benefit's decision to be the start of a "new" Newark.

A year later, the Prudential Insurance Company, Newark-centered since its founding in 1875, began a twenty-four-story white marble and glass home office, flanked by two seven-story wings. Between 1954 and 1957 nearly $250 million in public and private money was committed to rebuild the "new Newark."

Public agencies poured additional hundreds of millions of dollars into Newark. The Port of New York and New Jersey Authority (the "New Jersey" was added in the 1960s) handsomely improved Port Newark and its adjacent twin, Port Elizabeth.

Railroading's heyday was in the early 1950s, when railroad yards in Hoboken and Jersey City were filled with passenger and freight trains. Commuting was the way of life in scores of towns; passengers bound for city jobs waited morning and night on station platforms.

Railroading's demise was accelerated by the flood of automobiles and trucks that crossed bridges or drove through tunnels on the way to Philadelphia or New York. The busiest of all interstate links was the Lincoln Tunnel at Weehawken. Day and night, long lines of vehicles eased up or down the long approach ramp, moving into the lines of traffic that led to or from the attractions of New York City.

The Port Authority totally rebuilt Newark Airport making it one of the finest air facilities in the world. Newark's western hill glowed with new educational buildings for Rutgers, New Jersey Institute of Technology, Essex County College, and the sprawling complex of the New Jersey College of Medicine and Dentistry.

Tempers On The Boil

On the glassy surface, Newark seemed to be on its way up. The appearance was deceiving. Behind the facade of new construction and the dreams of the headlines, New Jersey's foremost city decayed faster than ever.

Fleeing businesses and industries took ratables off the city's tax rolls. As the leading businesses left, so did much of the pride and leadership they had created. Additionally, Newark was burdened by many government-owned areas and buildings — the large Essex County parks, the college and university campuses, Port Newark, Newark Airport, and many state,

county, and federal offices.

All of these were valuable assets, but they paid no city taxes. All relied on such city-paid services as streets, police, and fire protection.

County and state residents who benefited from the Newark-based parks and other facilities felt no obligation to share in local costs.

Worst of all, Newark's substandard housing deteriorated. Thousands of wretched apartments had no toilets, much less bathtubs. These were the only dwellings available to the rising tide of African American residents who arrived from southern states to seek opportunity.

An explosive situation was building, but in 1966 when Newark celebrated the 300th anniversary if its founding, city leaders congratulated themselves that the city had not been racked by the racial riots and disorders that swept other American cities.

Newark's turn came on July 12, 1967 when rioters tore apart much of the African American area of the city. Riot leaders charged that police and National Guardsmen heightened the disorder by indiscriminate

The photographs above, taken fifteen years apart, zeroed-in on a compelling story of the decline of railroads in New Jersey. The picture on the left showed Camden in 1952, when railroad trains frequently ran into and out of the big yards beside the Camden waterfront. Some locomotives still burned coal, accounting for the thick smoke that nearly obscured the round-house where engines were turned. Fifteen years later, the smoke was gone, but so were most evidences of railroad activity. Trucks now carried much of the freight loaded aboard or taken from ships that tied up at Camden's Delaware River port.

gunfire. When the much-publicized affair ended, twenty-six persons were dead and property damage was estimated in the millions of dollars. (That same night, smaller, simultaneous uprisings occurred in Plainfield and Englewood.)

The 1967 riots forced local political, business, and social service leaders to pay attention to the intense problems that Newark's minority populations suffered. However, a decade later, burned-out buildings and boarded-up store fronts continued as mute symbols of the neglect that had befallen America's cities.

"Concern Halts At City Boundaries"

By 1967, every major New Jersey city — every major city in the nation for that matter — presented the same picture: traffic-choked, littered streets; inadequate parking, appalling, expanding slums, rising crime rates, fleeing industry, soaring taxes, and worst of all, evidences of indifference and confusion on the part of governments at state and federal levels.

"Urban renewal" had become little more than a grandiose term for bulldozing away large areas of the cities. The bulldozers left only large patches of unused land where people once found homes, no matter how wretched. Sections of some cities, such as

in Newark, appeared to have received a heavy aerial bombing rather than any of the purported benefits of "renewal."

The Governor's Economic Recovery Commission, a panel of state leaders appointed in 1976 to study the state's serious economic depression, stressed the circle tightening the state's city populations:

> Most of the remaining [city] residents are confronted with loss of employment opportunities. They turn to unemployment compensation and ultimately to welfare (which adds to public cost burdens) because they haven't the means to follow the flight of jobs out of the cities.
>
> New Jerseyans are concerned with the human environment but, in too many respects, that concern seems to halt at the boundaries of our older cities — within which the environment is in a state of severe degradation and people are visibly suffering.
>
> This is a condition no state can afford to ignore.

The condemnation of "concerned New Jerseyans" was little more than rhetoric by 1980. Finding a way to weave city economic and social existence into the overall fabric of the state remained the most serious challenge facing New Jersey.

327

Chapter Fifteen - Adapting To A Changing World

United States			New Jersey
		1966	Sales Tax Approved
		1970	NJ DEP created
Arabs cut off oil supply	1973	1973	Long gasoline lines
America celebrates	1976	1976	State income tax begins
200th birthday		1978	Pinelands becomes 1st
Americans taken	1979		national reserve
hostage in Iran			
Arabs cut back oil	1979	1979	Price of gasoline tops
supplies			$1/gal
President Carter	1981		
negotiates release of		1983	NJ Transit begins train
hostages			& bus commuter lines
Berlin Wall comes down	1989		
Clean Air Act	1990		
Persian Gulf War	1991	1991	NJ-originated weapons
Dissolution of USSR	1991		used in war
		1994	1st NJ woman governor
Congress votes to bring	1998		takes office
USS New Jersey to NJ		2001	*USS New Jersey* opens
			for visitors in Camden
9/11 attacks on World	2001	2001	NJ commuters die in
Trade Center and			collapse of Twin Towers
Pentagon			
War on Terrorism	2001		
War on Iraq	2002		
9/11 commission	2004	2004	Former NJ Gov Tom
releases report			Kean chairs commission

As New Jersey prepared to join the rest of the country in celebrating the bicentennial of the Declaration of Independence, most New Jerseyans seemed to be relatively content. The divisive Vietnam War was finally over; wounds were beginning to heal. Patriotism timidly returned. Bicentennial celebration plans were in the works. The plans ranged from complex city events to simple backyard get-togethers, but America — decked in red, white, and blue right down to the flower gardens — would be ready to celebrate on July 4, 1976. There would be parades, speeches, barbecues, and — of course — fireworks, lots of fireworks.

All was not rosy in New Jersey, however. The state had ignored some of its problems for far too long; it would have to face them soon.

People Make Their Problems

There were the city problems to deal with, of course, but now many of the city problems had also extended outward from the cities. By 1975, New Jersey's population reached about 7.2 million, close to double the pre-World War II total. People so concentrated created or compounded problems merely by living close together in such a small area.

For one thing, the crowding brought New Jersey

How High Can It Go?

New Jersey motorists experienced a rude awakening in 1973 when gasoline suddenly became exceptionally scarce. Drivers grumbled over the consequent price rise, but found adjusting their budgets far preferable to waiting on long lines or, worse, doing without gasoline. Suburban New Jerseyans really had no choice; the automobile had become an indispensable part of their lives.

Over the remainder of the twentieth century and into the twenty-first, fuel conservation fluctuated. Some motorists conscientiously strove to be frugal; others never

bothered. Some were careful because they couldn't afford not to be; others refused to give up their powerful, gas-guzzling trucks and SUVs. Many took advantage of the strengthening transit system. The car industry responded with more fuel-efficient vehicles. Progress was made, but not enough.

Some expected the War in Iraq to lower oil prices, but during the summer of 2005, in the third year of the war, oil prices hit a new record-high. Americans, New Jerseyans most definitely included, were still much too dependent on gasoline.

Trenton underwent remarkable change in the 1960s when new structures provided modern accommodations for the State Library, State Museum, an education headquarters, and buildings for labor, industry, agriculture, and environmental control. All needed large parking lots for a rising tide of state employees.

crises in water and air pollution. The state reacted in the 1960s with antipollution laws as tough as any in the nation. Both industrialists and labor leaders blamed a deepening recession that began in 1973 partially on those laws, claiming they forced industry out of state. As energy supplies grew scarce by 1976, some of the regulations were at least temporarily relaxed.

Suburbia's nearly complete reliance on the automobile precipitated a totally new kind of crisis, in the winter of 1973-4, when Arab nations temporarily cut off petroleum supplies.

As gasoline became scarcer, motorists lined up at service stations to wait hours for a few gallons of precious fuel. For the first time, there was chilling awareness that the gasoline pumps might run dry and a realization of what the flight from mass transportation had brought.

Then, the Arabs relented and gasoline flowed again, at steeply higher prices. Arab embargoes were forgotten; Americans had plenty of money for the gasoline that had risen 200 to 300 percent in price in fifteen years.

Long before the oil shortage, the state faced a critical shortage of an even more precious liquid — water. A prolonged drought dangerously lowered the levels in existing reservoirs through the early 1950s. Voters approved a $46 million bond issue, in 1958, to build two giant new reservoirs at Round Valley and Spruce Run, both in Hunterdon County.

The reservoirs were ready in 1965, when the state experienced the worst water shortages in its history, but there were no pipelines to deliver the reservoir water to areas in need. Normal rainfalls resumed in 1966; the pipelines were not ready until 1977.

Round Valley and Spruce Run provided a double

Glassboro: LBJ's Summit

President Lyndon B. Johnson was in Washington on June 22, 1967. Soviet Prime Minister Aleksei Kosygin was in New York. They agreed to talk, if a halfway place could be found for a "Summit Meeting."

The place was found: the president's home on the campus of Glassboro State College (now Rowan University). Johnson and Kosygin met for three days, starting June 23. Glassboro was the center of world attention; feelings of good will radiated throughout the nation.

Glassboro proved to be a personal as well as an international summit for Johnson. When he became President, after the assassination of President John F. Kennedy in 1963, the United States had about 20,000 military personnel in Vietnam. By June 1967, the total exceeded 400,000.

Johnson's popularity plummeted. Students on college campuses began protests, usually peaceful, and on October 21, 1967 hundreds of New Jersey students joined a throng of 35,000 in a peace march at Washington.

Recognizing that the Vietnam War probably made his re-election impossible, Johnson withdrew as a candidate in March 1968. Violence erupted that year; both Dr. Martin Luther King and Senator Robert F. Kennedy were assassinated. Colleges seethed with dissent.

New Jersey voters showed a startling reversal of sentiment in 1968. Johnson had won the state in 1964 by a margin of 903,828 votes; Richard M. Nixon took New Jersey in 1968 by 61,261 votes — a switch of 965,089 votes in a four-year period! In 1972, Nixon swept New Jersey by a 743,291 vote margin.

Overwhelmed by the Watergate scandal, Nixon resigned on August 9, 1974, after the House Judiciary Committee headed by Congressman Peter Rodino of Essex County recommended impeachment. Nixon's two strongest committee supporters were Congressmen Charles Sandman of Cape May County and Joseph Maraziti of Morris.

benefit. The stored water was the first priority, but the reservoirs also served as parklands, open to the public for swimming, fishing, and boating. This was significant; reservoirs in the past had high fences to keep the public out.

Reservoirs, parklands, educational pressures, traffic problems, air and water pollution — New Jersey faced all of these and then some, in 1975. Thirty years had passed since World War II ended. Many things had gone radically wrong. New Jersey was in trouble.

Who Will Pay The Piper?

New Jersey's legislative halls seethed with anger, frustration, and fear on July 1, 1976. Ironically, the 1976 emotions stemmed from taxes, much as 200 years before, and because of the emotions, New Jersey faced the prospect of no budget — and therefore no means of conducting government.

The task of a 1976 budget was more explainable than solvable. The State Constitution required a balanced annual budget, but on June 30, 1976 the budget of $2.8 billion fell short of balance by about a billion dollars. The fiscal year ended at midnight on June 30, giving legislators a choice: raise taxes or close down the state.

New Jerseyans awakened the next morning to a state in a non-budget paralysis. Except for absolutely necessary services, state functions ceased. All public schools closed immediately, the first such closure ever known in the United States. The showdown finally came in the extended war of nerves between Democratic Governor Brendan T. Byrne and the two houses of legislature, both heavily weighted with members of his own party.

Three dreaded words resounded through Trenton: *State Income Tax.* Byrne risked his political future by insisting New Jersey must enact one. Legislators, fearful of losing their seats, twisted, compromised, and sought a way out, exactly as they had been doing for fifteen months. Opponents of income taxes, from legislators to newspaper editors, suggested Byrne must be called "One Term Byrne."

The tricky game of tax dodge played in New Jersey for decades, usually stalemated by enacting or increasing "nuisance taxes" and by keeping state services at one of the lowest levels in the nation. That worked for a half century, in an era when expectations were slight and pressures were minimal for state services and state financial support.

However, New Jerseyans demanded — and got

— ever-increasing state services as the 1950s wore on into the 1960s and 1970s. They wanted better schools and colleges, better roads, better pollution controls, better seaside jetties, and more "law and order." New Jersey political leaders, in turn, sought constantly to avoid the old adage that whoever danced must "pay the piper."

Time after time, legislators put off New Jersey's day of financial reckoning by a series of bond issues after World War II. (Voters rarely rejected any of them.) That "have now, pledge tomorrow" system of state bond financing built highways, revolutionized higher education, bought parkland, constructed reservoirs, acquired recreational land, and partially rebuilt prisons and state mental hospitals. It worked handsomely, but it hid the fact that eventually someone must pay.

Taxes always have hung over New Jersey like an ominous cloud. For more than three centuries, local property taxes paid for local services (schools, streets, water, sewers, garbage collection, etc.). Wealthy towns could have excellent services. Poor towns had to accept inferior services.

A few political leaders openly admitted, as early as the 1930s, that New Jersey needed a sound tax system. Republican Governor Harold G. Hoffman pushed a sales tax through the legislature in 1935 to underwrite increased costs created by the Depression. Anguished wails by taxpayer groups and newspaper editors across the state forced repeal of the tax within four months. Legislators from then on approached state taxes as if they were handling a loaded bomb.

Drink, Drive, Gamble? Pay Taxes

State budgets rose constantly, from $80 million in 1946 to more than $2 billion in 1975. To keep the state afloat, and to meet constitutional requirements that every annual budget must be balanced, many so-called "nuisance taxes" were inflicted on the public.

Levies were placed on alcoholic beverages, gasoline, motor vehicle licenses, cigarettes, racetrack betting, inheritances, and on a variety of businesses. Many businessmen, in the late 1950s and 1960s, labeled the industrial taxes as "Jersey Lightning;" there was no way of knowing when or where the next bolt might strike.

The nonpolitical New Jersey League of Women Voters surveyed state taxes in 1957. The League concluded: "Unless you smoke, drink, play the horses,

VOL. CXXII . . No. 42,137   © 1973 The New York Times Company

SANDMAN DEFEATS CAHILL IN NEW JERSEY'S PRIMARY; DEMOCRATS SELECT BYRNE

Governor William T. Cahill's support of a state income tax cost him a stunning upset loss in his party's primary election. Charles Sandman, antitax, was in turn overwhelmed by Democrat Brendan T. Byrne, at first noncommittal on the tax. However, despite later strong advocacy of an income tax, Byrne (represented below as standing on a strong fiscal platform) won re-election in 1977 by a 300,000 majority.

drive a car, or die, you, as an individual, pay no taxes directly to the state." The League suggested that a state income tax would be the most equitable tax for New Jerseyans. No politician seconded the motion.

Governor Richard J. Hughes convinced a Democratic legislature to enact a sales tax in 1966, at a rate of three percent. Income tax supporters protested that a sales tax struck most unfairly at poor people. Previous taxes continued, of course, with smokers, drinkers, drivers, and gamblers — the old dependables — paying rising rates.

The income tax continued to be rejected year after year. Then, Governors William T. Cahill, a Republican, and Brendan T. Byrne, a Democrat, both risked their political careers by strongly advocating a state income tax. Cahill's stand cost him his own party's renomination for a second term in 1973.

State government came to a virtual halt in 1975 when legislators, Republican and Democrat alike, agonized for weeks over the merits and faults of Governor Byrne's income tax proposals. Finally the legislature voted "no." Drastic cuts in government spending necessarily followed.

The deep cuts of 1975 merely postponed the crisis. The most urban state in the union needed a reasonable, fair tax program. It was not a matter of the state's residents being unable to bear taxes, for in 1976 New Jersey was second only to Alaska among all states in per capital income.

Closing The School Doors

Taxes roared back on center stage through a back door in the summer of 1976. The State Supreme Court ruled that every school district in New Jersey had to provide a "thorough and efficient education," and it ordered the state government to help hard-pressed local school boards get necessary funds for the program.

The legislators protested, stalled, and occasionally debated the issue rationally as their tempers rose to match the heat of late June 1976. Without state funding, all the state's public schools would be closed completely on July 1, 1976.

Even the legislature and the lobbyists could not withstand the fury of state residents and the ridicule of national headline. On July 9, a bitterly-divided legislature squeezed through a hastily-drawn bill authorizing a state income tax of two percent (rising to 3.5 percent) with agreement that the tax would end in June 1978. Byrne had won — or had he?

The schools reopened immediately. Simultaneously, well-financed antitax groups marshaled forces to fight for repeal of the income tax measure. Somewhere, in the maze of charges and counter-charges, bond issues and state needs, there had to be fair and reasonable answers.

A powerful answer came in 1977 when despite his vigorous support of an income tax, Byrne won a 300,000-vote victory over antitax Republican Raymond Bateman. Byrne had flaunted tradition and the public appreciated his courage. In December 1977,

the income tax became permanent.

The Old Order Changes

Votes on tax matters hinged on legislator awareness that angry voters might not return a lawmaker to office. Political maneuvering to retain office always has been a pertinent part in New Jersey government or — for that matter — any government entity from municipal to federal.

Through the years, New Jersey legislators shaped and reshaped voting districts to benefit whichever party held office. However, for 190 years after the state's first constitution in 1776, no reforming of district lines ever affected the time-honored custom that each of the state's counties must have one State Senator and two Assemblymen.

Rural counties dominated the state under such a system. Their sympathies were not geared to the city areas in the 1950s and 1960s, as urban crises accumulated far faster than attempts at solution. The problem was not New Jersey's alone; farm areas controlled much of government, including Congress, since the nation began and still hold a powerful influence in Washington.

The United States Supreme Court struck down the rural domination of state legislatures in its landmark "one man, one vote" decision of 1964, requiring that representation in state bodies must be based on population rather than on counties or on other whims of blocs of politicians.

New Jersey voters endorsed the Supreme Court philosophy in a November 1966 referendum. By 1973, the State Legislature was finally apportioned according to population, with forty Senators and eighty Assemblymen. Rural politicians no longer dominated the state's highest lawmaking chambers. At the same time, powerful old-time "county bosses" found their abilities to "deliver the votes" diminishing.

"Amateur" Conservationists Lead

Within New Jersey's changing political system, there emerged a core of legislators who fought to stem the rising environmental evils in a state hastening toward widespread overcrowding. They were responsible to a public that recognized far sooner than its political representatives that something had to be done to control wetlands, to combat pollution of air and water, and to face up to a state being wasted by "development."

Admirers of Morris County's Great Swamp owe a debt of gratitude to the Port of New York Authority. Until the Authority decided in 1959 that the swamp was the perfect place for a giant new jetport, the area was ignored and shunned. Unquestionably, the Great Swamp would have been lost in time to garbage dumps and housing developments. The jetport proposal solidified pro-Swamp support.

The Great Swamp history dates to about 40,000 years ago when a massive glacier retreated and left behind a thirty-mile long lake (the vanished Lake Passaic). Today the region is a place of great beauty, saved as a National Wildlife Refuge that encompasses 7,500 acres.

The late 1960s and the 1970s became a supreme time of environmental awakening. "Environmentalist" in earlier times generally meant only a professional social scientist interested in the effect of immediate surroundings (such as a home or community) on an individual or a group. By the mid-1960s, the emphasis among most people swung to despair over what humans were doing to their surroundings. It did not take a college degree to know that an environmentalist also was anyone who recognized that natural surroundings had to be respected and preserved.

"Amateur" environmentalists came in full perspective in late 1959 when the Port of New York Authority announced plans to build a jetport in Morris County's Great Swamp. Outraged local residents, joined by conservationists and environmentalists from around the nation, outfought and outmaneuvered their powerful antagonist, using enthusiasm and imagination to match Port Authority millions. The jetport was rejected. The region became the Great Swamp National Wildlife Refuge.

Similarly, a loosely-organized environmental coalition battled the even mightier Army Corps of Engineers to a standstill in the 1970s. The Corps planned a huge reservoir and recreational area in northwestern New Jersey. Conservationists went to work; by 1975 it was evident the dam would not be built, barring a catastrophic water shortage in the future.

New Jersey's conservationists were far more numerous than politicians suspected. Voters put their money where their concerns were in 1961 when they vigorously endorsed a landmark $60 million "Green Acres" bond issue to acquire land for recreational and conservation purposes. Voters continue to approve Green Acres bond issues and money for clean water, sewers, and other environmental needs.

Conservationists enjoyed their biggest victory in 1970 when the legislature created a Department of Environmental Protection. Until that time, the "environment" had been in a catchall Department of Conservation and Economic Development. Obviously, the same department could not both conserve and develop. The new department focused attention on matters that twenty years before were dismissed as of concern only to "nature lovers" or bird watchers.

The Pinelands National Reserve

The name Pinelands, or Pine Barrens, evokes varying thoughts and images. To travelers, it's a seemingly endless wooded area — where the Jersey Devil might lurk — on either side of the Garden State Parkway. Environmentalists recognize it as America's first national reserve guarding the Kirkwood-Cohansey Aquifer, believed to hold up to 17 trillion gallons of pure water, and myriad flora and fauna. Outdoors lovers enjoy the numerous recreational opportunities provided by the area's many state parks and forests. To blueberry lovers, it's that fruit's birthplace. All marvel that it comprises about one fourth of the most densely populated state in the nation.

Melting glaciers and ocean erosion created the Pinelands relatively level million acres. Sandy soils, acidic water, and frequent fires created a unique environment in which only those plants and animals that could adapt survived. Early colonists called the area the "Pine Barrens" because they considered its only value to be lumber.

The Pinelands is comprised of 56 towns and villages with over 700,000 permanent residents; farms; vast unbroken forests of pine, oak, and cedar; and the Pine Plains with its Pygmy Forest where the trees may attain a height of only about four feet at maturity. About a quarter of the Pinelands is covered by wetlands including rivers, streams, bogs, hardwood and cedar swamps, and pitch pine lowlands. Here there are more than 1,200 plant and animal species, almost 100 of which are threatened or endangered. State Forests include Wharton, Brendan T. Byrne (formerly Lebanon), Bass River, Penn State, and Belleplain. Batsto, Whitesbog, and Smithville Historic Villages demonstrate industries and ways of 19th century life. Blueberries and cranberries grow in abundance, providing livelihood for many Pinelands residents.

Congress established the Pinelands National Reserve in 1978. The original boundaries, loosely set by botanists, were changed to allow efficient management. The reserve now also includes parts of Barnegat Bay, the barrier islands, Delaware Bay, and the Maurice River.

The National Park Service defines a reserve as "an area of nationally significant resources that are protected through a program of local land use management supported by federal financial and technical assistance."

A year after the federal government established the Pinelands National Reserve, New Jersey passed the Pinelands Protection Act. The Pinelands Commission was established to develop and implement a plan to safeguard the reserve. Fifteen members were appointed to the commission — seven by the governor, one by each of the seven Pinelands counties (Burlington, Atlantic, Ocean, Cumberland, Camden, Cape May, and Atlantic), and one by the US Secretary of the Interior. The commission's Pinelands Comprehensive Management Plan went into effect on January 16, 1981. The Plan protects the Pinelands and guides future development. The commission implements the Plan with the help of local, state, and federal government. The mission of the commission is to preserve, protect, and enhance the natural and cultural resources of the reserve and encourage compatible economic and other human activities consistent with that purpose.

Pure water, parks and forests, wetlands, wildlife, mystery, and history — the Pinelands is undoubtedly worth protecting. Those who formed the Pinelands National Reserve were wise, indeed!

Pinelands and Wetlands

New Jersey's greatest environmental victory resulted from Governor Byrne's stubborn insistence that radical actions were needed to preserve the great pinelands in southern New Jersey familiarly called "The Pine Barrens."

The area selected for preservation was mostly in Burlington and Ocean counties, but also spilled over into portions of several other counties. Many towns fell into the region, creating strong opposition from the advocates of "home rule" (wherein local governments set their own policies independent of other towns).

Pro-preservation groups ranged from those who desired to save the region for its unique wildflowers, animals, and reptiles to those who appreciated the potential for parklands, and most telling of all, its huge reservoir of clean, fresh water that underlay the sandy soil. An estimated 17 trillion gallons of water are in that reservoir — enough to create a surface lake 2,000 square miles in area and thirty-seven feet deep.

Byrne led the way, confronting developers who insisted pineland protection would violate municipal and individual landowner rights. The cause received a major boost in 1978 when the United States Secretary of the Interior designated the region as the first National Reservation in the United States. The next year, the New Jersey legislature passed the Pinelands Preservation Act.

Equally important to environmentalists are the state's wetlands, particularly the 245,000 acres of wetland identified in eleven shore counties fronting on the Atlantic Ocean and the Hudson and Delaware rivers. Prior to 1970, developers built indiscriminately in the wetlands, ruining the areas for environmental uses.

The Wetlands Act, adopted in 1970, places supervision of the shore areas in the Department of Environmental Protection. Since then, coastal building has been reduced, but the act contained enough loopholes to permit much questionable construction.

Exit Byrne, Enter Kean

Outspoken Brendan Byrne acted according to deeply-held convictions often in conflict with standard political "wisdom." He demonstrated that a conscientious governor could enact a state income tax (and be re-elected) and he proved that intelligent leadership could bring a measure of agreement in sensitive environmental areas. Even those who remained unconvinced agreed that Byrne's powerful leadership set very high marks for succeeding governors to follow.

State budgets climbed from $2.6 billion in Byrne's first year to $5.1 billion in his eighth and final year. It was the sharpest rise to that time during any two-term governor's rule, presaging a trend of pressures for accelerated state services.

In 1981, New Jerseyans had to choose for governor between two attractive, if sharply contrasting, political leaders — veteran Republican State Assemblyman Thomas H. Kean (pronounced Kane) of Livingston and Democratic United States Congressman James J. Florio of Camden.

Kean, Princeton-educated, wealthy, and patrician, had been elected to the General Assembly five consecutive terms before seeking the Republican nomination for governor in the 1977 gubernatorial election. Kean lost in that primary to Raymond Bateman.

Florio, a Brooklyn-born, high school dropout who earned his General Equivalent Diploma while in the US Navy, graduated from Trenton State College and earned his law degree from Rutgers University. He served in the State Assembly for three terms, and then won election to Congress for seven terms.

Both candidates campaigned vigorously. Voters chose Kean by a scant margin of 1,797 votes out of 2.3 million cast — the closest gubernatorial election in New Jersey history. The official count was not certified until December 21, forty-five days after the election.

Kean made public school education and preservation of the environment primary focal points of his first term. Several of his proposals created major controversy, particularly a proposal inaugurated to permit alternative methods of certifying public school teachers. How to fund large increases in teachers' salaries also created considerable debate.

Kean's progressive policies and his frequent appearances on television as a commentator and as spokesman in the state's tourism ads pleased most New Jerseyans. He was re-elected in 1985 by the greatest margin ever recorded in a race for governor, swamping Democrat Peter Shapiro by 795,000 votes, a mandate if ever a governor received one.

Financially, the state careened through the Kean years. The budgets zoomed upward each year, rising from the $5.1 billion that Kean inherited to $12.1 billion when his two terms ended, a rise of nearly $1

Drumthwacket, The Executive Mansion,
354 Stockton Street (Route 206), Princeton

Drumthwacket *became New Jersey's official governor's mansion in 1981. Since then, the mansion served as primary residence for the families of Governor Florio and Governor McGreevey and part-time residence for Governor Whitman's family. Governor Kean entertained here; Acting Governor DiFrancesco and Acting Governor Codey used it for meetings and receptions.*

Morven *was New Jersey's first official executive mansion. Richard Stockton built it on land he acquired from his grandfather in 1754. Stockton's wife, Annis Boudinot, a poet, named the house after a mythical Gaelic kingdom.* **Morven,** *now a museum, is less than a mile from* **Drumthwacket** *and also on Route 206.*

William Olden bought the property, once owned by William Penn, on which **Drumthwacket** *stands in 1696. His grandson, Thomas Olden, built the small house,* **Olden House,** *still standing on the front of the property. Charles S. Olden, born in* **Olden House** *in 1799, built the main, center section of* **Drumthwacket** *in the mid 1830s. Serving as New Jersey Governor from 1860 to 1863, Charles S. Olden became the first governor to live in* **Drumthwacket.** *He died in 1876.*

Industrialist and banker Moses Taylor Pyne bought the property after Olden's wife, Phoebe, died in 1893. The deed used the name **Drumthwacket,** *Scottish Gaelic for "wooded hill." Pyne was a Princeton graduate who remained active in the university and pushed for Woodrow Wilson to be its president. He added the two-story wings to the east and west and extensively landscaped the grounds. He died in 1921.*

Russian immigrant Abram Spanel purchased **Drumthwacket** *after the death of Pyne's wife, Margaretta Stockton, 20 years later. Spanel was a scientist who produced rubber products crucial to the WW II effort. His engineering staff lived at* **Drumthwacket,** *and many of his inventions were conceived here.*

Mr. & Mrs. Spanel sold **Drumthwacket** *to the State of New Jersey in 1967, with the intention of it becoming the governor's residence. The New Jersey Historical Society accomplished this in the early 1980s by soliciting the funds necessary to renovate the historic mansion.*

billion per year. Early in his first term he signed a bill that raised the income tax.

New Jersey was exceptionally prosperous as the 1980s wound down, keying its industrial prosperity to "high tech" firms rather than traditional "blue collar" factories. Prosperity each year brought large collections in income and sales taxes; in 1990, income tax revenues totaled $2.9 billion, sales taxes produced $3.2 billion.

A Hard Act To Follow

Kean left Trenton after his second term expired to become president of Drew University in Madison, surprising many political pundits who believed he would take a federal appointment in Washington. The same pundits declared that Kean's two terms would be a hard act to follow.

Florio returned from Washington once more to seek the governor's chair. This time he faced Republican James A. Courter, conservative adherent to most Reagan policies. Although an attractive candidate, with a law degree from Duke University, a stint in the Peace Corps, and election to six terms in the United States Congress, Courter and his advisers ran a peculiarly inept campaign. Florio won a smashingly-easy victory by a margin of 543,000 votes

Florio faced vast problems from the day of his inauguration in January 1990. The once-proclaimed "surplus" of Kean's last year had melted away. Pressures for budget increases mounted. Tax revenues declined as a severe recession struck the nation, hitting particularly hard at the northeastern states. Federal funds to states had diminished since the start of the Reagan reign in 1981.

Entering Trenton like a whirlwind, Florio stirred controversy and anger. He pushed through a law to ban assault guns, legislation intended to reduce automobile insurance, and — most controversial of all — increases in both the income tax and the state sales tax. The gun ban angered the politically powerful National Rifle Association and his tax increases stirred negative passions across the state.

Florio ran into further complications as the economy stubbornly resisted improvement. "Downsizing" became a household word as many corporations attempted to remain profitable by merging and shutting down no longer needed departments and often entire companies. Many New Jerseyans lost their jobs. Finding new employment often meant a marked cut in pay. Few felt secure about their financial future.

When Herbert Norman Schwartzkopf's son was born, in 1934, he wanted to name him after himself, but he didn't like his own first name. He settled on H. Norman Schwarzkopf.

The senior Schwartzkopf, a West Point graduate, served in World War I. In 1921, he organized the New Jersey State Police and supervised it for 15 years. When the Lindbergh kidnapping fell to the state police because the crime took place in rural New Jersey and kidnapping was not yet a federal offense, he was the chief investigator. He was called back into the Army in 1940 and sent to Iran where he was eventually joined by his family.

H. Norman Schwarzkopf grew up in Lawrenceville and Princeton, New Jersey. He attended public schools there and Bordentown Military Academy. He graduated from West Point in 1956. He served two tours of duty in Vietnam and commanded the US forces in the invasion of Grenada. His many medals and awards include the Silver Star, Bronze Star Medal, Purple Heart, Distinguished Service Medal, Legion of Merit, and Army Commendation Medal.

Brenda Schwartzkopf helped pin the four stars of general on her husband on November 18, 1988. The ceremony, making Schwartzkopf the highest ranking officer in the US Army, took place in the Pentagon's Hall of Heroes.

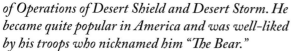

General Schwarzkopf is best known as Commander of Operations of Desert Shield and Desert Storm. He became quite popular in America and was well-liked by his troops who nicknamed him "The Bear."

General H. Norman Schwarzkopf retired in August 1991. His autobiography, **It Doesn't Take A Hero,** *begins with his words, "It doesn't take a hero to order men into battle. It takes a hero to be one of those men who goes into battle." It ends, "I shall always remain confident of the American people's ability to rise to* any *challenge."*

Television War

Early in 1991, New Jerseyans watched in awe as Persian Gulf War live action strikes and battles enfolded on television. Everyday citizens and veterans alike stared with amazement at modern war technology. All were astounded to see American Patriot missiles intercept and destroy Iraq's Scud missiles, Precision Guided Munitions (including Tomahawk missiles and "smart" bombs) find their marks, stealth fighters attack Baghdad targets, and howitzers self-propel themselves into battles — *as they watched!* No veterans of any war had seen the details now exposed by television cameras.

Most Americans supported the war, comforted that the United Nations backed us and convinced Iraq had no right to invade our ally, Kuwait. Besides, the war was successful and short, lasting only a few months.

The Persian Gulf War once again reminded Americans that dependence on the Middle East for oil was dangerous. Why was this still true after so many past warnings? Oil conservation efforts since the 1974 Arab oil cutback had been intermittent and poorly coordinated. The concern Americans exhibited in 1974 waned, and then resurfaced in 1979 when the Arabs again cut back the oil they supplied the United States — once more shaking the nation with shortages, conservation fears, and resolves. As before, the Arabs backed off once prices soared well over $1 a gallon.

Oil prices remained stable through the 1980s, with only a few advances in gasoline conservation. New Jersey city life became more attractive and lured many back to the cities. The establishment of the NJ Transit bus-rail system offered commuting alternatives to automobiles.

This was not enough, however, to compensate for the gas and oil-burning lifestyle that New Jerseyans had reestablished. Thermostat settings crept back up. Few people bothered with the 55 mile-per-hour speed limits on the Interstate Highways. Gasoline use in New Jersey soared throughout the 1980s. When OPEC (Organization of Petroleum Exporting Countries) again cut back oil production in 1990, New Jersey and all of America were totally unprepared, and later relieved, when prices and supply stabilized after the Persian Gulf War.

New Jersey was well connected to the Persian Gulf War. Picatinny Arsenal in Dover supplied weapons. Fort Dix trained reservists, guard members, and Kuwaitis. A New Jerseyan, General H. Norman Schwarzkopf, served as its commander. The Commander of Operations of Desert Shield and Desert Storm, as General Schwarzkopf was officially titled, grew up in Lawrenceville and Princeton. He attended Lawrenceville and Princeton Elementary Schools and Bordentown Military Academy.

A Woman Takes Charge

Christine Todd Whitman was well known to most New Jerseyans before she challenged Governor James Florio in the 1993 governor's race. She had come close to obtaining Senator Bill Bradley's seat in the 1990 election, gathering 49% of the vote.

The most important issue in Whitman's campaign was her promise to cut the state income tax by 30%. Voters appeared to be skeptical; polls continued to show Florio with a comfortable lead right up to Election Day. The polls were wrong, however, Christine Todd Whitman became New Jersey's 50th governor and its first woman to hold the office.

Governor Whitman set out immediately to lower the state income tax. She fulfilled her promise, cutting it by 30% for most taxpayers and completely eliminating it for low-income families. She also low-

In 1996, voters overwhelming approved money to dredge and clean up New Jersey's ports.
Port Camden (upper left) and Port Newark/Elizabeth (upper right) are the state's largest ports. Port Elizabeth specializes in container shipments and uses ExpressRail to transfer the containers from the ship unto a train (lower right). South Jersey Port Corporation owns Port Camden and the much smaller Port Salem (lower left).

A dream became reality on October 18, 1997 with the world premiere of the New Jersey Performing Arts Center in Newark. Since then, more than three and a half million people have enjoyed concerts, ballets, plays, operas, family programs, film festivals, performances by artists from around the world, and special events including Governor Christine Todd Whitman's inauguration.

It began with Governor Kean in 1986. Looking to promote New Jersey's performing arts organizations, he commissioned a consulting firm to study their needs. The commission reviewed existing facilities for potential expansion and or renovation and explored the feasibility of new construction. No satisfactory existing buildings could be found. None were adequate for performances by the New Jersey Symphony Orchestra, the New Jersey State Opera, the various New Jersey dance and theater companies, or national and international touring companies.

On June 30, 1987, the consultants recommended building a new performing arts complex in Downtown Newark. The arts center, they suggested, should become part of a cultural district. It should be located where there was room for new growth to support it — restaurants, retail establishments, and office buildings. It also should be close to people who would attend these performances.

Downtown Newark was ideal! An estimated 4.5 million people lived within a 25-mile-radius of Newark, and it was readily accessible by mass transportation and automobile. Organizations within one-quarter mile of the proposed sites included: Newark Museum, Newark Public Library, Rutgers University, NJ Institute of Technology, Seton Hall Law Center, and Essex County College. The nearby NJ Historical Society, it was suggested, could be (and was in 1997) moved to a new building in the area. The funding of this fantastic project was recommended to be a partnership between government and the private sector.

Governor Kean formally accepted the commission's recommendations in July 1987. The project was underway by April 1988. Generous individual and corporate donations, supplemented by state financing, allowed the purchase of the 12-acre site. Plans for Phase One, a large multi-use hall and a smaller theater, were presented in 1992.

In May of 1993, 1,400 invited guests and the viewing audience of WNBC-TV's Sunday Today witnessed the implosion of old Military Park Hotel — the only major building on the site. Governor Florio, the NJ Symphony Orchestra, and children from each of New Jersey's 21 counties were among those who attended the ground-breaking ceremonies later that year.

Corporate and individual donations continued and the Whitman administration provided an additional construction loan. When Prudential Insurance added 3.5 million to their original 3 million contribution, the NJPAC named the 2,750-seat multi-purpose theater Prudential Hall. The 514-seat theater was named the Victoria Theater in recognition of the Victoria Foundation's contributions.

New Jersey Performing Arts Center has been a remarkable boon for Newark. People now come from all over the world to Downtown Newark to see or participate in performances at the NJPAC.

ered small business corporate taxes and froze property taxes for low-income senior citizens and residents with disabilities.

Necessarily, jobs were lost and projects lost funding. A tax amnesty program replaced some of the needed tax revenue, as did allowing corporations to pay to rename public institutions. (The Garden State Arts Center became the PNC Bank Arts Center and Brendan Byrne Arena the Continental Airlines Arena. Governor Byrne later had a state forest named after him.)

Whitman attempted to make New Jersey more "business friendly" by relaxing many government-imposed regulations. Unions and environmental groups fought back. Her environmental challenges were especially difficult as the state struggled to meet the requirements of the Federal Clean Air Act. HOV (high-occupancy vehicle) lanes were tried, and then closed down when determined unsuccessful. Tougher vehicle emission control was mandated. Newly privatized NJ Division of Motor Vehicles regulated this with stricter emission sensors installed in inspection stations.

Governor Whitman created tough anti-crime legislation and reformed the state's juvenile justice system. She signed "Megan's Law" (community notification when a sex offender is released from prison) and laws requiring violent criminals to serve at least 85% of their sentences.

Decreased federal and state aid to municipalities led to increased property taxes. Property owners voted down school budgets attempting to keep their property taxes within reason. Schools were forced to make drastic spending cuts. To mollify taxpayers, Governor Whitman created a tax rebate program.

Funding public education again became a hot issue, further complicated by the New Jersey Supreme Court ruling that the T & E (thorough and efficient education) legislation of 1976 had not been satisfied. Cities and lower income towns were still not getting a fair education. Whitman voiced support for a "voucher" program that would allow parents to apply some of their tax money toward private school tuition or choose which public school they wished their children to attend. Attempts to improve the education system included implementing complex Core Curriculum Content Standards and Assessments and creating charter schools. To promote higher education, the governor created a college savings program. In 1998, the Supreme Court approved her school-funding plan.

Governor Whitman appointed the state's first African American Supreme Court Justice, the first female State Supreme Court Chief Justice, and the first female Attorney General. She reformed the state's civil justice and welfare systems and created an insurance program for children of low-income families.

During Governor Whitman's administration, voters decidedly approved several referendums. $340,000,000 was set aside for "Green Acres" land acquisition and development, farmland soil and water conservation projects, and recreation and conservation projects. Funding in the amount of $300 million was awarded for dredging and environmental cleanup of the Kill Van Kull, Arthur Kill, and other channels in the New Jersey/New York port area, lake restoration projects, and economic development in the Delaware River and Bay area. Municipalities were provided $200 million in low-interest loans for demolition and disposal of unsafe buildings in urban and rural centers. Half a billion dollars was allocated for rehabilitating and improving the state transportation system, including structurally deficient local bridges. In 1998, voters approved a constitutional amendment dedicating $98 million dollars annually, for State Fiscal Years 1999 to 2009, in sales and use tax revenues for open space, farmland, and historic preservation.

State spending increased by 40% while Ms. Whitman was in office. Her first year's budget dropped slightly from the year before to $15.3 billion dollars. Her last year's, however, spiked to $21.4 billion.

"Christie" Whitman, a successful, popular governor, attracted attention nationally. In 1995, she became the first governor to deliver the opposing response to the State of the Union, urging the return of power to the states. The media speculated she might be candidate for vice president.

She considered a 2000 bid for the US Senate but nixed the challenge, citing a desire to accomplish more as governor. A year later, she accepted President Bush's offer to head the EPA and ended her term as governor on January 31, 2001, a year early. Her cabinet term lasted until May 2003 and included some controversial "Ground Zero" World Trade Center clean-up decisions.

A Weakness in New Jersey's Constitution?

According to the New Jersey Constitution (Article V, Section I, Paragraph 6), the president of the Senate becomes acting governor when the governor

View from Liberty State Park, July 2001

resigns. So — an hour after Christine Todd Whitman left office, on January 31, 2001, Senate President Donald T. DiFrancesco was sworn in as acting governor of New Jersey.

This wasn't his first time — he had taken this oath many times before to fill in for Governor Whitman when she left the state, but it was the first time it would be for more than just a few days. The NJ Constitution requires an election for a vacant governorship unless it occurs during an election year, as 2001 was. Donald T. DiFrancesco would serve the remainder of Christine Todd Whitman's term.

All this added up to an unelected governor serving for almost a full year! He would be an unelected governor who would serve two roles — governor and president of the Senate. (Actually, he would serve a third role for a while — gubernatorial candidate. He withdrew from the race in April after drawing criticism for his business and real estate dealings.)

How could one man manage this? What were the writers of the 1947 Constitution thinking? In most other states the lieutenant governor fills a vacant gov-

ernor's spot. Maybe New Jersey needed a lieutenant governor.

Many worried about the amount of power Donald DiFrancesco would possess. The whole situation just seemed un-American! DiFrancesco, as senator, could propose a bill and vote for it; and then, as governor, sign it into law. New Jersey had long-term acting governors before (the most notable was to complete Woodrow Wilson's unexpired term when he left to become President), but not under the 1947 Constitution that grants so much power to the governor. New Jerseyans worried about all this and more as Acting Governor Donald T. DiFrancesco took office.

Ringside View on Terror

September 11, 2001, a beautiful late summer day, began as any normal Tuesday workday in New Jersey. As usual, commuters headed for work and jets departed from Newark International Airport. Commuters headed for the World Trade Center and passengers bound for San Francisco on United Flight

#93, however, were about to experience the most unusual day of their lives.

Shortly before 9 AM, New Jerseyans rushed to turn on their TVs after hearing a jet had crashed into one of the Towers of the World Trade Center. A few minutes later, they watched in stunned disbelief as another jet crashed into the other Tower. American Flight #11, out of Boston, had crashed into the North Tower of the World Trade Center at 8:47 AM. United Airlines Flight #175, also out of Boston, crashed into the South Tower at 9:03.

When one Tower and then the other crumbled to the ground later that morning, New Jerseyans miserably calculated how many lives could be lost. Many knew people or — worse yet — had relatives who worked in the Towers. "America Under Attack" raced across the bottoms of their television screens as the emergency grounding of all air crafts silenced the skies. New Jerseyans experienced their first enemy attack on US soil since December 7, 1941.

People scrambled to do something. They wanted to help, but how? Parents rushed to schools to pick up their children. Rescue workers headed for the city. Boaters cruised the city shoreline offering rides to stranded commuters. Acting Governor DiFrancesco declared a state of emergency. America watched as emergency personnel dug through the debris, searching for survivors.

As the rescue operation progressed, the survivors waited, some with pictures of missing relatives. Cars sat in New Jersey train stations awaiting drivers that never returned. New Jersey buzzed with stories. One had a sister who missed her flight — on one of the hijacked planes! Another talked to her husband, who was in one of the Towers, by cell phone after the attack, but never again. Yet another cancelled a meeting scheduled in the Trade Center that morning. Others shared tamer stories of horrific exodus from the paralyzed city.

Many New Jerseyans who commuted to the World Trade Center on the morning of September 11 never returned. All the passengers who left Newark International Airport (soon to be renamed Newark Liberty International Airport in honor of those lost on this day) on United Flight #93 died when they crashed in Shanksville, Pennsylvania.

The world had changed forever. Thoughts of the future, and even the present, were shadowed with confusion, doubt, and fear. Desperate for hope and reassurance, New Jerseyans joined all Americans in patriotic solidarity not seen since Pearl Harbor Day.

Mayor Vs. Mayor

Two mayors received the nod from their parties for the 2001 governor's race. Bret Schundler had been mayor of New Jersey's second largest city, Jersey City; Jim McGreevey was the mayor of Woodbridge, New Jersey's 6th largest municipality.

New Jerseyans knew McGreevey well. In 1997, he nearly rendered Christine Todd Whitman a one-term governor.

The mayors squared off as expected, each assuming the usual party agendas. McGreevey, a moderate Democrat, proposed closing the massive state budget deficit by cutting spending, but resisted the promise to not raise taxes until Schundler forced him into it later in the campaign. Schundler promised more services with fewer dollars through good management, citing his lowering of taxes in Jersey City.

Education was also a key issue. Schundler advocated vouchers and income tax credits to help families pay for private schools. McGreevey challenged the effectiveness of this, predicting it would undermine public education and cost the state too much. He proposed a partnership of education, business, labor, and government.

The candidates also debated discontinuing tolls on the Garden State Parkway. Schundler was for it; McGreevey called the plan dishonest. He cited the problem of finding a source of revenue to cover the $600 million existing debt.

McGreevey won decisively with 1,256,853 votes to Schundler's 928,174.

Five Governors in One Week

Acting Governor DiFrancesco's term as senator expired on January 8, 2002, thereby ending his term as acting governor a week before James McGreevey was to take office. The role of acting governor fell to Attorney General John Farmer for a few hours until the new Senate was sworn in that afternoon.

After oaths were administered, the new Senate President was to take over, but who would that be? The new Senate was split at 20 Republicans and 20 Democrats, denying either party claim to president of the Senate. Republican Leader John Bennett and Democratic Leader Richard Codey agreed to split the week's term and each served three and a half days.

To recap, New Jersey had five governors between January 7 and 15, 2002: Donald T. DiFrancesco (outgoing Senate President who served a few weeks short

A Battleship To Restore A City

On October 14, 2001, a ribbon cutting ceremony welcomed the USS New Jersey to its final resting place on the Camden Waterfront. This was the culmination of a many-years-long tough battle — an emotional roller-coaster ride — for a group that just knew the battleship belonged in Camden, New Jersey. The New Jersey in the address was not the area of contention; most had long agreed that the USS New Jersey belonged in the state for which it was named. Some, however, wanted it to be in Bayonne or Jersey City. How could they not see that the USS New Jersey belonged across the river from where it was built — in Camden?

The USS New Jersey was first launched from the Philadelphia Naval Shipyard on the first anniversary of Pearl Harbor Day, December 7, 1942. She served in World War II, the Korean War, the Vietnam War, and as part of President Reagan's 600-ship Navy. After being decommissioned a fourth and final time on February 8, 1991, she was moved to Pugent Sound Naval Yard in Bremerton, Washington.

The endeavor to bring the USS New Jersey to New Jersey began in 1980 when the State of New Jersey established the USS New Jersey Battleship Commission. One necessary step was to get the New Jersey on the Navy's donation list. The commission accomplished this in 1997 by arranging a swap with sister ship, Iowa, which had no takers. (There were four Iowa class ships: USS Iowa BB61, USS New Jersey BB62, USS Missouri BB63, and USS Wisconsin BB64.)

As progress continued, it appeared the commission would choose Bayonne or Jersey City, rather than Camden, as the site for the battleship. When the commission actually did confirm Bayonne as the spot, most accepted this as the final decision. A group of southern New Jerseyans, however, did not. Knowing that the final decision rested with the owner of the ship, the US Navy, the group organized as the Home Port Alliance and approached the Navy with a well-organized proposal. Their efforts paid off — the Navy liked their plan and chose Camden!

The USS New Jersey left Puget Sound Naval Shipyard on September 12, 1999 under tow. The 6,000-mile cruise included a squeeze, with only inches to spare, through the Panama Canal. (A few weeks later, passing through the canal would have been far more complicated, as control of the canal passed from the United States to Panama on December 31.) The battleship arrived in Camden on Veteran's Day 1999.

Restoration work soon began. There was much to do before the scheduled opening date of Summer 2001. "Big J" (as the crew affectionately called the ship) was painted inside and out. Parts of the river bottom were dredged. A closed circuit on-board television system, a phone system, and an integrated computer system were installed. Displays, exhibits, a ship store, and a snack bar were constructed and set up. Deck flooring was cleaned and sanded or replaced. Nearly 1,000 volunteers accomplished a major share of the renovation work. When the work was done, many remained as tour guides and support for overnight "camp-on-boards."

The USS New Jersey was moved from its renovation site to a new pier and dock on September 23, 2001. Her first visitors boarded on October 15th.

Today many visitors are attracted to Camden to see our nation's most decorated battleship. A docent provides background information for a fascinating 2-hour tour of the battleship. Mannequins throughout the ship add authenticity. Two exhibit areas relate the history of the battleship and the life of a battleship sailor. Port and starboard areas on the bridge display the ship's many ribbons. The tour includes the captain's and admiral's cabins; the quarters and mess halls of the officers and enlisted men; the communication and control rooms; loading and firing the guns and missiles; and a mock attack from the combat engagement center.

"Big J" has given Camden — a city in great need of economic growth — a reason for hope and pride.

In November 2002, the US Congress and President George W. Bush established by law the National Commission on Terrorist Attacks Upon the United States. The Commission was to be an independent, bipartisan panel directed to examine the facts and circumstances surrounding the September 11, 2001 attacks, including preparedness for and the immediate response to the attacks; identify lessons learned; and provide recommendations to safeguard against future acts of terrorism.

President Bush appointed former NJ Governor Thomas Kean, who was at the time Drew University President, to head the Commission. The Commission released The 9/11 Commission Report on July 22, 2004. Governor Kean travelled around the country and shared the commission's ideas. **(Bob Handelman Images)**

of a year), John Farmer (Attorney General who served a few hours), John Bennett and Richard Codey (party leaders of a newly-elected, split Senate who each served 3 1/2 days), and finally the elected Governor James McGreevey.

A Tumultuous Time

Governor James McGreevey's term turned rocky within weeks of its start. As his wife and newborn baby charmed New Jerseyans, accusations of his unscrupulous actions hung in the air, waiting to explode. The time itself was tumultuous. He had landed as governor in a period that challenged United States governors as most faced huge budget deficits like the multi-billion-dollar New Jersey deficit McGreevey inherited.

McGreevey managed to close the state deficit without raising sales or income taxes, and passed the blame to previous Republican governors and Legislatures. He signed legislation that reformed auto insurance, limited telemarketing calls, created a child-proof hand gun law, allowed stem cell research, recognized domestic partners, banned racial profiling, and protected New Jersey's drinking water.

For education, he started a reading coach program, a student book club, a school construction program,

and a plan to encourage cuts in administrative spending.

The Highlands Bill was an integral part of McGreevey's pet objective to control "sprawl." Signed in August 2004, it set aside 400,000 acres of open space in the New Jersey Highlands. Preserved farmland, lakes, residential communities, and forestland comprise the area that provides much of the state's drinking water. The triumph environmentalists enjoyed over the signing of this bill was tempered, however, by the passage of the fast-track bill. In designated growth areas of the state, developers could now pay an extra fee to speed up the construction permit process including overriding some environmental barriers.

August 12, 2004 marked an abrupt change in McGreevey's governorship. A few days after he signed the Highlands Bill, with his wife and parents at his side, he admitted to a homosexual affair. On national television, he pronounced himself a "Gay American" and tendered his resignation effective November 15th.

There's That Weakness Again

It was back to the Constitution for New Jerseyans after James McGreevey resigned. Article V, Section I, Paragraph 9 specifies that an election need not take place if the vacancy occurs within 60 days preceding a

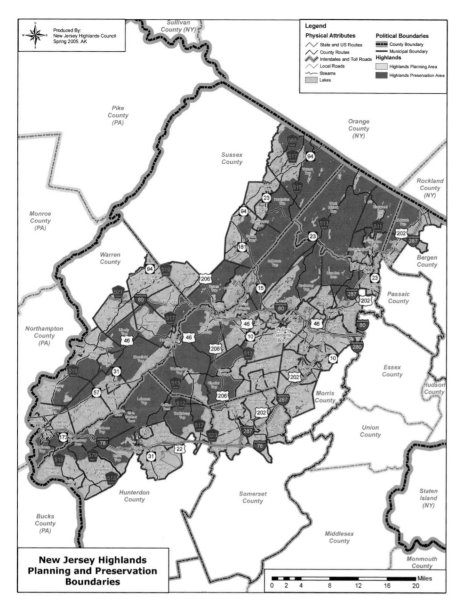

Legend

Physical Attributes
- State and US Routes
- County Routes
- Interstates and Toll Roads
- Local Roads
- Streams
- Lakes

Political Boundaries
- County Boundary
- Municipal Boundary

Highlands
- Highlands Planning Area
- Highlands Preservation Area

**New Jersey Highlands
Planning and Preservation
Boundaries**

Miles
0 2 4   8   12   16   20

In August 2004, Governor James McGreevey signed the Highlands Water Protection and Planning Act to preserve open space and protect a diversity of natural resources, recreational spots, and historic sites in the Highlands. The law protects wetlands and forests that supply important habitat for many species of plants and wildlife. Its main goal, however, is to conserve the drinking water the area supplies for more than half of the state's population — approximately 379 million gallons of water daily.

The area is divided into planning areas and preservation areas. The preservation areas allow little or no building. A council — the Highlands Water Protection and Planning Council — was created to develop a regional master plan, perform land use functions, and protect the region's critical environmental areas and high resource lands.

general election. Republicans argued to no avail that McGreevey's resignation be effective immediately — more than 60 days before the next general election — and a special election held.

New Jersey would now have its second unelected governor in less than four years! This time the unelected governor's term would be for more than a year. Senate President Richard Codey's term extended to January 2008, so he would remain in power until January 2006 when the newly elected governor would be sworn in.

Richard Codey stepped into the governorship with relative quiet and little of the fear and questioning of potential power created at the commencement of DiFrancesco's term. New Jerseyans were now inured to those doomsayers' predictions; DiFrancesco's

term had been comfortably unspectacular. Codey had acted as governor many times before, had worked well with Republicans and Democrats in his five terms in the Assembly and 23 years in the Senate, and was well liked.

Acting Governor Codey breakfasted at Greystone Psychiatric Hospital with patients and staff on his first day in office. He wished to make mental health reform a primary objective in his governorship, admitting his wife had battled the disease for most of her life.

Early in his term, he announced he would not run for governor in November. In his first annual message, he vowed to fight to keep New Jersey safe from terrorism, restore confidence in government, proposed moving the state's primary date earlier for influence

Christopher Reeve moved to Princeton, New Jersey in 1955 — on his third New Year's Eve — with his mother and younger brother. He attended Nassau Street School and Princeton Day School. His first stage appearance was at Princeton's McCarter Theater when he was 9. He later attended Lawrenceville School's summer theater workshop.

Reeve first became famous in 1978 for his movie role as Superman. He appeared in many other films, Broadway plays, and TV movies. Always eager to learn and master new skills, he performed his own stunts, earned his pilot's license and flew solo across the Atlantic Ocean twice, and was an excellent sailor, scuba diver, skier, and horseman. He was also a dedicated activist, fighting for environmental issues, AIDS, and the homeless.

On Memorial Day weekend 1995, Reeve was thrown off his horse and became completely paralyzed. He spent six months at the Kessler Institute for Rehabilitation in West Orange, NJ.

Reeve never gave up on the possibility of walking again. Believing his (and all those afflicted with spinal cord injuries) best hope was with stem cell research, he appeared before Congress, in an electric wheel chair that he operated by mouth with a straw, and appealed for funding. He also acted as chairman of the board of the Christopher Reeve Paralysis Foundation in Springfield, New Jersey.

Christopher Reeve died on October 10, 2004. His wife, Dana, continued the fight for stem cell research.

In January 2004, Governor James McGreevey signed legislation legalizing stem cell research and prohibiting human cloning in New Jersey. A few months later, the Stem Cell Institute of New Jersey was created. The Institute would be built in New Brunswick with the financial support of the State of New Jersey, Rutgers, and the University of Medicine and Dentistry of NJ. Rutgers and UMDNJ would jointly operate it.

New Jersey's pioneering role in stem cell research was further secured on October 18, 2005 when Acting Governor Codey signed an executive order making New Jersey the first state to create a public umbilical cord and placental blood bank for use in stem cell research.

in the presidential primaries, vowed to improve the health care system, and requested funds to support stem cell research.

Codey submitted one of the few budgets in New Jersey history that was lower than the year before, and he did it without raising the income tax, sales tax, or business taxes. He signed legislation that set aside more farmland and parkland, allocated bond money to improve existing state parks, made New Jersey the first state to establish a public umbilical cord and placenta blood bank to be used for stem cell research, created housing for the mentally ill, and restored the Office of Public Advocate.

Number One in Property Taxes

As the Corzine/Forrester gubernatorial campaign of 2005 got under way, property taxes, stem cell research, and ethics became major issues. New Jerseyans had reason for concern over property taxes; they were the highest in the nation. Many pushed for a special constitutional convention for property tax reform. Although a controversial issue to much of the United States, most New Jerseyans supported stem cell research even to the point of government funding. Everyone wanted an end to corruption in government.

Money was not an issue for either candidate; they both spent record-breaking amounts of their own money in their quests for New Jersey's top position. Jon Corzine had been CEO of a Wall Street brokerage house, Goldman Sachs. Doug Forrester had founded a benefit-supplying corporation in Lawrenceville, New Jersey.

Senator Jon Corzine, a Democrat, had served in the US Senate since 2001. Forrester, a Republican, had served as mayor of West Windsor Township, Assistant State Treasurer, and Pension Director for New Jersey. He appeared to be winning the New Jersey senatorial race in 2002 until Frank Lautenberg replaced Robert Torricelli as the Democratic candidate.

Doug Forrester proposed automatically cutting all property taxes by 30% over three years. Jon Corzine wanted to increase homestead rebates for families whose annual income was less than $200,000.

Corzine was for stem cell research. Forrester, at first against it, changed his view at the end of the campaign.

The candidates conversely accused each other of the unethical and defended their own actions. They both pledged to clean up New Jersey's government.

Other issues included homeland security, health care affordability, state spending, improving the business climate, and pledges to end "pay-to-play" lobbying practices.

On Election Day, New Jersey voters chose Senator Corzine decisively. They also ended that "weakness" in the NJ Constitution by voting for an amendment establishing the office of Lieutenant Governor.

Living In A New Millennium

So New Jersey raced onward in the 21st century. The transformation of the state since the onset of World War II was amazing. Everything had changed; even war itself, although shooting never seemed to cease. New Jersey troops went off to various wars — Korea in the early 1950s, Vietnam in the 1960s and 1970s, Iraq and Kuwait in the early 1990s and Afghanistan and Iraq again in the 2000s. Increasingly sophisticated weapons of war, many originated in New Jersey, went with them. Satellites circling the earth brought the cruel hurts of war and terrorism into the living room.

Millions of people had moved from the cities to "the country." As they moved, they transformed former fields into new cities and demanded more and more from their local and state governments. Demands were met, creating needs for increased taxes.

The price far exceeded dollars. It included onerous traffic tie-ups, pollution of air and waters, fouling of wetlands, destruction of forests, pressures to recycle, dumping of dangerous chemicals, disgusting filth strewn along the Jersey Shore, and the elimination of hundreds of thousands of valuable farm acres.

All was not lost — far from it. Nearly one million acres of land had been preserved in parklands and other areas set aside for the future. Close to a million acres of farmland remained as well as more than a million acres of forests. Vigorous conservation groups battled the forces of pollution in never ending skirmishes. Stricter environmental laws curbed and even reversed pollution. Mass transportation improved. City revitalization projects created inviting new housing in and close to the cities. Brownfield clean-ups reclaimed land once classified as too polluted for human use.

New Jersey long knew the dubious pleasure of being the most densely populated and the most urban of all the states. People mean problems. Problems mean opportunity. Ahead lay the challenges that an alert, intelligent population needed to face.

The Role Of A Peninsula

Time continues to write the state's role in history. Set between the two finest natural harbors on the East Coast, bordered by two of the nation's leading cities, and settled by people from nearly every corner of the world, this peninsula called New Jersey was destined from the start to become an urban center.

The twenty-first century vibrates with research and industry, and New Jersey has more than its share of both. A state that developed the transistor, weather satellites, and "miracle drugs" has no need to apologize for its modern role.

People have passed this way, from the Lenape to the newest refugees from foreign lands. They have brought problems. They have created answers. Here, as much an anywhere, is a synthesis of most of what makes America a challenging place in which to live.

History has never ignored New Jersey. Whatever the mood of the moment or the year, whatever the passion of the nation, it has been reflected here. New Jersey remains the small mirror reflecting most American history.

This site welcomes Cape May-Lewis Ferry passengers when they arrive from Delaware after crossing the Delaware Bay.

All entrances into New Jersey, the peninsula state, are over water, except the roads that cross the straight-line boundary that divides the north of New Jersey from New York State.

Index

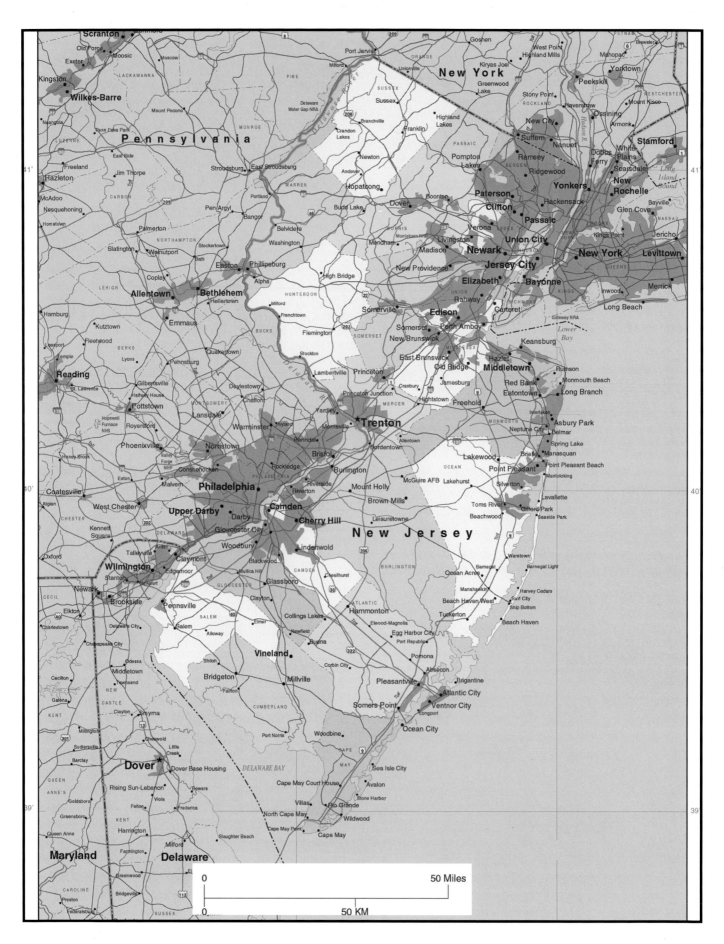